THE

UNDATED CIRCULAR MARKS

OF

THE MIDLAND COUNTIES

The Midland (GB) Postal History Society - No. 1

Published by

The Midland (GB) Postal History Society

ISBN 0 9513311 3 2

First Edition April 1985

Second (1986 Revised) Edition July 1986

Third Edition May 1989

Fourth Edition April 1996

CONTENTS

Foreword	4
Introduction	5
How to Use this Book	9
Derbyshire	14
Gloucestershire	29
Herefordshire	45
Leicestershire and Rutland	57
Northamptonshire	70
Nottinghamshire	83
Oxfordshire	94
Shropshire	106
Staffordshire	123
Warwickshire	143
Birmingham	156
Worcestershire	171
Railway Sub-Offices	186
Money Order Offices	187
Alphabetical Index	194

FOREWORD

In the final sentence of his Foreword to the Third Edition, our Chairman in 1989, Richard Farman, wrote of "some future unanticipated new edition in the 1990s or 21st century". Here we are, four years short of the millennium, and here it is.

Richard also wrote of the "quantum leap" between the Second and Third Editions. Perhaps the changes are less dramatic in this edition but they are still very considerable. Pride of place must be given to the inclusion of the County of Oxford for the first time. For several years, the Society has felt that its claim to cover the Midlands has been marred only by the omission of Oxfordshire. We searched for someone with the enthusiasm and knowledge to become its County Editor and we were fortunate, with the help of several philatelic societies, to discover Martin Scroggs. While usage data for Oxfordshire undated circular marks is included for the first time, well in excess of 500 new usage dates have been added to the other Midland counties. As before, hardly a page has remained unamended.

An important new feature of this edition has been the incorporation of data relating to the establishment of Money Order Offices and the concurrent issue of datestamps to about 200 Midland sub-offices that previously used an undated stamp. The task was considerably eased by Michael Raguin's excellent series of volumes detailing 'British Post Office Notices, 1666-1899', an essential reference tool for any postal historian. We also 'discovered' several previously unrecorded tiny 'Cresswell type' namestamps and an entirely new (and possibly unique) undated circular stamp from Staffordshire.

Dare I follow my predecessors and suggest that this may be the final edition of the book, at least in this form. The Coordinating Editor has indicated that the venerable typewriter and disk drive are on their last legs even if he (arguably) isn't. However we may choose to present information in the years ahead, I doubt that the enthusiasm of our many contributors will flag and I know that the County Editors will still be delighted to hear of new discoveries and usage dates. There's never a dull moment in the study of postal history and we shall never know half of what there is to learn.

Roger Broomfield

R.W. BROOMFIELD
Chairman
The Midland (GB) Postal History Society

INTRODUCTION

The aim of this publication is to provide a comprehensive list of the undated circular handstamps issued to and used at post offices in the Midland Counties between 1825 and 1860. Details of other undated marks, notably the straight line namestamps used between 1840 and 1860, are to be found in the Society's second book, 'The Undated Straight Line & Numbered Receiving House Marks of the Midland Counties, 1840-1860', published in December 1988.

The origin of the undated circular mark (hereafter abbreviated as 'UDC') is to be found in the mileage marks of the late 18th and early 19th centuries. These were originally in straight line form but, from 1803, circular handstamps began to appear with the office name and the mileage from London around the circumference. In the 1820s, postmasters were advised to excise the mileage figures from their handstamps. New handstamps were similar to the circular mileage marks but the gap created by the omission of mileage figures was neatly filled with two arcs or, in a very few instances, by a single arc or a fleuron device. Offices with an annual revenue of less than £1,000, whatever their status, were provided only with an undated stamp. Following a decision in 1838, by 1840 nearly all the principal offices in post towns had their undated stamps replaced with circular dated stamps. Fewer than 5% of the undated stamps listed in this book were issued before 1840 and, of that relatively small number, only half were issued to principal offices in post towns. The great majority of UDCs were issued to and used by minor offices (sub-offices and receiving offices) in the 1840s and the 1850s.

Minor offices were known as 'receiving offices' or 'receiving houses' because of their role in the pre-1840 Penny Posts as places where letters could be handed in. These offices normally had no handstamp to cancel the adhesive stamps introduced in 1840 nor were they permitted to do so. Those that held a cancelling stamp were the only offices correctly termed 'sub-offices' until about 1848. From then, all minor offices, whether previously sub-offices or receiving offices, that exchanged mailbags with a post town became known as sub-offices and it is that name which has survived to the present day. Minor offices were invariably run in conjunction with a small shop or business, the owner being termed the 'receiver'. The minor offices received their letters from their main town office for collection by the addressees or for local delivery and letters were put into the post at these offices for conveyance to the main office. The exceptions were the so-called 'town receiving offices' which had no responsibility for local delivery, this being made direct from the main office. Letters received at minor offices were forwarded to their post town main office for any adhesive stamps to be cancelled, for a circular datestamp (CDS) to be applied and for the letters to be sorted and distributed to other towns (if they were not for local delivery). It was also normal practice for main offices to apply their CDS to incoming mail from other post towns before it was sorted.

Before 1837, minor offices (particularly rural receiving offices) had not been provided with a standard or satisfactory means of identifying letters posted there. Whilst a handful of minor offices had UDCs of varying design and some sub-post towns still used mileage marks, the remainder more often than not used a numeral stamp or no stamp at all. In 1838, a proposal was put to the Postmaster General by the Secretary, Colonel W.L. Maberly, that every receiver should have a stamp bearing the name of his or her office which they could strike on each letter put into their office. This was agreed but since, in the previous September, the PMG had decided to establish a Penny Post for all local letters (for accounting reasons unnecessary to discuss here), the stamp proposed was to have the office name followed, on a second line, by the words 'Penny Post'. The script style of these stamps, often known inaccurately as the 'village type', was standardised throughout England. The consequence of this decision was that many Penny Post stamps were issued between 1837 and 1840 but few UDCs. The introduction of Uniform Penny Postage in January 1840 swept away the need for provincial penny posts and thus handstamps incorporating the words 'Penny Post' became obsolete. By then, the manufacture and issue of the 'village type' Penny Post handstamps was in full swing and, since the contracts could hardly be stopped abruptly, it continued into 1841. However, progressively from 1840, more and more UDCs were issued to minor offices, particularly to rural offices, where there had previously been no handstamp or where an obsolete Penny Post stamp had to be replaced. The town receiving offices were initially more likely to be issued with an undated straight line stamp but a UDC was substituted at many of these in the late 1850s. As new rural offices opened, a UDC was issued, usually within a month and sometimes before a receiver could be appointed!

The early UDCs, issued to both minor and some principal offices, varied in diameter from less than 24mm to more than 30mm. By the mid-1830s, a diameter of 29mm became standard. The lettering was, without exception, in seriffed form and this style (known here as type C2 or C3) remained in vogue until 1844 when sans-serif lettering found favour and remained in use until UDCs were withdrawn. With sans-serif lettering came a reduction in the diameter of UDCs to 25mm and this type (known as C1) can be said to dominate the UDC period. However, from 1857, the diameter of the stamps was progressively reduced and the last of the UDCs (types D1 and D2) were just 19mm across, designed for use with the Cresswell stamping apparatus which provided a continuously moist ink pad but employed smaller, neater handstamps using less ink than previous designs. The classification of the various stamps is explained in detail in the section headed 'How to Use this Book'. Between 1840 and 1860, almost 200 minor offices in the Midlands were empowered to transact Money Order business and became Money Order Offices (M.O.O.s). Money Orders required the office to use a dated stamp. Circular datestamps (CDSs) were therefore issued to Money Order Offices, usually a few weeks before they were officially established, and thereafter it was usual for the office to strike the dated stamp on both Money Orders and letters. At some offices, UDCs continued in use on letters for a short period and isolated examples may be found of dated stamps used with the date slugs removed.

It has been noted that the vast majority of minor offices had no stamp for cancelling adhesives nor were they empowered to cancel. A UDC was not provided for that purpose but to identify the place of posting. The 1853 Rules for Postmasters stated that the impression of the stamp had to be struck on the back of paid letters. Examples of UDCs on the front of letters are, perversely, more attractive to collectors and the mark can also be found, albeit very rarely indeed, cancelling an adhesive stamp. This occurred when a letter was collected by a letter carrier on the incoming ride to a minor office for local delivery. Since it could not then be cancelled at the post town, the receiver sometimes used his UDC rather than a pen to deface the adhesive. Some minor offices struck their UDC not only on outgoing letters but also on incoming mail and, in some rare instances where mail passed through two or even three receiving offices before reaching the post town, all the receivers apparently applied their undated namestamps.

Whilst it is more usual to find a UDC struck in black or blue ink, it would appear that there were no general requirements in the earlier years regarding the colour of ink used at receiving houses and receivers were obliged to provide their own ink and pads. This led to a variety of colours being used, presumably with tacit approval from Head Postmasters. The use of various colours, while adding charm to a collection of these namestamps, eventually caused official comment and the rules for sub-postmasters published in 1853 specifically stated:

" . . . stamping ink should be composed of indigo or prussian blue ground with olive oil until the consistency of cream."

By 1856 the rules had been amended and merely stated:

"You will be supplied with proper ink by your Head Postmaster and you must use no other."

On 10th December 1856, the Controller of the Circulation Department at the GPO, Mr W. Bokenham, issued a circular to receivers which read as follows:

"The Postmaster General has been pleased to firect you to be furnished with blue stamping ink, to be used in stamping the letters posted at your office; a supply will, therefore, be sent to you as soon as it can be prepared, and I have to request that in the meantime you will inform me if you will require a box or pad, and that you will be careful to let the impressions be made upon the letters as clearly as possible."

Following the issue of this circular, the vast majority of marks were struck in blue or black with only a very few green, red and yellow ink pads continuing in use at isolated offices. During the early 1850s in particular, experiments were put in hand for the principal offices to strike datestamps in differing colours at various towns and subsequently in different surveyors' districts. Although these trials were not intended to include the receivers of the minor offices, there can be little doubt they became involved, sometimes changing ink colour in concert with the post town but often following some pattern or whim of their own. Examples may be found in this book of UDCs struck in half a dozen or more different colours in the space of ten or twelve years and it is difficult to discern any logical plan. Surprisingly it is a topic that, even at this time, has received minimal study.

Although, for obvious reasons, collectors prefer to see UDCs struck on the front of letters, they have to accept that the majority appear on the back. In many instances the UDC is found to have been overstruck with another stamp, perhaps the datestamp of the post town or that of another major town along the route. This problem also troubled the Post Office of the day when it became difficult to read the name of the office at which the letter had been posted. Acknowledging that there was no general rule to prevent overstriking, it was suggested to the Postmaster General in 1853 that letters should be stamped to the right of the seal at the office where they were posted and that forward letters - if stamped at all - and letters received for delivery should be stamped to the left of the seal. It is unlikely that this proposal was ever generally adopted.

The era of undated receiving office stamps came to an end in 1859 and 1860. In 1856 the postmaster at Liverpool had persuaded the Postmaster General that, as an experiment, the stamping of letters by town receivers in Liverpool should cease. This decision was taken to lighten their workload and to avoid any pressure to increase their salaries. It was also taken on the distinct understanding that, if any inconvenience was caused, the previous system would be restored. Apparently no difficulties were reported and this isolated concession was to sow the seeds of change which led to the ultimate demise of undated namestamps. The question of their abolition was again raised in September 1859 when a meeting of the district surveyors recommended to the Postmaster General that the practice of stamping letters at town receiving offices (other than Money Order Offices) should be discontinued immediately but, because there was a difference of opinion about the propriety of such action at other minor offices, a six month trial should be conducted in the Shrewsbury area. An additional benefit of some magnitude was that, if stamping at town offices ceased, the cost of the proposed issue of the Cresswell stamping pad to all receiving offices would be materially reduced.

Following a circular to surveyors dated 14th September 1859, stamping by town receivers stopped immediately and the trial in the Shrewsbury area began on 1st October. This book records just one strike of a UDC in Shropshire after that date and, the trial having been judged a success, an Instruction to Postmasters dated 17th March 1860 finally abolished the practice of stamping letters at all offices using undated stamps. By then many letters were posted in pillar or wall boxes and identification of the place of posting had become less relevant. There can be little doubt, too, that the economies of abolition held considerable attraction. It was during the later years of the UDC era that the Post Office also experimented with 'double stamps' (the 'spoon' and 'duplex') which combined the canceller with the datestamp. The subsequent introduction of double stamps led to further appreciable economies in both handstamps and labour.

Some UDCs were not issued until late 1858 or even 1859 and examples of their use are extremely rare. It is ironic that early seriffed stamps, many of which had a long period of use, command a premium. An examination of the record of usage on the first and last page of any county listing of UDCs will tell its own story. UDCs used after March 1860 are extremely unusual and the recent discovery of one from Derbyshire used on 14th June 1860 is remarkable.

STAMPING OF LETTERS AT SUB POST OFFICES.

The practice of stamping letters is abolished at all Sub-offices, at which undated stamps only have hitherto been used.

Head Postmasters will see that this rule is carried out, and will collect all undated stamps from their Sub-offices to which the rule is applicable, and transmit them, with a list, to the Metropolitan Office, sending also a duplicate list to the District Surveyor.

The Instruction to Postmasters dated Saturday 17th March 1860
which brought the use of undated stamps to an end.

HOW TO USE THIS BOOK

The book is divided into twelve county sections and each section is made up of three lists. (Birmingham is treated as an individual county and may be found following Warwickshire.) The three lists in each county section are:

1. The Office List.
2. The Transfer List.
3. The Chronological List.

Each Office List serves as an index to its county's Chronological List. There is also an alphabetical index at the back of the book.

The Office List

The Office List functions as an index to the Chronological List by placing, against the name of each office, references to undated circular marks (UDCs) issued to that office. These references can be turned up in the same county's Chronological List to find issue and usage details of each UDC. The Office List does more than act as an index. It groups the minor offices under the post towns to which they were subordinate; the towns whose circular datestamps will normally be found on any cover struck with a UDC. However, during the currency of undated marks, postal arrangements sometimes changed and minor offices found themselves served from, and made subordinate to, a different post town. The Office List therefore puts the minor offices under the post town to which they were subordinate when their first UDC was issued and, by means of cross-reference to a Transfer List, indicates all the known changes that took place prior to 1860. By following these 'TL' cross-references, it should be possible to trace the postal history of a minor office through to the time that undated marks were withdrawn.

As a general rule, all minor offices under a post town have been listed even if some were in an adjacent county. Similarly, all minor offices within the county boundary served from a post town in another county are included. Some minor offices therefore appear in two, and sometimes more, sections of the book, particularly where they were affected by transfers or county boundary changes.

A new feature of this edition is the incorporation into the Office list of the dates of issue of Circular Datestamps (CDSs) to offices that previously used a UDC. Such an issue, intended to enable selected offices to transact Money Order business, usually brought UDC usage to an abrupt end. Very occasionally, a further UDC was issued after the issue of a CDS and, in these exceptional cases, it can be expected that Money Order Office status had been lost. Details of the establishment (and closure) of Money Order Offices may be found in a new section at the back of the book, immediately before the Alphabetical Index.

The Transfer List

A Transfer List follows each county's Office List. The dates shown are those on which the Inland Office changed the post town to which letters for a minor office were sent. The actual wording often used was "On and from the evening of . . ." Thus, as far as the minor office was concerned, the change came into force on the following day.

Only those transfers which took place after the issue of a UDC are shown. In some instances, the opening of a minor office was part of a major revision of rural posts in the area which resulted in the transfer of a village from the delivery of one post town to another. These changes have not been shown since no handstamp was used under the first post town and it is usually impossible to identify covers originating from a particular village.

Wherever possible, downgrading of a post town has been included as an entry in the Transfer List since the subordinate offices would have then been transferred to a new post town. For example, when Northleach (Glos) was downgraded and became a sub-office of Cheltenham, minor offices such as Aldsworth, previously under Northleach, came under Cheltenham.

In some cases, it has not been possible to find the exact date of a change of post town but, where the year can be deduced, it has been shown.

The Chronological List

The Chronological List for each county is based on the information contained in the Steel Impression Books, Volumes 1-18, of the Post Office Archives. These books were intended to record the issue of each and every handstamp by the GPO in London. Essentially, the Steel Impression Books (often referred to as the 'proof books') include a strike of the handstamp being issued together with the name of the office to which it was sent (usually the post town) and the date on which it was issued. At certain busy times, the information in the Steel Impression Books was incompletely entered: the date may be limited to the month and year or omitted altogether and, more rarely, all issue details are left out. It has been suggested that many stamps were issued without being recorded in the Steel Impression Books. This exercise has shown that very few indeed of the Midland UDCs have eluded the proof books with the exception of the small so-called "Creswell" UDCs issued to a few Birmingham, Coventry and Wolverhampton sub-offices in about 1857.

For those not familiar with the appearance of the Steel Impression Books, a reduced illustration of part of a typical page is shown here.

Information about usage of the issued handstamps was initially obtained from the collections formed by members of the Midland, Derbyshire and Shropshire Postal History Societies. Since the first edition of the publication appeared in 1985, many hundreds of new usage dates have been notified to the Society by dozens of contibutors and more than 500 new reports are included in this edition.

The Chronological List has seven columns:

A	B	C	D	E	F	G
BLAKENEY	C2	14AUG43	Newnham	5/176	R	3FEB44- 7JUN44
					GR	10AUG49
EASINGTON	C2	30AUG43	Stroud	5/177	B	11JUN45
					BL	8APR51-10SEP58
HORSEFERRY-BRIDGE	C2	4SEP43	Gloucester	5/180		
WOODSIDE	C2	23OCT43	Newnham	5/189	BL/GR	3SEP50
BIBURY	C2	16NOV43	Fairford	5/199	R	30NOV49-30JAN54.

COLUMN A. The undated stamp in its exact form so far as it can be reproduced in type.

COLUMN B. The Type Designation of the undated stamp. For the basic scheme of type numbers used, the Society is indebted to Michael Champness who, as long ago as 1973, produced a classification system for The London Postal History Group. Because the UDCs of the Midlands are generally more straightforward than those of London, the classification system has been very slightly modified so that 'Champness type' D1A is known simply as 'D1' and 'Champness type' D1B is referred to as 'D2', there being no true 'Champness type' D2 marks in the Midlands. Other changes are the addition of sub-types of types C1 and C2 which we call C1* and C2* to indicate that they are of distinctly smaller diameter than the normal marks and the further addition of a new sub-type C3D which, like type D6, is possibly unique. The full details of our classification are as follows:

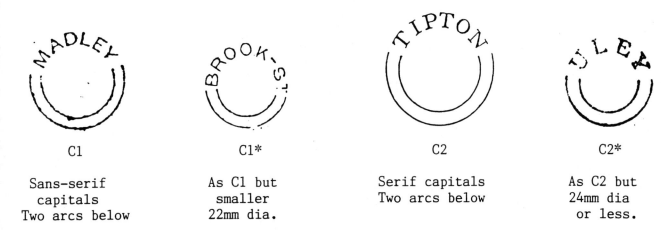

C1	C1*	C2	C2*
Sans-serif capitals Two arcs below	As C1 but smaller 22mm dia.	Serif capitals Two arcs below	As C2 but 24mm dia or less.

Note: C1M and C2M are dated stamps used without the date slugs.

C3 - Serif capitals with a dot, a small dash or no spacer at all. (Three examples).

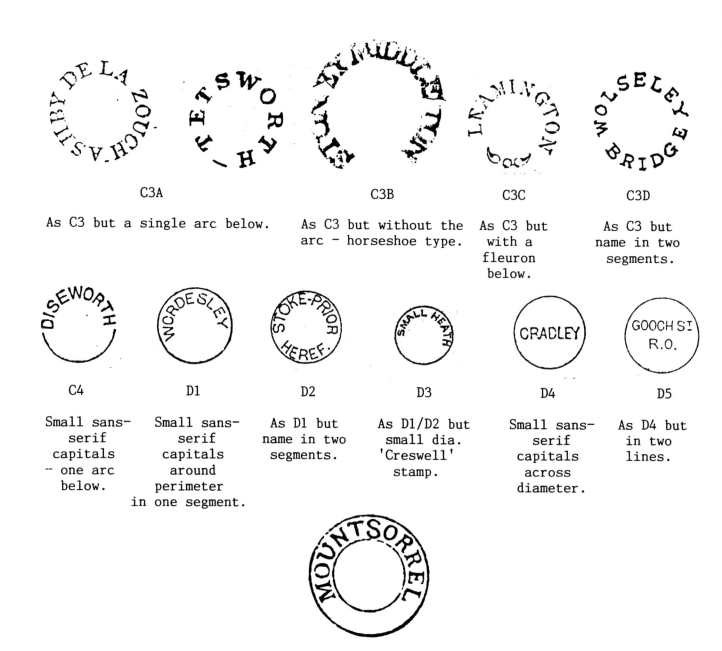

C3A	C3B	C3C	C3D	
As C3 but a single arc below.	As C3 but without the arc - horseshoe type.	As C3 but with a fleuron below.	As C3 but name in two segments.	

C4	D1	D2	D3	D4	D5
Small sans-serif capitals - one arc below.	Small sans-serif capitals around perimeter in one segment.	As D1 but name in two segments.	As D1/D2 but small dia. 'Creswell' stamp.	Small sans-serif capitals across diameter.	As D4 but in two lines.

D6

Unique to Mountsorrel.

COLUMN C. The date of issue of the handstamp as recorded in the Steel Impression Books. If the stamp pre-dates these books (i.e. was issued before 1825) or is not recorded in them, an approximate date of issue has been included where there is evidence to support it.

COLUMN D. The office (normally the post town) to which the handstamp was sent, as recorded in the Steel Impression Books. Where the issue is not recorded, this column will be blank.

COLUMN E. The reference number of the entry in the Steel Impression Books by Volume and Page number e.g. 9/120 represents Volume 9, Page 120. Certain volumes of the proof books contain only London and Overseas marks or information duplicated elsewhere and no reference to them appears in these lists. The Steel Impression Book reference numbers are, themselves, in chronological order except in the earliest volumes and therefore provide a convenient index for each mark or group of marks. In the Office Lists of this publication, each subordinate office name has been followed by the Steel Impression Book reference, enabling it to be found quickly in the Chronological List. Where a mark has been reported in use whose issue cannot be found in the proof books (a rare occurence), it has been indexed with an asterisk, e.g. 7/253*, and has been included in the Chronological List (without a Steel Impression Book reference, of course) immediately following 7/253, the point of insertion being determined by what is thought to have been its approximate date of issue.

COLUMNS F and G. These columns record the known usage of the marks as reported to The Midland (GB) PHS. In column F, the Colour of Ink has been abbreviated, typically as follows:

    B Black BL Blue GR Green R Red OR Orange Y Yellow BR Brown

Where necessary, a combination of these symbols is used, GR/BL indicating a 'greenish blue' shade.

Column G shows the Span of Dates (earliest and latest) for which use of a UDC has been reported. This does not mean that a particular mark has necessarily been struck continuously in the given colour over the stated period. Where possible the dates have been given in full but, since some reports indicate no more than the year of use, only that information can be included.

The Reports of Use form a very important part of this publication and have been updated in each new edition of the book. To simplify this task, the information in the Chronological Lists was stored on magnetic disks which could be amended at any time. (Incidentally, the full stops that occur after every few lines of the lists are solely for technical reasons and have no other significance.) Anyone with an interest in Midland UDCs is therefore requested to report unrecorded usage (giving the Steel Impression Book reference, the ink colour and the date of use) to the relevant County Editor. Details of the County Editors are given on the final page.

ACKNOWLEDGMENTS

The Society wishes to thank Jean Farrugia and the staff of Post Office Archives for their continued help and for permission to illustrate marks from the Steel Impression Books. Thanks are also expressed to the County Editors, to the members of the Society who continue to support this work enthusiastically and particularly to Mr M.V.D.Champness whose initial help and classification system was instrumental in launching the project.

The popularity of the information on the Birmingham receivers, their trades and locations which was included in the Society's book of Undated Straight Line Marks has prompted the inclusion of a greatly enlarged list in this publication. It will be found on pages 161-167. The Society acknowledges the valuable and original research undertaken by Mr and Mrs Eric Lewis.

Derbys

DERBYSHIRE

ALFRETON (6).

Brinsley 2 12/90
Butterley 7/39
Codnor 13/112
Crich 4/3 See TL11&15.
Greenhill Lane 12/90
Higham 7/145 18/30
Hucknall (Huthwaite) 2 12/90
Ironville 7/115 (CDS SEP52)
Normanton 12/90
Old Brinsley 2 12/90
Pinxton 7/159 18/31
Riddings 7/36
Ripley 7/39 (CDS 20FEB51)
Selston 2 9/127
South Wingfield 12/90
Swanwick 12/90
Tibshelf 7/145 13/288

ASHBOURNE (28). 1/2 (CDS 4FEB32)

Alstonefield 3 7/28 14/43
Ellastone 3 7/184 14/43
Hartington 10/58 (CDS 1DEC57)
Hulland 12/93
Ilam 3 7/28 14/43
Mappleton 12/194
Marston Montgomery 13/215
Mathfield/Mayfield 3 7/184 14/77
Osmaston 10/191 Note 1.
Parwich 9/35 12/304
Rocester 3 7/184
Snelston 13/144
Thorpe 13/144
Tissington 13/215

BAKEWELL (41). 1/155 (CDS 30MAR40)

Ashford 9/38
Bamford 13/258 See TL17.
Baslow 5/54 (CDS 14OCT56) Note 2.
Bradwell 9/36 See TL17.
Calver 13/191 See TL17.
Castleton + 5/16 13/276 (CDS 20JUL57) See TL17.
Cresbrook 13/191 See TL17.
Derwent 13/258 See TL17.
Edensor 7/278 18/42 See TL18.
Eyam 7/28 13/276 See TL17.
Great Longstone 10/8

Grindleford Bridge 13/191
 See TL17.
Hassop 13/191
Hathersage + 11/83 (CDS 16APR56)
 See TL17.
Litton 13/191 See TL17.
Money Ash 11/44
Stoney Middleton Pre-proof book
5/126 9/176 13/276 (CDS 9APR58)
 See TL1,2&17.
Taddington 9/38 13/276
Tideswell 4/102 10/78
 (CDS 20FEB51) See TL17.
Youlgrave 7/28 13/276

BELPER (64). 2/13 (CDS 3APR40)

Ambergate 12/90 See TL15.
Denby 12/291 16/69
Fritchley 12/151 12/181 See TL15.
Hazlewood 12/291
Heage 9/35 16/69
Heanor 7/123 (CDS 5MAR57)
Kilburn 16/69

BUXTON (155). 1/152 (CDS 1SEP38)

Chapel en le Frith 2/30 10/65
 (CDS 20FEB51) See TL5.
Fairfield 14/149
Longnor 3 7/227

CHESTERFIELD (186).

Ashover 5/195 16/148
Barlborough 7/42
Barlow 11/135
Bolsover 7/103 18/42
 (CDS 23JUL59)
Brampton Moor 9/7
Brimington 9/203
Clay Cross 5/195 (CDS 26DEC50)
Clown 11/53
Duckmanton 13/47
Eckington 7/42 (CDS 21SEP57)
Handley 13/47
Hasland 13/47
Heath 9/170

Notes: 1. Stamp sent to Derby.
 2. 5/54 was sent to Chesterfield: on the ride but not the post town.

+ indicates an office which used a straight line (or P.P.) stamp after 1840.

An underlined number, eg 2, indicates an office outside Derbys - see key at end.

Chesterfield (Cont'd)

Holymoorside 13/47
Killamarsh 13/213
Mosborough 13/213
Newbold 11/135
Old Brampton 14/228
Ridgway 9/115 See TL14&15.
Staveley 7/42 (CDS 26DEC50)
Stone Gravels 16/86
Tupton 11/232
Whittington 9/115
Whitwell 5/106 See TL8&9.
Wingerworth 13/47

DERBY (242).

Alvaston 7/11 13/214
Borrowash 11/43
Brailsford 7/216 (CDS 26JUN50) 13/96
Bramcote $\underline{2}$ 9/252 13/201 See TL7.
Breadsall 7/143
Brook Street + 13/221
Burnaston 13/239 13/292
Castle Donnington $\underline{1}$ 7/11 (CDS 26SEP49)
Cavendish Bridge + $\underline{1}$ 7/11
Chaddesden 10/140 10/146
Chellaston 9/7
Church Broughton 14/116
Draycott 18/25
Duffield 5/73 (CDS 26DEC50)
Gotham $\underline{2}$ 9/94
Green Lane 12/80
Holbrook 14/140
Kegworth + $\underline{1}$ 7/11 (CDS 16APR56)
Kingstone $\underline{2}$ 9/94
Kirk Langley 7/216
Little Eaton 7/218
Littleover 13/239
Lockington $\underline{1}$ 9/152
Long Eaton 13/150 (CDS 21SEP57)
Longford 7/216 13/160
Mackworth 10/42
Melbourne (243) 4/32 9/165 (CDS 26SEP49)
Mickleover 9/27
Milford 9/120
Muggington 10/20
Ockbrook 7/20 (CDS 26DEC50)
Osmaston 13/239 13/292
Quarndon 7/278.

Radbourne 13/239 14/158
Risley 11/43
St Mary's Bridge 10/128 13/259
Sandiacre 9/9 See TL3,4,6&7.
Sawley 7/169
Shardlow 7/66 13/120
Smalley 7/143 (CDS 31JAN56)
Spondon 7/20 13/262
Stanton by Dale 14/90
Stapleford $\underline{2}$ 5/81 14/140
    (CDS 5JUN58) See TL3,4&7.
Sutton (on the Hill) 11/44
    13/169
Swarkestone 9/7
Thulston 12/280
Ticknall (244) 5/73
Turnditch 10/21
West Hallam 10/43 13/259

MATLOCK BATH (520). 2/90
    (CDS 3APR40)

Bonsall 5/179
Cromford 7/153
Darley 7/176
Holloway 12/242
Lea 7/161 12/242
Matlock Bridge (B86) Note 3.
Matlock Village 5/129
Rowsley 7/176 See TL12.
Tansley 12/242
Winster 5/179

WIRKSWORTH (895).

Brassington 9/47 See TL13&19.
Kirk Ireton 11/119
Middleton 14/206

ASHBY DE LA ZOUCH (30), Leics

Breedon 9/63
Netherseal 11/105
Overseal 11/124
Packington 11/161
Ravenstone 5/197
Stretton en le Fields 11/105

Notes: 3. No undated stamp known.

+ indicates an office which used a straight line (or P.P.) stamp after 1840.

An underlined number, eg $\underline{2}$, indicates an office outside Derbys - see key at end.

Derbys

ATHERSTONE (33), Warks

Appleby + 9/210 (CDS 24MAR59)
Measham + 9/210 16/51

BURTON ON TRENT (152), Staffs

Caldwell 12/198 16/86
Egginton 10/7
Hartshorne 11/197 16/86
Hilton 12/275 16/87 See TL20.
Lullington 7/75 16/86
Midway 11/105
Milton 13/103
Newhall 7/75 16/87
Newton Solney 7/6 16/86
Repton 7/6 16/87
Rosliston 12/272 12/288
Stapenhill 7/75 16/86
Swadlincote 10/192
Walton on Trent 10/274 18/30
Willington 10/7 16/86
Winshill 13/103
Woodville 7/75 9/117

LOUGHBOROUGH (475), Leics

Diseworth 9/101 14/61

MANCHESTER (498), Lancs

Broadbottom 9/30
Charlesworth 10/176
Glossop (499) + 5/50 (CDS 23MAY47)
Hadfield 9/152
Old Glossop 10/115
Tintwistle 9/151
Whitfield 14/132.

MANSFIELD (504), Notts

Langwith 12/181
Norton 12/181
Pleasley 9/114
Scarcliffe 9/114
Shirebrook 16/139

NOTTINGHAM (583), Notts

Ilkeston 5/2 (CDS 23MAY51)

SHEFFIELD (700), Yorks

Beighton 11/125
Dore 10/90
Dronfield 4/36 (CDS 29JUL56)
Greenhill 18/73
Hackenthorpe 9/122 16/103
Heeley 11/125
Hope 14/204
Intake 9/124 16/103
Norton 4/77 7/112 11/119 13/250
Unston 14/256

STOCKPORT (733), Ches

Compstall 9/30 14/134
Hayfield 4/98 13/236
Marple 4/98 13/266
Mellor 9/187
New Mills 4/98 10/117 (CDS FEB54)
Peak Forrest 18/98
Whaley Bridge 7/72 14/210

UTTOXETER (827), Staffs
See TL16.

Cubley 13/38 See TL16.
Doveridge 11/224 See TL10.
Etwall 7/16 13/278 See TL10.
Sudbury (829) + 13/201 See TL10.

+ indicates an office which used a straight line (or P.P.) stamp after 1840.

KEY to offices not in Derbyshire

<u>1</u> is in Leicestershire
<u>2</u> is in Nottinghamshire
<u>3</u> is in Staffordshire.

TRANSFERS - Derbyshire

TL 1. Stoney Middleton from Bakewell to Sheffield in DEC40.

2. Stoney Middleton from Sheffield to Bakewell on 3JUL41.

3. Stapleford and Sandiacre from Derby to Nottingham on 3JAN48.

4. Stapleford and Sandiacre from Nottingham to Derby on 18JAN48.

5. Chapel en le Frith from Buxton to Stockport on 7NOV48.

6. Sandiacre from Derby to Nottingham on 14MAR49.

7. Stapleford, Sandiacre and Bramcote letters sent to Derby by Night Mail but to Nottingham by Day Mail from 19MAY49.

8. Whitwell from Chesterfield to Worksop on 22MAY50.

9. Whitwell from Worksop to Chesterfield on 30APR52.

10. Etwall, Doveridge and Sudbury from Uttoxeter to Derby on 18JUL53.

11. Crich from Alfreton to Belper on 5AUG54.

12. Rowsley from Matlock to Bakewell on 22OCT55.

13. Brassington from Wirksworth to Ashbourne c1855.

14. Ridgway from Chesterfield to Belper at an unknown date between 1855 and 1857.

15. Ambergate, Fritchley, Crich and Ridgway from Belper to Derby on 5OCT57.

16. The reduction in status of Uttoxeter (Staffs) to a sub-office under Derby on 23NOV57 would have involved the transfer of Cubley also.

17. Bamford, Bradwell, Castleton, Calver, Cresbrook, Derwent, Eyam, Litton, Grindleford Bridge, Stoney Middleton, Tideswell and Hathersage from Bakewell to Sheffield on 29APR58.

18. Edensor from Bakewell to Chesterfield on 29APR58.

19. Brassington from Ashbourne to Wirksworth c1858.

20. Hilton from Burton on Trent to Derby on 8AUG59.

DERBYSHIRE

Name	Type	Date	Town	Ref	Colour	Period
STONEY MIDDLETON	C3B				B	30- 46
ASHBOURN	C2*	9MAR29	Ashbourne	1/2	B	23FEB31-27JAN52
					R	22JAN46- 6JAN48
					GR	8NOV48
					BL	30NOV57
BUXTON	C2*	11NOV31	Buxton	1/152	B	26APR33- 7MAY38
BAKEWELL	C2*	14DEC31	Bakewell	1/155	B	25JUN32- 9JUL49
BELPER	C2*	13MAR35	Belper	2/13	B	11APR37-11DEC38.
CHAPEL-IN-LE-FRITH	C2	14SEP38	Chapel	2/30	B	31MAR40-18MAR45
MATLOCK BATH	C2	31AUG35	Matlock Bath	2/90	B	24FEB36-20FEB40
CRICH	C2	9JAN41	Alfreton	4/3	B	3JAN45-14MAY48
MELBOURNE	C2	6MAY39	Derby	4/32	OR	27NOV40-13APR42
					B	18JUL42-10AUG46
					BL	19JAN48-12FEB48
DRONFIELD	C2	28APR41	Sheffield	4/36	R	10SEP41- 1AUG54
					GR	25SEP47- 4MAY56.
NORTON-SHEFFIELD	C2	1MAY41	Sheffield	4/77	B	4NOV41-26JAN43
HAYFIELD	C2	13FEB41	Stockport	4/98	B	23APR51
MARPLE	C2	13FEB41	Stockport	4/98	B	6OCT43-11JUN48
NEW-MILLS	C2	13FEB41	Stockport	4/98	B	14OCT46
TIDESWELL	C2	3DEC40		4/102	B	29JUL42-25DEC44.
					BL	20JUN45
ILKESTON	C2	8JUN41	Nottingham	5/2	B	4JUL42- 56
						Note 1.
CASTLETON-DERBY^SH	C2	26JUL41	Bakewell	5/16	B	26JUL41- 54
					GR	24AUG47-23JAN57
						Note 2.
GLOSSOP	C2	25NOV41	Manchester	5/50	B	28JAN43- 9APR48
					BL/GR	26JAN44- 9AUG48
BASLOW	C2	11DEC41	Chesterfield	5/54	B	23MAY42- NOV53
DUFFIELD-DERBY	C2	8FEB42	Derby	5/73	B	6JUN42-21AUG43
					BL/GR	30OCT49-24DEC49
TICKNALL	C2	8FEB42	Derby	5/73	B	3AUG42-13FEB51
					BL	7NOV52
STAPLEFORD	C2	17MAR42	Derby	5/81	B	31JUL42
					BL	6JUL49
					GR	26JAN58
WHITWELL	C2	11JUL42	Chesterfield	5/106	B	30MAY43- 6JAN48
					GR	13APR58
STONY-MIDDLETON	C2	8DEC42	Bakewell	5/126		Note 3.
MATLOCK·VILLAGE	C2	14DEC42	Matlock	5/129	OR/R	6OCT43-31OCT43
					B	28OCT44- 7FEB58
					R	OCT44-15AUG46
					BL	13FEB54- 1JAN58.
					GR	10OCT58
BONSALL	C2	30AUG43	Matlock	5/179	Grey	15NOV46
					GR	6MAR47
WINSTER	C2	30AUG43	Matlock	5/179	B	30AUG43- 4JUL46
					BL	12FEB50- 9JUN55
CLAYCROSS	C2	16NOV43	Chesterfield	5/195	B	10JUL43-21MAR49
ASHOVER	C2	16NOV43	Chesterfield	5/195	R	50-20OCT53
					B	19JUN57
RAVENSTONE	C2	16NOV43	Ashby de la Z	5/197	B	MAR44-28NOV47

Notes: 1. The two arcs usually fail to strike.
2. The 'SH' is in small capitals.
3. Wrong spelling - probably not used.

Derbys

Name	Class	Date	Location	Ref	Code	Date Range
NEWTON	C2	19DEC43	Burton on Trent	7/6	B	19DEC44- 45
REPTON	C2	19DEC43	Burton on Trent	7/6	B	22FEB44-10FEB53
ALVASTON	C2	30DEC43	Derby	7/11	B	16DEC44-16MAY52.
CAVENDISH-BRIDGE	C2	30DEC43	Derby	7/11		
CASTLE-DONNINGTON	C2	30DEC43	Derby	7/11	B	44- 7APR49
					BL/GR	9MAY44
KEGWORTH	C2	30DEC43	Derby	7/11	BL	2DEC44-28OCT49
					BL/GR	8AUG51-31JUL56
ETWALL	C2	13JAN44	Uttoxeter	7/16	B	27FEB44-29MAR47
					BL/GR	2DEC44
					GR	4APR53- 7FEB56
SPOONDON	C2	19JAN44	Derby	7/20	BL/GR	4FEB45-28FEB55
OCKBROOK	C2	19JAN44	Derby	7/20	GR	24APR49
					B	24APR51
ALSTONEFIELD	C2	21FEB44	Ashbourne	7/28	R	22JAN46- 9FEB53.
					B	5OCT47
					GR	8NOV48
ILAM	C2	21FEB44	Ashbourne	7/28	R	11NOV45-12JUL55
EYAM	C2	21FEB44	Ashbourne	7/28	B	17DEC44-12JAN53
					R	10MAY46-18NOV49
					OR	12NOV52
					BL/GR	24MAY56
					GR	26JUN56
YOULGRAVE	C2	21FEB44	Bakewell	7/28	R/BR	18MAR45- 9SEP47
					GR	15MAY45-11JUN45
					BL	10MAY48-14OCT48
					B	31DEC53- 55
RIDDINGS	C2	6MAR44	Alfreton	7/36		
BUTTERLEY	C2	18MAR44	Alfreton	7/39	R	31OCT44- 4JUN48
					BL/GR	31MAY49- 7FEB50.
					BL	7APR51
RIPLEY	C2	18MAY44	Alfreton	7/39	B	26FEB46
					R	24DEC46-13AUG47
BARLBOROUGH	C2	1APR44	Chesterfield	7/42	R	3MAR45
					BL/B	26MAR58
ECKINGTON	C2	1APR44	Chesterfield	7/42	R	6FEB45-26MAY49.
					BL	27AUG46-13FEB51
					B	10JUN50-11MAR54
					GR	12JUN57
STAVELEY	C2	1APR44	Chesterfield	7/42	B	16FEB46
					R	24MAY46-27MAY49
SHARDLOW	C1	31MAY44	Derby	7/66	BL	6JUL44- 53
					BL/GR	6APR45
					GR	1AUG53
					B	13JUN54
WHALEY-BRIDGE	C1	15JUN44	Stockport	7/72	BL/GR	24JAN45
					R	49- 54
					BL	28JUN54-18JUN55
NEWALL	C1	28JUN44	Burton on Trent	7/75	B	21JUN45-25AUG47
LULLINGTON	C1	28JUN44	Burton on Trent	7/75	B	18SEP45-23MAY49.
STAPENHILL	C1	28JUN44	Burton on Trent	7/75	B	4DEC50
WOODEN-BOX	C1	28JUN44	Burton on Trent	7/75		
BOLSOVER	C1	30OCT44	Chesterfield	7/103		
NORTON	C1	29NOV44	Sheffield	7/112	BL	24JUN47- 2SEP49
IRONVILLE	C1	10DEC44	Alfreton	7/115	B	5JUL45-13MAR48
HEANOR	C1	29JAN45	Belper	7/123	R	9MAR54- 6FEB56
BREADSALL	C1	8MAY45	Derby	7/143		
SMALLEY	C1	8MAY45	Derby	7/143	BL	10AUG47-11AUG47

Derbys   20.

Name		Date	Place	Ref		
HIGHAM	C1	14MAY45	Alfreton	7/145		
TIBSHELF	C1	14MAY45	Alfreton	7/145	OR/R	45
					B	24APR46-10MAY50
					BL	MAY48-17MAY52
					GR	6FEB50
CROMFORD	C1	14JUN45	Matlock Bath	7/153	R	20JUL45-22SEP47
					BL/GR	14AUG49
					GR	21JUN53
PINXTON	C1	28JUN45	Alfreton	7/159		
LEA	C1	7JUL45	Matlock Bath	7/161		
SAWLEY	C1	13AUG45	Derby	7/169	B	27JUN47- 1MAR49
DARLEY DALE	C1	18SEP45	Matlock	7/176	BL/GR	25JUN50-13NOV51
					B	17NOV53
ROWSLEY	C1	18SEP45	Matlock	7/176	BR	19SEP54-30DEC54
					B	21NOV54- 5JAN55
					BL/GR	5MAR55-29OCT56
MATHFIELD	C1	25OCT45	Ashbourne	7/184	B	18AUG54
					BL	26JUN56 Note 4.
ELLASTONE	C1	25OCT45	Ashbourne	7/184	B	25SEP48- 5APR58
					BL	18DEC5?
					BR	53
ROCESTER	C1	25OCT45	Ashbourne	7/184	B	15APR50-14OCT51
LONGFORD	C1	4MAR46	Derby	7/216		
KIRK-LANGLEY	C1	4MAR46	Derby	7/216	B	6FEB49-15NOV58.
					GR	8JUL56
					BL	23MAR60
BRAILSFORD	C1	4MAR46	Derby	7/216	BL	6AUG46-14DEC46
					B	13NOV55-30SEP58
					GR	10NOV56
LITTLE-EATON	C1	10MAR46	Derby	7/218	B	7JAN51-27JAN59.
LONGNOR	C1	8APR46	Buxton	7/227	BR/R	28JUN48
					R/OR	10JUL52
EDENSOR	C1	10NOV46	Bakewell	7/278	B	18OCT54
QUORNDON	C1	13NOV46	Derby	7/278	GR	14NOV51 Note 5.
BRAMPTON	C1	28JAN47	Chesterfield	9/7	B	3JAN49
					GR	8JUN59
CHELLASTON	C1	28JAN47	Derby	9/7	GR	8JUL48- 3MAY51
					BL	24AUG57
SWARKESTONE	C1	28JAN47	Derby	9/7	R/OR	28MAR48
					BL/GR	2NOV56
SANDIACRE	C1	9FEB47	Derby	9/9	GR	19AUG47-16NOV58
MICKLEOVER	C1	3APR47	Derby	9/27	BL	6FEB55-25DEC57.
					B	9MAR59
BROADBOTTOM	C1	19APR47	Glossop	9/30	B	5JUN49
					BL/GR	2JAN50
COMPSTALL	C1	19APR47	Stockport	9/30		
HEAGE	C1	6MAY47	Belper	9/35	BL	4NOV48
PARWICK	C1	6MAY47	Ashbourne	9/35		Note 6.
BRADWELL	C1	6MAY47	Bakewell	9/36	R	26NOV47
					B	10FEB59
ASHFORD	C1	18MAY47	Bakewell	9/38	B	16SEP47- 9JUL59.
					BL	22MAY48- 4DEC54
					GR	8NOV48-12JUN57
TADDINGTON	C1	18MAY47	Bakewell	9/38	B	7DEC53
BRASSINGTON	C1	1JUN47	Wirksworth	9/47	GR	18JUN55
					B	10JAN59

Notes: 4. A spelling variant of Mayfield (14/77).
5. Also a Quorndon in Leics - Derbys spelling is Quarndon.
6. Spelling error.

Derbys

BREEDON	C1	24JUL47	Ashby de la Z	9/63			
GOTHAM	C1	28OCT47	Derby	9/94			
KINGSTONE	C1	28OCT47	Derby	9/94	BL	8AUG51-31JUL56	
DISEWORTH	C1	22NOV47	Loughborough	9/101	B	20JAN49- 51	
					BL/B	51	
					BL	20DEC51	
SCARCLIFFE	C1	8JAN48	Mansfield	9/114			
PLEASLEY	C1	8JAN48	Mansfiled	9/114	BL	?	
RIDGEWAY	C1	8JAN48	Chesterfield	9/115	R	22APR52	
					B	6DEC59	
WHITTINGTON	C1	8JAN48	Chesterfield	9/115			
WOODVILLE	C1	27JAN48	Burton on Trent	9/117		Note 7.	
MILFORD	C1	5FEB48	Derby	9/120			
HACKENTHORPE	C1	12FEB48	Sheffield	9/122	GR	JUN48	
					R	20APR49-18JAN53	
INTAKE	C1	12FEB48	Sheffield	9/124	R	10JAN52- 7DEC53	
					B	16OCT58	
SELSTON	C1	12FEB48	Alfreton	9/127			
TINTWISTLE	C1	24MAY48	Manchester	9/151			
HADFIELD	C1	24MAY48	Manchester	9/152	BL/GR	6JUN49- 7AUG54	
LOCKINGTON	C1	24MAY48	Derby	9/152			
MELBOURNE	C1	30JUN48	Derby	9/165	BL	23MAR49-25JUN49	
HEATH	C1	29JUL48	Chesterfield	9/170	BL/GR	16JUL50-31MAY54.	
					BL	16JUL54-20SEP56	
STONEY-MIDDLETON	C1	24AUG48	Bakewell	9/176	B	11APR50	
					BL	2AUG54- 1JUN55	
MELLOR	C1	16OCT48	Stockport	9/187			
BRIMINGTON	C1	8JAN49	Chesterfield	9/203	GR	7FEB56	
APPLEBY	C1	1FEB49	Atherstone	9/210	B	19FEB50-27MAR52.	
MEASHAM	C1	1FEB49	Atherstone	9/210			
BRAMCOTE	C1	11MAY49	Derby	9/252	BL	10JAN55	
WILLINGTON	C1	4JUN49	Burton on Trent	10/7	B	4JUL49	
EGGINTON	C1	4JUN49	Burton on Trent	10/7			
GREAT-LONGSTONE	C1	6JUN49	Bakewell	10/8	B	10JUN50-28DEC53.	
					BL	25JUN51-12JUN57	
MUGGINGTON	C1	5JUL49	Derby	10/20			
TURNDICH	C1	5JUL49	Derby	10/21			
MACKWORTH	C1	26SEP49	Derby	10/42	BL	10NOV57	
WEST-HALLAM	C1	29SEP49	Derby	10/43	B	10JAN52	
					BL	4JUL52	
HARTINGTON	C1	13DEC49	Ashbourne	10/58	B	14MAY51-28DEC55.	
					GR	23MAY56	
CHAPEL-EN-LE-FRITH	C1	31JAN50	Stockport	10/65			
TIDESWELL	C1	28MAR50	Bakewell	10/78	BL	27JUN50- 6DEC52	
					BL/GR	7OCT53	
					B	25DEC53- 5OCT54.	
DORE	C1	16MAY50	Sheffield	10/90	BL/GR	19AUG54-19MAY56	
OLD-GLOSSOP	C1	8NOV50	Manchester	10/115	BL	19MAR53-31DEC56	
NEW-MILLS	C1	8NOV50	Stockport	10/117	B	2AUG51-12FEB52	
ST MARYS BRIDGE	C1	26DEC50	Derby	10/128	B	20JAN58	
CHADDESDEN	C1	9JAN51	Derby	10/146			
CHADDESDEN	C1	29JAN51	Derby	10/146			
CHARLESWORTH	C1	19MAR51	Manchester	10/176			
OSMASTON	C1	24APR51	Derby	10/191			
SWADLINGCOTE	C1	24APR51	Burton on Trent	10/192	GR	11OCT51	
WALTON·ON·TRENT	C1	6OCT51	Burton on Trent	10/274	B	20DEC51-25JUN53.	
BORROWASH	C1	26APR52	Derby	11/43	GR	?	
RISLEY	C1	26APR52	Derby	11/43	GR	27SEP53	
MONEY-ASH	C1	26APR52	Bakewell	11/44			

Notes: 7. Formerly Wooden Box - see 7/75.

Derbys

Name	Type	Date	Office	Ref	Colour	Date2
SUTTON-ON-THE-HILL	C1	26APR52	Derby	11/44	BR	19FEB53
CLOWN	C1	18MAY52	Chesterfield	11/53	BL	6MAR57- 9SEP58
HATHERSAGE	C1	SEP52	Bakewell	11/83	GR	5OCT52- 5OCT56
					B	16MAY53- 7NOV54.
NETHERSEAL	C1	SEP52	Ashby de la Z	11/105	GR	8APR56
MIDWAY	C1	SEP52	Burton on Trent	11/105		
STRETTON-EN-LE-FIELDS	C1	SEP52	Ashby de la Z	11/105		
KIRK-IRETON	C1	NOV52	Wirksworth	11/119		
NORTON	C1	NOV52	Sheffield	11/119	B	21MAY53
					BL	23JUL55
OVERSEAL	C1	DEC52	Ashby de la Z	11/124	B	28OCT53-23DEC54.
BEIGHTON	C1	28DEC52	Sheffield	11/125		
LOWER-HEELEY	C1	28DEC52	Sheffield	11/125		
NEWBOLD	C1	JAN53	Chesterfield	11/135		
BARLOW	C1	JAN53	Chesterfield	11/135	BL	10JUN56
PACKINGTON	C1	APR53	Ashby de la Z	11/161	B	14AUG58.
HARTSHORNE	C1	15SEP53	Burton on Trent	11/197		
DOVERIDGE	C1	SEP53	Uttoxeter	11/224	GR	25OCT59
TUPTON	C1	7OCT53	Chesterfield	11/232		
GREEN-LANE	C1	cJUL54		12/80	BL/GR	30DEC57
					?	2AUG59
GREENHILL-LANE	C1	cJUL54		12/90		
SWANWICK	C1	cJUL54		12/90		
NORMANTON	C1	cJUL54		12/90	?	24OCT55
					BL/GR	11OCT58
SOUTH-WINGFIELD	C1	cJUL54		12/90		
AMBER-GATE	C1	cJUL54		12/90		
BRINSLEY	C1	cJUL54		12/90		Note 8.
HUCKNALL	C1	cJUL54		12/90	BL/GR	54
					B	17NOV56 Note 8.
HULLAND	C1	20JUL54		12/93	BL/GR	14APR55
					BL	2MAY55
FRICHLEY	C1	23JAN55	Belper	12/151		Note 9.
FRITCHLEY	C1	30MAR55	Belper	12/181		
LANGWITH	C1	30MAR55	Mansfield	12/181		
NORTON	C1	30MAR55	Mansfield	12/181	B	6DEC58
MAPPLETON	C1	5MAY55	Ashbourne	12/194	B	24JUL56- 6OCT59
					GR	24OCT59
					BL	18FEB60
CALDWELL	C1	17MAY55	Burton on Trent	12/198		
LEA-BRIDGE	C1	17SEP55	Matlock Bath	12/242	B	24FEB59- 2DEC59
HOLLOWAY	C1	17SEP55	Matlock Bath	12/242	GR	26APR56
					?	2DEC59
TANSLEY	C1	17SEP55	Matlock Bath	12/242		
ROSLINGTON	C1	30NOV55	Burton on Trent	12/272		Note 10.
HILTON	C1	4DEC55	Burton on Trent	12/275		
THULSTON	C1	15DEC55	Derby	12/280		
ROSLISTON	C1	28DEC55	Burton on Trent	12/288		
DENBY	C1	5JAN56	Belper	12/291		
HAZLEWOOD	C1	5JAN56	Belper	12/291		
PARWICH	C1	31JAN56	Ashbourne	12/304		
CUBLEY	C1	11JUL56	Uttoxeter	13/38		
WINGERWORTH	C1	29JUL56	Chesterfield	13/47		
DUCKMANTON	C1	29JUL56	Chesterfield	13/47		
HASLAND	C1	29JUL56	Chesterfield	13/47		
HANDLEY	C1	29JUL56	Chesterfield	13/47		
HOLYMOORSIDE	C1	29JUL56	Chesterfield	13/47	BL	2NOV56

Notes:
8. Probably sent to Alfreton.
9. Spelling error - see next line.
10. Spelling error - see 12/288.

BRAILSFORD	C1	13NOV56	Derby	13/96	BL/GR	26MAY57-29SEP58
					BL	21MAY58
MILTON	C1	2DEC56	Burton on Trent	13/103		
WINSHILL	C1	2DEC56	Burton on Trent	13/103		
CODNOR	C1	19DEC56	Alfreton	13/112	B	26MAY58-29MAY58
SHARDLOW	C1	1JAN57	Derby	13/120		
SNELSTON	C1	12FEB57	Ashbourne	13/144		
THORPE	C1	12FEB57	Ashbourne	13/144		
LONG-EATON	C1	16FEB57	Derby	13/150		
LONGFORD	C1	24FEB57	Derby	13/160		
SUTTON·ON·THE·HILL	C1	12MAR57	Derby	13/169		
HASSOP	C1	23MAR57	Bakewell	13/191		
LITTON	C1	23MAR57	Bakewell	13/191		
CALVER	C1	23MAR57	Bakewell	13/191		
GRINDLEFORD-BRIDGE	C1	23MAR57	Bakewell	13/191		
CRESBROOK	C1	23MAR57	Bakewell	13/191		
SUDBURY	C1	1APR57	Derby	13/201	GR	12DEC58
					B	9JAN59-16MAY59
BRAMCOTE	C1	1APR57	Derby	13/201		
KILLAMARSH	C1*	12APR57	Chesterfield	13/213	B	4JUL57-24DEC59.
					GR	57- 58
					BL	12DEC57- 59
MOSBOROUGH	C1	12APR57	Chesterfield	13/213		
ALVASTON	C1*	12APR57	Derby	13/214	BL	27JAN60
TISSINGTON	C1*	12APR57	Ashbourne	13/215	B	11SEP57-29SEP59
MARSTON-MONTGOMERY	C1*	12APR57	Ashbourne	13/215		
BROOK ST	C1*	29APR57	Derby	13/221	BL	17JUN58
					GR	21JUN58
HAYFIELD	C1*	16MAY57	Manchester	13/236		
ASMASTON	C1*	25MAY57	Derby	13/239		Note 11.
BARNASTON	C1*	25MAY57	Derby	13/239		Note 11.
LITTLEOVER	C1*	25MAY57	Derby	13/239		
RADBOURNE	C1*	25MAY57	Derby	13/239		
NORTON	C1*	8JUN57	Sheffield	13/250	BL	4JUL57
DERWENT	C1*	13JUN57	Bakewell	13/258		
BAMFORD	C1*	13JUN57	Bakewell	13/258		
WEST-HALLAM	C1*	15JUN57	Derby	13/259	BL	22DEC59.
ST-MARYS-BRIDGE	C1*	15JUN57	Derby	13/259	BL	24JUN57
					B	20JAN58
SPONDON	C1*	19JUN57	Derby	13/262		
MARPLE	C1*	23JUN57	Stockport	13/266		
EYAM	C1*	10JUL57	Bakewell	13/276		
STONEY-MIDDLETON	C1*	10JUL57	Bakewell	13/276		
CASTLETON-DERBY	C1*	10JUL57	Bakewell	13/276		Note 12.
TADDINGTON	C1*	10JUL57	Bakewell	13/276	BL	15FEB60
YOULGREANE	C1*	10JUL57	Bakewell	13/276	B	14JUN60 Note 13.
ETWALL	C1*	15JUL57	Derby	13/278	GR	1JUN58
					?	22MAR59
TIBSHELF	C4	25JUL57	Alfreton	13/288		
OSMASTON	C4	1AUG57	Derby	13/292		
BURNASTON	C4	1AUG57	Derby	13/292		
ILAM	C4	6OCT57	Ashbourne	14/43		
ALSTONEFIELD	C4	6OCT57	Ashbourne	14/43	BL	30NOV57.
ELLASTONE	C4	6OCT57	Ashbourne	14/43	B	3NOV57-12JAN59
DISEWORTH	C4	22OCT57	Loughborough	14/61		

Notes:
11. Spelling error – see 13/292.
12. Wrongly made and never used – a CDS was issued on 21JUL57 to Castleton.
13. Spelling error – left leg of 'N' apparently filed off when used.

Derbys   24.

MAYFIELD	C4	12NOV57	Ashbourne	14/77			
STANTON·BY·DALE	C4	27NOV57	Derby	14/90			
CHURCH-BROUGHTON	C4	30DEC57	Derby	14/116			
WHITFIELD	C4	27JAN58	Manchester	14/132			
COMPSTALL	D1	3FEB58	Stockport	14/134			
STAPLEFORD	D1	5FEB58	Derby	14/140			
HOLBROOK	C4	5FEB58	Derby	14/140			
FAIRFIELD	D1	18FEB58	Buxton	14/149	BL	6JAN60	
RADBOURNE	D1	4MAR58	Derby	14/158			
HOPE	D4	22APR58	Sheffield	14/204	B	6JAN60	
MIDDLETON	D1	22APR58	Wirksworth	14/206			
WHALEY-BRIDGE	D1	22FEB58	Stockport	14/210			
OLD-BRAMPTON	D1	4JUN58	Chesterfield	14/228	GR	8JUN59-	60
UNSTON	D4	15JUN58	Sheffield	14/256			
MEASHAM	D4	30SEP58	Atherstone	16/51	B	?	
KILBURN	D4	25OCT58	Belper	16/69			
HEAGE	D4	25OCT58	Belper	16/69			
DENBY	D4	25OCT58	Belper	16/69			
STONE-GRAVELS	D1	8NOV58	Chesterfield	16/86	BL	14JUN59	
					B	16SEP59	
WILLINGTON	D1	8NOV58	Burton on Trent	16/86			
NEWTON-SOLNEY	D1	8NOV58	Burton on Trent	16/86			
STAPENHILL	D1	8NOV58	Burton on Trent	16/86	B	23JUN59.	
LULLINGTON	D1	8NOV58	Burton on Trent	16/86			
HARTSHORNE	D1	8NOV58	Burton on Trent	16/86			
CALDWELL	D1	8NOV58	Burton on Trent	16/86			
NEWHALL	D4	8NOV58	Burton on Trent	16/87			
REPTON	D4	8NOV58	Burton on Trent	16/87	GR	20JAN59	
					B	2AUG59	
HILTON	D4	8NOV58	Burton on Trent	16/87			
INTAKE	D4	17DEC58	Sheffield	16/103	BL	18AUG59	
HACKENTHORPE	D1	17DEC58	Sheffield	16/103			
SHIREBROOK	D1	14JAN59	Mansfield	16/139			
ASHOVER	D4	27JAN59	Chesterfield	16/148			
DRAYCOTT	D1	11APR59	Derby	18/25			
HIGHAM DERBYSHIRE	D2	20APR59	Alfreton	18/30			Note 14.
WALTON·ON·TRENT	D1	20APR59	Burton on Trent	18/30	B	3MAY59	
PINXTON	D4	20APR59	Alfreton	18/31			
BOLSOVER	D1	14MAY59	Chesterfield	18/42			
EDENSOR	D4	14MAY59	Chesterfield	18/42			
GREENHILL	D1	14JUL59	Sheffield	18/73			
PEAK·FORREST	D1	26AUG59	Stockport	18/98			

Notes: 14. The only example from Derbyshire of a type D2 mark.

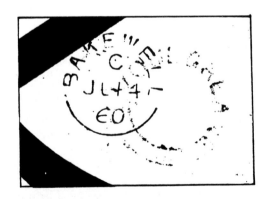

Very late use on 24th June 1860 of YOULGREA<u>N</u>E (13/276). The 'N' appears to have had the left leg removed to make the stamp read as 'YOULGREAVE'.

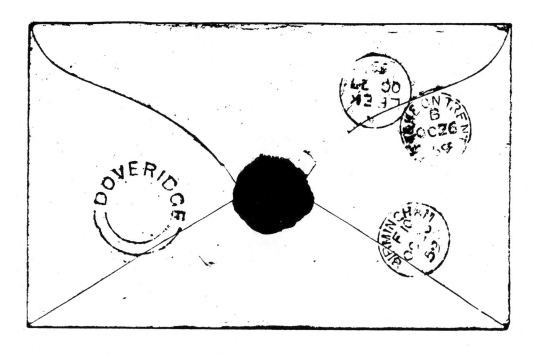

DOVERIDGE (11/224)

A Derbyshire office but under Uttoxeter (Staffs) when the stamp was issued.

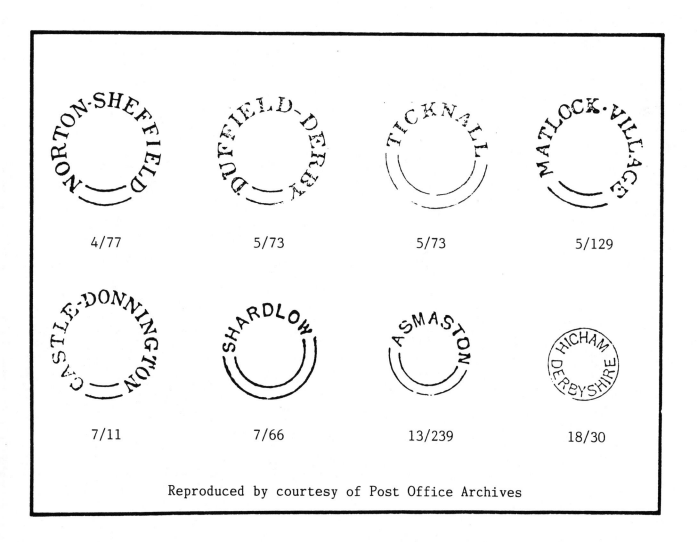

Reproduced by courtesy of Post Office Archives

Derbys 26.

Similar Sans-serif (C1) Marks of Derbyshire

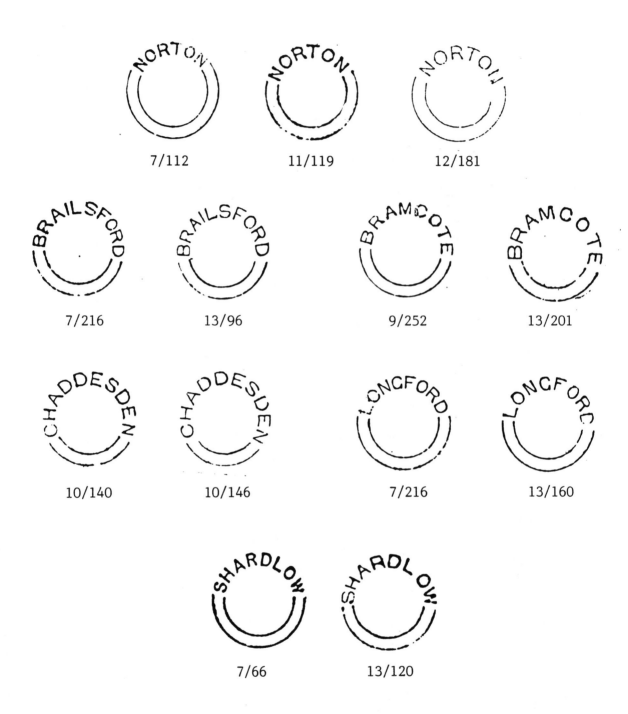

7/112	11/119	12/181

7/216	13/96	9/252	13/201

10/140	10/146	7/216	13/160

7/66	13/120

Reproduced by courtesy of Post Office Archives

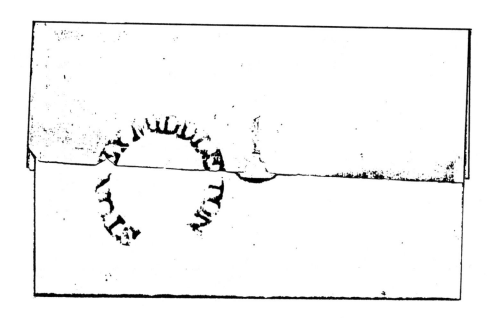

STONEY MIDDLETON (Pre-proof books) used in 1842.

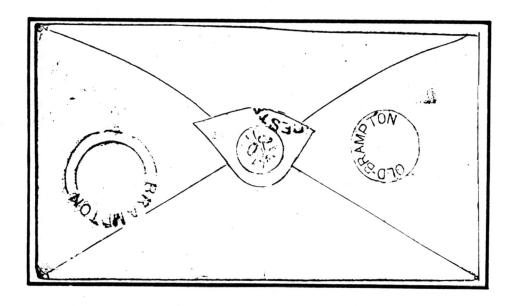

BRAMPTON (9/7) and OLD BRAMPTON (14/228) struck on the same cover in 1859.

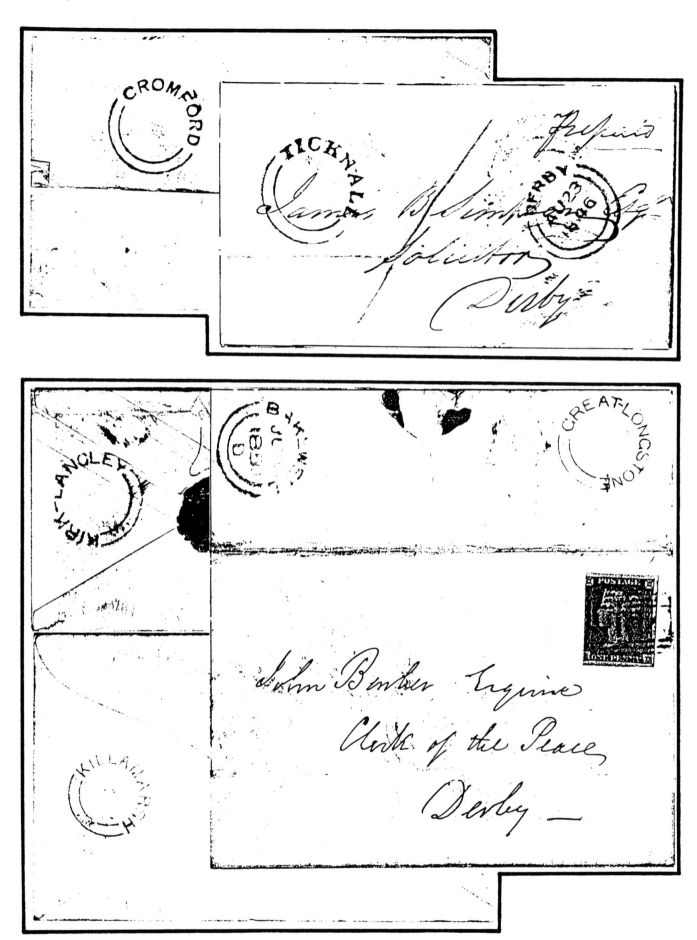

Above: CROMFORD (7/153) and TICKNALL (5/73).

Below: KIRK LANGLEY (7/216), GREAT LONGSTONE (10/8) and KILLAMARSH (13/213).

GLOUCESTERSHIRE
(excluding the Bristol area)

BERKELEY (270). 1/19 4/32 (CDS 9JUL47) See TL6.

Purton 11/192
Stone 9/160 12/324
Whitfield 9/143

CHELTENHAM (177).

Alderton 11/167 12/83
Andoversford (572) 2/4 See TL2.
Bath Road + 11/56
Bishops Cleeve 5/67
Boddington 7/231
Charlton Kings 5/67
Chedworth 11/147 14/245
Colesbourne 9/33 12/135
Combe Hill 9/63 (replaced Uckington in 1847)
Cowley 9/67
Ford 11/160
Fossbridge 10/63
Hawling 9/183
Leckhampton 7/21
London Road + 13/13
Montpellier + 9/160 14/245
Pittville + 9/187 14/245
Prestbury 5/67 13/15
Shurdington 7/21
Staverton 13/13
St Pauls + 13/13
Tewkesbury Rd +
Uckington 7/252 (replaced by Combe Hill)
Winchcombe (536) 2/157 (CDS 12SEP49)
Withington 11/147
Woolstone 9/182 14/245

CIRENCESTER (204).

Ampney Crucis 11/150
Ashton Keynes 7/22
Barnsley 7/22
Daglingworth 7/22
Edgworth 7/22
Harnhill 9/218
Miserden 7/22
North Cerney 7/22
Oaksey 9/29 12/51
Sapperton 9/32 See TL16&30.
Siddington 10/141
South Cerney 9/42
Stratton 11/150
Winstone 10/163.

COLEFORD (212). 1/28
(CDS 14JUN39)

English Bicknor 10/112
Llandogo _1_ 7/218 11/83
See TL15&23.
Stanton 11/168
Whitebrook _1_ 11/168

DURSLEY (269).

Cambridge + 10/68 12/82
See TL24.
Coaley 11/171
Frampton on Severn + 10/116
(CDS 28MAR51) See TL24.
Slimbridge 10/67 See TL24.

GLOUCESTER (312).

Ashleworth 9/2
Barton St Michael(s) 9/33 16/51
Brimpsfield 7/146 See TL13.
Brockthorpe 7/249
Brockworth 14/154
Haresfield 7/84 See TL24.
Hartpury 10/44
Hasfield 7/7
Hempstead 13/203
Highnam 12/16
Hope Mansell _2_ 9/175 See TL31.
Horseferry Bridge 5/180
Hucclecote 12/16
Huntley 9/49 See TL31&39.
Lea (313) + _2_ 5/159 (CDS 28MAR51)
13/194 See TL37.
Longhope 9/49 14/114 See TL19.
Longney 12/17
Maisemore 7/53 16/57
Minsterworth 7/222
Mitcheldean + 5/39 (CDS 28MAR51)
See TL31.
Newent + 7/69 (CDS 28MAR50)
Northgate Street + 13/101
Norton 9/26
Quedgeley 12/17
Redmarley _3_ 5/159 7/92
See TL4&36.
Sandhurst 10/167 14/56
Southgate Street + 13/101
Staunton _3_ 7/163 (CDS 28MAR51)
14/90
Taynton 9/56.

+ Indicates an office which used a straight line (or P.P.) stamp after 1840.

An underlined number, eg _1_, indicates an office outside Glos - see key at end.

Glos

Gloucester (Cont'd)

Thornbury (315) 4/42 (CDS 29JAN49)
Tuffley 12/17 16/51
Upton St Leonards 7/92 12/15 16/51
Westbury on Severn 5/157 14/73 See TL11.
Weston Under Penyard 2 7/174 See TL5.
Witcombe 16/57

LYDNEY (559). 1/53* (CDS 14SEP49)

Ailburton 11/168
Parkend 12/32 (CDS 30DEC58)

MORETON IN MARSH (534). 1/116 (CDS 21OCT39)

Barton in/on the Heath 4 10/162
Blockley 5/101 10/65 (CDS 1SEP57) See TL28&29.
Bourton on the Hill 5/123 11/148
Bourton on the Water 7/3
Broadwell 11/62
Lower Guiting 9/17 14/245 See TL21.
Mickleton 9/160 See TL22.
Stow on/in the Wold Pre-proof books, (CDS 31MAY49)
Toddenham 11/131

NEWNHAM (558). 1/124 (CDS 21SEP39)

Awre 9/168
Blakeney 5/176 (CDS 11JUN56) See TL12.
Brookend + 10/44 See TL12.
Cinderford 11/160 (CDS 7MAR51)
Littledean 7/280
Newerne 10/175 See TL12.
Respidge 14/144
Ruardean 11/160
The Flat 10/267
Whitecroft 9/85
Woodside 5/189
Yorkley 10/175 See TL12.

NORTHLEACH (571). 1/124 (CDS 21SEP39) See TL18.

Aldsworth 9/140 See TL18.
Aston Blank 11/147 See TL18.
Salperton 10/125 14/245 See TL17.
Sherborne 9/140 See TL18.
Winson 11/147 See TL18&33.

STONEHOUSE (024). 7/19 (CDS cDEC53) See TL24.

Leonard Stanley 12/339
Saul 13/233.

STROUD (757).

Arlingham 11/167 See TL24.
Avening 7/106
Beverstone 9/140
Bisley 7/19 13/259
Bowbridge 11/167
Brimscombe (Port) 7/19 7/50 14/43
Cainscross 7/19 14/154
Chalford (171) 2/25 (CDS 9AUG36)
Coates 11/167 See TL30.
Dudbridge 11/167
Eastcombe 11/167
Eas(t)ington 5/177 14/78
    See TL24.
Fretherne 9/101 See TL24.
Frocester 11/167 See TL24.
Horsley 7/48 9/188
Kings Stanley 7/19 See TL24.
Littleworth 9/113
Minchinhampton (172) 1/114
Nailsworth 4/75 (CDS 16JAN49)
Nympsfield 9/140 See TL24.
Pagenhill 11/167
Painswick (314) + 7/7
(CDS 16JAN49) 13/259
(further CDS 15JUL57) See TL1&13.
Pitchcombe 11/101
Randwick 11/167
Rodborough 11/167
Rudge (now Edge) 11/167
Sheepscombe 9/24
Shortwood 11/167
Stroud Green 7/270 See TL38.
Uley (759) 1/189 See TL3.
Whitminster + 9/242 See TL24.
Woodchester 5/3 16/49

TETBURY (786).

Badminton 5/165 9/183
    (CDS 28MAR51) See TL7.
Brokenborough 5 12/83
Burton Hill 5 11/186 18/39
Charlton 5 9/57 18/14 See TL40.
Crudwell 5 9/23 16/62
Didmarton 9/48 See TL9&26.
Dunkirk (205) 5/144 See TL9&26.
Little Sodbury 9/127 See TL9&26.
Little Somerford 5 11/186
    See TL27.
Long Newnton 18/85
Luckington 5 7/254 See TL26.
Minety 5 9/57 9/93 16/61
Nettleton 5 7/253
Sherstone 5 7/254 12/33 12/71
Shipton Moyne 11/186
West Kington 5 7/254
Westonbirt 9/140.

+ indicates an office which used a straight line (or P.P.) stamp after 1840.

An underlined number, eg 5, indicates an office outside Glos - see key at end.

Glos

TEWKESBURY (788).

Apperley 14/277
Aston Cross 11/247 16/58
Beckford 3 9/4
Bredon 3 9/170 12/315 16/58
Corse Lawn 7/13 16/151
Eldersfield 3 14/277
Forthampton 14/277
Kemerton 3 9/4 16/57
Longdon 3 7/33 16/58
Overbury 3 9/70 16/58
Strensham 3 7/79 12/315 16/58
Tirley 7/279 14/32
Twining Green 11/247 16/58

WOTTON UNDER EDGE (915). 1/208 (CDS 22AUG39)

Alderley 10/163
Charfield 11/178
Cromhall 10/30
Hawkesbury Upton 10/31 See TL26.
Kingscote (758) + 12/324 12/332
Kingswood 9/24 12/317
Leighterton 10/31
North Nibley 5/160 10/84 See TL25.
Old Sodbury 10/31 16/163 See TL26.
Pitt Court 11/178
Stinchcombe 11/178 See TL25.
Tortworth 7/23 12/317 12/332
Wickwar (917) 1/202 (CDS 28MAR51)
Yate 11/179 18/13

BROADWAY (137), Worcs

Stanton 10/163
Weston sub Edge 10/198

BURFORD (149), Oxon

Barrington 11/186 14/35 See TL20.
Little Rissington 10/70 See TL20.
Swinbrook 11/186 14/245 See TL20.

CHEPSTOW (178), Mon

Lydney See TL10&12.
Tiddenham 7/110

CHIPPENHAM (191), Wilts

Chipping Sodbury (193) 1/28 (CDS 28MAR50)
Crosshands 7/85
Dyrham 11/179
Marshfield 7/85

CHIPPING NORTON (195), Oxon

Oddington 9/164 14/275

EVESHAM (284), Worcs

Dumbleton 7/21 13/281

FARINGDON (293), Berks

Bibury 5/199
Eastleach Turville 9/19
Fairford (294) 1/53 (CDS 20AUG39)
Hatherop 11/152
Kempsford 9/80
Lechlade (296) 1/105
    (CDS 20AUG39)
Quennington 11/152

LEDBURY (446), Herefs

Dymock 7/151 See TL36.
Much Marcle 2 7/151 See TL36.

MONMOUTH (532), Mon

Clearwell 7/128 13/142 13/162
    See TL14.
Dingeston 10/90
May(s) Hill 11/172 14/65
Newland 7/128 9/236 9/243
    See TL14.
Redbrook 11/57 See TL23.
St Briavels 7/128 11/83
    See TL14.

PERSHORE (611), Worcs

Eckington 3 7/70 See TL8&32.

ROSS (654), Herefs

Lydbrook 7/13

SWINDON (766), Wilts

Down Ampney 11/172 See TL35.
Meysey Hampton 9/10 10/242
    See TL35.

WORCESTER (918), Worcs

Ripple 3 10/35 See TL34.

KEY to offices not in Gloucestershire

1 is in Monmouth, 2 is in Herefs, 3 is in Worcs, 4 is in Warks, 5 is in Wilts.

TRANSFERS - Gloucestershire

TL 1. Painswick letters to be sent to Gloucester by the Night Mail and to Stroud by the Day Mail from 5OCT41.

2. Andoversford reduced in status from a sub-post town to a sub-office (under Cheltenham) in 1842.

3. Uley from Stroud to Dursley on 17AUG44.

4. Redmarley from Gloucester to Ledbury on 19OCT44.

5. Weston under Penyard from Gloucester to Ross on Wye on 27APR46.

6. Berkeley became a post town on 10OCT47.

7. Badminton from Tetbury to Chippenham by 1848.

8. Eckington from Pershore to Tewkesbury on 22MAY48.

9. Didmarton, Dunkirk and Little Sodbury from Tetbury to Wotton under Edge on 8DEC49.

10. Lydney from Chepstow to Newnham on 5OCT51.

11. Westbury on Severn from Gloucester to Newnham on 10NOV51.

12. Lydney became a post town on 11NOV51. Newerne, Yorkley Brookend and Blakeney from Newnham to Lydney at that time.

13. Brimpsfield and Painswick from Gloucester to Stroud on 29MAR52.

14. Newland, Clearwell (and St Briavels?) from Monmouth to Coleford on 30JUN52.

15. Llandogo from Coleford(?) to Monmouth on 30JUN52.

16. Sapperton from Cirencester to Stroud in MAR53.

17. Salperton from Northleach to Cheltenham on 21JUL53.

18. Northleach reduced to a sub-office under Cheltenham on 5AUG53. (Day Mail to come through Oxford.) Aldsworth, Aston Blank, Sherborne and Winson would have transferred at the same time.

19. Longhope from Gloucester to Newnham on 21SEP53.

20. Barrington, Little Rissington and Swinbrook from Burford to Cheltenham on 5OCT53 when Burford ceased to be a post town.

21. Lower Guiting from Moreton in Marsh to Cheltenham on 29OCT53.

22. Mickleton from Moreton in Marsh to Broadway on 1NOV53.

23. Llandogo and Redbrook from Monmouth to Coleford on 3NOV53.

TL24. Stonehouse (previously under Stroud) became a post town on 5DEC53. Arlingham, Cambridge, Frampton-on-Severn, Slimbridge Haresfield, Eastington, Fretherne, Frocester, Kings Stanley, Nympsfield and Whitminster were all transferred to Stonehouse, probably at that time. Whitminster (and perhaps others) may have been further transferred to Dursley at a later date.

25. North Nibley (and probably Stinchcombe) from Wotton under Edge to Dursley on 22DEC53.

26. Didmarton, Dunkirk, Little Sodbury, Old Sodbury, Luckington and Hawkesbury Upton to Chippenham on 26DEC53.

27. Little Somerford from Tetbury to Chippenham, perhaps in 1854.

28. Blockley from Moreton in Marsh to Broadway, at an unknown date, probably in the early 1850s.

29. Blockley from Broadway to Moreton in Marsh on 24JAN54.

30. Coates and Sapperton from Stroud to Cirencester on 15MAR54.

31. Mitcheldean, Huntley and Hope Mansell from Gloucester to Newnham on 13JUL54.

32. Eckington from Tewkesbury to Pershore on 18JUL54.

33. Winson from Cheltenham to Faringdon on 25JUL54.

34. Ripple from Worcester to Tewkesbury on 31AUG54.

35. Cricklade (Wilts) became a post town on 1FEB55. Down Ampney and Meysey Hampton were probably transferred to Cricklade at the same time.

36. Much Marcle, Dymock and Redmarley from Ledbury to Gloucester on 3NOV55.

37. Lea from Gloucester to Ross on Wye on 9MAY56.

38. Stroud Green from Stroud to Stonehouse on 28FEB57.

39. Huntley from Newnham to Gloucester on 2OCT57.

40. Charlton (Wilts) from Tetbury to Chippenham by 1859.

GLOUCESTERSHIRE (excluding the Bristol area)

STOW IN THE WOLD	C3				B	12NOV29- 2MAY49
WICKWAR	C2*	21JAN28	Wickwar	1/202	B	31-28SEP46
					BL	5MAY49-30JAN51
MINCHINHAMPTON	C2*	5JUN28	Minchinhampton	1/114	B	11OCT28- 7SEP46
					BL	52
					GR	53
					R	26FEB54-21APR56.
					GY/B	59
ULEY	C2*	2MAR29	Uley	1/189	B	8AUG29-20MAR49
NEWNHAM	C2*	9MAR29	Newnham	1/124	B	29-27JUL39
NORTHLEACH	C2*	4MAY29		1/124	B	11FEB35-18MAR39
BERKELEY	C2*	13FEB30	Berkeley	1/19	OR	17JAN31
					B	11MAY33- 6SEP39
MORETON IN MARSH	C2	11MAR30		1/116	B	8APR30- 9MAR39
COLEFORD	C2*	3JUL30	Coleford	1/28	B	7SEP31- 39
TETBURY	C2*	30JUL30	Tetbury	1/182	B	11DEC31- 5JUL38.
CHIPPING·SODBURY	C2	10AUG30	Chipping Sodbury	1/28	B	16NOV30-10MAR47
					OR	29DEC39
WOTTON·UNDER·EDGE	C2	17AUG30	Wotton U Edge	1/208	B	17JAN32-25JUN39
LECHLADE	C2*	27SEP30		1/105	B	22NOV32- 39
FAIRFORD	C2*	15FEB31	Fairford	1/53	B	31-16MAY35.
LYDNEY	C3*				R	8NOV31- 7NOV40
					B	26JUN39-24APR49
					BL/GR	11SEP49
WINCHCOMB	C2	3JUL34	Winchcomb	2/157	B	12MAR37-28FEB47
					R	MAR45
					BL	7JUN48- 5SEP49
CHALFORD	C2	25JAN36	Chalford	2/25	B	36-28MAR41
ANDOVERSFORD	C2M	6NOV38	Andoversford	2/4	B	30JUN48-11NOV57 Note 1.
BERKELEY	C2	21SEP39	Dursley	4/32	B	16DEC39-12FEB47
THORNBURY	C2	11NOV39	Gloucester	4/42	B	20APR41-14FEB43
NAILSWORTH	C2	10OCT40	Nailsworth	4/75	B	5APR41-11SEP48
WOODCHESTER	C2	11JUN41	Stroud	5/3	B	16AUG41-10NOV54
					BL	22JUL54
MITCHELDEAN	C2	30OCT41	Gloucester	5/39	B	4AUG42-19MAR50.
BISHOPS-CLEEVE	C2	11JAN42	Cheltenham	5/67	OR/R	30AUG43
CHARLTON-KINGS	C2	11JAN42	Cheltenham	5/67	B	23OCT46
					BL	4APR50-15MAY55
					GY/B	4DEC58- 3APR59.
PRESTBURY	C2	11JAN42	Cheltenham	5/67	B	18SEP44
BLOCKLEY	C2	4JUN42	Moreton in M	5/101	OR/R	24AUG43-10AUG50
					BR	3MAR48
					GR/BL	21OCT52-26JAN53
					GR	26MAR55- 56.
BOURTON·ON·THE·HILL	C2	7NOV42	Moreton in M	5/123		
DUNKIRK	C2	25FEB43	Tetbury	5/144		
WESTBURY-ON-SEVERN	C2	9MAY43	Gloucester	5/157	B	2MAR47-16AUG53
					R	17NOV56
LEA	C2	13MAY43	Gloucester	5/159	B	15JUL44-11SEP45
REDMARLEY	C2	13MAY43	Gloucester	5/159		
NORTH-NIBLEY	C2	19MAY43	Wootton U Edge	5/160		
BADMINTON	C2	23JUN43	Tetbury	5/165	B	31AUG43-20NOV46.

Notes: 1. Issued as a CDS when Andoversford was a sub Post Town. Later used as a UDC with slugs removed when it was reduced to a sub-office in 1842.

Glos

BLAKENEY		C2	14AUG43	Newnham	5/176	R	3FEB44- 7JUN44
						GR	16AUG49
EASINGTON		C2	30AUG43	Stroud	5/177	B	11JUN45 Note 2.
						BL	8APR51-10SEP58?
HORSEFERRY-BRIDGE		C2	4SEP43	Gloucester	5/180		
WOODSIDE		C2	23OCT43	Newnham	5/189	BL/GR	3SEP50
BIBURY		C2	16NOV43	Fairford	5/199	BL	30NOV49- 9DEC51
						R	30JAN54
						B	14JUN58
BOURTON-ON- THE-WATER		C2	6DEC43	Moreton in M	7/3	R	17SEP51
HASFIELD		C2	19DEC43	Gloucester	7/7	B	18JAN45
PAINSWICK		C2	19DEC43	Stroud	7/7	B	<u>14DEC43</u>-19FEB49.
CORSE-LAWN		C2	3JAN44	Tewkesbury	7/13		
LYDBROOK		C2	3JAN44	Ross	7/13	B	5FEB48-17MAY50
						GR	7DEC52
						R	10APR55
						BL/B	2JUL58
BRINSCOMB-PORT		C2	19JAN44	Stroud	7/19		Note 3.
BISLEY		C2	19JAN44	Stroud	7/19	R	16AUG44-13JUN57
						BL	27JAN44-22JUN55
CAINS-CROSS		C2	19JAN44	Stroud	7/19	B	30DEC44-30OCT51
						OR	11SEP54
KINGS-STANLEY		C2	19JAN44	Stroud	7/19	B	27AUG44-17FEB48
						BL	5NOV51- 9JUN53
STONEHOUSE		C2	19JAN44	Stroud	7/19	B	22MAY45- 48
						BL	23DEC50
LECKHAMPTON		C2	20JAN44	Cheltenham	7/21	B	28JUN44-17NOV46.
SHURDINGTON		C2	20JAN44	Cheltenham	7/21	OR/R	28MAR47-16MAR48
DUMBLETON		C2	20JAN44	Evesham	7/21	B	2MAR45-15JAN48
						BL	20DEC54
ASHTON-KEYNES		C2	29JAN44	Cirencester	7/22	B?	?
BARNSLEY		C2	29JAN44	Cirencester	7/22		
DAGLINGWORTH		C2	29JAN44	Cirencester	7/22		
EDGEWORTH		C2	29JAN44	Cirencester	7/22		
MISERDEN		C2	29JAN44	Cirencester	7/22		
NORTH-CERNEY		C2	29JAN44	Cirencester	7/22	B	28MAY51
TORTWORTH		C2	29JAN44	Wotton U Edge	7/23	B	28APR49
LONGDON		C2	26FEB44	Tewkesbury	7/33	BR	24MAY47
						BL	5DEC51
HORSLEY		C1	19APR44	Stroud	7/48		
BRIMSCOMB-PORT		C2	1MAY44	Stroud	7/50	R	19APR45-28OCT47.
						BL	8JAN54
MAISMORE		C1	11MAY44	Gloucester	7/53	B	10AUG48-23MAY55
NEWENT		C1	8JUN44	Gloucester	7/69	B	20JUN44-24AUG46
						BL	4JUN49
						GR	8JUN52
ECKINGTON		C1	8JUN44	Pershore	7/70	B	29NOV59
STRENSHAM		C1	10JUL44	Tewkesbury	7/79		
HARESFIELD		C1	9AUG44	Gloucester	7/84	B	17JUL50-10AUG58
CROSSHANDS		C1	9AUG44	Chippenham	7/85	BL/GR	27JUL53- 54
MARSHFIELD		C1	9AUG44	Chippenham	7/85		
UPTON ST LEONARDS		C1	22AUG44	Gloucester	7/92	B	10DEC44- 3MAR49.
						BL/GR	10JAN51- 3APR53
REDMARLEY		C1	22AUG44	Ledbury	7/92	BR	26SEP46
						B	15AUG45-14OCT52
AVENING		C1	9NOV44	Stroud	7/106	B	24JAN48-25APR50
						GR	10NOV49- 7JUL51
TIDDENHAM		C1	19NOV44	Chepstow	7/110	B	27APR46-27NOV48

Notes: 2. Correct name is 'Ea<u>s</u>tington'.
3. Almost certainly not used - see 7/50.

Glos   36.

IRNHAM	C1	6DEC44	Cheltenham	7/114		Note 4.
CLEARWELL	C1	21FEB45	Newport, Mon	7/128		
NEWLAND	C1	21FEB45	Newport, Mon	7/128	B	28APR47
ST BRIAVELS	C1	21FEB45	Newport, Mon	7/128		
BRIMPSFIELD	C1	14JUN45	Gloucester	7/146		
DYMOCK	C1	2JUN45	Ledbury	7/151	B	20JUN50-16AUG59
					BR/B	25JUL50
					R	23JAN56- 4OCT56
					BL/B	16AUG57-15DEC58.
MUCH-MARCLE	C1	2JUN45	Ledbury	7/151	B	15NOV46-10MAR50
					BL	10JUL51-16AUG57
					R	14MAR56
					BL/B	15DEC58
STAUNTON	C1	16JUL45	Gloucester	7/163		
WESTON·UNDER. PENYARD	C1	9SEP45	Gloucester	7/174	B	26SEP46
					BL/B	16AUG59
					R	2APR56
LANDOGO	C1	10MAR46	Coleford	7/218	B	17SEP48
MINSTERWORTH	C1	17MAR46	Gloucester	7/222		
BODDINGTON	C1	24APR46	Cheltenham	7/231		
BROCKTHORPE	C1	30JUN46	Gloucester	7/249		
UCKINGTON	C1	13JUL46	Cheltenham	7/252		
NETTLETON	C1	13JUL46	Tetbury	7/253		
WEST-KINGTON	C1	13JUL46	Tetbury	7/254		
LUCKINGTON	C1	13JUL46	Tetbury	7/254	BR/B	7JUN51-28MAR54
					BL/B	28JUN56
SHERSTONE	C1	13JUL46	Tetbury	7/254		
STROUD-GREEN	C1	29SEP46	Stroud	7/270		
TIRLEY	C1	18NOV46	Tewkesbury	7/279	B	23APR54
LITTLE-DEAN	C1	21NOV46	Newnham	7/280	BR	26NOV48
					BL	20DEC52
ASHLEWORTH	C1	1JAN47	Gloucester	9/2		
BECKFORD	C1	12JAN47	Tewkesbury	9/4	GR	23MAR55
KEMERTON	C1	12JAN47	Tewkesbury	9/4	B	19AUG47-20AUG47.
					GR	18OCT52-30APR55
MEYREY-HAMPTON	C1	16FEB47	Swindon	9/10		Note 5.
LOWER-GUITING	C1	2MAR47	Moreton in M	9/17		
EASTLEACH-TURVILLE	C1	3MAR47	Faringdon	9/19	GR	22FEB53
					BL	25AUG54
					B	24JAN60
CRUDWELL	C1	29MAR47	Tetbury	9/23		
KINGSWOOD	C1	29MAR47	Wootton U Edge	9/24		
SHEEPSCOMBE	C1	29MAR47	Stroud	9/24	B?	9JUN59
NORTON	C1	3APR47	Gloucester	9/26		
OAKSEY	C1	17APR47	Cirencester	9/29	BR	19AUG48
SAPPERTON	C1	24APR47	Cirencester	9/32		
COLESBOURNE	C1	5MAY47	Cheltenham	9/33		
BARTON-ST-MICHAELS	C1	5MAY47	Gloucester	9/33		
SOUTH-CERNEY	C1	22MAY47	Cirencester	9/42		
DIDMARTON	C1	7JUN47	Tetbury	9/48	BL	2JUN51-21JUN51.
HUNTLEY	C1	7JUN47	Gloucester	9/49		
LONGHOPE	C1	7JUN47	Gloucester	9/49	B	17OCT47-24SEP48
TAYNTON	C1	21JUN47	Gloucester	9/56	BR	13SEP48
MINESY	C1	30JUN47	Tetbury	9/57		Note 6.
CHARLTON	C1	30JUN47	Tetbury	9/57		
COMB-HILL	C1	22JUL47	Cheltenham	9/63		
COWLEY	C1	26JUL47	Cheltenham	9/67	Y/BR	13AUG55
OVERBURY	C1	13AUG47	Tewkesbury	9/70		
KEMPSFORD	C1	13SEP47	Faringdon	9/80	BL	15MAR52

Notes: 4. Probably intended for Grantham.
5. Spelling error - see 10/242.
6. Spelling error - see 9/93.

Glos

WHITECROFT	C1	10OCT47	Newnham	9/85	B	?
MINETY	C1	19OCT47	Tetbury	9/93		
FRETHERNE	C1	22NOV47	Stroud	9/101		
LITTLEWORTH	C1	8JAN48	Stroud	9/113		
LITTLE-SODBURY	C1	12FEB48	Tetbury	9/127		
WESTON-BIRT	C1	18APR48	Tetbury	9/140		
BEVERSTONE	C1	18APR48	Stroud	9/140		
NYMPSFIELD	C1	18APR48	Stroud	9/140		
ALDSWORTH	C1	18APR48	Northleach	9/140		
SHERBORNE-GLOS	C1	18APR48	Northleach	9/140	BL/GR	25MAY54
WHITFIELD	C1	4MAY48	Berkeley	9/143		
MICKLETON	C1	20JUN48	Campden	9/160	B	7JAN49-21JUL55.
					BL	27APR50
					R	3JUL57
MONTPELLIER	C1	20JUN48	Cheltenham	9/160	B	5JUL48-23OCT49
					BL	7APR49-19NOV56
					BL/B	8OCT50-13APR56.
STONE	C1	20JUN48	Berkeley	9/160	R	10JAN49
ODDINGTON	C1	29JUN48	Chipping Norton	9/164		
AWRE	C1	29JUN48	Newnham	9/168		
BREDON	C1	29JUL48	Tewkesbury	9/170	B	25MAY50-14JUN52.
					BR	20DEC53
HOPE-MANSELL	C1	24AUG48	Gloucester	9/175		
WALSTONE	C1	22SEP48	Cheltenham	9/182		Note 7.
WOLSTONE	C1	22SEP48	Cheltenham	9/182	B	21JUN51-28MAY53
BADMINTON	C1	4OCT48	Chippenham	9/183	BL	18AUG49- 4SEP49
HAWLING	C1	22SEP48	Andoversford	9/183	B	18MAY49
					BL/GR	15NOV54
PITTVILLE	C1	16OCT48	Cheltenham	9/187	BL	4DEC48-16AUG55.
					B	2FEB58
HORSELEY	C1	26OCT48		9/188	BL	22NOV54-27APR55
						Note 8.
HARNHILL	C1	15FEB49	Cirencester	9/218		
NEWLAND	C1	28MAR49	Monmouth	9/236	GR/B	26DEC50
					R	17SEP55
					BL	8JAN59
WHITMINSTER	C1	5APR49	Stroud	9/242	GR	21FEB53-21DEC53
					OR/R	13DEC56- 9NOV59
					BL	17DEC56
					B	2FEB58-10JAN59
NEWLAND	C1	14APR49	Monmouth	9/243		
CROMHALL	C1	8AUG49	Chippenham	10/30		
OLD-SODBURY	C1	8AUG49	Wootton U Edge	10/31	B	25JUL56-29JUN57
LEIGHTERTON	C1	8AUG49	Wootton U Edge	10/31	B	21JUN52
HAWKESBURY-UPTON	C1	8AUG49	Wootton U Edge	10/31	BL	2JUN51-21JUN52.
					B	25JUL56
RIPPLE	C1	23AUG49	Worcester	10/35		
BROOKEND	C1	9OCT49	Newnham	10/44	BL	22MAY56
HARTPURY	C1	9OCT49	Gloucester	10/44	Albino	13DEC54
					GR	20JUN55
FOSSBRIDGE	C1	31JAN50	Cheltenham	10/63		
BLOCKLEY	C1	31JAN50	Moreton in M	10/65		Note 9.
SLIMBRIDGE	C1	15FEB50	Dursley	10/67	BL/B	18JUL59
CAMBRIDGE	C1	15FEB50	Dursley	10/68		
LITTLE-RISSINGTON	C1	21FEB50	Burford	10/70		
NORTH-NIBLEY	C1	17APR50	Wootton U Edge	10/84	B	26AUG58
DINGESTON	C1	16MAY50	Monmouth	10/90		

Notes: 7. May not have been used.
8. Only known used as 'HORS LEY'.
9. See usage of C2 mark - 5/101.

Glos

ENGLISH-BICKNOR	C1	2OCT50	Coleford	10/112	BL	31JUL54?
					B	21JAN55-19JUL55
FRAMPTON-ON-SEVERN	C1	8NOV50	Dursley	10/116		
SALPERTON	C1	26NOV50	Northleach	10/125		
SIDDINGTON	C1	29JAN51	Cirencester	10/141		
BARTON-IN-THE-HEATH	C1	1MAR51	Moreton in M	10/162	B	12AUG58
WINSTONE	C1	1MAR51	Cirencester	10/163	B	28MAY51
ALDERLEY	C1	1MAR51	Wotton U Edge	10/163	BL	17JAN55
STANTON	C1	1MAR51	Broadway	10/163	BL	12JUN51-20MAY55
SANDHURST	C1	4MAR51	Gloucester	10/167		
NEWERNE	C1	17MAR51	Newnham	10/175	BL	18SEP58
YORKLEY	C1	17MAR51	Newnham	10/175		
WESTON-SUB-EDGE	C1	18MAY51	Broadway	10/198	BL	23JUN51
MEYSEY-HAMPTON	C1	27AUG51	Swindon	10/242		
THE-FLAT	C1	5OCT51	Newnham	10/267		
BATH-ROAD	C1	26MAY52	Cheltenham	11/56	BL	1SEP52-15NOV54
					R	13NOV55-18AUG56
					B	1APR55-22JUL58.
BROADWELL	C1	5JUN52	Moreton in M	11/62	BL	2OOCT55
					B	4AUG59
REDBROOK	C1	JUN52	Monmouth	11/62	R	14OCT56
LLANDOCO	C1	JUL52	Monmouth	11/83		Note 10.
ST-BRIAVELS	C1	JUL52	Coleford	11/83		
PITCHCOMBE	C1	SEP52	Stroud	11/101		
TODDENHAM	C1	JAN53	Moreton in M	11/131		
WINSON	C1	FEB53	Northleach	11/147	BL	21NOV54
ASTON-BLANK	C1	FEB53	Northleach	11/147		
CHEDSWORTH	C1	FEB53	Cheltenham	11/147		
WITHINGTON	C1	FEB53	Cheltenham	11/147		
BOURTON·ON·THE·HILL	C1	FEB53	Moreton in M	11/148	GR	8MAR55
STRATTON	C1	FEB53	Cirencester	11/150		
AMPNEY-CRUCIS	C1	FEB53	Cirencester	11/150		
HATHEROP	C1	MAR53	Faringdon	11/152		
QUENNINGTON	C1	MAR53	Faringdon	11/152		
FORD	C1	APR53	Cheltenham	11/160	B	2FEB60
ANDERFORD	C1	APR53	Newnham	11/160		Note 11.
RUARDEAN	C1	APR53	Newnham	11/160		
ALDERTON	C1	APR53	Cheltenham	11/166	R	4NOV57-30NOV57
PAKEN-HILL	C1	APR53	Stroud	11/167		
RANDWICK	C1	APR53	Stroud	11/167	BL/GR	15JUN54-12JUL54
RUDGE	C1	APR53	Stroud	11/167		Note 12.
BOWBRIDGE	C1	APR53	Stroud	11/167	R	26APR56
					BL	18SEP57
EASTCOMBE	C1	APR53	Stroud	11/167	R	30SEP56
					BL	13DEC58
					B	17FEB59
COATES	C1	APR53	Stroud	11/167		
SHORTWOOD	C1	APR53	Stroud	11/167		
DUDBRIDGE	C1	APR53	Stroud	11/167		
RODBOROUGH	C1	APR53	Stroud	11/167		
FROCESTER	C1	APR53	Stroud	11/167	BL	10MAY54
					R	26FEB56-15MAR56.
ARLINGHAM	C1	APR53	Stroud	11/167	BL	30JUN54
					B	1MAY58
WHITEBROOK	C1	APR53	Coleford	11/168		
STANTON	C1	APR53	Coleford	11/168		
AILBURTON	C1	APR53	Lydney	11/168		

Notes: 10. The 'C' may be a defective 'G'.
11. Intended as 'Cinderford'?
12. The village is now known as 'Edge'.

COALEY	C1	MAY53	Dursley	11/171			
MAYS-HILL	C1	MAY53	Monmouth	11/172			
DOWN·AMNEY	C1	MAY53	Swindon	11/172			Note 13.
PITT-COURT	C1	MAY53	Wotton U Edge	11/178			
CHARFIELD	C1	MAY53	Wotton U Edge	11/178	OR	16NOV54	
					BL	21SEP59	
STINCHCOMBE	C1	MAY53	Wotton U Edge	11/178			
YATE	C1	MAY53	Chippenham	11/179			
DYRHAM	C1	MAY53	Chippenham	11/179			
SHIPTON·MOYNE	C1	JUN53	Tetbury	11/186			
LITTLE-SOMERFORD	C1	JUN53	Tetbury	11/186			
BARRINGTON	C1	JUN53	Burford	11/186			
SWINBROOK	C1	JUN53	Burford	11/186			
BURTON-HILL	C1	JUN53	Tetbury	11/186			
PURTON-GLOS	C1	JUL53	Berkeley	11/192	R	30OCT55	
ASTON·CROSS	C1	OCT53	Tewkesbury	11/247			
TWINING·GN	C1	OCT53	Tewkesbury	11/247			
UPTON-ST-LEONARDS	C1	JAN54	Gloucester	12/15	GR	16AUG54	
					R	12APR56	
HUCCLECOTE	C1	JAN54	Gloucester	12/16	B	16MAR59	
HIGHNAM	C1	JAN54	Gloucester	12/16	R	18FEB57	
QUEDGELEY	C1	JAN54	Gloucester	12/17			
TUFFLEY	C1	JAN54	Gloucester	12/17			
LONGNEY	C1	JAN54	Gloucester	12/17			
PARKEND	C1	MAR54	Lydney	12/32			
SHERSTONE	C1	MAR54	Tetbury	12/33			
OAKSEY	C1	APR54	Cirencester	12/51			
SHERSTONE·WILTS	C1	JUN54	Tetbury	12/71			
CAMBRIDGE·GLOS	C1			12/82	B	27OCT57	Note 14.
ALDERTON	C1	cJUN54		12/83			Note 15.
BROCKENBOROUGH	C1	cJUN54		12/83			Note 16.
COLESBOURNE	C1	15NOV54	Cheltenham	12/135			
STRENSHAM	C1	17FEB56	Tewkesbury	12/315			
BREDON	C1	17FEB56	Tewkesbury	12/315	BL	16NOV57	
					B	16JUN58	
FORTHWORTH	C1	27FEB56	Wotton U Edge	12/317			Note 17.
KINGSWOOD	C1	27FEB56	Wotton U Edge	12/317			
KINGSCOTE	C1	25MAR56	Wotton U Edge	12/324			Note 18.
STONE	C1	22MAR56	Berkeley	12/324			
KINGSCOTE	C1	25MAR56	Wotton U Edge	12/332	R	21MAY57- 1JUN57	
					BL	1JUL57-20MAR60	
							Note 19.
TORTWORTH	C1	25MAR56	Wotton U Edge	12/332			
LEONARD-STANLEY	C1	16APR56	Stonehouse	12/339			
STAVERTON	C1	3JUN56	Cheltenham	13/13			
LONDON.RD.	C1	3JUN56	Cheltenham	13/13	B	15NOV56-25NOV59.	
					OR/R	13JAN57- 3JAN60	
ST-PAULS	C1	3JUN56	Cheltenham	13/13	BR/R	15FEB57	
PRESTBURY	C1	3JUN56	Cheltenham	13/15	B	31JAN58-29APR59.	
					BL	5DEC59	

Notes:
13. Intended as 'Ampney'.
14. Probably sent to Dursley.
15. Probably sent to Cheltenham - all use shown against 11/166.
16. Probably sent to Tetbury.
17. Probably not used - see 12/332.
18. All use shown against 12/332.
19. Mileage mark in use until at least 14DEC54.

Glos

NORTHGATE-ST	C1	20NOV56	Gloucester	13/101	BL	11MAR59
SOUTHGATE-ST	C1	20NOV56	Gloucester	13/101		
CLEARWELL	C1	12FEB57	Coleford	13/142		
CLEARWELL	C1	4MAR57	Coleford	13/162		
LEA	C1	25MAR57	Ross	13/194		
HEMPSTEAD	C1	2APR57	Gloucester	13/203		
SAUL	C1	16MAY57	Stonehouse	13/233		
PAINSWICK	C1*	15JUN57	Stroud	13/259		
BISLEY	C1*	15JUN57	Stroud	13/259	OR/R	18JUN57- 4APR58.
					B	7JUL57-24DEC58
DUMBLETON	C4	10JUL57	Evesham	13/281	B	11SEP58-19APR59
TIRLEY	D4	25SEP57	Tewkesbury	14/32		
BARRINGTON	C4	30SEP57	Cheltenham	14/35		
BRIMSCOMBE	C4	5OCT57	Stroud	14/43		
SANDHURST-GLOS	C4	19OCT57	Gloucester	14/56		
MAY-HILL	C4	30OCT57	Monmouth	14/65		
WESTBURY·ON-SEVERN	C4	10NOV57	Newnham	14/73		
EASTINGTON	C4	14NOV57	Stonehouse	14/78		
STAUNTON	C4	27NOV57	Gloucester	14/90	B	28JAN59- 8APR59.
LONGHOPE	C4	28DEC57	Newnham	14/114	BL/B	10JUL59
RESPIDGE	D1	13FEB58	Newnham	14/144		
CAINS CROSS	D1	25FEB58	Stroud	14/154	B	?
BROCKWORTH	D1	25FEB58	Gloucester	14/154		
LOWER·GUITING	D1	1JUN58	Cheltenham	14/245	B	2FEB60
WOOLSTONE GLOS	D2	1JUN58	Cheltenham	14/245		
CHEDWORTH	D1	1JUN58	Cheltenham	14/245		
SWINBROOK	D1	1JUN58	Cheltenham	14/245	B	30JUN58
MONTPELLIER	D1	1JUN58	Cheltenham	14/245	BL	7OCT58
					B	7OCT58-13MAR60
SALPERTON	D1	1JUN58	Cheltenham	14/245		
PITTVILLE	D1	1JUN58	Cheltenham	14/245	B	30OCT58-31OCT59.
ODDINGTON	D1	9JUL58	Chipping Norton	14/275		
FORTHAMPTON	D1	14JUL58	Tewkesbury	14/277		
ELDERSFIELD	D1	14JUL58	Tewkesbury	14/277		
APPERLEY	D1	14JUL58	Tewkesbury	14/277	B	15APR59
WOODCHESTER	D1	24SEP58	Stroud	16/49	B	21DEC58
TUFFLEY	D4	30SEP58	Gloucester	16/51		
BARTON-ST-MICHAEL	D1	30SEP58	Gloucester	16/51		
UPTON-ST-LEONARDS	D1	30SEP58	Gloucester	16/51		
WITCOMB	D4	7OCT58	Gloucester	16/57		
MAISEMORE	D1	7OCT58	Gloucester	16/57		
KEMERTON	D1	7OCT58	Tewkesbury	16/57	B	14NOV58-30NOV59.
BREDON	D4	7OCT58	Tewkesbury	16/58		
LONGDON	D4	7OCT58	Tewkesbury	16/58		
ASTON-CROSS	D1	7OCT58	Tewkesbury	16/58		
OVERBURY	D1	7OCT58	Tewkesbury	16/58		
STRENSHAM	D1	7OCT58	Tewkesbury	16/58		
TWINING-GREEN	D1	7OVT58	Tewkesbury	16/58		
MINETY	D4	16OCT58	Chippenham	16/61		
CRUDWELL	D1	16OCT58	Chippenham	16/62	B	9FEB59
CORSE-LAWN	D1	1FEB59	Tewkesbury	16/151		
OLD-SODBURY	D1	23FEB59	Chippenham	16/163		
CHARLTON WILTS.	D2	31MAR59	Chippenham	18/14		
YATE	D4	2APR59	Yate	18/18		
BURTON-HILL	D1	4MAY59	Chippenham	18/39		
LONG·NEWNTON	D1	3AUG59	Tetbury	18/85		

Glos

Similar Sans-serif (C1) Marks of Gloucestershire (1)

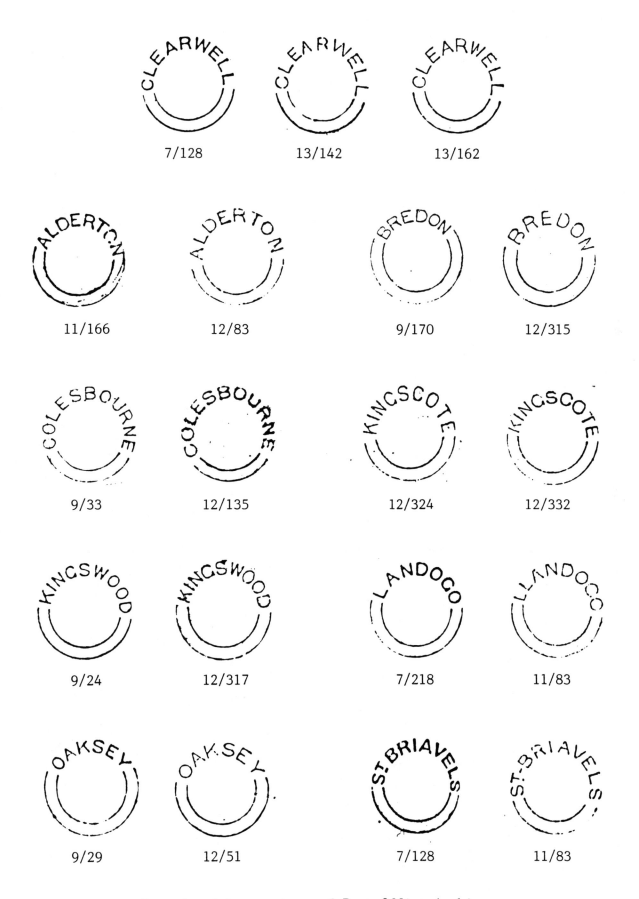

Reproduced by courtesy of Post Office Archives

Similar Sans-serif (C1) Marks of Gloucestershire (2)

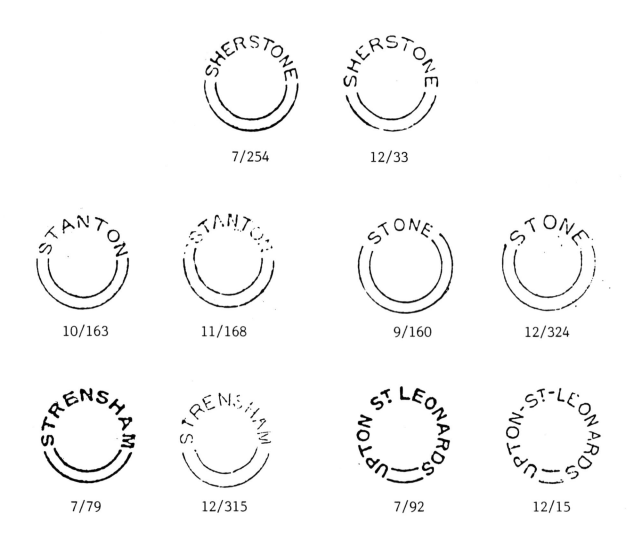

Reproduced by courtesy of Post Office Archives

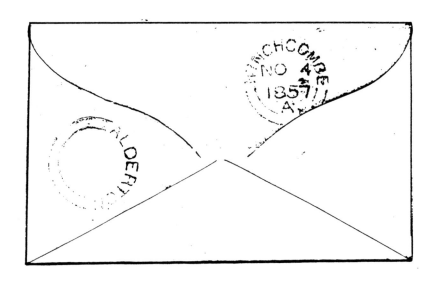

ALDERTON (11/166) in red ink.

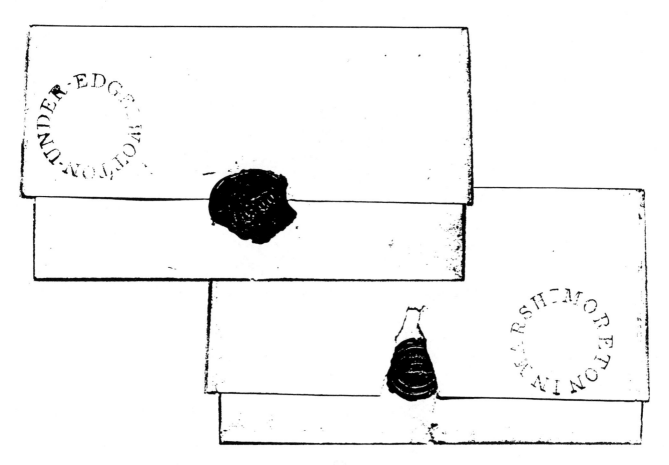

WOTTON·UNDER·EDGE (1/208) and MORETON IN MARSH (1/116)

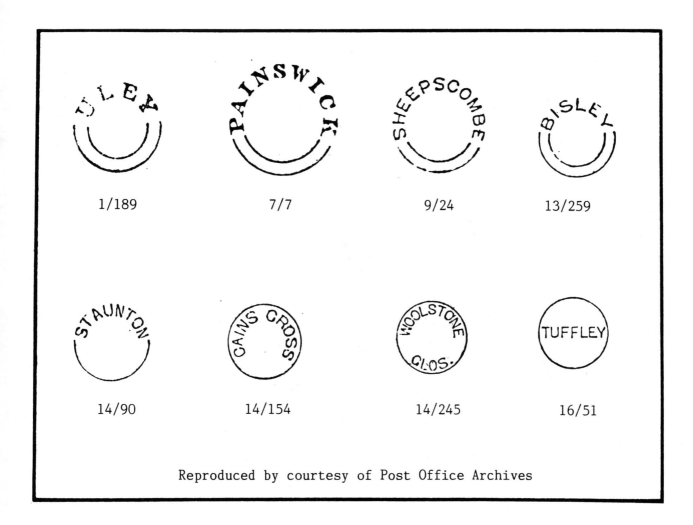

| 1/189 | 7/7 | 9/24 | 13/259 |

| 14/90 | 14/154 | 14/245 | 16/51 |

Reproduced by courtesy of Post Office Archives

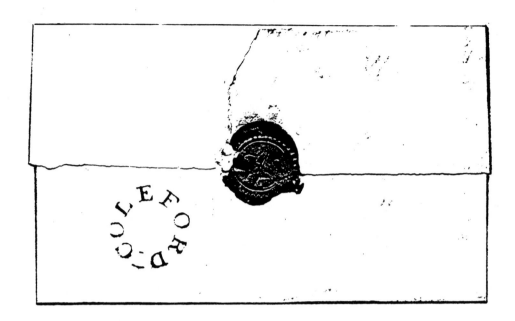
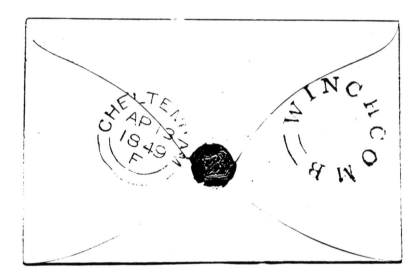
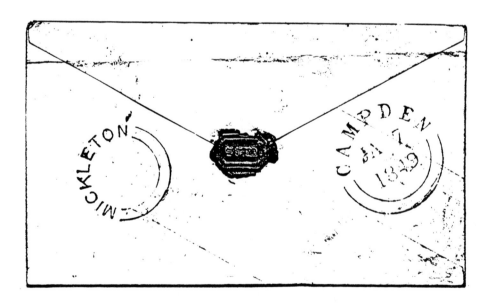

Above: COLEFORD (1/28)

Centre: WINCHCOMB (2/157) in blue ink.

Below: MICKLETON (9/160)

HEREFORDSHIRE

BROMYARD (138). 1/15 (CDS 27FEB39) See TL3.

Bishops Frome 10/267 See TL3.

HEREFORD (357).

Abbey Dore 9/126
Allensmore 12/14
Bartestree 10/274
Bishopstone 11/171 12/97?
Blackmarston(e) 12/14 12/166 Note 1.
Borlestree 10/67 Note 2.
Bredwardine 12/14 14/225
Bridge Street 9/125
Burghill 16/64
Canon Pyon 10/163
Clifford 12/14
Credenhill 5/113 9/33
Dormington 13/271 Note 3.
Eardisley + (358) 7/77 (CDS 26DEC50)
Eaton Bishop 16/60
Eign 12/121
Eign Street 9/125
Fownhope 7/83
Grosmont 2 12/180
Hampton Bishop 14/244
High Town 9/125
Holme Lacey 9/39
Holmer 11/150
Kentchurch + (CDS 26DEC50)
Kings Acre 12/14
Letton + 9/84 10/130 (CDS 26DEC50)
Lionshall 12/14 See TL16.
Llangorse 14/254
Madley 7/205 14/222
Marden 9/47
Moreton on Lug 11/64 Note 3.
Norton Cannon 12/14
Peterchurch + 10/255.

Pontrilas 12/14
Portway 11/171
Skenfrith 2 10/30 18/79 See TL8.
Staunton on Wye 9/125 Note 4.
Sugwas Pool 9/125 Note 4.
Sutton St Nicholas 9/36 Note 3.
Vowchurch 16/80*
Wellington + 12/14
Weobly + 9/80 (CDS 26DEC50)
Westhide 7/247 Note 3.
Whitney 12/14
Withington 14/244
Woonton 12/14 See TL16.
Wormbridge 7/24 12/329

KINGTON (419). 1/92 (CDS 2SEP39)

Evenjobb 3 14/56
Hundred House 16/105
Llanbadarn Fyndd 3 12/199
                14/103
Nantmel 3 11/47
Pen y Bont + 3 12/192
      (CDS 5MAY55)
Radnor + 3 (CDS 28JUN55)
Titley + 10/84 See TL19.
Walton 3 10/61

LEDBURY (446). 1/104 (CDS 2SEP39)

Berrow 4 7/252
Dymock 5 7/151 See TL11.
Eastnor 18/103
Greenway 12/251
Little Marcle 12/304
Lower Eagleton 12/304
Much Marcle 7/151 See TL11.
Shucknell 13/35 Note 1.
Tarrington 7/249 16/103
The Trumpet 12/82
Woolhope 12/82

Notes:
1. Office not in the 1860 list.
2. Not in the 1855 or 1860 lists - Bartestree?
3. Not in the 1855 or 1860 lists.
4. Entry in proof book marked 'cancelled'.

+ indicates an office which used a straight line (or P.P.) stamp after 1840.

An underlined number, eg 2, indicates an office outside Herefs - see key at end.

Herefs

LEOMINSTER (454). (CDS 4/10 6JUL38) 4/58

Bodenham 10/68 (CDS 21MAY51)
Cock Gate 9/176
Dilwyn 9/11
Docklow 9/146
Eardisland + 9/129
Eye 12/304 Note 1.
Kingsland 7/255 (CDS 5APR59)
Pembridge (455) 9/129 9/135 (CDS 21MAY51)
Shobden (456) 9/129 12/271 (CDS 23JUL59)
Staunton Arrow 12/304 (CDS 16JAN60)
Stoke Prior 16/173
The Broad 12/304
Wigmore 7/255

ROSS (654).

Birch + 7/187
Carey 11/241
Crow Hill 10/162 10/162*
Garway Common 12/308
Goodrich + 7/187 14/253
Harewood End + 7/187
Hoarwithey 11/19
How Caple 11/241
Kings Caple 11/241
Linton 7/205
Llangarran 11/191
Llangrove Common 11/241
Lydbrook 5 7/13
Much Dewchurch 11/241
Pencraig + 7/187
Pooll Hill 11/19
St Weonards 9/107
Walford 10/224
Whitchurch + 7/187 (CDS 28MAR51)
        See TL4.
Wilton 11/241

ABERGAVENNY (1), Mon

Longtown + 11/101

BRECON (116), Brecon

Beulah 1 13/15 See TL15&17.
Llangammarch 1 13/15 See TL15&17.
Llyswen 1 11/96 See TL9,12&15.

GLOUCESTER (312), Glos

Hope Mansell 9/175 See TL7.
Lea (313) + 5/159 (CDS 28MAR51)
       13/194 See TL13.
Redmarley 4 5/159 7/92
            See TL1&11.
Weston under Penyard 7/174
            See TL2.

GREAT MALVERN (497), Worcs

Bosbury 7/44 See TL6.
Colwall 7/44
Colwall Green 14/70
Cradley 7/49 14/70
Stifford(s) Bridge 12/92 Note 1.

HAY (347), Brecon See TL14.

Bronyllys (348) 1 1/18 1/174
   5/120 14/205 See TL12&15.
Clyro 1 12/16 See TL14.
Erwood 1 12/222 See TL12&15.
Glasbury (349) 1 1/62 See TL14.

LLANDOVERY (468), Carms

Llanwrtyd 3 11/135 See TL18.

LUDLOW (479), Salop

Brampton Bryan 7/24 (CDS 23DEC57)
          See TL5.
Brimfield 9/92
Leintwardine (481) (CDS 23DEC57)
          Note 5.
Orleton 12/317
Richards Castle 10/153

RHAYADER (639), Radnor

Newbridge on Wye 5 9/126
     See TL10,12,15&17.

Notes: 5. Circular mileage mark still in use in AUG57.

+ indicates an office which used a straight line (or P.P.) stamp after 1840.

An underlined number, eg 4, indicates an office outside Herefs - see key at end.

TENBURY (783), Worcs

Little Hereford 12/15

WORCESTER (918), Worcs

Much Cowarne 12/106
Pencombe 18/82
Stoke Lacey 14/154
Tedstone Wafer 12/6
Upper Sapey 12/3

KEY to offices not in Herefordshire

1 is in Breconshire
2 is in Monmouthshire
3 is in Radnorshire
4 is in Worcestershire
5 is in Gloucestershire.

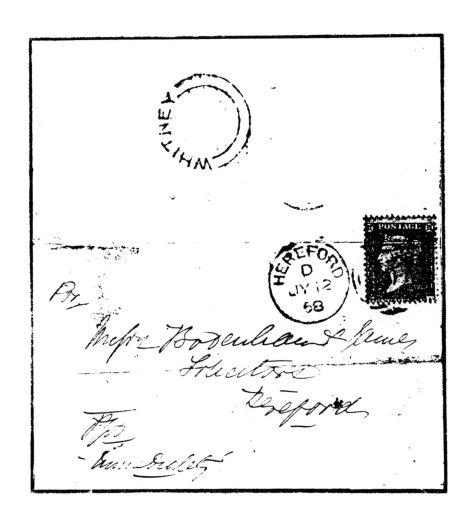

WHITNEY (12/14)

TRANSFERS - Herefordshire

TL 1.   Redmarley from Gloucester to Ledbury on 19OCT44.

2.   Weston under Penyard from Gloucester to Ross on 27APR46.

3.   Bromyard reduced to a sub-office (under Worcester) on 6AUG50. Bishops Frome would have transferred to Worcester at the same time.

4.   Whitchurch from Ross on Wye to Monmouth on 5FEB51.

5.   Brampton Bryan from Ludlow to Shrewsbury on 28OCT52.

6.   Bosbury from Malvern to Ledbury on 15MAR53.

7.   Hope Mansell from Gloucester to Newnham on 13JUL54.

8.   Skenfrith from Hereford to Monmouth on 17OCT54.

9.   Llyswen from Brecon (?) to Hay on 1OCT55.

10.   Newbridge on Wye from Rhayader to Hay on 1OCT55.

11.   Much Marcle, Dymock and Redmarley from Ledbury to Gloucester on 3NOV55.

12.   Erwood, Newbridge on Wye, Llyswen and Bronllys from Hay to Brecon on 30NOV55.

13.   Lea from Gloucester to Ross on 9MAY56.

14.   Hay reduced to a sub-office (under Hereford) on 1JAN58. Clyro and Glasbury would have transferred at the same time.

15.   Beulah, Llangammarch, Newbridge on Wye, Erwood, Llyswen and Bronllys from Brecon to Hereford on 1JAN58.

16.   Lionshall and Woonton from Hereford to Kington on 1JAN58.

17.   Beulah, Llangammarch and Newbridge on Wye from Hereford to Kington on 10AUG58.

18.   Llanwrytd from Llandovery to Brecon to Hereford at unknown dates. To Kington on 10AUG58.

19.   Titley from Kington to Leominster by MAR60.

Herefs

HEREFORDSHIRE

BUNTLESS	C2*	26MAR28	Buntless	1/174			Note 1.
BROMYARD	C2*	5MAY28	Bromyard	1/15	B	13OCT28-29DEC37	
					Y	29- 33	
					GR	30-30MAR34	
GLASBURY	C2*	5MAY28	Glasbury	1/62	R	13MAY40	
					B	21SEP44-11SEP53	
					GR	9APR58	
					Grey	28APR58- 2MAR59	
LEDBURY	C2*	7FEB29	Ledbury	1/104	R	7JAN30-15AUG39	
KINGTON	C2*	9MAR29	Kington	1/92	B	29-29DEC38	
BROYNTLISS	C2*	10JUN29	Broyntliss	1/18	R	23AUG29-31DEC33	
					B	17FEB39-31DEC33	
					B	17FEB39-21JAN40	
							Note 1.
LEOMINSTER	C2M?	27NOV39	Leominster	4/58			
CREDENHILL	C2	20AUG42	Hereford	5/113	B	12NOV43-22APR44	
BRYNNLLIS	C2	5OCT42	Hay	5/120	B	6JUL45-11OCT48	
LEA	C2	13MAY43	Gloucester	5/159	B	15JUL44-11SEP45	
REDMARLEY	C2	13MAY43	Gloucester	5/159			
LYDBROOK	C2	3JAN44	Ross	7/13	B	5FEB48-17MAY50.	
					GR	7DEC52	
					R	10APR55	
					BL/B	2JUL58	
WORMBRIDGE	C2	2FEB44	Hereford	7/24	B	8AUG46-28DEC50	
BRAMPTON-BRYAN	C2	2FEB44	Ludlow	7/24	B	3APR44-28JAN54.	
					BR	11JAN53- 2FEB53	
					BL/GR	26SEP53-29JAN54	
BOSBURY	C1	15APR44	Great Malvern	7/44	B	26DEC47	
					BL	19APR55-24OCT55	
					R	25APR56-25NOV56	
					BL/B	8SEP59	
COLWALL	C1	15APR44	Great Malvern	7/44	B	23DEC46- 6OCT57	
					BL	9MAY49- 9MAR50	
					B/GR	6OCT57	
CRADLEY	C1	19APR44	Great Malvern	7/49	B	11MAR45-21MAR50	
					GR	16JUN49	
					BL	13JAN52-16SEP52	
					R	30JAN56-28JUL56	
					OR	26MAR57 Note 2.	
EARDISLEY	C1	1JUL44	Hereford	7/77	B	2JAN46- 6FEB46.	
FOWNHOPE	C1	25JUL44	Hereford	7/83	B	29DEC45- 9APR47	
REDMARLEY	C1	22AUG44	Ledbury	7/92	BR	26SEP46	
					B	15AUG45-14OCT52	
DYMOCK	C1	2JUN45	Ledbury	7/151	B	20JUN50-16AUG59	
					BR/B	25JUL50	
					R	23JAN56- 4OCT56	
					BL/B	16AUG57-15DEC58	
MUCH-MARCLE	C1	2JUN45	Ledbury	7/151	B	15NOV46-10MAR50	
					BL	10JUL51-16AUG57	
					R	14MAR56	
					BL/B	15DEC58	
WESTON·UNDER· PENYARD	C1	9SEP45	Gloucester	7/174	B	26SEP46-14JAN54	
					R	2APR56	
					BL/B	16AUG59	
WHITCHURCH	C1	10NOV45	Ross	7/187			
PENCRAIG	C1	10NOV45	Ross	7/187	R	4AUG56	
HAREWOOD-END	C1	10NOV45	Ross	7/187	B	3JUN50	
					BL	3NOV58	

Notes: 1. Probably intended as Bruntless/Bronllys. See also 5/120 and 14/205.
2. There is another Cradley in Worcs.

Herefs 50.

Office	Type	Date	Head Office	Ref	Colour	Dates
GOODRICH	C1	10NOV45	Ross	7/187		
BIRCH	C1	10NOV45	Ross	7/187	R	15NOV46-18OCT52
					BL	5NOV57-19NOV59
LINTON	C1	10JAN46	Ross	7/205	B	30OCT48
					BL/B	1FEB60
MADLEY	C1	10JAN46	Hereford	7/205	R	16SEP47-27MAR48
					B	28FEB54-22JAN55.
WEST-HIDE	C1	27JUN46	Hereford	7/247	B	27DEC48
					BL/GR	29JAN50
					BL	23JUL55
TARRINGTON	C1	30JUN46	Ledbury	7/249	B	15JAN48-10MAR52
					BL/B	14JUN49-18SEP50
					B/GR	29AUG53
					OR/R	7DEC57-10DEC57
BERROW	C1	13JUL46	Ledbury	7/252	GR	31MAY54
					R	11DEC55-28DEC57
					BL/B	2AUG58
					BL	29NOV58
					B	17JAN59- 4OCT59.
WIGMORE	C1	15JUL46	Leominster	7/255	B	1JAN51- 1SEP53
					R	3DEC55
KINGSLAND	C1	15JUL46	Leominster	7/255	B	1JAN51-27JUL56.
					R	16JUN56-17MAR57
					BL/B	31DEC57- 8JAN59
CREDENHILL	C1	1MAY47	Hereford	9/33	B	30MAR54-31JUL54.
					B/R	22DEC56
SUTTON-ST-NICHOLAS	C1	6MAY47	Hereford	9/36		
HOLME-LACEY	C1	23MAY47	Hereford	9/39		
MARDEN	C1	1JUN47	Hereford	9/47	B	3SEP49-19APR55
WEOBLY	C1	13SEP47	Hereford	9/80	B	19DEC47-19DEC49
LETTON	C1	10OCT47	Hereford	9/84	B	25JAN48
BRIMFIELD	C1	19OCT47	Ludlow	9/92	B	58-14MAY59
ST-WEONARDS	C1	16DEC47	Ross	9/107	R	4MAR57-16MAR57
					BL/B	14FEB59
					B	15FEB59
DILWYN	C1	24DEC47	Leominster	9/111	BL	8FEB53
					R	?
EIGN-ST	C1	12FEB48	Hereford	9/125	B	5MAR50-12MAY58
					Purple	56
					R	3JAN56-24SEP56
BRIDGE-ST	C1	12FEB48	Hereford	9/125	B	8JUL51
HIGH-TOWN	C1	12FEB48	Hereford	9/125	B	27AUG48- 5JUL52.
					B/GR	10MAR49- 8FEB50
					BR	23MAR50-12APR51
					BL	7AUG54- 9APR59
					R	31MAY56
SUGWAS-POOL	C1	12FEB48	Hereford	9/125		Note 3.
STAUNTON-ON-WYE	C1	12FEB48	Hereford	9/125		Note 3.
ABBEY-DORE	C1	17FEB48	Hereford	9/126		
NEWBRIDGE-ON-WYE	C1	17FEB48	Rhayader	9/126		
EARDISLAND	C1	3MAR48	Leominster	9/129	B	14NOV54
SHOBDEN	C1	3MAR48	Leominster	9/129	BL	50- 4MAY52
						Note 4.
PEMBRIGDE	C1	3MAR48	Leominster	9/129		
PEMBRIDGE	C1	19MAR48	Leominster	9/135	BL	31MAR51-14MAY51
DOCKLOW	C1	4MAY48	Leominster	9/146	BL/B	53-25JUN57
HOPE-MANSELL	C1	24AUG48	Gloucester	9/175		
COCK-GATE	C1	24AUG48	Leominster	9/176	GR/BR	5OCT54
					Grey	15DEC54

Notes: 3. Issue in doubt as entry in Proof Book is marked 'cancelled'.
4. See also C1 Shobdon (12/271).

Herefs

Name	Class	Date	Office	Ref	Type	Dates
SKENFRITH	C1	8AUG49	Hereford	10/30	B	1AUG50
					GR	30JUN51
WALTON	C1	14JAN50	Kington	10/61	B	30OCT51-11JUL59
					BL	20MAR51- 5OCT53
BORLESTREE	C1	15FEB50	Hereford	10/67		
BODENHAM	C1	15FEB50	Leominster	10/68	BL/GR	?
TITLEY	C1	17APR50	Kington	10/84	BL/B	26JUL50
					R	11OCT52
					R/BR	22JUN53-22APR54.
LETTON	C1M	26DEC50	Hereford	10/130	B	30SEP58
RICHARDS-CASTLE	C1	12FEB51	Ludlow	10/153		
CROW-HALL	C1	1MAR51	Ross	10/162		
CROW-HILL	C1				BL	10FEB52-14OCT54
CANON-PYON	C1	1MAR51	Hereford	10/163	BL	12AUG51- 55
					B	16FEB52-21DEC57.
WALFORD	C1	5AUG51	Ross	10/224	BL	AUG55
					BL/B	10AUG55
					R	30AUG58
PETERCHURCH	C1	29SEP51	Hereford	10/255	B	8AUG57
BISHOPS·FROME	C1	5OCT51	Bromyard	10/267	BL	8MAR52-30MAY55
					BL/GR	6JUN55
BARTESTREE	C1	6OCT51	Hereford	10/274	BL	13JUL55-20AUG55
					R	12MAR56- 9AUG56.
HOARWITHY	C1	6FEB52	Ross	11/19		
POOLL-HILL	C1	6FEB52	Ross	11/19		
NANTMEL	C1	28APR52	Kington	11/47	BL	25MAR53
MORETON·ON·LUG	C1	15JUN52	Hereford	11/64		
LLYSWEN	C1	SEP52	Brecon	11/96		
LONGTOWN·HERE	C1	SEP52	Abergavenny	11/101		
LLANWRTYD	C1	JAN53	Llandovery	11/135		
HOLMER	C1	FEB53	Hereford	11/150	BL	11JUL53-10MAY55.
					B	29MAR58- 1JUL59
BISHOPSTONE	C1	MAY53	Hereford	11/171		
PORTWAY	C1	MAY53	Hereford	11/171	R	10DEC55
LLANGARRAN	C1	JUN53	Ross	11/191	R	4AUG56- 4MAY58.
HOW·CAPLE	C1	OCT53	Ross	11/241	GR	5DEC54
					R	19DEC55-20DEC56
					BL/B	29JUN58- 3NOV58
KINGS·CAPLE	C1	OCT53	Ross	11/241		
CAREY	C1	OCT53	Ross	11/241	BL	3DEC57
WILTON	C1	OCT53	Ross	11/241		
MUCH·DEWCHURCH	C1	OCT53	Ross	11/241		
LLANGROVE·COMMON	C1	OCT53	Ross	11/241		
UPPER-SAPEY	C1	DEC53	Worcester	12/3	R	16MAY57-29SEP57.
					B	18NOV58
TEDSTONE-WAFER	C1	DEC53	Worcester	12/6	R	15OCT56-11AUG57
					BL	58
CLIFFORD	C1	JAN54	Hereford	12/14	B	30OCT55-12AUG58
					BL/B	31MAY59
NORTON-CANNON	C1	JAN54	Hereford	12/14		
WOONTON	C1	JAN54	Hereford	12/14	B	14MAR59-17MAR59.
WELLINGTON	C1	JAN54	Hereford	12/14		
ALLENSMORE	C1	JAN54	Hereford	12/14	BL/B	17MAR58
					B	31DEC58
PONTRILAS	C1	JAN54	Hereford	12/14	R	7APR55
BLACKMARSTON	C1	JAN54	Hereford	12/14		Note 5.
KINGS-ACRE	C1	JAN54	Hereford	12/14	R	10JUL56-19MAY57
					BL/B	14JUL59
BREDWARDINE	C1	JAN54	Hereford	12/14		

Notes: 5. See also C1 Blackmarstone (12/166).

Herefs

Name	Class	Date	Office	Ref	Colour	Date Range
WHITNEY	C1	JAN54	Hereford	12/14	B	12JUL58
LIONSHALL	C1	JAN54	Hereford	12/14	BL	4APR55- AUG55
					R	27FEB56- 3MAY56
					B	23APR59-25MAY59
LITTLE-HEREFORD	C1	JAN54	Tenbury	12/15	GR	3MAY57
CLYRO	C1	JAN54	Hay	12/16	BL/B	23JAN57
					B/GR	13MAY59
					B	18AUG59
THE-TRUMPET	C1	cJUN54		12/82	GR/B	23JUN54-21NOV54
					GR/BR	9NOV54
					R	15OCT56-16MAR58
					BL/B	21OCT58-20SEP59.
					BL	15OCT59 Note 6.
WOOLHOPE	C1	cJUN54		12/82	GR	16MAR58 Note 6.
STIFFORD·BRIDGE	C1	cJUL54		12/92	R	3JAN55
					OR/R	5MAY57 Note 7.
BISHOPSTONE	C1	12AUG54		12/97		Note 8.
MUCH-COWARNE	C1	22AUG54		12/106		Note 9.
EIGN	C1	OCT54	Hereford	12/121		
BLACKMARSTONE	C1	27FEB55	Hereford	12/166		
GROSMONT	C1	30MAR55	Hereford	12/180	BL	10SEP57
					GR/B	15SEP57
					BL/B	27AUG57-31MAR58
PEN-Y-BONT	C1M	5MAY55	Kington	12/192	B	14AUG58
LLANBADWRNFYNYDD	C1	17MAY55	Kington	12/199		Note 10.
ERWOOD	C1	26JUL55	Hay	12/222		
GREENWAY	C1	5OCT55	Ledbury	12/251	R	10CT57
SHOBDON	C1	24NOV55	Leominster	12/271	B	1JAN59
STAUNTON-ARROW	C1	31JAN56	Leominster	12/304	BL/B	21SEP57.
EYE	C1	31JAN56	Leominster	12/304		
THE-BROAD	C1	31JAN56	Leominster	12/304		
LOWER-EAGLETON	C1	31JAN56	Ledbury	12/304		
LITTLE-MARCLE	C1	31JAN56	Ledbury	12/304		
GARWAY-COMMON	C1	31JAN56	Ross	12/308	R	4MAR57
ORLETON	C1	27FEB56	Ludlow	12/317	B	2FEB58-14SEP58.
WORMBRIDGE	C1	22MAR56	Hereford	12/329		
BEULAH	C1	3JUN56	Builth	13/15		
LLANGAMMARCH	C1	3JUN56	Brecon	13/15		
SHUCKNELL	C1	27JUN56	Ledbury	13/35		
LEA	C1	25MAR57	Ross	13/194		
DORMINGTON	C1*	14JUL57	Hereford	13/271		
EVENJOBB	C4	29AUG57	Kington	14/56		
CRADLEY	D4	10NOV57	Great Malvern	14/70	BL	11FEB59-24FEB59.
COLWALL-GREEN	D1	10NOV57	Great Malvern	14/70		
LLANBADARN-FYNYDD	C4	10NOV57	Kington	14/103		
STOKE LACEY	D1	25FEB58	Worcester	14/154		
BRONLLYS	D1	22APR58	Hereford	14/205		
MADLEY	D4	10MAY58	Hereford	14/222		
BREDWARDINE	D1	12MAY58	Hereford	14/225	BL	26MAY58.
					B	7SEP58-12FEB59
HAMPTON-BISHOP	D1	31MAY58	Hereford	14/244		
WITHINGTON	D1	31MAY58	Hereford	14/244	B	31AUG58
GOODRICH	D1	9JUN58	Ross	14/253		
LLANGORSE	D1	9JUN58	Hereford	14/254		
BURGHILL	D1	23OCT58	Hereford	16/64	B	4JUL59

Notes:
6. Probably sent to Ledbury.
7. Probably sent to Malvern.
8. May not be a Herefs UDC.
9. Probably sent to Worcester.
10. See also C4 Llanbadarn-Fynydd (14/103).

EATON·BISHOP	D1	1NOV58	Hereford	16/80			
VOWCHURCH	D1				B		?
TARRINGTON	D1	7DEC58	Ledbury	16/103	B		20FEB60
HUNDRED-HOUSE	D1	8DEC58	Kington	16/105			
STOKE·PRIOR HEREF	D2	9MAR59	Leominster	16/173			
SKENFRITH	D1	19JUL59	Monmouth	18/79			
PENCOMBE	D1	28JUL59	Worcester	18/82			
EASTNOR	D4	8SEP59	Ledbury	18/103			

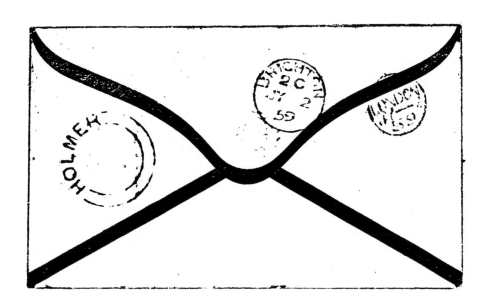

HOLMER (11/150)

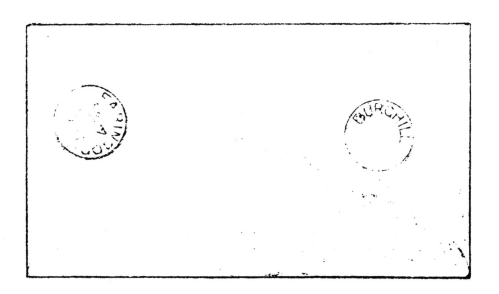

BURGHILL (16/64) - the only recorded example.

Herefs 54.

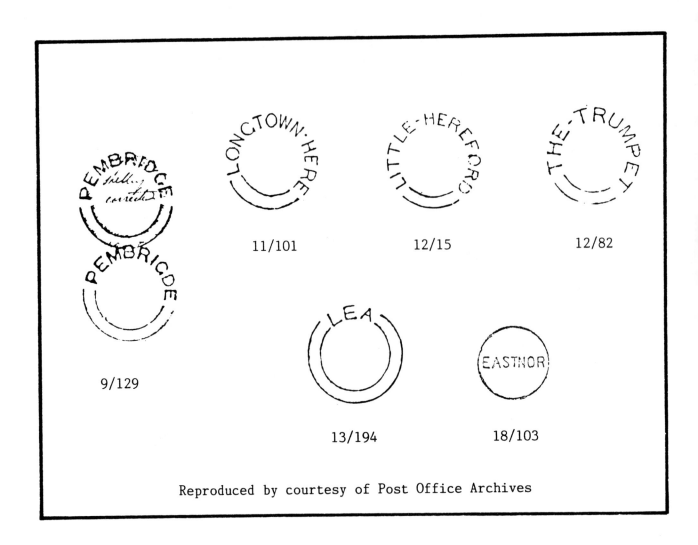

Similar Sans-serif (C1 & C1M) Marks of Herefordshire

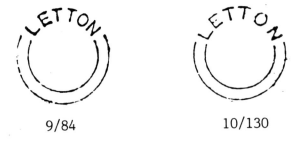

Reproduced by courtesy of Post Office Archives

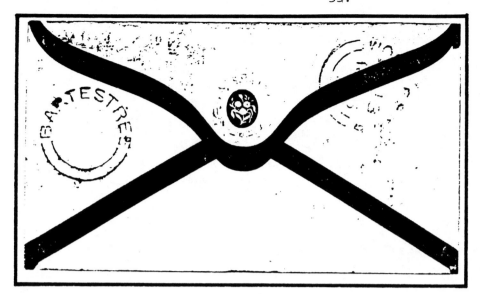
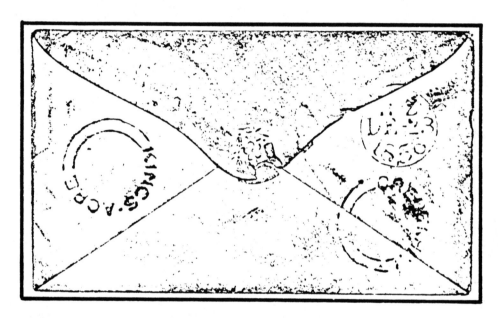
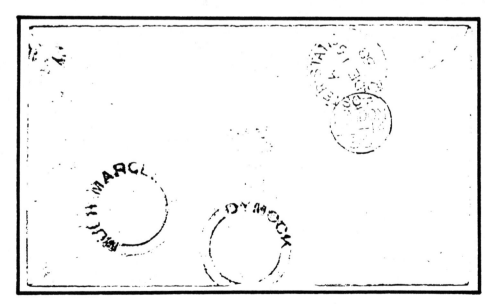

Above: BARTESTREE (10/274)

Centre: KINGS ACRE (12/14) and CREDENHILL (9/33)

Below: MUCH MARCLE and DYMOCK (both 7/151)

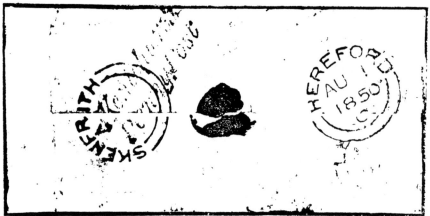

SKENFRITH (10/30), under Hereford at this time.

WIGMORE and KINGSLAND (both 7/255) - a cover with more than one UDC is invariably worth a premium.

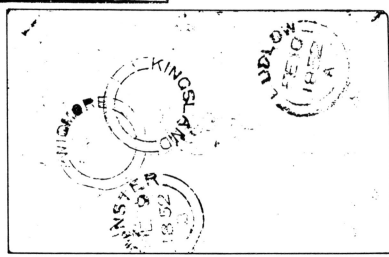

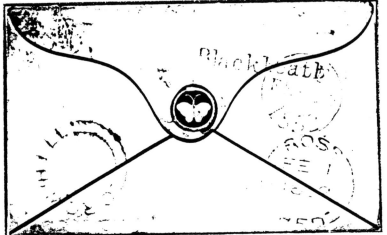

CROW-HALL (10/162) was the stamp sent to Ross in 1851 but it was corrected to read CROW-HILL (10/162*), a fact not recorded in the Steel Impression Books.

CRADLEY (14/70), one of only three D4 stamps in the county, struck in blue ink in 1859.

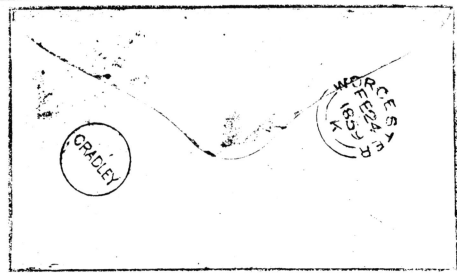

LEICESTERSHIRE & RUTLAND

ASHBY-DE-LA-ZOUCH (30). 1/3 (CDS 24MAR40)

Breedon 9/63
Coalville 11/105
Coleorton 10/153
Hugglescote 11/181 11/191
Ibstock 5/172 16/127
Netherseal 11/105
Overseal + 11/124
Packington 11/161
Ravenstone 5/197
Snarestone 11/105
Stretton-en-le-Fields 11/105
Swannington 16/148
Thringstone 12/235 12/244
Whitwick 5/197 (CDS 15JUL56)

HINCKLEY (365).

Barwell 14/63
Burbage 7/161 11/101
Croft 14/63
Earl Shilton 2/38 13/102
Higham on the Hill 9/58 9/63
Market Bosworth 5/113 (CDS 28MAR50)
Nailstone 14/63
Newbold Verdon 12/261 14/43
Stoney Stanton 7/161
Thornton 9/97 16/32
Thurlaston 12/171
Wolvey 3 7/161 16/160 See TL18&26.

LOUGHBOROUGH (475).

Barrow on Soar 7/159 9/166
Cossington 7/82 14/61
Diseworth 9/101 14/61
East Leake 2 7/233
Hathern 7/170
Hoton 7/91 7/139
Mountsorrel (476) 2/91 12/312 (CDS 20MAR57)
Normanton on Soar 2 13/69
Quorn(don) 7/82 14/61
Ratcliffe-on-the-Wreake 9/82 See TL25.
Rempstone 2 7/233 14/61
Rothley 7/159 14/61
Seagrave 9/82
Shepshed 5/196 14/65 (CDS 17MAR58)
Sileby 9/184 14/61
Stanford 2 13/69
Sutton Bonnington 2 7/170 14/61
Swithland 13/70
Woodhouse Eaves 7/159 14/61
Wymeswold 7/91 7/94 13/127 13/145.

LEICESTER (449).

Allexton 5/179 (closed 1844)
Anstey 12/200
Belgrave 7/158
Belgrave Gate 4/63 13/237
Billesdon 5/179 14/126
                        See TL2&10.
Blaby 9/151
Braunstone 18/24
Burton Overy 10/35 14/145
Desford 9/19 (CDS 29SEP58)
Enderby 12/200
Glenfield 10/141 10/146
Great Glen 4/63 14/126
Groby 7/118
High Cross Street 4/63 13/230
Houghton on the Hill 16/139
Humberstone 9/26
Humberstone Gate 12/62
Hungarton 9/26
Kibworth 7/171 (CDS 2MAY56)
                        See TL8.
Markfield 7/118 14/126
Narborough 7/36 14/126
Oxford Street 4/63 14/126
Rearsby 5/59 11/19 See TL1&6.
South Croxton 9/93
Syston 7/136
Thrussington 18/38
Thurmaston 16/138
Thurnby 7/213
Tilton on the Hill 14/93
Tugby 5/179 14/126 See TL2&10.
Wanlip 7/158 (closed 1859)
Waterloo Street + 13/200 13/214
Wigston 4/63 13/172 (CDS 15JUN58)

LUTTERWORTH (483). 1/104 2/79
                        (CDS 21FEB40)

Ashby Parva 2/2 14/185
Bitteswell 14/234
Bruntingthorpe 7/75 16/133
Claybrooke 12/244
Cosby 12/10
Countesthorpe 9/80
Frowlesworth 7/246
Gilmorton 16/96
Leire 9/80
Swinford 7/229 See TL21.
Ullesthorpe 2/149 14/185
Walcote 16/96
Walton 9/146
Wibtoft 3 10/192 14/183
Wiley 3 16/143

+ indicates an office which used a straight line (or P.P.) stamp after 1840.

An underlined number, eg 3, indicates an office outside Leics - see key at end.

Leics

MARKET HARBOROUGH (511).

Arthingworth <u>1</u> 11/158 See TL20.
Clipston(e) <u>1</u> 7/10 See TL4.
Great Bowden 16/142
Lubenham 7/39 14/207 16/161 See TL3&15 and Note 1.
Mowsley 9/80
Oxendon <u>1</u> 7/10 See TL4.
Saddington 12/172
Shearsby 9/193 14/184
Slawston 10/122 10/145
Theddingworth 7/39 14/197 See TL3&15 and Note 1.
Thorpe Langton 12/199
Tur Langton 7/282 14/184
Wilbarston <u>1</u> 5/132

MELTON MOWBRAY (522). + 1/116 (CDS 13MAR40)

Ab Kettleby 9/136 16/33
Asfordby 9/64
Burrough on the Hill 9/93
Coston 10/184 14/120
Eastwell 9/101
Gaddesby 9/190
Hickling <u>2</u> 13/47
Hoby 9/64
Nether Broughton 9/136
Scalford 11/202

OAKHAM (587). 1/132 (CDS 1SEP38)

Braunston 9/184
Cold Overton 7/31
Cottesmore 7/81 14/121
Exton 10/254
Greetham 7/81
Hambleton 9/243
Langham 7/31
Market Overton 7/121
Somerby 7/31 14/121
Whissendine 7/215 14/121
Wymondham 7/71

UPPINGHAM (825). 2/149 (CDS 24MAR40)

Belton 9/166
Hallaton 7/265 12/313
Laxton <u>1</u> 13/249
Lyddington 9/101
Lyndon 9/18
Manton 9/18 14/247
Medbourne 7/265 18/94 See TL13.
Morcott 9/18 14/247
North Luffenham 16/155 See TL24.

ATHERSTONE (33), Warks

Appleby Magna + 9/210
  (CDS 24MAR59)
Measham + 9/210 16/51
Sheepy + 9/210
Sibson 9/51
Swepstone 7/190 See TL14.
Twycross + 9/210

BURTON-ON-TRENT (152), Staffs

Wooden Box 7/75
Woodville 9/117

DERBY (242), Derbys

Castle Donington 7/11
  (CDS 26SEP49)
Cavendish Bridge +? 7/11
Kegworth + 7/11 (CDS 16APR56)
Lockington 9/152

GRANTHAM (321), Lincs

Branston 11/210
Buckminster 9/150
Croxton Kerrial 7/143 18/47?
Harby 7/251 16/33 See TL7.
Waltham-on-the-Wolds 5/168
  16/33 See TL5.

NOTTINGHAM (583), Notts

Barkestone 9/144
Bottesford 7/144 (CDS 6JUN56)
Muston 13/246
Redmile 13/246

NUNEATON (957), Warks
  (CDS 14JUN43)

Shenton 13/20

ROCKINGHAM (652), Northants
  See TL12.

Great Easton 9/18 14/248
Gretton <u>1</u> 9/144 See TL16.

+ indicates an office which used a straight line (or P.P.) stamp after 1840.

An underlined number, eg <u>2</u>, indicates an office outside Leics - see key at end.

RUGBY (659), Warks (CDS 9JAN40)

Catthorpe 9/27 13/208
Cotesbach 12/292 See TL22.
Monks Kirby 3 9/178 18/80 See TL23.
Pailton 3 7/142 See TL23.
South Kilworth 12/210

STAMFORD (742), Lincs

Bridge Casterton 7/126 18/52
Empingham 7/126 7/138
Ketton 7/89 18/52
Ryhall 9/30 18/52
South Luffenham 7/102 18/28 See TL9,11,19&24.
Stretton 7/263 See TL17.

WELFORD (857), Northants
                (CDS 9MAR40)

North Kilworth 7/230 14/197
          See TL15 and Note 1.
Husbands Bosworth 7/75 18/88
          (CDS 14OCT59)
       See TL15 and Notes 1 and 2.

Notes: 1. These villages, although coming under Rugby on 7MAR53, were still served via Welford until 1JUN55.
         2. 7/75 was sent to Lutterworth but the minute authorising the official post and the opening of an S.O. mentioned the village being served from Welford. No Lutterworth-Welford transfer found.

KEY to offices not in Leicestershire

1 is in Northamptonshire.
2 is in Nottinghamshire.
3 is in Warwickshire.

On 30 September 1897, Overseal, Netherseal and part of Woodville were transferred from Leicestershire to Derbyshire whilst Stretton-en-le-Fields and Measham were transferred to Leicestershire from Derbyshire.

Thorpe Langton and Saddington (under Market Harborough) closed in 1856 and 1858 respectively. Morcott (under Uppingham) closed in 1861.

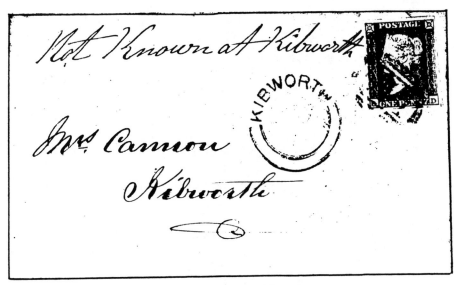

KIBWORTH (7/171)

TRANSFERS - Leicestershire

TL 1. Rearsby from Leicester to Melton Mowbray on 1DEC42.

2. Billesdon and Tugby from Leicester to Uppingham on 26DEC43.

3. Lubenham and Theddingworth from Market Harborough to Welford on 11JUL44.

4. Oxendon and Clipston(e) from Market Harborough to Northampton on 29AUG45.

5. Waltham from Grantham to Melton Mowbray on 7APR46.

6. Rearsby from Melton Mowbray to Leicester on 9APR46.

7. Harby from Grantham to Melton Mowbray on 30JUL46.

8. Kibworth from Leicester to Market Harborough on 5JUL48.

9. South Luffenham from Stamford to Uppingham on 31JUL48.

10. Billesdon and Tugby from Uppingham to Leicester on 1SEP48.

11. South Luffenham from Uppingham to Stamford on 31JAN49.

12. Letters for Rockingham (and its delivery) to be sent to Leicester from 6MAR49.

13. Medbourne from Uppingham to Market Harborough on 13AUG51.

14. Swepstone from Atherstone to Ashby de la Zouch on 21JUN53.

15. Welford was reduced to a sub-office under Rugby on 7MAR53.

16. Gretton to Uppingham in 1854.

17. Stretton from Stamford to Oakham on 25APR54.

18. Wolvey and Bulkington from Hinckley to Nuneaton on 18JUL54.

19. South Luffenham from Stamford to Uppingham on 9OCT54.

20. Arthingworth from Market Harborough to Northampton in 1855/56?

21. Swinford from Lutterworth to Rugby on 24FEB56.

22. Cotesbach from Rugby to Lutterworth on 17MAR56.

23. Monk's Kirby and Pailton from Rugby to Lutterworth on 16AUG58.

24. North Luffenham and South Luffenham from Uppingham to Leicester on 28JAN59.

25. Ratcliffe-on-the-Wreake from Loughborough to Leicester on 1AUG59.

26. Wolvey from Nuneaton to Hinckley on 16AUG59.

Leics

LEICESTERSHIRE and RUTLAND

Office	Type	Date	Town	Ref	Colour	Dates
LUTTERWORTH	C2*	22MAY29	Lutterworth	1/104		
MELTON MOWBRAY	C3	31MAY30	Melton Mowbray	1/116	B	2MAY31- 8JAN39
ASHBY DE LA ZOUCH	C3A	30AUG30	Ashby de la Z	1/3	B	28APR31-11JAN40
OAKHAM	C2*	12SEP30	Oakham	1/132	B	34- 38
LUTTERWORTH	C3	4FEB32		2/79	B	19DEC32- 1AUG38.
UPPINGHAM	C2	16MAR33	Uppingham	2/149	B	34- 40
ULLESTHORPE	C2	12OCT37	Lutterworth	2/149	B	21FEB38- 6JAN39
ASHBY	C2	11OCT37	Lutterworth	2/2	B	19MAR38-10AUG49
					BL/GR	12MAY57
EARL-SHILTON	C2	3APR38	Earl Shilton	2/38	B	12MAY40
MOUNTSORREL	D6	25MAY37	Mountsorrel	2/91	B	14APR38-19AUG45.
					BL	43- 54
					GR	55
GREAT-GLENN	C2	19MAR41	Leicester	4/63	OR	15SEP44
					R	45- 6DEC47.
BELGRAVE-ST LEICESTER	C2	23FEB41	Leicester	4/63	B	30MAR46
OXFORD-ST LEICESTER	C2	23FEB41	Leicester	4/63	B	16JUL46- 47
HIGH·CROSS-ST LEICESTER·	C3	23FEB41	Leicester	4/63	B	16JUN41- 4APR47.
WIGSTONE	C2	19MAR41	Leicester	4/63	B	15DEC45- 7DEC46
					BL	50
					GR	5MAR50-18NOV55
REARSBY	C2	21DEC41	Leicester	5/59	R/OR	2JAN44-13MAR45
MARKET-BOSWORTH	C2	20AUG42	Hinckley	5/113	R	23SEP42- 48
					OR/BR	10JUL49
WILBARSTON	C2	24DEC42	Mkt Harborough	5/132	B	23JUL45-15SEP48
					BL	20SEP53
WALTHAM	C2	5JUL43	Grantham	5/168	B	17SEP43-15SEP48
IBSTOCK	C2	27JUL43	Ashby de la Z	5/172	B	15OCT43-10MAY52
ALLEXTON	C2	30AUG43	Leicester	5/179		
BILLESDON	C2	30AUG43	Leicester	5/179	R	2AUG45- 9APR53.
					BL/GR	11JAN58
TUGBY	C2	30AUG43	Leicester	5/179	B	44
					BL/GR	6MAY48-12JUN49
SHEEPSHEAD	C2	16NOV43	Loughborough	5/196	B	25SEP44-16JUL49
					BL	9JUN56- 7MAR57
RAVENSTONE	C2	16NOV43	Ashby de la Z	5/197	B	MAR44-28NOV47
WHITWICK	C2	16NOV43	Ashby de la Z	5/197	B	1MAY44-21MAR52.
					BL	57
					GR	10FEB57-14AUG57
CLIPSTONE	C2	30DEC43	Mkt Harborough	7/10	B	5SEP47
					OR	2JAN52-21MAR53
					BL	27FEB57
OXENDON	C2	30DEC43	Mkt Harborough	7/10	B	16AUG45
					BR	21OCT47
					R	20NOV48
CASTLE-DONNINGTON	C2	30DEC43	Derby	7/11	B	44- 7APR49.
					BL/GR	9MAY44
KEGWORTH	C2	30DEC43	Derby	7/11	BL	2DEC44-28OCT49
					BL/GR	8AUG51-31JUL56
CAVENDISH-BRIDGE	C2	30DEC43	Derby	7/11		
COLD-OVERTON	C2	24FEB44	Oakham	7/31	BL/GR	51.
LANGHAM	C2	24FEB44	Oakham	7/31		
SOMERBY	C2	24FEB44	Oakham	7/31		
NARBOROUGH	C2	6MAR44	Leicester	7/36	BL	18APR57
LUBBENHAM	C2	18MAR44	Mkt Harborough	7/39	B	44-13MAR55

Leics

THEDDINGWORTH	C2	18MAR44	Mkt Harborough	7/39	B	14DEC44-	55
					GR	27AUG56-28FEB57.	
WYMONDHAM	C1	13JUN44	Oakham	7/71	B	26MAY49	
WOODEN-BOX	C1	28JUN44	Burton on Trent	7/75		Note 1.	
BRUNTINGTHORPE	C1	28JUN44	Lutterworth	7/75	B	25DEC46- 5JUL55	
HUSBANDS-BOSWORTH	C1	28JUN44	Lutterworth	7/75	B	31OCT45-14NOV49	
					GR	8JAN56-12MAR57.	
COTTESMORE	C1	20JUL44	Oakham	7/81			
GREETHAM	C1	20JUL44	Oakham	7/81			
QUORNDON	C1	23JUL44	Loughborough	7/82	B	19OCT44	
					BL	14NOV44-16SEP45	
					GR	30APR50- 56.	
COSSINGTON	C1	23JUL44	Loughborough	7/82	B	45- 9SEP47	
					GR	17JUL51-24JUL54	
KETTON	C1	22AUG44	Stamford	7/89			
WIMESWOULD	C1	22AUG44	Chesterfield	7/91		Note 2.	
HOOTON	C1	22AUG44	Chesterfield	7/91		Note 3.	
WIMESWOULD	C1	10SEP44	Loughborough	7/94	B	23DEC53	
SOUTH-LUFFENHAM	C1	22OCT44	Stamford	7/102	B	23SEP46	
					GR	46	
GROBY	C1	24DEC44	Leicester	7/118	R	24APR45	
					GR	25FEB59	
MARKFIELD	C1	24DEC44	Leicester	7/118	BL	22NOV54- 6JAN57	
MARKET-OVERTON	C1	22JAN45	Oakham	7/121			
EMPRINGHAM	C1	8FEB45	Stamford	7/126		Note 4.	
BRIDGE-CASTERTON	C1	8FEB45	Stamford	7/126			
SYSTON	C1	10APR45	Leicester	7/136	R	21MAY46	
					GR	26AUG58	
EMPINGHAM	C1	14APR45	Stamford	7/138	R	47-29JAN50	
HOTON	C1	18APR45	Loughborough	7/139	BR	17JAN46-29JAN50.	
					B	26DEC46	
PAILTON	C1	8MAY45	Rugby	7/142	B	22JUL55	
					GR	OCT56	
CROXTON	C1	8MAY45	Grantham	7/143			
BOTTESFORD	C1	8MAY45	Nottingham	7/144	BL	21OCT51- 56	
WANLIP	C1	28JUN45	Leicester	7/158	BL	27MAY57-21AUG57.	
BELGRAVE	C1	28JUN45	Leicester	7/158	BL	28FEB46- 3JAN52	
BARROW	C1	28JUN45	Loughborough	7/159	BR	6JAN46	
					GR	25AUG57	
ROTHLEY	C1	28JUN45	Loughborough	7/159	B	27MAY49-13DEC52	
WOODHOUSE-EAVES	C1	28JUN45	Loughborough	7/159	BL	24AUG53	
BURBAGE	C1	7JUL45	Hinckley	7/161			
STONY-STANTON	C1	7JUL45	Hinckley	7/161			
WOLVEY	C1	7JUL45	Hinckley	7/161	OR	3DEC50	
					R	25AUG51	
					BL/GR	19MAY52	
					GR	54	
HATHERN	C1	13AUG45	Loughborough	7/170	BL/GR	13JUN49-16NOV52.	
SUTTON	C1	13AUG45	Loughborough	7/170	BL	12MAY49-31MAR52	
KIBWORTH	C1	25AUG45	Leicester	7/171	R	6OCT45-14APR52.	
					BR	13FEB47- 3AUG53	
SWEPSTON	C1	18NOV45	Atherstone	7/190	B	12DEC46	
					BR	51	
					GR	3MAR56- 3MAR57	

Notes:
1. Later known as Woodville. Now entirely in Derbyshire - see 9/117.
2. Sent in error to Chesterfield - see 7/94.
3. Sent in error to Chesterfield. Sent to Loughborough on 10SEP44 but not used? See 7/139.
4. Probably not used - see 7/138.

THURNBY	C1	20FEB46	Leicester	7/213			
WISSENDINE	C1	4MAR46	Oakham	7/215			
SWINFORD	C1	20APR46	Lutterworth	7/229			
NORTH-KILWORTH	C1	20APR46	Welford	7/230	B	16MAR50-24AUG53	
REMPSTONE	C1	24APR46	Loughborough	7/233	BL?	14NOV49	
					BL/GR	13SEP55	
EAST-LEAKE	C1	24APR46	Loughborough	7/233	GR	13JAN46-17JUL46.	
FROWLESWORTH	C1	27JUN46	Lutterworth	7/246			
HARBY	C1	2JUL46	Grantham	7/251	BL	14SEP48.	
STRETTON	C1	2SEP46	Stamford	7/263	R	28NOV52	
HALLATON	C1	5SEP46	Uppingham	7/265	B	5NOV53	
MEDBOURNE	C1	5SEP46	Uppingham	7/265	BL/GR	18FEB59	
TARLANGTON	C1	27NOV46	Mkt Harborough	7/282			
GREAT-EASTON	C1	3MAR47	Rockingham	9/18			
LYNDON	C1	3MAR47	Uppingham	9/18			
MANTON	C1	3MAR47	Uppingham	9/18			
MORCOTT	C1	3MAR47	Uppingham	9/18			
DESFORD	C1	3MAR47	Leicester	9/19	OR	4JAN49	
					GR	12DEC56-10JAN57	
CALTHORPE	C1	12MAR47	Rugby	9/27	B	17NOV48-10APR55	
HUMBERSTON	C1	3APR47	Leicester	9/26	B	16FEB48- 9OCT50.	
HUNGARTON	C1	3APR47	Leicester	9/26	BL	25AUG57- AUG58	
RYALL	C1	19APR47	Stamford	9/30			
SIBSON	C1	11JUN47	Atherstone	9/51			
HIGHAM	C1	2JUL47	Hinckley	9/58	OR	9JAN52	
HIGHAM	C1	24JUL47	Hinckley	9/63			
BREEDON	C1	24JUL47	Ashby de la Z	9/63			
HOBY	C1	24JUL47	Melton Mowbray	9/64	BL	59	
ASFORDBY	C1	24JUL47	Melton Mowbray	9/64	B	3MAY59	
COUNTESTHORPE	C1	13SEP47	Lutterworth	9/80			
LEIRE	C1	13SEP47	Lutterworth	9/80	BL	18MAR50.	
					BL/GR	24SEP51	
MOUSLEY	C1	13SEP47	Mkt Harborough	9/80	BL/GR	28NOV57	
					B	6SEP59	
SEAGRAVE	C1	30SEP47	Loughborough	9/82			
RATCLIFFE	C1	30SEP47	Loughborough	9/82			
BURROW-ON-THE-HILL	C1	19OCT47	Melton Mowbray	9/93			
SOUTH-CROXTON	C1	20OCT47	Leicester	9/93	BL	5DEC51	
STOCKINGFORD	C1	12NOV47	Hinckley	9/96		Note 5.	
THORNTON	C1	12NOV47	Hinckley	9/97			
DISEWORTH	C1	22NOV47	Loughborough	9/101	B	20JAN49-	51
					BL	20DEC51	
EASTWELL	C1	22NOV47	Melton Mowbray	9/101			
LYDDINGTON	C1	22NOV47	Uppingham	9/101			
WOODVILLE	C1	27JAN48	Burton on Trent	9/117			
NETHER-BROUGHTON	C1	26MAR48	Melton Mowbray	9/136			
KETTLEBY	C1	26MAR48	Melton Mowbray	9/136			
BARKSTONE	C1	4MAY48	Grantham	9/144			
GRETTON	C1	4MAY48	Rockingham	9/144	BL	18MAR50-25JUL54	
WALTON	C1	4MAY48	Lutterworth	9/146	GR	22FEB49	
					OR/BR	27JAN51	
BUCKMINSTER	C1	24MAY48	Grantham	9/150			
BLABY	C1	24MAY48	Leicester	9/151	BL	15NOV56-	59.
LOCKINGTON	C1	24MAY48	Derby	9/152			
BARROW	C1	4JUL48	Loughborough	9/166	OR	10FEB51	
BELTON	C1	4JUL48	Uppingham	9/166			
MONKSKIRBY	C1	28AUG48	Rugby	9/178	B	5OCT50	
BRANSTON	C1	20OCT48	Oakham	9/184			
SILEBY	C1	20OCT48	Loughborough	9/184	B	9OCT49	

Notes: 5. In Warks - no other record of it being served from Hinckley.

Leics

GADDESBY	C1	14NOV48	Melton Mowbray	9/190			
SHEARESLEY	C1	19NOV48	Mkt Harborough	9/193		Note 6.	
SHEEPY	C1	1FEB49	Atherstone	9/210			
APPLEBY	C1	1FEB49	Atherstone	9/210	B	19FEB50-27MAR52.	
TWYCROSS	C1	1FEB49	Atherstone	9/210	GR	8JUL57-26DEC57	
					B	14MAY58-27OCT59	
MEASHAM	C1	1FEB49	Atherstone	9/210			
HAMBLETON	C1	14APR49	Oakham	9/243			
BURTON-OVERY	C1	23AUG49	Leicester	10/35			
SHAWSTON	C1	18NOV50	Mkt Harborough	10/122		Note 7.	
GLENFIELD	C1	29JAN51	Leicester	10/141			
SLAWSTON	C1	29JAN51	Mkt Harborough	10/145			
GLENFIELD	C1	29JAN51	Leicester	10/146			
COLEORTON	C1	12FEB51	Ashby de la Z	10/153			
COSTON	C1	28MAR51	Melton Mowbray	10/184			
WEBTOFT	C1	24APR51	Lutterworth	10/192		Note 8.	
EXTON	C1	29SEP51	Oakham	10/254			
REARSBY	C1	6FEB52	Leicester	11/19	R	45	
BURBAGE	C1	SEP52	Hinckley	11/101	B	19MAR53	
					GR	18MAR59-13OCT59.	
STRETTON·EN·LE·FIELDS	C1	SEP52	Ashby de la Z	11/105			
COALVILLE	C1	SEP52	Ashby de la Z	11/105	B	30MAR56-24JUN59	
NETHERSEAL	C1	SEP52	Ashby de la Z	11/105	GR	8APR56	
SNARSTON	C1	SEP52	Ashby de la Z	11/105			
OVERSEAL	C1	DEC52	Ashby de la Z	11/124	B	28OCT53-23DEC54	
ARTHINGWORTH	C1	APR53	Mkt Harborough	11/158			
PACKINGTON	C1	APR53	Ashby de la Z	11/161	B	14AUG58	
HUGGLESCOTE	C1	JUN53	Ashby de la Z	11/181			
HUGGLESCOTE	C1	JUN53	Ashby de la Z	11/191	B	30MAR58-11DEC58.	
SCALFORD	C1	AUG53	Melton Mowbray	11/202			
BRANSTONE	C1	AUG53	Grantham	11/210			
COSBY	C1	DEC53	Lutterworth	12/10	GR	19JUL59-23DEC59	
HUMBERSTONE-GATE	C1	MAY54	Leicester	12/62	B	26OCT57	
THURLASTON	C1	20MAR55	Hinckley	12/171			
SADDINGTON	C1	20MAR55	Mkt Harborough	12/172			
THORPE-LANGTON	C1	17MAY55	Mkt Harborough	12/199			
ANSTEY	C1	17MAY55	Leicester	12/200			
ENDERBY	C1	17MAY55	Leicester	12/200			
SOUTH·KILWORTH	C1	15JUN55	Rugby	12/210			
THRINGSTONE	C1	1SEP55	Ashby de la Z	12/235			
CLAYBROOK	C1	18SEP55	Lutterworth	12/244	B	19MAR59	
THRINGSTONE	C1	18SEP55	Ashby de la Z	12/244			
NEWBOLD-VERNON	C1	5NOV55	Hinckley	12/261	B	14JUL57	
COTESBACH	C1	5JAN56	Rugby	12/292			
MOUNT-SORREL	C1	13FEB56	Loughborough	12/312			
HALLATON	C1	17FEB56	Uppingham	12/313			
SHENTON	C1	11JUN56	Nuneaton	13/20			
HICKLING	C1	29JUL56	Melton Mowbray	13/47			
NORMANTON	C1	12SEP56	Loughborough	13/69	B	15APR59	
STANFORD	C1	12SEP56	Loughborough	13/69		Note 9.	

Notes:
6. Should be 'Shearsby' but no such C1 stamp.
7. Probably not used - see 10/145.
8. Spelling error - W<u>i</u>btoft.
9. Possibly never used since "Authority for an office at Stanford cancelled" (Post 35/649/1857).

Leics

SWITHLAND	C1	12SEP56	Loughborough	13/70	B	9MAR59
EARL-SHILTON	C1	27NOV56	Hinckley	13/102	GR	12FEB57-16FEB58
WYMESWOLD	C1	30JAN57	Loughborough	13/127		Note 10.
WYMESWOLD	C1	14FEB57	Loughborough	13/145		
WIGSTON	C1	16MAR57	Leicester	13/172		
WATERLOO-ST	C1	31MAR57	Leicester	13/200	BL/GR	57
					BL/B	1AUG59
CATTHORPE	C1	7APR57	Rugby	13/208		
WATERLOO-ST	C1*	12APR57	Leicester	13/214		
HIGH-CROSS-ST	C1*	9MAY57	Leicester	13/230	GR	MAY58-19JAN59
BELGRAVE-GATE	C1*	16MAY57	Leicester	13/237	GR	3AUG59
LAXTON	C1*	3JUN57	Uppingham	13/249		
MUSTON	C1*	8JUN57	Nottingham	13/246		
REDMILE	C1*	8JUN57	Nottingham	13/246	B	25NOV57
NEWBOLD-VERDON	C4	6AUG57	Hinckley	14/43	GR	30OCT57-30DEC57.
					B	21NOV59
COSSINGTON	C4	22OCT57	Loughborough	14/61		
DISEWORTH	C4	22OCT57	Loughborough	14/61		
QUORNDON	C4	22OCT57	Loughborough	14/61		
REMPSTONE	C4	22OCT57	Loughborough	14/61		
ROTHLEY	C4	22OCT57	Loughborough	14/61	GR	8SEP58-10SEP58.
SILEBY	C4	22OCT57	Loughborough	14/61	BL/GR	60
SUTTONBONNINGTON	C4	22OCT57	Loughborough	14/61		
WOODHOUSE·EAVES	C4	22OCT57	Loughborough	14/61	GR	5NOV57
BARWELL	D4	22OCT57	Hinckley	14/63		
NAILSTONE	D1	22OCT57	Hinckley	14/63	B	16NOV58.
CROFT	D4	22OCT57	Hinckley	14/63		
SHEEPSHED	C4	30OCT57	Loughborough	14/65	BL	7MAR57- 9FEB58
TILTON ON THE HILL	C4	1DEC57	Leicester	14/93		
COSTON	C4	2JAN58	Melton Mowbray	14/120		
SOMERBY	C4	7JAN58	Oakham	14/121		
COTTESMORE	C4	7JAN58	Oakham	14/121		
WHISSENDINE	C4	7JAN58	Oakham	14/121		
BASTON	C4	7JAN58	Oakham	14/121		Note 11.
OXFORD.ST.LEICESTER	C4	18JAN58	Leicester	14/126		
TUGBY	C4	18JAN58	Leicester	14/126	GR	24MAR58
NARBOROUGH	C4	18JAN58	Leicester	14/126		
MARKFIELD	C4	18JAN58	Leicester	14/126		
GREAT-GLENN	C4	18JAN58	Leicester	14/126		
BILLESDON	C4	18JAN58	Leicester	14/126	GR	5DEC59.
BURTON OVERY	D1	13FEB58	Leicester	14/145	B	10NOV59
WIBTOFT	D4	3MAR58	Lutterworth	14/183		
TUR-LANGTON	D1	31MAR58	Mkt Harborough	14/184		
SHEARSBY	D1	31MAR58	Mkt Harborough	14/184		
ASHBY-PARVA	D1	1APR58	Lutterworth	14/185		
ULLESTHORPE	D1	1APR58	Lutterworth	14/185		
NTH-KILWORTH	D1	13APR58	Rugby	14/197		
THEDDINGWORTH	D1	13APR58	Rugby	14/197	GR	28FEB57
					B	18JUN59-12DEC59.
LUBBENHAM	D1	22APR58	Rugby	14/207	B	30AUG58
BITTESWELL	D1	26MAY58	Lutterworth	14/234	B	4APR59
MORCOTT	D4	1JUN58	Uppingham	14/247		
MANTON	D4	1JUN58	Uppingham	14/247		
GREAT-EASTON	D1	4JUN58	Uppingham	14/248		

Notes: 10. 'Y' looks like 'V' - never used? See 13/145.
11. Probably Baston in Lincolnshire.

Leics

THORNTON	D1	8SEP58	Hinckley	16/32	B	21DEC58.
HARBY	D4	10SEP58	Melton Mowbray	16/33		
WALTHAM	D4	10SEP58	Melton Mowbray	16/33		
AB·KETTLEBY	D1	10SEP58	Melton Mowbray	16/33		
MEASHAM	D4	30SEP58	Atherstone	16/51	B	?
GILMORTON	D1	2DEC58	Lutterworth	16/96		
WALCOTE	D4	2DEC58	Lutterworth	16/96	BL	59
IBSTOCK	D4	31DEC58	Ashby de la Z	16/127		
BRUNTINGTHORPE	D1	5JAN59	Lutterworth	16/133		
THURMASTON	D1	13JAN59	Leicester	16/138	BL	JUL59.
HOUGHTON LEICESTER	D2	14JAN59	Leicester	16/139		
GREAT-BOWDEN	D1	21JAN59	Mkt Harborough	16/142		
WILLY	D4	21JAN59	Lutterworth	16/143		Note 12.
SWANNINGTON	D1	27JAN59	Ashby de la Z	16/148		
NORTH LUFFENHAM	D1	5FEB59	Uppingham	16/155		
WOLVEY	D4	18FEB59	Nuneaton	16/160		
LUBENHAM	D1	18FEB59	Rugby	16/161	B	4APR59-30DEC59
BRAUNSTONE	D1	9APR59	Leicester	18/24		
SOUTH·LUFFENHAM	D1	15APR59	Leicester	18/28		
THRUSSINGTON	D1	4MAY59	Leicester	18/38		
CROXTON-LINC.	D1	21MAY59	Grantham	18/47		Note 13.
RYHALL	D4	MAY59	Stamford	18/52		
BRIDGE-CASTERTON	D1	2JUN59	Stamford	18/52		
KETTON	D4	3JUN59	Stamford	18/52		
MONKS·KIRBY	D1	19JUL59	Lutterworth	18/80		
HUSBAND'S·BOSWORTH	D1	12AUG59	Rugby	18/88		
MEDBOURNE	D1	17AUG59	Mkt Harborough	18/94		

Notes: 12. Probably intended for Wil<u>e</u>y (Warks).
       13. Intended for Croxton (Kerrial)
           in Leicestershire (see 7/143).

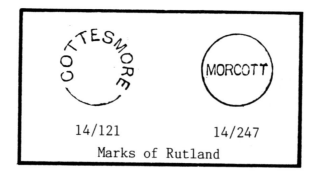

Marks of Rutland

Leics

Similar Sans-serif (C1) Marks of Leicestershire

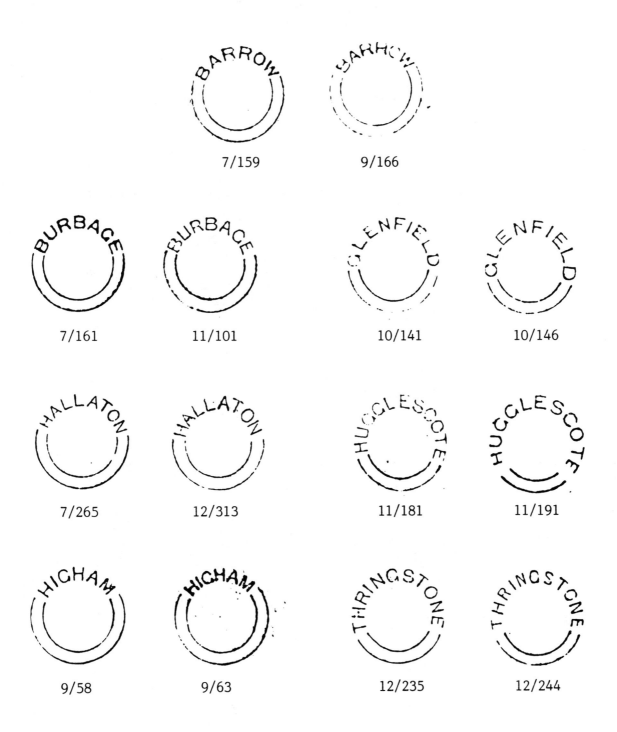

Reproduced by courtesy of Post Office Archives

Leics 68.

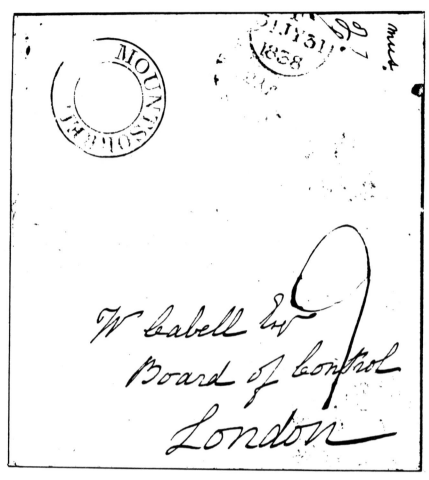

The distinctive mark of MOUNTSORREL (2/91)

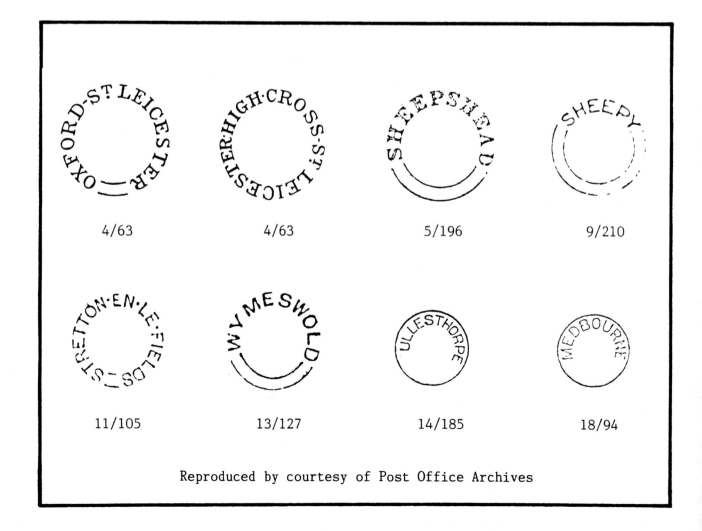

| 4/63 | 4/63 | 5/196 | 9/210 |
| 11/105 | 13/127 | 14/185 | 18/94 |

Reproduced by courtesy of Post Office Archives

TUGBY (5/179) and QUORNDON (7/82)

EMPINGHAM (7/138) and COALVILLE (11/105)

NORTHAMPTONSHIRE

BRACKLEY (104). 2/9 (CDS 9NOV39)

Aynho 5/159
Croughton 12/22
Evenley 12/22
Farthinghoe 11/110
Helmdon 9/96 16/56
Marston St Lawrence 11/110
Souldern 1 10/67 16/56
Syresham 9/96 (CDS 7DEC58)
Whitfield 9/96

DAVENTRY (238). Pre proof books (CDS 11NOV31)

Badby 12/306
Barby 12/129 See TL14.
Boddington 10/208
Braunston + (CDS 24MAY51) See TL17.
Byfield 5/182 116/133
Crick 7/246 See TL11.
Drayton 13/132
Eydon 7/270 14/267
Hellidon 9/5
Kilsby + 12/232 See TL5,12&14.
Long Buckby + 7/68 (CDS 24MAY51)
Preston Capes 9/32
Watford 7/246
Welton 12/292
West Haddon + 7/211 (CDS 11JUL56) See TL16.
Whilton 9/193 9/193*

HIGHAM FERRERS (363). 2/58 (CDS 7MAR40)

Burton Latimer 10/283 See TL7&18.
Finedon 10/283
Irthlingborough 12/141
Riseley 2 10/283 14/22
Rushden 10/283 14/28
Stanwick 12/278

KETTERING (414).

Barton Seagrave 10/241
Broughton 10/241 See TL18.
Cranford 10/241 18/24
Desborough 7/167 10/241 (CDS 30SEP57)
Geddington 10/241
Rothwell 7/167 10/241 (CDS 20FEB58)
Rushton 12/141 13/23 18/23
Thorpe Malsor 10/241.

NORTHAMPTON (570).

Blisworth 7/108 14/159
Boughton 7/166
Bridge St 12/223
Brixworth 7/166 (CDS 24FEB51)
Chapel Brampton 11/242
Cottesbrooke 11/211
Creaton 7/166 16/163
East Haddon 11/242 11/252
Easton Maudit 9/108 16/163
Ecton 7/208
Gt Billing 12/288
Gt Brington 12/289
Grendon 13/57
Guilsborough 7/166 (CDS 24FEB51)
Hackleton 7/148 14/184
Hannington 7/209
Hardingstone 7/108
Harlestone 9/120
Harrington 11/161
Hartwell 11/242
Haselbech 11/137
Kelmarsh 11/137
Kingsthorpe 7/239
Lamport 9/63
Little Brington 13/24
Little Houghton 7/215 14/183
Maidwell 7/166
Mears Ashby 7/267
Milton 11/137 16/163 16/171
Moulton 7/209
Old 9/63
Pitsford 7/166
Roade 7/108
Scaldwell 10/205
Spratton 7/166 14/159
Walgrave 12/289
Wellingborough Rd 12/223
Wellington Place 12/223
Weston Favell 7/208 14/69
Wilby 7/267
Wootton 12/288 13/3
Yardley Hastings 7/215

OUNDLE (601). 1/132 (CDS 1SEP38)

Barnwell 10/251
Benefield 12/244
Chesterton 3 10/251 See TL13.
Elton 3 10/251
Fotheringhay 10/251
Lower Benefield 18/24

+ indicates an office which used a straight line (or P.P.) stamp after 1840.

An underlined number, eg 3, indicates an office outside Northants - see key at end.

Northants

Oundle (Cont'd)

Luddington 10/251
Polebrook 16/119
Wadenhoe 14/197
Warmington 13/221

PETERBOROUGH (612). 1/142 (CDS 1/144 30MAR30)

Alwalton 3 10/270
Castor 9/79
Coates 4 12/135
Connington 3 12/206
Crowland 5 4/83 7/111 9/237 (CDS JUL52)
Eye 9/79 10/270
Glatton 3 18/39
Holme 3 12/206 12/247 14/247
Millfield 12/247 14/248
New Fletton 11/214
Sawtry 3 10/270 14/247
Stanground 3 10/270
Thorney 4 4/83 9/237 9/245
Werrington 10/270
Whaplode Drove 5 12/206
Whittlesey 4 4/83 (CDS 8FEB49)
Yaxley 3 10/270 14/247

ROCKINGHAM (652). See TL6.

Great Easton 6 9/18 14/248 See TL21.
Gretton 9/144 See TL9.
Middleton 9/18 See TL9.

THRAPSTON (798). 1/182 (CDS 14MAR40)

Brigstock 10/260
Corby 11/40
Islip 14/117
Little Addington 14/117
Lowick 10/259
Molesworth 3 10/260 13/23 18/4
Raunds 10/260 14/11
Ringstead 12/56
Sudborough 10/259
Titchmarsh 10/260
Woodford 10/260.

TOWCESTER (808). 2/140
                    (CDS 22JAN40)
Abthorpe 9/117
Blakesley 7/210
Fosters Booth 7/1
Greens Norton 11/116
Lois Weedon 9/117
Pattishall 12/261
Paulerspury 9/109
Silverstone 9/108
Stoke Bruerne 9/230
Tiffield 9/230
Whittlebury 9/109

WANSFORD (839). 1/208
                    (CDS 13JUN40)

Apethorpe 10/259 14/248
Deene 4/112 10/258 14/247
Kingscliffe (no mark found)
                    (CDS 19AUG51)
Nassington 11/15
Water Newton 3 10/258
Weldon 4/112 10/251 See TL4&20.

WEEDON (851).

Bugbrook 7/143
Farthingstone 7/271 16/127
Flore 10/122
Harpole 7/143 13/89
Heyford 12/58

WELFORD (857). 1/206 (CDS 9MAR40)
                    See TL8.

Husbands Bosworth 6 7/75 18/88
(CDS 14OCT59) See TL8, Notes 1&2.
Naseby 7/185 12/204
            14/207 See TL8.
North Kilworth 6 7/230
            See TL8 & Note 1.

WELLINGBOROUGH (858).

Bozeat + 18/2
Cransley 14/104
Earls Barton 7/209* See TL3.
Great Harrowden 14/104
Irchester 12/26
Isham 11/118
Little Harrowden 10/256 18/24
Orlingbury 12/244
Wollaston 10/256 13/23 18/24

+ indicates an office which used a straight line (or P.P.) stamp after 1840.

An underlined number, eg 5, indicates an office outside Northants - see key at end.

Northants

BANBURY (46), Oxon

Chipping Warden 7/249
Culworth 7/12
Middleton Cheney 7/12
Thorpe Mandeville 11/191 16/16

MARKET DEEPING (508), Lincs

Blatherwick 12/103 14/248 See TL10.
Bulwick 12/103 See TL10.
Helpston 10/251
Newborough 10/251

MARKET HARBOROUGH (511), Leics

Arthingworth 11/158 See TL15.
Clipston 7/10 See TL2.
Lubenham 6 7/39 14/207 16/161 See TL1&8.
Oxendon 7/10 See TL2.
Theddingworth 6 7/39 14/197 See TL1&8.
Wilbarston 5/132

RUGBY (659), Warks

Ashby St Legers 12/210
Yelvertoft 7/270.

ST NEOTS (686), Hunts

Hargrave 10/247

STAMFORD (742), Lincs

Barnack 7/138 18/52
Duddington 7/102 18/52
Easton 7/102

STONY STRATFORD (749), Bucks

Cosgrove 7/16 14/215
Deanshanger 7/216
Potterspury 7/149
Wicken 7/216
Yardley Gobion 13/154

UPPINGHAM (825), Rutland

Laxton 13/249

WOODSTOCK (910), Oxon

Charlton 9/210
Kings Sutton 13/221 14/11
        See TL19.

Notes:
1. These villages, although coming under Rugby on 7MAR53, were still served via Welford until 1JUN55.
2. 7/75 was sent to Lutterworth but the minute authorising the official post and the opening of an S.O. mentioned the village being served from Welford. No Lutterworth to Welford transfer found.

KEY to offices not in Northamptonshire

1 is in Oxfordshire
2 is in Bedfordshire
3 is in Huntingdonshire
4 is in Cambridgeshire
5 is in Lincolnshire
6 is in Leicestershire.

TRANSFERS - Northamptonshire

TL 1. Lubenham and Thedingworth from Market Harborough to Welford on 11JUL44.

2. Oxendon and Clipston from Market Harborough to Northampton on 29AUG45.

3. Earl's Barton from Wellingborough to Northampton on 26JAN46.

4. Weldon from Wansford to Oundle on 16NOV46.

5. Kilsby from Daventry to Rugby on 27NOV46.

6. Letters for Rockingham (and its delivery) to be sent to Leicester from 6MAR49.

7. Burton Latimer from Higham Ferrers to Kettering on 5JAN53.

8. Welford reduced to a sub-office under Rugby on 7MAR53.
(The Welford sub-offices would have moved at the same time.)

9. Gretton and Middleton to Uppingham in 1854.

10. Blatherwick and Bulwick from Market Deeping to Wansford c1854 unless their 1854 stamps were sent to Market Deeping in error. They were under Wansford by April 1855.

11. Crick from Daventry to Rugby on 9FEB55.

12. Kilsby from Rugby to Daventry on 9FEB55.

13. Chesterton from Oundle to Peterborough on 7MAY55.

14. Barby and Kilsby from Daventry to Rugby on 1JUN55.

15. Arthingworth from Market Harborough to Northampton in 1855/56?

16. West Haddon from Daventry to Rugby on 24FEB56.

17. Braunston from Daventry to Rugby on 21FEB57.

18. Burton Latimer and Broughton from Kettering to Wellingborough on 30JAN58.

19. Kings Sutton from Woodstock to Banbury on 8FEB58.

20. Weldon from Oundle to Wansford on 1AUG59.

21. Great Easton from Rockingham to Uppingham at unknown date.

NORTHAMPTONSHIRE

DAVENTRY	C3				B	14APR30-22OCT32
PETERBOROUGH	C2	29OCT27	Peterborough	1/142		
PETERBOROUGH	C2M	30MAY30	Peterborough	1/144	B	24NOV34-18JAN36
WELFORD	C2*	11MAR30	Welford	1/206	B	24MAY30-23MAR38
OUNDLE	C2*	31MAY30	Oundle	1/132	B	31-14OCT36
THRAPSTONE	C3	31MAY30	Thrapstone	1/182	B	1NOV30-25NOV34.
					R	17JUN38- 9JUL38
WANDSFORD	C2	11NOV31		1/208	B	1OCT30- 40
BRACKLEY	C2*	7JAN32	Brackley	2/9	B	21JUL33-25DEC36
HIGHAM FERRERS	C2	4JAN33	Higham Ferrers	2/58	R	23JUN34- 3DEC34
TOWCESTER	C2	19OCT35	Towcester	2/140	B	6NOV35-13JUN40.
DEANE-NORTHTn	C2	4MAR41	Wansford	4/112	B	50
WELDON-NORTHTn	C2	4MAR41	Wansford	4/112	B	23JUL45-15SEP48
					GR	24JAN50
CROWLAND	C2	15MAR41	Peterborough	4/83		
THORNEY	C2	15MAR41	Peterborough	4/83	B	28JAN49
WHITTLESEA	C2	15MAR41	Peterborough	4/83	B	SEP43- 49.
WILBARSTON	C2	24DEC42	Mkt Harborough	5/132	B	23JUL45-15SEP48
					BL	20SEP53
AYNHO	C2	13MAY43	Brackley	5/159	GR	11MAR55
BYFIELD	C2	19SEP43	Daventry	5/182	B	27DEC43-27APR44
					GR	55
FOSTERS-BOOTH	C2	29NOV43	Towcester	7/1	B	45- 5JAN46.
					BL	2JAN51- 6SEP51
OXENDON	C2	30DEC43	Mkt Harborough	7/10	B	16AUG45
					BR	21OCT47
					R	20NOV48.
CLIPSTONE	C2	30DEC43	Mkt Harborough	7/10	B	5SEP47
					OR	2JAN52-21MAR53
					R	4MAR53
					BL/GR	27FEB57
CULWORTH	C2	3JAN44	Banbury	7/12	R	14APR56-30OCT56.
					BL	13DEC59
MIDDLETON-CHENEY	C2	3JAN44	Banbury	7/12	OR	5JUL46
					BL	21OCT52
COSGROVE	C2	13JAN44	St'y Stratford	7/16		
LUBBENHAM	C2	18MAR44	Mkt Harborough	7/39	B	44-13MAR55
THEDDINGWORTH	C2	18MAR44	Mkt Harborough	7/39	B	14DEC44- 55
					GR	27AUG56-28FEB57
LONG-BUCKBY	C1	6JUN44	Daventry	7/68	R	8JUL44-20MAY47.
					OR	24DEC49
HUSBANDS-BOSWORTH	C1	28JUN44	Lutterworth	7/75	B	31OCT45-14NOV49
					GR	8JAN56-12MAR57
DUDDINGTON	C1	22OCT44	Stamford	7/102		
EASTON	C1	22OCT44	Stamford	7/102	Y	5DEC44.
HARDINGSTONE	C1	16NOV44	Northampton	7/108	B	22FEB45
ROADE	C1	16NOV44	Northampton	7/108	B	5JUN46
BLISWORTH	C1	16NOV44	Northampton	7/108	GR	12JAN58
CROWLAND	C1	29NOV44	Peterborough	7/111	B	7JUL45
BARNACK	C1	14APR45	Stamford	7/138	B	11MAR47
BUGBROOK	C1	8MAY45	Weedon	7/143	R	3NOV47- 1DEC53.
					BL	58
HARPOLE	C1	8MAY45	Weedon	7/143	B	21MAR48
HACKLETON	C1	22MAY45	Northampton	7/148	B	45- 5NOV47
POTTERSPURY	C1	22MAY45	St'y Stratford	7/149	R	21MAY49
BRIXWORTH	C1	24JUL45	Northampton	7/166	B	46- 5NOV50.

Northants

BROUGHTON	C1	24JUL45	Northampton	7/166	R	5AUG45 Note 1.
					B	18NOV54
					GR	10DEC56
					BL	7AUG57
GREAT-CREATON	C1	24JUL45	Northampton	7/166	B	20MAR47
					R	26MAR48
					BL	10OCT56- 58.
GUILSBOROUGH	C1	24JUL45	Northampton	7/166	R	27SEP49- 50
MAIDWELL	C1	24JUL45	Northampton	7/166	B	10AUG58
PITSFORD	C1	24JUL45	Northampton	7/166	B	20SEP45- 53
					GR	10DEC56
SPRATTON	C1	24JUL45	Northampton	7/166	B	3NOV47-17AUG55
					R	23APR49
					GR	15DEC57
DESBOROUGH	C1	5AUG45	Kettering	7/167	R	15JUN49
					BR	20NOV50
					GR	22JUL54
ROTHWELL	C1	5AUG45	Kettering	7/167	B	20SEP47
					GR	8DEC47
NASEBY	C1	25OCT45	Welford	7/185	B	46- 5MAR55.
ECTON	C1	27JAN46	Northampton	7/208	BL	27NOV57
WESTON-FAVELL	C1	27JAN46	Northampton	7/208	B	2MAR48
HANNINGTON	C1	28JAN46	Northampton	7/209		
MOULTON	C1	28JAN46	Northampton	7/209		
EARLS BARTON	C1		Northampton		BL	20AUG56
BLAKESLEY	C1	5FEB46	Towcester	7/210	B	APR46-19JUL46.
WEST-HADDON	C1	14FEB46	Daventry	7/211	OR	29OCT49
					R	27JUL50- 51
LITTLE-HOUGHTON	C1	4MAR46	Northampton	7/215	R	20APR49
YARDLEY-HASTINGS	C1	4MAR46	Northampton	7/215	B	24FEB48
DENSHANGER	C1	4MAR46	St'y Stratford	7/216		
WICKEN	C1	4MAR46	St'y Stratford	7/216		
NORTH-KILWORTH	C1	20APR46	Welford	7/230	B	16MAR50-24AUG53.
KINGSTHORPE	C1	27MAY46	Northampton	7/239	BL	24JAN47
					B	12MAR60
CRICK	C1	27JUN46	Daventry	7/246	BL	28FEB60
WATFORD	C1	27JUN46	Daventry	7/246	B	50- 58.
					BL/B	27DEC58
CHIPPING-WARDEN	C1	30JUN46	Banbury	7/249		
MEARS-ASHBY	C1	16SEP46	Northampton	7/267	B	21DEC46- 2JUL57
WILBY	C1	16SEP46	Northampton	7/267	B	3NOV46-17JUL47.
					GR	8DEC56- 2JUL57
EYDON	C1	29SEP46	Daventry	7/270	GR	27JUN51
YELVERTOFT	C1	29SEP46	Rugby	7/270	OR	12OCT49.
FARTHINGSTONE	C1	29SEP46	Weedon	7/271		
FARTHINGSTONE	C?	(Locally made?)			GR	27MAR56 Note 2.
HELLIDON	C1	19JAN47	Daventry	9/5	B	31JUL47
					GR	27APR56-27MAY57.
					BL	17OCT59
MIDDLETON	C1	3MAR47	Rockingham	9/18	OR	30AUG47
					BL	31AUG54
GREAT-EASTON	C1	3MAR47	Rockingham	9/18		
PRESTON-CAPES	C1	27APR47	Daventry	9/32	GR	29JUN57-24NOV57
					B	59

Notes: 1. Issued to Boughton. The 'R' was removed locally, leaving a gap, and only in this form is it known used.
2. Seriffed letters; narrow arcs.

Northants

OLD	C1	22JUL47	Northampton	9/63	BL	29SEP55-10DEC57
LAMPORT	C1	22JUL47	Northampton	9/63		
CASTOR	C1	13SEP47	Peterborough	9/79	B	28MAY56
EYE	C1	13SEP47	Peterborough	9/79		
HELMDON	C1	9NOV47	Brackley	9/96	BL	25JUL57.
WHITFIELD	C1	9NOV47	Brackley	9/96		
SYRESHAM	C1	9NOV47	Brackley	9/96	GR	2NOV49
					BL	54
EASTON-MAUDIT	C1	16DEC47	Northampton	9/108	R	24JUL48
SILVERSTONE	C1	20DEC47	Towcester	9/108	BL	27APR59
PAULERSPURY	C1	20DEC47	Towcester	9/109		
WHITTLEBURY	C1	20DEC47	Towcester	9/109	BL	24OCT52- 54.
LOIS WEEDON	C1	15JAN48	Towcester	9/117	BL/GR	15APR56- 57
ABTHORPE	C1	15JAN48	Towcester	9/117	BL	7SEP52
HARLESTON	C1	5FEB48	Northampton	9/120	B	53
					BL	16OCT57
GRETTON	C1	4MAY48	Rockingham	9/144	BL	18MAR50-25JUL54
WHITTON	C1	19NOV48	Daventry	9/193		Note 3.
WHILTON	C1	19NOV48	Daventry	9/193	BL	2AUG51
					BR	51- 52
					B	1MAY52-24JUN54.
					GR	24MAR57
CHARLTON	C1	1FEB49	Woodstock	9/210	R	4FEB56
STOKE BRUEN	C1	10MAR49	Towcester	9/230		
TIFFIELD	C1	10MAR49	Towcester	9/230	B	7JAN59-23MAR59
THORNEY	C1	28MAR49	Peterborough	9/237	see 9/245 below	
CROWLAND	C1	28MAR49	Peterborough	9/237		
THORNEY	C1	16APR49	Peterborough	9/245	BL	17MAY55
SOULDERN	C1	15FEB50	Brackley	10/67		
FLOOR	C1	18NOV50	Weedon	10/122	GR	16DEC55
SCALDWELL	C1	27MAY51	Northampton	10/205	BL	2JAN55-23MAR56
BODDINGTON	C1	8JUN51	Daventry	10/208	BL	8JAN58
					B	59
FINEDON	C1	19AUG51	Higham Ferrers	10/283	B	2AUG54
					BL/GR	20AUG57.
BURTON LATIMER	C1	19AUG51	Higham Ferrers	10/283	BL	12FEB59
					GR	24MAR59
RUSHDEN	C1	19AUG51	Higham Ferrers	10/283		
RISELEY	C1	19AUG51	Higham Ferrers	10/283		
ROTHWELL	C1	27AUG51	Kettering	10/241	B	57
					BL	24DEC57
DESBOROUGH	C1	27AUG51	Kettering	10/241	BL/GR	11FEB56-15FEB56
THORPE-MALSER	C1	27AUG51	Kettering	10/241		
BROUGHTON	C1	27AUG51	Kettering	10/241		
GEDDINGTON	C1	27AUG51	Kettering	10/241	BL	13AUG55-21SEP55
					GR	FEB55-22JAN56.
					BL/GR	11DEC57
BARTON-SEGRAVE	C1	27AUG51	Kettering	10/241		
CRANFORD	C1	27AUG51	Kettering	10/241	BL	10JUN55
HARGRAVE	C1	29SEP51	St Neots	10/247		
HELPSTONE	C1	29SEP51	Market Deeping	10/251		
NEWBOROUGH	C1	29SEP51	Market Deeping	10/251		
WELDON	C1	29SEP51	Oundle	10/251	BL	MAR55
ELTON	C1	29SEP51	Oundle	10/251	B	10OCT55-30AUG59.
CHESTERTON	C1	29SEP51	Oundle	10/251	B	53
BARNWELL-ST-ANDREW	C1	29SEP51	Oundle	10/251	B	20MAR54- 9FEB58
					BL	JUL59
FOTHERINGAY	C1	29SEP51	Oundle	10/251	GR	12FEB57
LUDDINGTON	C1	29SEP51	Oundle	10/251		

Notes: 3. See below - probably amended locally.

WOLLASTON	C1	10OCT51	Wellingborough	10/256			
LITTLE-HARROWDEN	C1	10OCT51	Wellingborough	10/256	GR	29JUN52.	
DEANE	C1	10OCT51	Wansford	10/258			
WATER-NEWTON	C1	10OCT51	Wansford	10/258			
APETHORPE	C1	10OCT51	Wansford	10/259			
LOWICK	C1	10OCT51	Thrapstone	10/259	BL	54	
SUDBOROUGH	C1	10OCT51	Thrapstone	10/259	B	20NOV53-	55.
BRIGSTOCK	C1	10OCT51	Thrapstone	10/260	GR	7OCT58	
TITCHMARSH	C1	10OCT51	Thrapstone	10/260	B	55	
MOLESWORTH	C1	10OCT51	Thrapstone	10/260			
RAUNDS	C1	10OCT51	Thrapstone	10/260	R	31DEC51-	1SEP53.
					OR	29DEC51-	53
WOODFORD	C1	10OCT51	Thrapstone	10/260			
EYE	C1	6OCT51	Peterborough	10/270			
ALWALTON	C1	6OCT51	Peterborough	10/270			
STANGROUND	C1	6OCT51	Peterborough	10/270			
WERRINGTON	C1	6OCT51	Peterborough	10/270			
SAWTRY	C1	6OCT51	Peterborough	10/270			
YAXLEY	C1	6OCT51	Peterborough	10/270			
NASSINGTON	C1	16JAN52	Wansford	11/15	BL	3FEB53.	
CORBY	C1	10APR52	Thrapstone	11/40			
FARTHINGHOE	C1	OCT52	Brackley	11/110			
MARSTON·ST·LAWRENCE	C1	OCT52	Brackley	11/110			
GREENS-NORTON	C1	OCT52	Towcester	11/116	GR	21MAR59	
ISHAM	C1	OCT52	Wellingborough	11/118	BL	7JAN58	
MILTON	C1	FEB53	Northampton	11/137	BL	19OCT57	
KELMARSH	C1	FEB53	Northampton	11/137	BL/GR	21NOV58.	
					B	16DEC59	
HASELBEECH	C1	FEB53	Northampton	11/137			
ARTHINGWORTH	C1	APR53	Mkt Harborough	11/158			
HARRINGTON	C1	APR53	Northampton	11/161	BL	24JUN57	
THORPE MANDEVILLE	C1	29JUN53	Banbury	11/191			
COTTESBROOK	C1	AUG53	Northampton	11/211	BL	12OCT54	
NEW-FLETTON	C1	AUG53	Peterborough	11/214			
CHAPEL-BRAMPTON	C1	OCT53	Northampton	11/242			
HARTWELL	C1	OCT53	Northampton	11/242			
EART HADDON	C1	OCT53	Northampton	11/242			Note 4.
EAST HADDON	C1	NOV53	Northampton	11/252	BL	14MAR54-	7AUG57.
EVENLEY	C1	JAN54	Brackley	12/22			
CROUGHTON	C1	JAN54	Brackley	12/22			
IRCHESTER	C1	FEB54	Wellingborough	12/26	BL	18DEC59	
RINGSTEAD	C1	MAY54	Thrapstone	12/56	B	24NOV55.	
HEYFORD	C1	MAY54	Weedon	12/58	GR	55	
					BL	24APR58	
BLATHERWICK	C1	22AUG54	Market Deeping	12/103			
BULWICK	C1	22AUG54	Market Deeping	12/103			
BARBY	C1	27OCT54	Daventry	12/129	BL/GR	13APR57	
					BL	3SEP59.	
COATES	C1	15NOV54	Peterborough	12/135			
RUSHTON	C1	11DEC54	Kettering	12/141			
IRTHLINGBOROUGH	C1	11DEC54	Higham Ferrers	12/141			
NASEBY	C1	20MAY55	Welford	12/204	B	7MAR57	
WHAPLODE-DROVE	C1	5JUN55	Peterborough	12/206			
HOLME	C1	5JUN55	Peterborough	12/206			
CONNINGTON	C1	5JUN55	Peterborough	12/206			
ASHBY-ST-LEDGERS	C1	15JUN55	Rugby	12/210	GR	57	
BRIDGE-ST	C1	27JUL55	Northampton	12/223	BL	56	
					GR	25MAR56	
WELLINGBOROUGH-RD	C1	27JUL55	Northampton	12/223	BL/GR	56-26SEP57.	

Notes: 4. Probably not used - see 11/252 below.

Northants

WELLINGTON-PLACE	C1	27JUL55	Northampton	12/223	BL/GR	3DEC57-29MAR58
KILSBY	C1	11AUG55	Rugby	12/232	GR	56- 57
					B	25APR59
					BL	26APR59- 60
ORLINGBURY	C1	19SEP55	Wellingborough	12/244	GR	18DEC55-19JUL56
BENEFIELD	C1	19SEP55	Oundle	12/244		
MILL-FIELD	C1	19SEP55	Peterborough	12/247		
HOLME	C1	19SEP55	Peterborough	12/247		
PATTISHALL	C1	5NOV55	Towcester	12/261	BL	11JUL56
STANWICK	C1	17DEC55	Higham Ferrers	12/278		
WOOLTON	C1	28DEC55	Northampton	12/288		Note 5.
GT-BILLING	C1	28DEC55	Northampton	12/288		
GT-BRINGTON	C1	28DEC55	Northampton	12/289	GR	11SEP56-18SEP56.
WALGRAVE	C1	28DEC55	Northampton	12/289		
WELTON	C1	5JAN56	Daventry	12/292	GR	15NOV56
					BL/GR	25AUG57
BADBY	C1	31JAN56	Daventry	12/306		
WOOTTON	C1	29APR56	Northampton	13/3	BL	20JAN58
					B	58
MOLESWORTH	C1	21JUN56	Thrapstone	13/23		
WOOLASTON	C1	21JUN56	Wellingborough	13/23		
RUSHTON	C1	21JUN56	Kettering	13/23		
LITTLE-BRINGTON	C1	21JUN56	Northampton	13/24	GR	11OCT56-10JAN57.
GRENDON	C1	8AUG56	Northampton	13/57		
HARPOLE	C1	28AUG56	Weedon	13/89		
DRAYTON	C1	12FEB57	Daventry	13/132		
YARDLEY-GOBION	C1	23FEB57	St'y Stratford	13/154		
KINGS-SUTTON	C1	29APR57	Woodstock	13/221	B	3DEC58
WARMINGTON	C1*	29APR57	Oundle	13/221	B	31JUL58
LAXTON	C1*	15JUN57	Uppingham	13/249		
KINGS-SUTTON	C4	1SEP57	Banbury	14/11		
RAUNDS	C4	1SEP57	Thrapstone	14/11	BL	30NOV59
RISELY	C4	10SEP57	Higham Ferrers	14/22		
RUSHDEN	C4	21SEP57	Higham Ferrers	14/28		
WESTON-FAVELL	D1	22OCT57	Northampton	14/69		
GREAT HARROWDEN	D1	10DEC57	Wellingborough	14/104	B	1SEP59.
CRANSLEY	D4	10DEC57	Wellingborough	14/104		
ISLIP	D4	2JAN58	Thrapstone	14/117		
LITTLE-ADDINGTON	D1	2JAN58	Thrapstone	14/117	B	60.
SPRATTON	D1	11MAR58	Northampton	14/159	B	9SEP59
					BL	28JUL59
BLISWORTH	D1	11MAR58	Northampton	14/159		
LITTLE HOUGHTON	D1	31MAR58	Northampton	14/183		
HACKLETON	D1	31MAR58	Northampton	14/184		
WADENHOPE	D1	13APR58	Oundle	14/197		
NTH-KILWORTH	D1	13APR58	Rugby	14/197		
THEDDINGWORTH	D1	13APR58	Rugby	14/197	GR	28FEB57
					B	18JUN59-12DEC59.
NASEBY	D1	22APR58	Rugby	14/207		
LUBBENHAM	D1	22APR58	Rugby	14/207	B	30AUG58.
COSGROVE	D1	28APR58	St'y Stratford	14/215		
YAXLEY	D4	4JUN58	Peterborough	14/247		
SAWTRY	D4	4JUN58	Peterborough	14/247		
HOLME	D4	4JUN58	Peterborough	14/247		
DEENE	D4	4JUN58	Wansford	14/247		
BLATHERWYKE	D1	4JUN58	Wansford	14/248		
MILL-FIELD	D1	4JUN58	Peterborough	14/248		
APETHORPE	D1	4JUN58	Wansford	14/248		

Notes: 5. Spelling error - see 13/3 below.

GREAT-EASTON	D1	4JUN58	Uppingham	14/248			
EYDON	D4	23JUN58	Daventry	14/267	B		59.
THORPE-MANDEVILLE	D1	17AUG58	Banbury	16/16			
SOULDERN	D1	7OCT58	Brackley	16/56			
HELMDON	D4	7OCT58	Brackley	16/56			
POLEBROOK	D1	20DEC58	Oundle	16/119			
FARTHINGSTONE	D1	31DEC58	Weedon	16/127			
BYFIELD	D4	5JAN59	Daventry	16/133	B		59
LUBENHAM	D1	18FEB59	Rugby	16/161	B		4APR59-30DEC59
MILTON NORTHAMPTONSHIRE	D2	23FEB59	Northampton	16/163			Note 6.
EASTON-MAUDIT	D1	23FEB59	Northampton	16/163			Note 7.
GREAT-CREATON	D1	23FEB59	Northampton	16/163			
MILTON NORTHAMPTON	D2	7MAR59	Northampton	16/171			
BOZEAT	D4	15MAR59	Wellingborough	18/2			
MOLESWORTH	D1	17MAR59	Thrapstone	18/4			
RUSHTON	D4	9APR59	Kettering	18/23			
CRANFORD-ST-JOHN	D1	9APR59	Kettering	18/24			
LOWER-BENEFIELD	D1	9APR59	Oundle	18/24			
LITTLE-HARROWDEN	D1	9APR59	Wellingborough	18/24			
WOLLASTON NOR.	D2	9APR59	Wellingborough	18/24	B		FEB60.
GLATTON	D4	4MAY59	Peterborough	18/39			
BARNACK	D4	21MAY59	Stamford	18/52			
DUDDINGTON	D1	21MAY59	Stamford	18/52			
HUSBAND'S·BOSWORTH	D1	12AUG59	Rugby	18/88			

Notes: 6. Annotated "Not sent" - see 16/171.
7. Annotated "Sent 2 March 59".

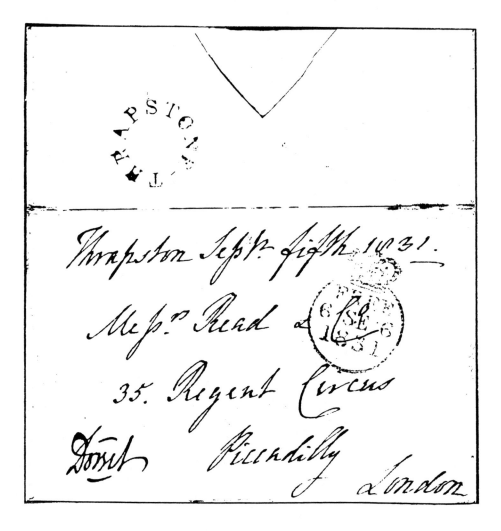

THRAPSTONE (1/182)

Similar Sans-serif (C1) Marks of Northamptonshire

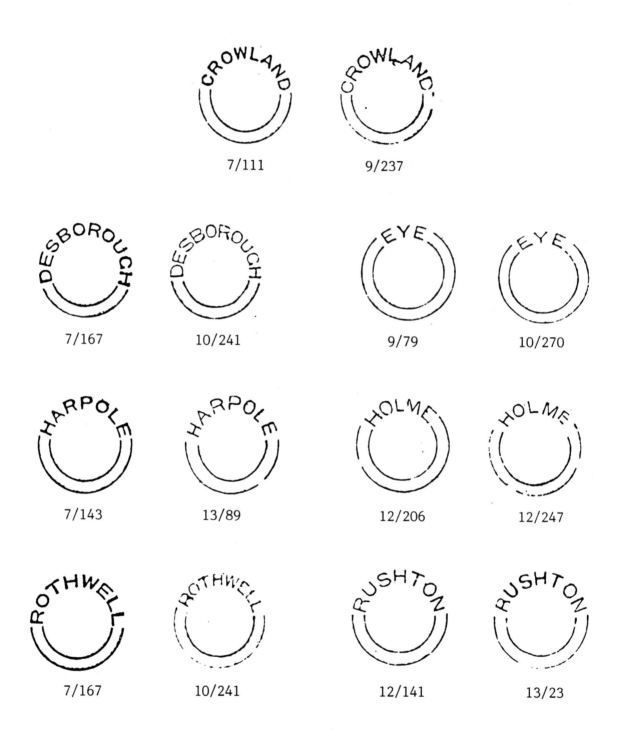

Reproduced by courtesy of Post Office Archives

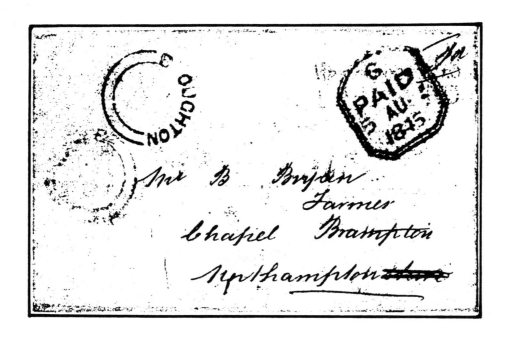

B OUGHTON — Issued as BROUGHTON (7/166), the 'R' was removed (probably locally) leaving a gap and it is only known used in this form.

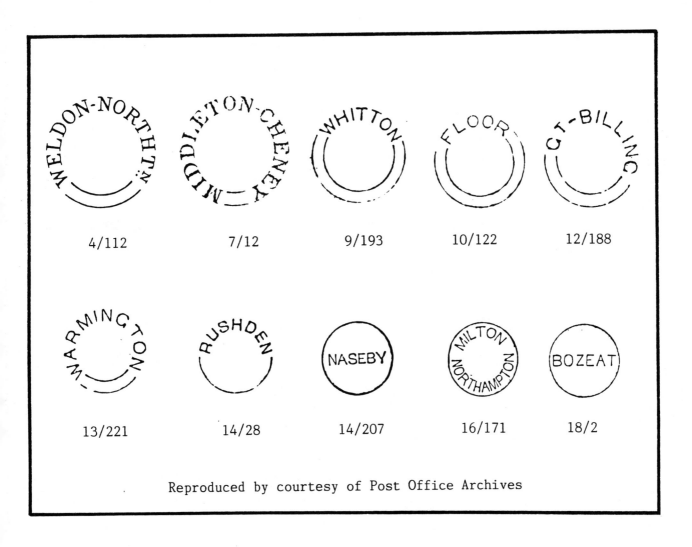

Reproduced by courtesy of Post Office Archives

Northants 82.

From top to bottom:

WILBY (7/267)
GEDDINGTON (10/241)
BLAKESLEY (7/210)
SPRATTON (14/159)

NOTTINGHAMSHIRE

MANSFIELD (504).

Bagthorpe 16/60
Blidworth 10/92
Cuckney 7/82 10/140
Fackley 16/60
Kirkby 10/8
Langwith 12/181
Mansfield Woodhouse 7/82 14/37
Norton 1 12/181
Pleasley 1 9/114
Scarcliffe 1 9/114
Shirebrook 1 16/139
Skegby 16/60
Sutton in Ashfield 5/72 (CDS 20FEB51)
Warsop 12/181 (CDS 11JUN56)

NEWARK (541).

Balderton 10/127 14/106
Bassingham 3 7/276 14/106
Beckingham 3 7/30
Besthorpe 5/63
Brant Broughton 3 7/30
Carlton upon Trent (543) 5/87
Caunton 7/279 14/116
Claypole 3 7/265 14/106
Clifton 11/158
Collingham 5/62 (CDS 24SEP58)
Dunham on Trent 5/106
Eagle 10/194
Eakring 9/33 10/207 14/116
East Stoke 9/167 14/106
Egmanton 7/276
Farndon 13/111
Farnsfield 7/209 See TL8.
Fiskerton 9/100
Flintham 9/167 14/106
Kelham 9/100
Kirklington 9/108 See TL8.
Kneesal 9/33 13/48
Newton 3 5/61 9/163* 14/105
Norwell 13/111
Oxton 9/184 See TL8&12.
Rampton 13/21
Shelton 9/163
South Muskham 7/279 14/112
Stoke (East) 9/167
Sutton 7/200
Swinderby 3 13/111
Thurgarton 9/101
Upton 9/108 See TL8.
Wellow 12/21
West Markham (no mark found)
Winthorpe 5/61.

NOTTINGHAM (583).

Arnold 7/105 14/14
Barkestone 2 9/144
Barton (in Fabis) 9/243
Basford 7/18 12/253 (CDS 10OCT55)
Basingfield 14/183
Beeston 7/90 (CDS 26MAY52)
Bingham (584) 5/55 (CDS 27APR43)
Bobbers Mill 13/246
Bottesford 2 7/144 (CDS 6JUN56)
Bulwell 7/18 14/14
Bunny 7/29
Burton Joyce 7/90 14/14
Calverton 7/105 14/14
Carlton 7/90
Carrington 7/105 14/14
Chilwell 13/246
Cinder Hill 12/46
Colston Bassett 7/146
Cotgrave 9382 9/100 14/11
Cropwell Butler 7/146
Derby Road 14/12
East Bridgeford 7/90 14/8
Eastwood 7/18 (CDS 26DEC50)
Elton 11/87
Epperstone 7/105 See TL8.
Hoveringham 9/150
Hucknall Torkard 7/18 14/12
        (CDS 1DEC57)
Hyson Green 9/137 (CDS 8NOV58)
Ilkeston (585) 1 5/2
        (CDS 23MAY51)
Kimberley 12/45
Lenton 7/90 (CDS 21MAR60)
Linby 13/246
Lowdham 9/150
Mansfield Road 7/107
Mapperley 14/14
Moor Green 9/183
Muston 2 13/246
New Basford 13/57
New Lenton 14/12
Newthorpe 13/246
Nuttall 12/45
Old Lenton 13/246
Old Radford 9/137 14/12
Orston 7/170 14/22
Plumtree 7/201 14/11
Radcliffe 7/105 14/8
        (CDS 20FEB58)
Radford 7/107 13/152
Redmile 2 13/246
Ruddington 7/30
Saxondale 10/128
Sneinton 7/107 13/152
        (CDS 21MAR60)

An underlined number, eg 2, indicates an office outside Notts - see key at end.

Notts

Nottingham (Cont'd)

Sneinton Elements 13/97
Strelly 13/246
Thoroton 10/91 10/97 14/22
Tollerton 9/82
Trowell 13/47
West Bridgford 13/246
Watnall 7/18 14/14
Whatton 7/170 14/22
Wollaton 10/223
Wysall 18/139

OLLERTON (592). Pre proof books (CDS 28JUL40) See TL10.

Edwinstowe 7/228 See TL10.
Rufford 7/228
Walesby 9/39 See TL10.

RETFORD (638). 1/163 (CDS 7AUG40)

Babworth 12/90
Barnby Moor 12/90
Clarborough 12/90 16/151
Elkesley 12/90
Gamston 7/186
Lound 10/16
Ordsall 14/56
Ranby 12/90 16/151
Saundby 7/186
South Leverton 9/164
Sturton 9/164

SOUTHWELL (542). 2/130 (CDS 5/22 20AUG41) See TL8.

Westhorpe 18/73
Woodborough 14/145 See TL11.

TUXFORD (821). See TL9.

East Markham 10/20 See TL9.

WORKSOP (922). 1/207 (CDS 31AUG40)

Blyth 7/81 16/82
Carlton 7/81 12/105
Letwell 10/117
Station Road 13/262.

ALFRETON (6), Derbys.

Brinsley 12/90
Hucknall (Huthwaite) 12/90
Selston 9/127

BAWTRY (55), Yorks.

Clayworth 12/160
Everton 9/136 14/221
Gringley (56) 5/81 14/99
Mattersey 7/71 14/221
Misson 9/136 14/221
Ranskill 10/111 14/221

CHESTERFIELD (186), Derbys.

Whitwell $\underline{1}$ 5/106 See TL5&6.

DERBY (242), Derbys.

Bramcote 9/252 13/201 See TL4.
Gotham 9/94
Kingstone 9/94
Sandiacre $\underline{1}$ 9/9 See TL1,2,3&4.
Stapleford (586) 5/81 14/140
                              See TL1,2&4.

GAINSBOROUGH (307), Lincs.

Beckingham 13/201
Misterton 12/155
Stockwith 7/30
Walkeringham 7/30 18/24
West Stockwith 18/24

GRANTHAM (321), Lincs

Granby 9/144

LOUGHBOROUGH (475), Leics.

East Leake 7/233
Normanton on Soar 13/69
Rempstone 7/233 14/61
Stanford 13/69
Sutton Bonnington 7/170 14/61

MELTON MOWBRAY (522), Leics.

Hickling 13/47

ROTHERHAM (655), Yorks.

Harthill <u>4</u> 9/122 See TL7.

KEY to offices not in Nottinghamshire

<u>1</u> is in Derbyshire
<u>2</u> is in Leicestershire
<u>3</u> is in Lincolnshire
<u>4</u> is in Yorkshire

TRANSFERS - Nottinghamshire

TL 1. Stapleford and Sandiacre from Derby to Nottingham on 3JAN48.

2. Stapleford and Sandiacre from Nottingham to Derby on 18JAN48.

3. Sandiacre from Derby to Nottingham on 14MAR49.

4. Stapleford, Sandiacre and Bramcote letters sent to Derby by Night Mail but to Nottingham by Day Mail from 19MAY49.

5. Whitwell from Chesterfield to Worksop on 22MAY50.

6. Whitwell from Worksop to Chesterfield on 30APR52.

7. Harthill from Rotherham to Worksop on 30APR52.

8. Southwell (previously under Newark) became a post town on 5DEC53. Several minor offices were transferred to it.

9. Tuxford reduced to a sub-office under Newark on 6DEC53. East Markham would have been transferred with it.

10. Ollerton reduced to a sub-office under Newark on 6DEC53. Edwinstowe and Walesby were probably transferred at the same time.

11. Woodborough from Southwell to Nottingham on 16MAR58.

12. Oxton from Southwell to Nottingham on 16NOV58.

NOTTINGHAMSHIRE

Office	Type	Date	Post Town	No.	Mark	Dates
OLLERTON	C2*				B	24DEC32- 2JAN40
					GR	29MAY40
RETFORD	C2*	31MAY30	Retford	1/163	B	27JUN33-26MAY40
WORKSOP	C2*	31MAY30	Worksop	1/207	B	3SEP32-12JUN38
SOUTHWELL	C2	3JUL34	Southwell	2/130	B	13MAR36-18OCT38.
ILKESTON	C2	3JUN41	Nottingham	5/2	B	4JUL42- 56
SOUTHWELL	C2M	20AUG41	Southwell	5/22	B	8JUN44-17FEB45
						Note 1.
BINGHAM	C2	11DEC41	Nottingham	5/55	B	23AUG42-31JAN43
NEWTON	C2	29DEC41	Newark	5/61	B	30APR42- 7JAN50
WINTHORPE	C2	29DEC41	Newark	5/61		
COLLINGHAM	C2	29DEC41	Newark	5/62	B	30JUL45-16AUG51
BESTHORPE	C2	29DEC41	Newark	5/63	B	19NOV50- 9DEC51.
SUTTON-IN-ASHFIELD	C2	3FEB42	Mansfield	5/72	B	25APR42
					BL/GR	11JAN49-24AUG49
STAPLEFORD	C2	17MAR42	Derby	5/81	B	31JUL42
					BL	6JUL49
					GR	26JAN58
GRINGLEY	C1	17MAR42	Bawtry	5/81		
CARLTON-UPON-TRENT	C2	22APR42	Newark	5/87	B	14MAR44- 1JAN51
DUNHAM	C2	11JUL42	Newark	5/106	B	48-27APR50
WHITWELL	C2	11JUL42	Chesterfield	5/106	B	30MAY43- 6JUN48
					GR	13APR58
BASFORD	C2	17JAN44	Nottingham	7/18	B	45-30NOV48
BULWELL	C2	17JAN44	Nottingham	7/18	B	23JUL48
EASTWOOD	C2	17JAN44	Nottingham	7/18	OR/R	29MAR47- 50
HUCKNALL-FORKARD	C2	17JAN44	Nottingham	7/18		Note 2.
WATNALL	C2	17JAN44	Nottingham	7/18	B	45-13DEC46
					R	18APR48-27APR48
BUNNY	C2	21FEB44	Nottingham	7/29	R	30NOV45- 2FEB46
RUDDINGTON	C2	24FEB44	Nottingham	7/30	R	2SEP48
					BL	28OCT59- 3DEC59.
BECKINGHAM	C2	24FEB44	Newark	7/30		
BRANT-BROUGHTON	C2	24FEB44	Newark	7/30	B	6AUG59
STOCKWITH	C2	24FEB44	Guisborough	7/30	B	27JUN48 Note 3.
WALKERINGHAM	C2	24FEB44	Guisborough	7/30		Note 3.
MATTERSEA	C1	13JUN44	Bawtry	7/71		Note 4.
BLYTH	C1	20JUL44	Worksop	7/81	BL	51-17MAR57
CARLTON	C1	20JUL44	Worksop	7/81	BR	49
					B	9AUG52-23JUL59
					BL	19DEC57 Note 5.
CUCKNEY	C1	23JUL44	Mansfield	7/82		
MANSFIELD-WOODHOUSE	C1	23JUL44	Mansfield	7/82	B	12AUG47-21MAR54
					BL/GR	10FEB56-14APR57
EAST-BRIDGEFORD	C1	22AUG44	Nottingham	7/90	B	29JUN45-10MAY48
					GR	48
					BL	6JAN54
LENTON	C1	22AUG44	Nottingham	7/90	R	11SEP49-19MAR52
BEESTON	C1	22AUG44	Nottingham	7/90	R	30NOV48-24JUN50.
					GR	52
BURTON-JOYCE	C1	22AUG44	Nottingham	7/90	B	23NOV52

Notes:
1. UDC 2/130 fitted with date slugs but not used as CDS before 1846.
2. Spelling error - Hucknall <u>T</u>orkard.
3. Post Town likely to be <u>Gai</u>nsborough.
4. Spelling error - should be Matterse<u>y</u>.
5. Carlton in Linderick.

CARLTON	C1	22AUG44	Nottingham	7/90	B	46-29AUG49
ARNOLD	C1	7NOV44	Nottingham	7/105	BL	23NOV49
EPPERSTONE	C1	7NOV44	Nottingham	7/105	BL/GR	10MAY52
					BL	52
CARRINGTON	C1	7NOV44	Nottingham	7/105	BL/GR	56
RADCLIFFE	C1	7NOV44	Nottingham	7/105	R	24FEB57 Note 6.
CALVERTON	C1	7NOV44	Nottingham	7/105		
SNEINTON	C1	13NOV44	Nottingham	7/107	R	6JUN55- 59
					B	24AUG57
RADFORD	C1	13NOV44	Nottingham	7/107	R	30JAN45
					BL	12NOV55
MANSFIELD-ROAD	C1	13NOV44	Nottingham	7/107		
BOTTESFORD	C1	8MAY45	Nottingham	7/144	BL	21OCT51- 56.
COLSTON-BASSETT	C1	14MAY45	Nottingham	7/146	BL	?
CROPWELL-BUTLER	C1	14MAY45	Nottingham	7/146	B	24FEB54
					BL	27NOV56
SUTTON	C1	13AUG45	Loughborough	7/170	BL	12MAY49-31MAR52 Note 7.
ORSTON	C1	13AUG45	Bingham	7/170	BL/GR	24APR49- 53
WHATTON	C1	13AUG45	Bingham	7/170		
GAMSTON	C1	1NOV45	Retford	7/186	R	2NOV48
SAUNDBY	C1	1NOV45	Retford	7/186	R	27MAY46
					BL	48
SUTTON	C1	22DEC45	Newark	7/200	BR	7JAN51 Note 8.
PLUMTREE	C1	22DEC45	Nottingham	7/201		
FARNSFIELD	C1	28JAN46	Newark	7/209	GR	1NOV55
EDWINSTOWE	C1	8APR46	Ollerton	7/228		
RUFFORD	C1	8APR46	Ollerton	7/228		
REMPSTONE	C1	24APR46	Loughborough	7/233	BL	14NOV49
					BL/GR	13SEP55
EAST-LEAKE	C1	24APR46	Loughborough	7/233	GR	13JAN46-17JUL46 Note 9.
CLAYPOLE	C1	5SEP46	Newark	7/265	B	18SEP56
BASSINGHAM	C1	5NOV46	Newark	7/276		
EGMANTON	C1	5NOV46	Newark	7/276		
CAUNTON	C1	13NOV46	Newark	7/279		
SOUTH-MUSKHAM	C1	13NOV46	Newark	7/279	B	7APR49- 6NOV55.
SANDIACRE	C1	9FEB47	Derby	9/9	GR	19AUG47-16NOV58
KNEESAL	C1	1MAY47	Newark	9/33	B	23OCT51
EAKRING	C1	1MAY47	Newark	9/33		
WALESBY	C1	23MAY47	Ollerton	9/39	GR	51
COLGRAVE	C1	30SEP47	Nottingham	9/82		Note 10.
TOLLERTON	C1	30SEP47	Nottingham	9/82		
GOTHAM	C1	28OCT47	Derby	9/94		
KINGSTONE	C1	28OCT47	Derby	9/94	BL	8AUG51-31JUL56
COTGRAVE	C1	22NOV47	Nottingham	9/100		
KELHAM	C1	22NOV47	Newark	9/100	B	12JAN49-21OCT59.
FISKERTON	C1	22NOV47	Newark	9/100	B	26MAR49-23AUG51
THURGARTON	C1	22NOV47	Newark	9/101		
KIRKLINGTON	C1	16DEC47	Newark	9/108		
UPTON	C1	16DEC47	Newark	9/108	B	21DEC48-10FEB51
PLEASLEY	C1	8JAN48	Mansfield	9/114	BL	?
SCARCLIFFE	C1	8JAN48	Mansfield	9/114		
HARTHILL	C1	12FEB48	Sheffield	9/122		

Notes:
6. Radcliffe on Trent.
7. Sutton Bonnington.
8. Sutton on Trent.
9. Reported JAN46 usage is suspect.
10. Spelling error - Cotgrave. See 9/100 below.

Notts

Office	Type	Date	Sent to	Ref	Mark	Date/Period
SELSTON	C1	12FEB48	Alfreton	9/127		
EVERTON	C1	26MAR48	Bawtry	9/136	BL	53
MISSON	C1	26MAR48	Bawtry	9/136	R	2NOV49
HYSON-GREEN	C1	26MAR48	Nottingham	9/137	GR	26MAY56- 8JUL58.
OLD-RADFORD	C1	26MAR48	Nottingham	9/137	R	31MAY58
					BL	51
BARKSTONE	C1	4MAY48	Grantham	9/144		Note 11.
GRANBY	C1	4MAY48	Grantham	9/144	GR	?
HOVERINGHAM	C1	24MAY48	Nottingham	9/150	GR	4JAN55
LOWDHAM	C1	24MAY48	Nottingham	9/150		
SHELTON	C1	29JUN48	Newark	9/163		
NEWTON	C1				B	7DEC50- 8NOV53
						Note 12.
SOUTH-LEVERTON	C1	29JUN48	Retford	9/164	BR	58
STURTON	C1	29JUN48	Retford	9/164		
FLINTHAM	C1	4JUL48	Newark	9/167		
EAST-STOKE	C1	4JUL48	Newark	9/167	B	29DEC49- 51.
MOOR-GREEN	C1	4OCT48	Nottingham	9/183		
OXTON	C1	20OCT48	Newark	9/184		
BARTON	C1	14APR49	Nottingham	9/243	BL	15SEP52
					B	16JAN54
BRAMCOTE	C1	11MAY49	Derby	9/252	BL	10JAN55
KIRKBY	C1	6JUN49	Mansfield	10/8		
LOUND	C1	19JUN49	Retford	10/16		
EAST-MARKHAM	C1	5JUL49	Tuxford	10/20	BL/GR	18SEP52
THORNTON	C1	10MAY50	Nottingham	10/91		Note 13.
BLIDWORTH	C1	11JUN50	Mansfield	10/92	R	52
THOROTON	C1	JUL50		10/97		
RANSKILL	C1	20OCT50	Bawtry	10/111	B	24MAR52
LETWELL	C1	8NOV50	Worksop	10/117	B	27JUL59
BALDERTON	C1	6DEC50		10/127		Note 14.
SAXONDALE	C1	12DEC50	Nottingham	10/128		
CUCKNEY	C1	9JAN51	Mansfield	10/140		
EAGLE	C1	24APR51	Newark	10/194		
EAKRING	C1	28MAY51	Newark	10/207		
WOLLATON	C1	24JUL51	Nottingham	10/223	BL	52- 53.
ELTON	C1	JUL52	Nottingham	11/87	BL/GR	53
					B	57-26NOV60
CLIFTON	C1	APR52	Newark	11/158		
WELLOW	C1	JAN54	Newark	12/21	BL	6OCT54- 7MAR59
NUTTALL	C1	APR54	Nottingham	12/45		Note 15.
KIMBERLEY	C1	APR54	Nottingham	12/45		
CINDERHILL	C1	APR54	Nottingham	12/46		
BRINSLEY	C1	cJUL54		12/90		Note 16.
HUCKNALL	C1	cJUL54		12/90	BL/GR	54
					B	17NOV56 Note 16.
BABWORTH	C1	cJUL54		12/90		Note 17.
RANBY	C1	cJUL54		12/90		Note 17.
CLARBOROUGH	C1	cJUL54		12/90		Note 17.

Notes:
11. Intended for Bark<u>e</u>stone (Leics) and not Barkston, near Grantham.
12. Appears to be the C2 mark (5/61) re-cut.
13. Spelling error - Thor<u>o</u>ton - see 10/97 below.
14. Probably sent to Newark.
15. Spelling error - should be Nut<u>h</u>all.
16. Probably sent to Alfreton. ('Hucknall' is Hucknall Huthwaite.)
17. Probably sent to Retford.

Notts

Name	Class	Date	Location	Ref	Code	Date2
BARMBY-MOOR	C1	cJUL54		12/90	B	19JAN58 Notes 17&18.
ELKESLEY	C1	cJUL54		12/90		Note 17.
CARLTON	C1	cAUG54		12/105	B	5JAN60 Note 19.
MISTERTON	C1	1FEB55	Gainsborough	12/155		
CLAYWORTH	C1	1FEB55	Bawtry	12/160		
WARSOP	C1	30MAR55	Mansfield	12/181		
LANGWITH	C1	30MAR55	Mansfield	12/181		
NORTON	C1	30MAR55	Mansfield	12/181	B	6DEC58
BASFORD	C1	5OCT55	Nottingham	12/253		
RAMPTON	C1	11JUN56	Newark	13/21	B	29APR57-29JUN58
HICKLING	C1	29JUL56	Melton Mowbray	13/47		
TROWELL	C1	29JUL56	Nottingham	13/47		
KNEESAL	C1	29JUL56	Newark	13/48	BL/GR	6JAN58
NEW-BASFORD	C1	8AUG56	Nottingham	13/57		
NORMANTON	C1	12SEP56	Loughborough	13/69	B	15APR59 Note 20.
STANFORD	C1	12SEP56	Loughborough	13/69		
SNEINTON-ELEMENTS	C1	13NOV56	Nottingham	13/97		
NORWELL	C1	17DEC56	Newark	13/111		
SWINDERBY	C1	17DEC56	Newark	13/111		
FARNDON	C1	17DEC56	Newark	13/111		
SNEINTON	C1	20FEB57	Nottingham	13/152		
RADFORD	C1	20FEB57	Nottingham	13/152		
BRAMCOTE	C1	1APR57	Derby	13/201		
BECKINGHAM	C1	2APR57	Gainsborough	13/201		
NEWTHORPE	C1*	8JUN57	Nottingham	13/246		
LINBY	C1*	8JUN57	Nottingham	13/246	B	15AUG58-24AUG59.
WEST-BRIDGEFORD	C1*	8JUN57	Nottingham	13/246		
MUSTON	C1*	8JUN57	Nottingham	13/246		
REDMILE	C1*	8JUN57	Nottingham	13/246	B	25NOV57
ROBBERS-MILL	C1*	8JUN57	Nottingham	13/246		Note 21.
STRELLY	C1*	8JUN57	Nottingham	13/246		
OLD-LENTON	C1*	8JUN57	Nottingham	13/246	B	11JAN58-28OCT58.
CHILWELL	C1*	8JUN57	Nottingham	13/246	B	26OCT59
STATION-RD	C1*	19JUN57	Worksop	13/262		
EAST-BRIDGEFORD	C4	7AUG57	Nottingham	14/8		
RADCLIFFE-ON-TRENT	C4	7AUG57	Nottingham	14/8		
NEW-LENTON	C4	7AUG57	Nottingham	14/12	GR	13JUL58-13JAN59 Note 22.
HUCKNELL-TORKARD	C4	7AUG57	Nottingham	14/12		
DERBY-RD	C4	27AUG57	Nottingham	14/12	B / BL	4JUN58-16AUG59. / 59
OLD-RADFORD	C4	27AUG57	Nottingham	14/12	R / BL	31MAY58 / 58
BULWELL	C4	27AUG57	Nottingham	14/14		
BURTON-JOYCE	C4	27AUG57	Nottingham	14/14	B	14APR59
MOOR-GREEN	C4	27AUG57	Nottingham	14/14		
WATNALL	C4	27AUG57	Nottingham	14/14		
CARRINGTON	C4	27AUG57	Nottingham	14/14	B	22JAN59.
ARNOLD	C4	27AUG57	Nottingham	14/14		
CALVERTON	C4	27AUG57	Nottingham	14/14		
MAPPERLEY	C4	27AUG57	Nottingham	14/14		
PLUMTREE	C4	1SEP57	Nottingham	14/11	BL	59.
COTGRAVE	C4	1SEP57	Nottingham	14/11		
THOROTON	C4	10SEP57	Nottingham	14/22		
WHATTON	C4	10SEP57	Nottingham	14/22		
ARSTON	C4	10SEP57	Nottingham	14/22		Note 23.

Notes:
18. Spelling error - now Bar**n**by Moor.
19. Probably sent to Worksop.
20. Normanton on Soar.
21. Spelling error: **B**obbers Mill.
22. Spelling error: Huckn**a**ll Torkard.
23. Spelling error: **O**rston.

Notts

MANSFIELD·WOODHOUSE	C4	28SEP57	Mansfield	14/37	BL	8NOV57-26MAR58
					B/GR	27MAR58-14APR58
					B	10SEP59
ORDSALL	C4	20OCT57	Retford	14/56		
REMPSTONE	C4	22OCT57	Loughborough	14/61		
SUTTONBONNINGTON	C4	22OCT57	Loughborough	14/61		
GRINGLEY	C4	10DEC57	Bawtry	14/99	GR	58
NEWTON	C4	10DEC57	Newark	14/105	?	1JUN58
					BL/GR	8MAR60
BASSINGHAM	C4	11DEC57	Newark	14/106		
BALDERTON	C4	11DEC57	Newark	14/106		
CLAYPOLE	C4	11DEC57	Newark	14/106		
EAST-STOKE	C4	11DEC57	Newark	14/106		
FLINTHAM	C4	11DEC57	Newark	14/106		
SOUTH-MUSKHAM	C4	30DEC57	Newark	14/112		
EAKRING	C4	30DEC57	Newark	14/116		
CAUNTON	C4	30DEC57	Newark	14/116		
STAPLEFORD	D1	5FEB58	Derby	14/140		
WOODBOROUGH	D1	13FEB58	Nottingham	14/145		
BASINGFIELD	D1	31MAR58	Nottingham	14/183		
MISSON	D4	10MAY58	Bawtry	14/221		
EVERTON	D4	14MAY58	Bawtry	14/221		
RANSKILL	D1	10MAY58	Bawtry	14/221		
MATTERSEY	D1	10MAY58	Bawtry	14/221		
SKEGBY	D4	17OCT58	Mansfield	16/60		
FACKLEY	D4	17OCT58	Mansfield	16/60		
BAGTHORPE	D1	18OCT58	Mansfield	16/60		
BLYTH	D4	5NOV58	Worksop	16/82		
BURNHAM/NOTTS	D2	7DEC58	Bawtry	16/104	Note 24.	
BURNHAM/ LINCOLNSHIRE	D2	15DEC58	Bawtry	16/114	Note 24.	
SHIREBROOK	D1	14JAN59	Mansfield	16/139		
CLARBOROUGH	D1	1FEB59	Retford	16/151		
RANBY	D4	1FEB59	Retford	16/151		
WALKERINGHAM	D1	19APR59	Gainsborough	18/24		
WEST-STOCKWITH	D1	19APR59	Gainsborough	18/24		
WYSALL	D4	4MAY59	Nottingham	18/39		
WESTHORPE	D1	13JUL59	Southwell	18/73		

Notes: 24. Returned wrongly engraved 'Notts' and a new stamp sent 15 December 58.

Notts

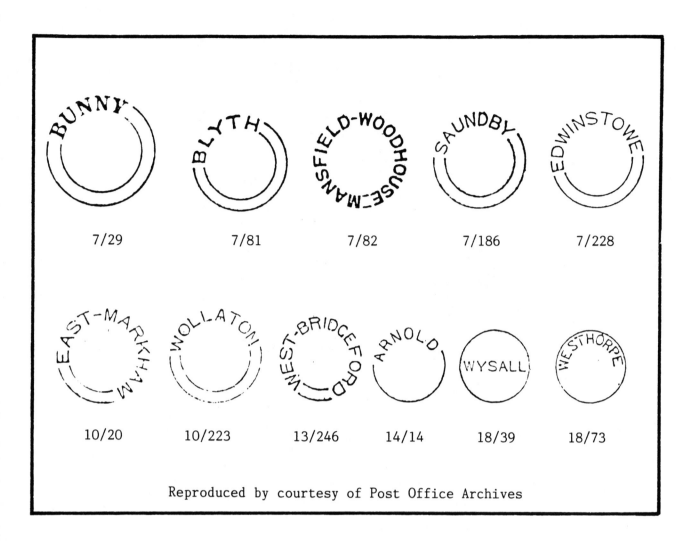

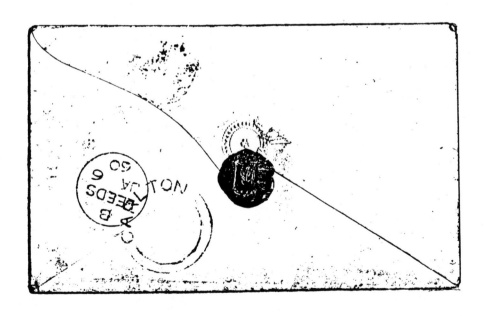

CARLTON (12/105), under Nottingham.
One of three similar type C1 UDCs.

Similar Sans-serif (C1) Marks of Nottinghamshire

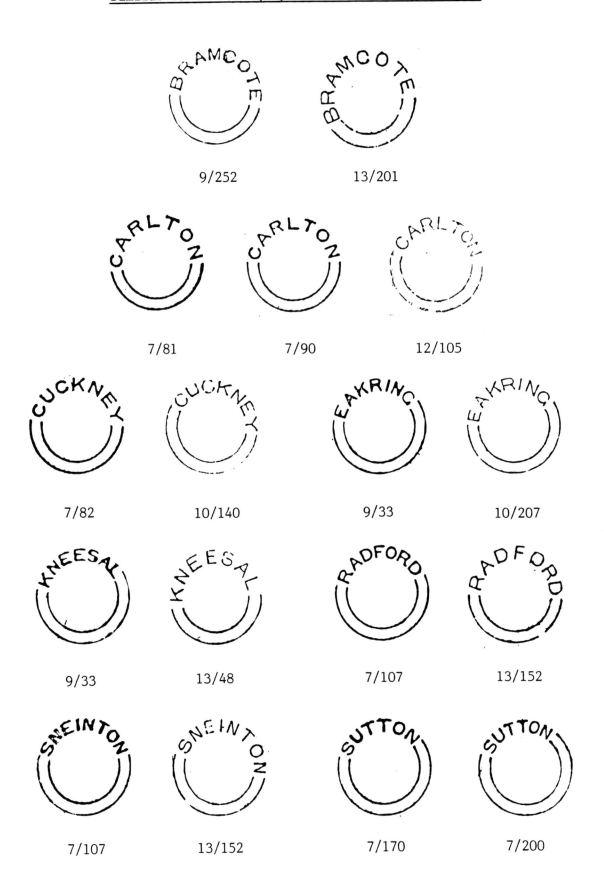

Reproduced by courtesy of Post Office Archives

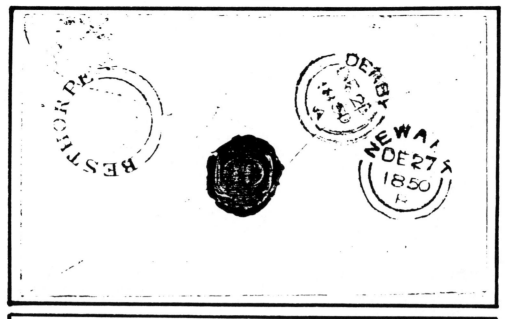

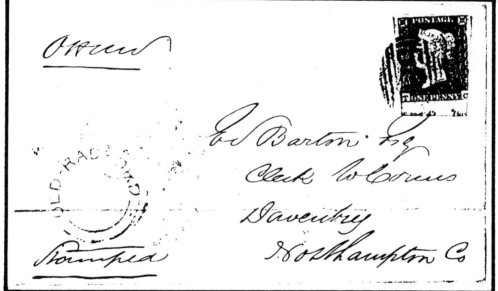

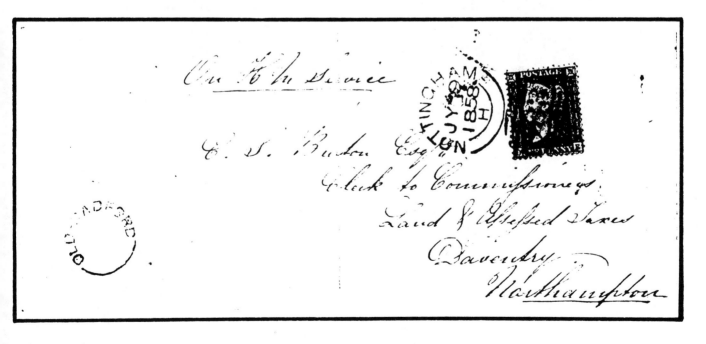

Above: BESTHORPE (5/63) on a letter to Breadsall Priory, Derbys.

Centre: OLD RADFORD (9/137)

Below: OLD RADFORD (14/12)

OXFORDSHIRE

BANBURY (46)

Avon Dassett 2 9/150
Bloxham 9/163
Bodicott 9/138
Chipping Warden 1 7/249
Claydon 9/139 See TL16.
Cropredy 9/139 9/142
Culworth 1 7/12 See TL8&9.
Farnborough 2 11/191
Fenny Compton 2 11/191 See TL17.
Middleton Cheney 1 7/12 See TL8&9.
Neithrop 11/191
North Newington 11/191
Radway 2 10/100
Shenington 7/12 7/34
Sibford 7/20
South Newington 7/23
Thorpe Mandeville 1 11/191 16/16 See TL8&9.
Wardington 9/168
Warmington 2 11/121
Wroxton 7/12 13/192

BICESTER (69).

Blackthorn 11/166
Fritwell 11/166
Hethe 9/24 16/96
Marsh Gibbon 3 10/190
Stratton Audley 11/208

BURFORD (149). See TL14&37.

Barrington 4 11/186 See TL14&37.
Little Rissington 4 10/70 See TL14&27.
Shipton-under-Wychwood 9/61 14/275 See TL6.
Swinbrook 11/186 14/245 See TL14&37.

CHIPPING NORTON (195). 1/25 (CDS 3OCT39)

Ascot Wychwood 9/113 See TL7.
Churchill 9/67 14/275
Fifield 10/84
Hook Norton 7/2
Kingham 10/153
Long Compton 2 5/168 See TL24.
Lower Milton/Milton-under-Wychwood 10/247
　　　　　　　　　　　　　　　　　　　14/275
Oddington 4 9/164 14/275

ENSTONE (278). 1/41 (CDS 28SEP38)

Chadlington 13/135
Charlbury 5/103 (CDS 26DEC50)
Great Tew 7/136

HENLEY-ON-THAMES (355). 1/75
　　　　　　　　　　　(CDS 2SEP39)

Checkendon 5/159
Hambledon 3 5/161
Nettlebed (356) 1/126
　　　　(CDS 13SEP39) See TL1.
Park Corner 10/58
Remenham Hill 5 12/307
Rotherfield Greys 12/307
Rotherfield Peppard 5/159
Stoke Row 11/206
Swyncombe 13/288
Turville 3 5/159
Upper Assendon 12/307
Wargrave 5 5/159
Woodcote 10/34 See TL22.

OXFORD (603).

Beckley 5/194
Bletchington 12/137
Botley/Botley Green 5 14/177
　　　　　　　　　　　　14/221
Ensham 7/22 10/35 (CDS 26DEC50)
Gosford 7/22 See TL22.
Headington 5/194
Holywell St 12/183
Iffley 7/22 14/43
Islip 7/105
Kidlington 10/188 (CDS 24APR51)
Kirtlington 12/112
Littlemore 9/16
Middleton Stoney 7/211 16/57
　　　　　　　　　　See TL12.
New Hincksey 14/177 14/221
Nuneham 7/22 13/24
Park End St 11/202 12/183
St Clements 5/194 12/183
　　　　　　　(CDS 8NOV56)
St Giles 12/183 14/43
Sommerstown/Summertown 7/136
　　　　　　　　　　　　16/60
Upper Wolvercote 13/173

An underlined number, eg 2, indicates an office outside Oxon - see key at end.

Oxford (Cont'd)

Weston-on-the-Green 10/213 See TL12.
Woolvercot 16/62
Wytham 5 7/136
Yarndon/Yarnton 11/96 16/64

TETSWORTH (787). 1/75 2/139 (CDS 2NOV39)

Britwell Salome 12/173 See TL19.
Chalgrove 7/217 12/333
Chilton 3 13/3
Chinnor 7/33
Cuxham 7/217
Great Hazeley 7/33 See TL3&21.
Ickford 3 11/118 See TL13&20.
Kingstone Blount 7/33
Lewknor 13/3
Ludgershall 3 14/188
Oakley 3 5/117 16/57 See TL5&18.
Stokenchurch (738) 1/210 (CDS 23OCT39)
                  See TL23.
Watlington 5/117 7/221 (CDS 4MAR51)

THAME (789). See TL18.

Brill 3 5/117 (CDS 16APR56) See TL18.
Long Crendon 3 5/118 10/269 16/57
                  See TL18.

WHEATLEY (874). 1/207 (CDS 2NOV39)

Cuddesden 7/262
Garsington 12/339
Great Milton 12/198 See TL21.
Horsepath 10/111
Stanton St John 12/319
Waterstock 7/33

WITNEY (902). 1/203 (CDS 7FEB34)

Bampton (050) 7/247 (CDS 26DEC50)
                  See TL36.
Brize Norton 9/219
Carlbridge/Curbridge 11/202 16/82
                  See TL36.
Charterville 9/219 See TL22.
Clanfield 12/70 See TL36.
Leafield 9/113
Lew 11/25 See TL36.
Minster Lovell 11/202
Newland 16/169 18/5

Witney (Cont'd)

North Leigh 11/202 13/134
Ramsden 10/129 See TL15.
Shilton 9/219
Standlake 7/103
Stanton Harcourt 10/20

WOODSTOCK (910). 1/208
                  (CDS 9NOV39)

Adderbury 5/102 10/198
                  See TL25&31.
Bladon 11/191
Charlton 1 9/210 See TL26.
Deddington (912) 7/69
          (CDS 19JAN47) See TL30.
Heyford Warren 7/281 See TL29.
Holt 5/102 See TL11.
Kiddington 11/191
Kings Sutton 1 13/221 14/11
                  See TL26.
Lower Heyford 10/162 (CDS 6OCT57)
                  See TL29.
North Aston 7/281 See TL29.
Sandford 7/221 See TL29.
Steeple Aston 10/162 See TL29.
Stonesfield 9/63
Tackley 7/249 12/251 See TL4.
Upper Worton 11/191 See TL29.
Wooton 11/191

ABINGDON (3), Berks

Clifton Hampden 9/160
Cumnor 5 7/223 See TL33.

AYLESBURY (38), Bucks

Haddenham 3 7/226 See TL10&18.

BRACKLEY (104), Northants

Souldern 10/67 16/56

BUCKINGHAM (145), Bucks

Mixbury 10/97 See TL32.

An underlined number, eg 5, indicates an office outside Oxon - see key at end.

Oxon

FARINGDON (293), Berks

Alvescot 7/53
Filkins 11/152 See TL35.

HIGH WYCOMBE (364), Bucks.

Ibston 3 9/155 See TL28.
Lane End 3 9/155 See TL28.

READING (635), Berks.

Bingfield Heath 12/109 See TL34.
Caversham 7/109 13/42
Caversham Hill 12/313
Goring 9/70
Goring Heath 11/54
Kidmore End 11/185
Maple Durham 7/279
Shiplake (097) 12/109 (CDS 18JAN58)
Shiplake Row 10/159
Whitchurch 5/37

WALLINGFORD (832), Berks.

Benson (833) 16/91 See TL2.
Crowmarsh 12/307
Dorchester 7/251 (CDS 24FEB51)
Drayton 12/308
Ewelme 7/150 16/104
Ipsden 12/307
North Stoke 9/8
South Stoke 9/8
Stadhampton 7/46 13/230 16/91
Warborough 7/46

KEY to offices not in Oxfordshire

1 is in Northamptonshire
2 is in Warwickshire
3 is in Buckinghamshire
4 is in Gloucestershire
5 is in Berkshire

TRANSFERS - Oxfordshire

TL 1. Nettlebed ceased to be a post town and was reduced to a sub-office under Henley on Thames on 23JUN40.

2. Benson reduced from a post town to a sub-office of Wallingford at an unknown date between 1840 and 1843.

3. Great Hazeley from Tetsworth to Wheatley on 5MAR44.

4. Tackley from Woodstock to Oxford on 5AUG46.

5. Oakley from Tetsworth to Thame, probably on 27MAR47.

6. Shipton under Wychwood from Burford to Chipping Norton on 19OCT47.

7. Ascot Wychwood from Chipping Norton to Enstone on 31JUL48.

8. Culworth, Middleton Cheney and Thorpe Mandeville from Banbury to Brackley on 25MAY50.

9. Culworth, Middleton Cheney and Thorpe Mandeville back to Banbury from Brackley on 31JUL50.

10. Haddenham from Aylesbury to Thame, probably on 6OCT51.

11. Holt closed 19MAY52.

12. Middleton Stoney and Weston on the Green from Oxford to Bicester on 31AUG52.

13. Ickford from Thame to Tetsworth on 29NOV52.

14. Burford ceased to be a post town on 5OCT53; Day Mail sent to Oxford and Night Mail to Cheltenham. Barrington, Little Rissington and Swinbrook transferred with Burford.

15. Ramsden from Witney to Enstone on 8NOV53.

16. Claydon closed 16FEB54.

17. Fenny Compton to Rugby on 31AUG54 (probably from Banbury).

18. Thame ceased to be a post town on 12FEB55; reduced to a sub-office under Aylesbury for its Day Mail and under Tetsworth for its Night Mail. Brill, Haddenham, Long Crendon and Oakley transferred with Thame.

19. Britwell Salome from Tetsworth to Wallingford on 14APR55.

20. Ickford from Tetsworth to Wheatley on 23JUN55.

21. Great Hazeley and Great Milton from Wheatley to Tetsworth on 23JUN55.

22. Charterville, Gosford and Woodcote closed by 1856.

23. Stokenchurch ceased to be a post town on 18AUG56 and was reduced to a sub-office under Tetsworth.

Oxon

TL24. Long Compton may have transferred from Chipping Norton to Shipston on Stour, either in 1854 or between 1856 & 1859, or it may have been subordinate to both offices.

25. Adderbury Day Mail from Woodstock to Banbury on 22APR57; Night Mail to be retained under Woodstock.

26. Kings Sutton and Charlton from Woodstock to Banbury on 8FEB58. Charlton was closed during 1858, possibly at the time of the transfer.

27. Little Rissington to Moreton in Marsh on 28MAY58.

28. Ibstone and Lane End from High Wycombe to Tetsworth on 4SEP58.

29. Heyford Warren, Lower Heyford, North Aston, Sandford, Steeple Aston and Upper Worton from Woodstock to Oxford on 22JAN59.

30. Deddington Day Mail from Woodstock to Banbury and Night Mail from Woodstock to Oxford on 22JAN59.

31. Adderbury Night Mail from Woodstock to Oxford on 22JAN59; Day Mail to remain under Banbury.

32. Mixbury from Buckingham to Brackley on 5MAR59.

33. Cumnor from Abingdon to Oxford on 25JUN59.

34. Binfield Heath from Reading to Henley on Thames on 9JUL59.

35. Filkins Night Mail from Faringdon to Swindon on 31MAR60.

36. Bampton, Clanfield, Curbridge and Lew from Witney to Faringdon on 31MAR60.

37. Night Mail for Burford, (Great) Barrington and Swinbrook from Cheltenham to Faringdon on 31MAR60.

Oxon

OXFORDSHIRE

WITNEY	C2*	26MAR28	Witney	1/203	B	2JUN29- 6MAR33
CHIPPING·NORTON	C2*	26MAY28	Chipping Norton	1/25	B	22SEP29-30APR39
HENLEY-ON-THAMES	C2*	2MAR29	Henley-on-T	1/75	B	19JAN32-29JAN39
TETSWORTH	C2*	7SEP29	Tetsworth	1/75	B	22JAN30-23DEC31
ENSTONE	C2*	20MAR30	Enstone	1/41	B	29JAN31-21MAR38.
WHEATLEY	C2	31MAY30	Wheatley	1/207		
WOODSTOCK	C2	17AUG30	Woodstock	1/208	B	9NOV33-21MAY39
STOKENCHURCH	C2	30AUG30	Stokenchurch	1/210		
NETTLEBED	C2*	28OCT31	Nettlebed	1/126	B	7AUG34
TETSWORTH	C3A	5OCT32	Tetsworth	2/139	B	30DEC32-14FEB38
WHEATLEY	C3A	5OCT32	Wheatley	2/155	B	28AUG33-28OCT38.
BENSON	C2M	22JUL37	Benson	1/20	B	18NOV46
					BL	29JUN53
					GR	1MAY57- 7DEC57
WHITCHURCH-OXON	C2	16OCT41	Reading	5/37	B	25MAR49
					BL	3JUN57- 7APR59
ADDERBURY	C2	20JUN42	Woodstock	5/102	B	29FEB44
HOLT	C2	20JUN42	Woodstock	5/102		
CHARLBURY	C2	20JUN42	Enstone	5/103	OR	22AUG44- 4AUG47.
OAKLEY	C2	13SEP42	Tetsworth	5/117		
WATLINGTON	C2	13SEP42	Tetsworth	5/117	R	16APR43
BRILL	C2	13SEP42	Thame	5/117	R	8NOV44-19MAY51
LONG-CRENDON	C2	20SEP42	Thame	5/118	Purp	24SEP58
CHECKENDON	C2	13MAY43	Henley-on-T	5/159	B	2JUL44-31JUL49
ROTHERFIELD-PEPPARD	C2	13MAY43	Henley-on-T	5/159		
TURVILLE	C2	13MAY43	Henley-on-T	5/159		
WARGRAVE	C2	13MAY43	Henley-on-T	5/159	B	5MAY45
HAMBLEDON	C2	23MAY43	Henley-on-T	5/161		
LONG-COMPTON	C2	5JUL43	Chipping Norton	5/168	B	8NOV44-20JUL46.
					BL	22NOV56
BECKLEY	C2	9NOV43	Oxford	5/194	BL/B	16NOV58
HEADINGTON	C2	9NOV43	Oxford	5/194	B	21SEP53-23MAY59
STCLEMENTS	C2	9NOV43	Oxford	5/194		
HOOK-NORTON	C2	29NOV43	Chipping Norton	7/2	BL	1SEP49-16APR53
					GR	27MAY52-26OCT52
CULWORTH	C2	3JAN44	Banbury	7/12	R	14APR56-30OCT56
					BL	13DEC59
MIDDLETON-CHENEY	C2	3JAN44	Banbury	7/12	OR	5JUL46
					BL	21OCT52
SHENNINGTON	C2	3JAN44	Banbury	7/12		Note 1.
WROXTON	C2	3JAN44	Banbury	7/12		
SIBFORD	C2	19JAN44	Banbury	7/20		
ENSHAM	C2	29JAN44	Oxford	7/22	B	7JUN44- 2MAY45
GOSFORD	C2	29JAN44	Oxford	7/22	B	7AUG44
IFFLEY	C2	29JAN44	Oxford	7/22	B	27MAR48- 3JUN55
NUNEHAM	C2	29JAN44	Oxford	7/22	B	26FEB48-18APR53.
SOUTH-NEWINGTON	C2	2FEB44	Banbury	7/23	BL	21MAR53
CHINNOR	C2	26FEB44	Tetsworth	7/33		
KINGSTONE-BLOUNT	C2	26FEB44	Tetsworth	7/33	OR	22JUN45-20MAR47
GREAT-HAZELEY	C2	26FEB44	Wheatley	7/33	B	30DEC45- 9SEP49.
WATERSTOCK	C2	26FEB44	Wheatley	7/33		
SHENINGTON	C2	29FEB44	Banbury	7/34		
STADHAMPTON	C1	8APR44	Wallingford	7/46		
WARBOROUGH	C1	8APR44	Wallingford	7/46		
ALVESCOT	C1	11MAY44	Lechlade	7/53	B	15FEB??
DEDDINGTON	C1	8JUN44	Woodstock	7/69	B	1JUN46- 1JAN47

Note: 1. Spelling error - She<u>n</u>ington (see 7/34 below).

Oxon

STANDLAKE	C1	30OCT44	Witney	7/103	BL	15JUL51
ISLIP	C1	6NOV44	Oxford	7/105	B	20DEC48- 4JUN49
CAVERSHAM	C1	19NOV44	Reading	7/109		
GREAT-TEW	C1	5APR45	Enstone	7/136	B	18JUN47
					BL	10DEC54
SOMMERSTOWN	C1	7APR45	Oxford	7/136	B	23OCT46- 1MAY49.
WYTHAM	C1	7APR45	Oxford	7/136		
EWELME	C1	29MAY45	Wallingford	7/150	BL	28JUL51
MIDDLETON-STONEY	C1	14FEB46	Oxford	7/211	R	13FEB47-19JAN49.
					BR	24FEB57
CHALGROVE	C1	5MAR46	Tetsworth	7/217	R	28JUL51
CUXHAM	C1	5MAR46	Tetsworth	7/217	R	16MAY47
					BL	5OCT55
WATLINGTON	C1	13MAR46	Tetsworth	7/221	R	27DEC49
SANDFORD	C1	13MAR46	Woodstock	7/221		
CUMNOR	C1	20MAR46	Abingdon	7/223		
HADDENHAM	C1	7APR46	Aylesbury	7/226		
BAMPTON-OXON	C1	27JUN46	Witney	7/247	B	13AUG46-23JUL48.
					BL	23JUL49
CHIPPING-WARDEN	C1	30JUN46	Banbury	7/249		
TACKLEY	C1	30JUN46	Oxford	7/249		
DORCHESTER	C1	4JUL46	Wallingford	7/251	OR	17SEP46-24NOV46.
CUDDESDEN	C1	25AUG46	Wheatley	7/262	B	7FEB60
MAPLE-DURHAM	C1	18NOV46	Reading	7/279	BL	21JUN54
HEYFORD-WARREN	C1	27NOV46	Woodstock	7/281		
NORTH-ASTON	C1	27NOV46	Woodstock	7/281		
NORTH-STOKE	C1	9FEB47	Wallingford	9/8		
SOUTH-STOKE	C1	9FEB47	Wallingford	9/8		
LITTLEMORE	C1	24FEB47	Oxford	9/16	B	4JUN51- 7JAN59.
HETHE	C1	29MAR47	Bicester	9/24	B	25MAY55
					R	5DEC55
SHIPTON-UNDER-WICHWOOD	C1	9JUL47	Chipping Norton	9/61		
STONESFIELD	C1	22JUL47	Woodstock	9/63		
CHURCHILL	C1	26JUL47	Chipping Norton	9/67		
GORING	C1	13AUG47	Reading	9/70		
ASCOT-WYCHWOOD	C1	8JAN48	Enstone	9/113		
LEAFIELD	C1	8JAN48	Witney	9/113		
BODICOTT	C1	29MAR48	Banbury	9/138	BL	1AUG51
CLAYDON	C1	29MAR48	Banbury	9/139	Y	5MAR49
CROPEDY	C1	29MAR48	Banbury	9/139		Note 2.
CROPREDY	C1	24APR48	Banbury	9/142	BL	26OCT49-24MAR54
AVON-DASSETT	C1	24MAY48	Bristol	9/150	B	27MAR49
					BL	? Note 3.
IBSTON	C1	3JUN48	High Wycombe	9/155		
LANE-END	C1	3JUN48	High Wycombe	9/155		
CLIFTON-HAMPDEN	C1	9JUN48	Abingdon	9/160	B	23SEP49
BLOXHAM	C1	29JUN48	Banbury	9/163	BL	20NOV49- 9JUL50.
ODDINGTON	C1	29JUN48	Chipping Norton	9/164		
WARDINGTON	C1	15JUL48	Banbury	9/168		
CHARLTON	C1	1FEB49	Woodstock	9/210	R	4FEB56
BRIZE-NORTON	C1	14FEB49	Witney	9/219	BL	11JAN51-22SEP54.
CHARTERVILLE	C1	14FEB49	Witney	9/219		
SHILTON	C1	14FEB49	Witney	9/219		
STANTON-HARCOURT	C1	5JUL49	Witney	10/20		
WOODCOTE	C1	23AUG49	Henley-on-T	10/34		

Notes: 2. Spelling error - Crop<u>r</u>edy (see 9/142 below).
3. Sent to Bristol in error - should be Banbury.

Oxon

ENSHAM	C1	3SEP49	Oxford	10/35			
PARK-CORNER	C1	13DEC49	Henley-on-T	10/58			
SOULDERN	C1	15FEB50	Brackley	10/67			
LITTLE-RISSINGTON	C1	21FEB50	Burford	10/70			
FIFIELD	C1	17APR50	Chipping Norton	10/84			
MIXBURY	C1	10JUL50	Buckingham	10/97			
RADWAY	C1	6AUG50	Banbury	10/100			
HORSEPATH	C1	20OCT50	Wheatley	10/111			
RAMSDEN	C1	26DEC50	Witney	10/129			
KINGHAM	C1	12FEB51	Chipping Norton	10/153			
SHIPLAKE-ROW	C1	25FEB51	Reading	10/159	BL/B	20NOV51	
LOWER-HEYFORD	C1	1MAR51	Woodstock	10/162			
STEEPLE-ASTON	C1	1MAR51	Woodstock	10/162	BL/B	4SEP54- 5SEP54.	
KIDLINGTON	C1	12APR51	Oxford	10/188			
MARSH-GIBBON	C1	24APR51	Bicester	10/190			
ADDERBURY	C1	18MAY51	Woodstock	10/198	B	7JAN54	
					OR	4FEB56	
WESTON·ON·THE·GREEN	C1	4JUL51	Oxford	10/213			
LOWER·MILTON	C1	29SEP51	Chipping Norton	10/247	B	24SEP55-30SEP55	Note 4.
LONG-CRENDON	C1	6OCT51	Thame	10/269			
LEW	C1	6MAR52	Witney	11/25			
GORING-HEATH	C1	18MAY52	Reading	11/54			
YARNDON	C1	SEP52	Oxford	11/96			Note 5.
ICKFORD	C1	NOV52	Tetsworth	11/118	B	10AUG55	
					BL/B	21JAN57	
WARMINGTON	C1	DEC52	Banbury	11/121			
FILKINS	C1	MAR53	Faringdon	11/152			
BLACKTHORN	C1	APR53	Bicester	11/166			
FRITWELL	C1	APR53	Bicester	11/166	BL	11OCT53.	
KIDMORE-END	C1	JUN53	Reading	11/185			
BARRINGTON	C1	JUN53	Burford	11/186			
SWINBROOK	C1	JUN53	Burford	11/186			
FARNBOROUGH	C1	JUN53	Banbury	11/191	BL/GR	21OCT57	
FENNY-COMPTON	C1	JUN53	Banbury	11/191	B	25OCT59.	
NEITHROP	C1	JUN53	Banbury	11/191			
NORTH-NEWINGTON	C1	JUN53	Banbury	11/191			
THORPE-MANDEVILLE	C1	JUN53	Banbury	11/191			
BLADON	C1	JUN53	Woodstock	11/191			
KIDDINGTON	C1	JUN53	Woodstock	11/191			
UPPER-WORTON	C1	JUN53	Woodstock	11/191	BL/B	4SEP54- 5SEP54.	
WOOTON	C1	JUN53	Woodstock	11/191			
PARKEND-ST	C1	AUG53	Oxford	11/202	B	18DEC54	
CARLBRIDGE	C1	AUG53	Witney	11/202			Note 6.
MINSTER-LOVELL	C1	AUG53	Witney	11/202			
NORTH-LEIGH	C1	AUG53	Witney	11/202			
STOKE-ROW	C1	AUG53	Henley-on-T	11/206			
STRATTON-AUDLEY	C1	AUG53	Bicester	11/208			
CLANFIELD	C1	JUN54	Witney	12/70			
KNOT·MILL	C1	JUN54	Witney	12/70			Note 7.
BINGFIELD-HEATH	C1	AUG54		12/109			Note 8.
SHIPLAKE	C1	AUG54		12/109			Note 8.
KIRTLINGTON	C1	SEP54		12/112			Note 9.
BLETCHINGTON	C1	7DEC54	Oxford	12/137			
BRITWELL-SALOME	C1	20MAR55	Wallingford	12/173			
HOLYWELL-ST	C1	28MAR55	Oxford	12/183	BL	3APR55-23OCT58	

Notes:
4. Known later as Milton-under-Wychwood.
5. Spelling error - Yarnton (see 16/54).
6. The old name for Curbridge.
7. Unknown location - probably sent in error.
8. Unallocated but under Reading.
9. Unallocated but under Oxford.

Oxon

Name	Class	Date	Office	Ref		
PARK·END-ST	C1	28MAR55	Oxford	12/183		
ST-CLEMENTS	C1	28MAR55	Oxford	12/183		
ST-GILES	C1	28MAR55	Oxford	12/183	BR	9FEB56
GREAT-MILTON	C1	17MAY55	Wheatley	12/198	B	10DEC58.
TACKLEY	C1	5OCT55	Oxford	12/251		
REMENHAM-HILL	C1	31JAN56	Henley-on-T	12/307	B	19OCT56
ROTHERFIELD-GREYS	C1	31JAN56	Henley-on-T	12/307		
UPPER-ASSENDON	C1	31JAN56	Henley-on-T	12/307		
CROWMARSH	C1	31JAN56	Wallingford	12/307		
IPSDEN	C1	31JAN56	Wallingford	12/307		
DRAYTON-OXON	C1	31JAN56	Wallingford	12/308		
CAVERSHAM-HILL	C1	17FEB56	Reading	12/313		
STANTON-ST-JOHN	C1	27FEB56	Wheatley	12/319		
CHALGROVE	C1	25MAR56	Tetsworth	12/333		
GARSINGTON	C1	16APR56	Wheatley	12/339		
CHILTON	C1	29APR56	Tetsworth	13/3		
LEWKNOR	C1	29APR56	Tetsworth	13/3	BL	23AUG58.
NUNEHAM	C1	21JUN56	Oxford	13/24		
CAVERSHAM	C1	15JUL56	Reading	13/42	BL/GR	3AUG57
NORTH-LEIGH	C1	3FEB57	Witney	13/134		
CHADLINGTON	C1	3FEB57	Enstone	13/135		
UPPER-WOLVERCOTE	C1	17MAR57	Oxford	13/173		
HEATH	C1	17MAR57	Bicester	13/174		Note 10.
WROXTON	C1	25MAR57	Banbury	13/192		
KINGS-SUTTON	C1*	29APR57	Woodstock	13/221	B	3DEC58
STADHAMPTON	C1*	9MAY57	Wallingford	13/230		
SWYNCOMBE	C4	25JUL57	Henley-on-T	13/288		
KINGS-SUTTON	C4	1SEP57	Banbury	14/11		
IFFLEY	C4	6OCT57	Oxford	14/43		
ST-GILES-ST	C4	6OCT57	Oxford	14/43	B	4SEP58-30MAR59
BOTLEY-GREEN	D1	31MAR58	Oxford	14/177		Note 11.
NEW-HINCKLEY	D1	31MAR58	Oxford	14/177		Note 12.
LUDGERSHALL BUCKS	D2	1APR58	Tetsworth	14/188		
BOTLEY BERKS	D2	10MAY58	Oxford	14/221		
NEW-HINKSEY	D2	10MAY58	Oxford	14/221		
SWINBROOK	D1	1JUN58	Cheltenham	14/245	B	30JUN58
CHURCHILL OXON	D2	9JUL58	Chipping Norton	14/275		
MILTON·UNDER· WYCHWOOD·	D1	9JUL58	Chipping Norton	14/275		
ODDINGTON	D1	9JUL58	Chipping Norton	14/275		
SHIPTON·UNDER· WYCHWOOD	D1	9JUL58	Chipping Norton	14/275		
THORPE·MANDEVILLE	D1	7AUG58	Banbury	16/16		
SOULDERN	D1	7OCT58	Brackley	16/56		
MIDDLETON-STONEY	D1	7OCT58	Bicester	16/57	BL	5JAN60-25JAN60.
LONG-CRENDON	D1	7OCT58	Tetsworth	16/57		
OAKLEY-BUCKS	D1	7OCT58	Tetsworth	16/57		
SUMMER-TOWN	D1	16OCT58	Oxford	16/60		
WOLVERCOT	D1	16OCT58	Oxford	16/62		
YARNTON	D4	21OCT58	Oxford	16/64		
CURBRIDGE	D1	5NOV58	Witney	16/82		
BENSON	D4	25NOV58	Wallingford	16/91		
STADHAMPTON	D1	25NOV58	Wallingford	16/91		
HETHE	D4	2DEC58	Bicester	16/96		
EWELME	D4	7DEC58	Wallingford	16/104		
NEWLAND·GLOS	D1	4MAR59	Witney	16/169		Note 13.
NEWLAND·OXON	D2	19MAR59	Witney	18/5		

Notes:
10. Unknown location - probably sent in error.
11. Incorrect name for Botley (see 14/221 below).
12. Spelling error - New Hinksey (see 14/221).
13. Error in county - see 18/5 below.

Oxon

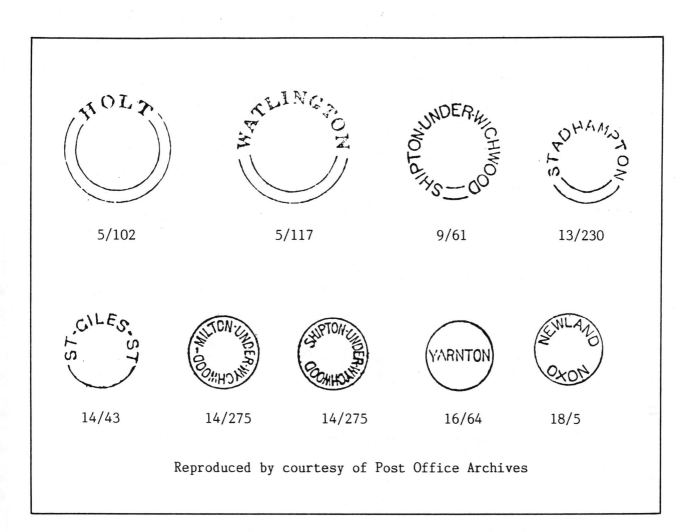

Similar Sans-serif (C1) Marks of Oxfordshire

Oxon 104.

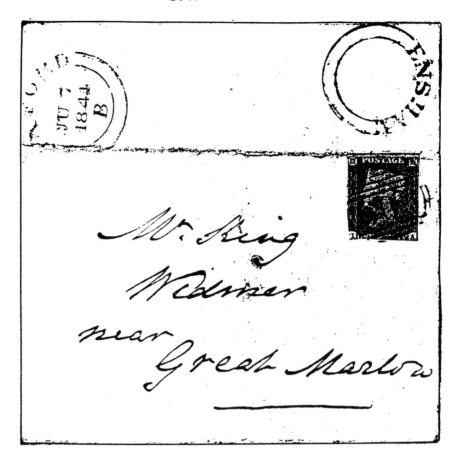

ENSHAM (7/22) to
Great Marlow on
7th June 1844.

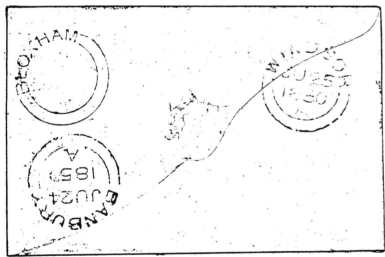

BLOXHAM (9/163) to Windsor
on 24th June 1850.

UPPER-WORTON (11/191)
and
STEEPLE-ASTON (10/162)
under Woodstock.

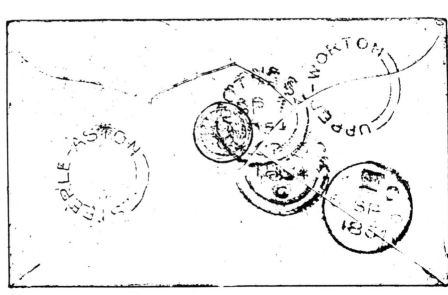

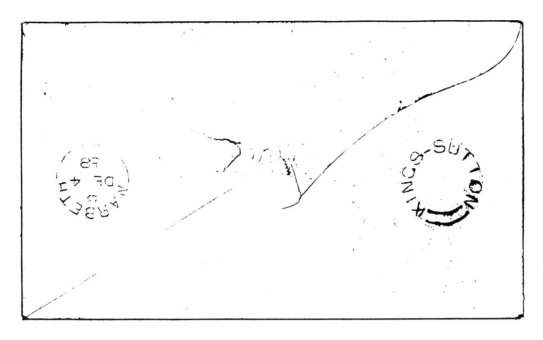

KINGS-SUTTON (13/221) to Narbeth on 3rd December 1858.
(Continued use of the C1* stamp although a C4 stamp had been issued.)

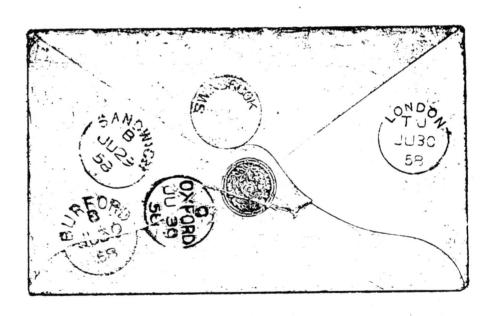

SWINBROOK (14/245) under Cheltenham but sent in the day mail via Burford and Oxford.

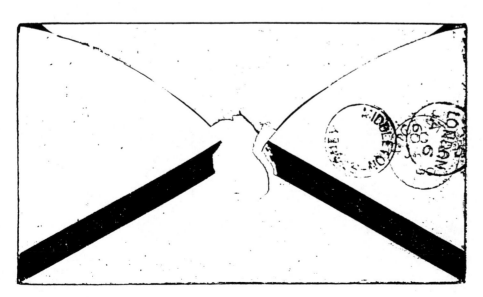

MIDDLETON-STONEY (16/57) under Bicester.

SHROPSHIRE

BRIDGNORTH (122). 1/18 (CDS 21DEC39)

Ackleton 13/213
Alveley 7/246 11/244 13/116
Billingsley 13/213
Bridgnorth Low Town + 9/75
Burwarton + 11/244
Chelmarsh 9/178
Glazeley 12/136
Harpswood 13/213
Hig(h)ley 13/213
Monk Hopton 7/181
Morville 13/214
Neenton 13/231
Newton 13/213
Oldbury 13/213
Quat 13/213
Quatford 13/213
Willey 13/214
Wyken 12/235

ELLESMERE (274). 2/37 See TL18.

Cockshutt 10/119 See TL18.

LUDLOW (479).

Ashford Carbonel 12/317
Aston on Clun 7/62 10/92 (CDS 4JUL51) See TL7.
Beguildy 4 13/258
Brampton Bryan 8 7/24 (CDS 23DEC57) See TL17.
Brimfield 8 9/92
Bromfield 7/246 13/258 (CDS 23DEC57)
Clee Hill 9/85 12/278
Clun 7/62 12/325 (CDS 7FEB57) See TL7.
Diddlebury 7/246 18/54 See TL7.
Felindre 4 13/271
Hopton Castle 10/153 See TL17.
Knighton 4 1/92 (CDS 21MAY51) See TL4&17.
Leintwardine (481/082) 8 Circ Mil (CDS 23DEC57)
Llanvair (Waterdine) 13/111 See TL17.
Lydbury (N) 7/41 12/325 (CDS 23DEC57) See TL7.
Middleton 12/241
Onibury 5/123 (CDS 18JAN58) See TL7.
Orleton 8 12/317
Richards Castle 8 10/153
Stanton Lacey 11/241

MARKET DRAYTON (509).

Adderley 12/50
Ashley 5 9/78.

Cheswardine 9/107
Childs Ercal 12/173
Hinstock 9/107
Hodnet 7/66 (CDS 24MAY51)
Norton 13/214
Woore (510) Pre-proof books 9/199

NEWPORT, Salop (565). 2/102
 (Skel used 26DEC39, CDS 31DEC39)

Adbaston 12/180
Donington 7/164
Edgmond 11/137
Lilleshall (Lillies Hall) 14/124
Moreton 12/317 18/28
Sheriff Hales 5 12/48

OSWESTRY (595).

Arleen 3 18/84
Felton 7/142
Gobowen 12/191
Hengoed 18/84
Kinnerley 9/131 13/91
Knockin 18/84
Llandrinio 3 9/55
Llanfecham 3 11/248
Llanfyllin 3 5/115 (CDS 29JAN51)
Llangedwin 9 11/51
Llangynog 3 12/188
Llanrhaiadr-yn-Mochnant 9
        5/115 11/230 13/69
Llanrwst (597) + 7/78
        (CDS 20FEB49)
Llansaintffraid-yn-Mechan 3
        5/115 7/8 11/230
Llansillin 9 9/43 9/43* 13/63
Llanwddyn 3 11/45
Llanyblodwell 5/115
Llanymynech 5/115 11/230 13/91
        (CDS 20FEB58)
Llwydiarth 3 12/190
Llynclys 11/157
Maesbury 18/83
Morda 12/57
Pant 18/84
Penybont Fawr 3 18/83
Rhydycroesan 18/83
Sarnan 3 18/84
Selattyn 11/158
Trefonnen 3 18/84
Welch Frankton 18/83
Whittington + 10/66.

+ Indicates an office which also used a straight line (or P.P.) stamp after 1840.

An underlined number, eg 3, indicates an office outside Salop - see key at end.

Salop

SHIFNAL (705).

Beckbury 7/179
Broseley 2/16 7/50 (CDS 12MAR51) See TL1,10&16).
Dawley 9/186 (CDS 12MAR51) See TL10&16.
Dawley Green + 9/76
Ironbridge (406) 2/70 (CDS 4JAN40)
      See TL1,5,10&16).
Madeley 2/92 (CDS 24MAY51) See TL10&16.
Norton 7/194
Priors Lee 12/191
Tong 12/98
Wenlock/Much Wenlock 2/159 5/183 (CDS 14OCT44)
      See TL1,5,10&16.
Weston (-under-Lizard) 12/98

SHREWSBURY (708).

Abbey Foregate 9/86
Acton Burnell 7/16 13/169 (CDS 8DEC58)
Alberbury 9/53 13/227
Albrighton 12/231
Baschurch + 12/213 (CDS 16OCT58)
Bayston Hill 11/132 13/249
Berriew 3 11/173 (CDS 7DEC58) See TL22.
Berrington 12/20
Bicton Heath 12/169 13/191
Bomere Heath 12/210
Bucknell 14/132
Burlton 11/248 12/20
Can(n) Office 3 1/28 See TL14.
Cardington 16/26
Castle Foregate 9/86 16/83
Cemmaes 3 12/266 (CDS 22APR58) See TL22.
Church Stretton (709) + 9/96 (CDS 14SEP49)
Clungunford 12/189
Coleham 9/86
Commins Coch 3 14/86
Condover 12/108
Corris 1 7/281
Cressage 7/194 16/64
Criggion 3 12/21
Cross Houses 12/76 18/33
Dinas Mowddy 1 11/62 13/180
Dorrington 7/16 14/204
Dylife (Delife) 3 18/85
Easthope 12/74 See TL27.
Edstaston 18/42
Ford 9/54
Frankwell 9/86
Frodesley 13/63
Garthmill 3 7/130 10/68 11/159 See TL22.

Gravel 12/231 13/216
Grinshill 12/27
Hadnall 12/229
Halfway House 12/231
Hanwood 11/132
Harmer Hill 12/294
Lea Cross 12/231
Leebotwood 12/20
Little Brampton/Brompton 11/124
    11/147 (CDS 23DEC57)
Llanymawddy 1 16/84
Loppington 10/2
Manaughty 14/177
Marshbrook 11/248
Meole Brace 14/37
Middle 9/44
Minsterley 7/16 (CDS 8APR56)
Montford 9/207A
Munslow 9/155 13/122
Nescliffe 7/190
Newton 10/191 (CDS 23DEC57)
Old Hall 4 13/258
Penegoes 3 13/35
Penley 6 11/248 14/69
Perkins Green 14/177
Pontesbury 5/182 11/132
Pontesford Bridge 12/231
Prees 7/5 (CDS 9DEC56)
      See TL3,6&8.
Preston Brockhurst 14/86
Preston Gubballs 12/20 12/20*
    13/216 13/216*
Pulverbatch 9/44
Rodington 9/98
Rushbury 11/124
Ruyton + 13/208
Shawbury 5/197 12/266 13/216
Smethcott 9/129
Stanton 13/64
Stapleton 12/20
The Bridges 16/149
Upton Magna 12/20
Wem (711) 2/157 (CDS 20FEB49)
Wentnor 13/30
Westbury + 10/191 16/134
Weston (-under-Red-Castle?) 10/78
West Felton 13/85
Wistanstow 9/97 10/42
   (CDS 23SEP57)
Worthen 10/122
Wroxeter 7/162
Yockleton 10/122 12/21.

+ Indicates an office which also used a straight line (or P.P.) stamp after 1840.

An underlined number, eg 6, indicates an office outside Salop - see key at end.

Salop

WELLINGTON (859).

Admaston 14/90
Burton 14/91
Coalbrookdale 11/82
Coalport 12/47
Dawley Bank 12/192
Eaton Constantine 12/274
Eyton 14/91
Great Bolas 14/90
Hadley 11/50
Harley 12/176
High Ercall 7/16
Horsehays 12/192
Jackfield 12/287
Ketley 5/171
Kinnersley 11/50
Leighton 14/91
Little Dawley 12/192
Long Stanton 14/90
Oakengates 5/171 (CDS 8AUG56)
Pains Lane 13/162
Preston 14/91
Trench Lane 14/90
Uppington 7/230
Waters Upton 12/74
Wrockwardine 14/90

WHITCHURCH (876). 1/202
(Skel used 22JAN40, CDS 23JAN40)

Ash 16/2
Bettisfield 6 16/2
Bickerton 7 11/160 See TL20&29.
Calverhall 9/177 16/49
Chorlton 16/2
Grindley Brook 12/330
Hanmer 6 9/178 (CDS 27JAN58)
Marbury 7 9/129 14/91
Redbrook 16/2
Tilstock 10/176 See TL8&30.
Wixhall 18/81

ABERYSTWYTH (2), Cardigan

Borth 2 10/103 See TL32.
Bow Street 2 12/153 See TL28.
Tal-y-Bont 2 12/27 See TL32.

BEWDLEY (68), Worcs

Ditton 12/79
Stottesdon 13/15

CORWEN (219), Merioneth

Capel Arthog 1 14/61 See TL31.
Llwyngwril 1 14/8 See TL31.

NEWTOWN (568), Montgomery

Abermule 3 11/45 See TL26.
Caersws 3 11/82 12/292
            See TL13&21.
Carno 3 11/82 See TL13&21.
Llanbrynmair 3 7/17 16/68
    (CDS 17SEP59) See TL13&21.
Llandinam 3 7/281 13/216
            See TL13&21.
New Mills 3 11/189 See TL23.
Tregynon 3 10/6 See TL24.

RUABON (197), Denbigh

Bronygarth 13/277
Dudleston 10/87
St Martins 10/87
The Lodge 11/50

WELSHPOOL (852), Montgomery

Chirbury (855) 2/27 16/48
            See TL2,15&19.
Church Stoke (856) 3 2/27
    (CDS 27AUG56) 16/160 See TL2.
Eglwysfach 2 11/52 See TL22.
Llandyssil 3 11/52 See TL32.
Llanegryn 1 11/52 See TL32.
Pennal 1 11/52 See TL32.
Pontfathew (now Bryncrug) 1
            12/288 See TL32.
Taliesin 2 9/54 See TL22.
Tallyllyn 1 11/52 See TL32.

WOLVERHAMPTON (905), Staffs

Albrighton 4/106 (CDS 28MAR50)
            See TL11&25.
Claverley 7/171 11/244
        (CDS 1JAN57) See TL9.
Pattingham 5 7/66 See TL11&12.
Worfield 5/88 5/108 5/113
        10/14 13/106 See TL9.

KEY to offices not in Shropshire

1 is in Merionethshire
2 is in Cardiganshire
3 is in Montgomeryshire
4 is in Radnorshire
5 is in Staffordshire
6 is in Flintshire
7 is in Cheshire
8 is in Herefordshire
9 is in Denbighshire

TRANSFERS – Shropshire

TL 1. Ironbridge (under Shifnal) became a post town in MAR38. Broseley and Wenlock were placed under Ironbridge.

2. Chirbury and Churchstoke from Welshpool(?) to Shrewsbury on 5APR45.

3. Prees from Shrewsbury to Market Drayton on 5APR47.

4. Knighton (and delivery) from Ludlow to Presteigne on 29JUN48. TL17 must raise doubts that this transfer went ahead.

5. Ironbridge reduced to a sub-office, probably under Shifnal from which it was served, on 5MAY49. Much Wenlock and Broseley would have been transferred at the same time.

6. Prees from Market Drayton to Whitchurch on 5APR50.

7. Clun, Aston, Diddlebury, Onibury and Lydbury from Ludlow to Shrewsbury on 30APR50.

8. Tilstock and Prees from Whitchurch to Shrewsbury on 7APR51. (Both offices are shown under Whitchurch in the 1855 P.O. List but see also TL30.)

9. Claverley and Worfield from Wolverhampton to Bridgnorth on 9JUN51.

10. Madeley, Dawley, Much Wenlock, Broseley and Ironbridge from Shifnal to Newport on 9JUN51.

11. Albrighton and Pattingham from Wolverhampton to Shifnal on 9JUN51.

12. Pattingham from Shifnal to Wolverhampton on 26NOV51.

13. Caersws, Llandinam, Carno and Llanbrynmair from Newtown to Shrewsbury on 5APR52 (but see also TL21.)

14. Cann Office from Shrewsbury to Welshpool on 14APR52.

15. Chirbury from Shrewsbury to Welshpool on 5JUN52.

16. Ironbridge, Madeley, Dawley, Much Wenlock and Broseley from Newport to Wellington on 28JUN52.

17. Knighton, Llanvair Waterdine, Brampton Bryan and Hopton Castle from Ludlow to Shrewsbury on 28OCT52.

18. Ellesmere reduced to a sub-office under Shrewsbury on 6AUG53. Cockshutt would have transferred at the same time.

19. Chirbury from Welshpool to Shrewsbury on 10DEC53.

20. Bickerton from Whitchurch to Chester on 10JAN54.

Salop 110.

TL21. Caersws, Llandinam, Carno and Llanbrynmair, which had been served partly from Shrewsbury and partly from Newtown, to be served from Shrewsbury only from 5FEB54.

22. Cemmaes, Taliesin, Eglwysfach, Garthmill and Berriew, which were served partly from Shrewsbury and partly from Welshpool, to be served from Shrewsbury only from 5FEB54.

23. New Mills from Newtown to Shrewsbury on 31MAR54.

24. Tregynon from "Welshpool" (but perhaps it was intended as Newtown) to Shrewsbury on 31MAR54.

25. Albrighton from Shifnal to Wolverhampton on 27JUL55.

26. Abermule from Newtown to Shrewsbury on 25FEB56.

27. Easthope from Shrewsbury to Wellington on 31MAR56.

28. Bow Street from Aberystwyth to Shrewsbury on 1DEC56.

29. Bickerton from Chester to Whitchurch on 27AUG58.

30. Tilstock from Shrewsbury to Whitchurch on 18JUL59.

31. Llwyngwril and Capel Arthog from Corwen to Shrewsbury on 10OCT59.

32. Borth and Tal-y-Bont (from Aberystwyth) and Llandyssil, Pennal, Llanegryn, Pontfathew and Tallyllyn (from Welshpool) to Shrewsbury by 1860.

Note: There are a number of minor offices in Wales which, perhaps surprisingly, were under Shrewsbury. It is probable that Shrewsbury was chosen as the town at which bags were made up for the villages so as not to delay the Shrewsbury-Aberystwyth mailcoach at intermediate points and to provide an earlier delivery. However, it seems likely that, for administrative purposes, a receiver would have referred to the nearest post town: for instance, if the receiver at Bow Street required more adhesive stamps, he would have obtained them from Aberystwyth.

CAERSWS (12/292) struck in blue ink in 1858 when the office was under Shrewsbury.

Salop

SHROPSHIRE

Name	Class	Date	Office	Ref	Colour	Period
WOORE	C3C	25?			B	11MAY39-17OCT48
WHITCHURCH-S	C2*	29OCT27	Whitchurch	1/202	B	28-23OCT39
CAN·OFFICE	C3A	21JUN28	Can Office	1/25	B	40-25FEB58
BRIDGENORTH	C2*	22MAY29	Bridgnorth	1/18	B	11DEC29- 9DEC39
KNIGHTON	C2*	11MAR30		1/92	B	16JUN38-20MAR51
					Y	11SEP45
					R	?
WEM	C2*	9AUG36	Wem	2/157	R	1APR37-30SEP37
					B	26DEC37-13FEB49.
					BL	42- 2APR44
NEWPORT-SALOP	C2	26SEP36	Newport	2/102	B	11NOV36-19NOV39
ELLESMERE	C2	8MAR37	Ellesmere	2/37	B	4JUL37-27NOV39
BROSELEY	C2	15FEB38	Shifnal	2/16	B	9JUL38- 5JAN43
IRON-BRIDGE	C2	15FEB38	Ironbridge	2/70	B	1JAN40- 2JAN40
MADELEY	C2	15FEB38	Shifnal	2/92	B	25MAY38-16NOV48.
WENLOCK	C2	15FEB38	Shifnal	2/159	R/BR	8MAR38
					BL	12AUG38-11DEC40
					B	30NOV41-21JUL43
CHURCHSTOKE	C2	13MAR38	Oswestry	2/27	BR/B	25NOV41
					B	21MAY42-26APR50
					GR	28OCT54
CHIRBURY	C2	13MAR38	Welshpool	2/27	B	30DEC44-19AUG50.
					BL	17JUN49-18JUN49
					GR	26JAN50- 7JUN56
IRONBRIDGE	C2	21MAR38	Ironbridge	2/70	B	15AUG39-17AUG39
ALBRIGHTON	C2	30MAR39	Wolverhampton	4/106	B	20SEP39- 2SEP48
					R	22APR41
WARFIELD	C2	23APR42	Wolverhampton	5/88		Note 1.
WORFIELD	C2	26JUL42	Bracknell	5/108		Sent in error.
WORFIELD	C2	3SEP42	Wolverhampton	5/113	B	10SEP42- 30CT49.
LLANFYLLIN	C2	13SEP42	Shrewsbury	5/115	R	22FEB43-12JAN45
					BR	6MAY46
					BL	14OCT47-14DEC50
LLANRHAIADR	C2	13SEP42	Shrewsbury	5/115	B	27DEC43-18APR50
LLANSAINTFRAID	C2	13SEP42	Shrewsbury	5/115	B	28MAR43-10APR43
					BL	27JUL48 Note 1.
LLAN-Y-BLODWELL	C2	13SEP42	Shrewsbury	5/115		
LLANYMYNECH	C2	13SEP42	Shrewsbury	5/115	B	7FEB43-18AUG53
					BL	27NOV47- 2JAN48
ONIBURY	C2	7NOV42	Ludlow	5/123	B	5NOV44- 6JUL55
					Drab	27JUL49
KETLEY	C2	27JUL43	Wellington	5/171	B	4JAN45- 2AUG56.
					GR	2AUG56- 8OCT56
OAKEN-GATES	C2	27JUL43	Wellington	5/171	B	9MAR44-24FEB54
PONTESBURY	C2	19SEP43	Shrewsbury	5/182	B	23NOV43-10JAN54
MUCH-WENLOCK	C2	28SEP43	Ironbridge	5/183	B	5OCT43-18JUL44
SHAWBURY	C2	16NOV43	Shrewsbury	5/197	B	18DEC43- 4JAN51.
					BL	27DEC52
PREES	C2	13DEC43	Shrewsbury	7/5	B	6APR48- 57
LLANSAINTFFRAID	C2	21DEC43	Oswestry	7/8	BL	27NOV47- 9MAY49
ACTON-BURNELL	C2	13JAN44	Shrewsbury	7/16	B	29JUL45-22APR49
DORRINGTON	C2	13JAN44	Shrewsbury	7/16	B	20MAR44-12SEP56.
					GR	19JAN56
					BL/GR	24SEP57
HIGH-ERCALL	C2	13JAN44	Wellington	7/16	B	10OCT44- 59
MINSTERLEY	C2	13JAN44	Shrewsbury	7/16	BL	56
LLANBRYNMAIR	C2	13JAN44	Newtown	7/17	Drab	29MAR45
BRAMPTON-BRYAN	C2	2FEB44	Ludlow	7/24	B	3APR44-28JAN54
					BR	11JAN53- 2FEB53
					BL/GR	26SEP53-29JAN54
LYDBURY-NORTH	C2	18MAR44	Ludlow	7/41	B	24APR47- 3MAR51

Notes: 1. Spelling error - see correction below.

Salop

Name	Class	Date	Location	Ref	Colour	Date Range
BROSELEY	C1	1MAY44	Shifnal	7/50	B	20JUN44- 51
ASTON	C1	17MAY44	Ludlow	7/62	B	11JUL45-23JAN50
CLUN	C1	17MAY44	Ludlow	7/62	B	8NOV45- 2APR53
HODNET	C1	31MAY44	Market Drayton	7/66	B	31OCT45- 9NOV50
PATTINGHAM	C1	31MAY44	Wolverhampton	7/66	OR	3NOV48-12JUN50
LLANRWST	C1	3JUL44	Oswestry	7/78	B	13AUG44-26JAN47.
GARTHMILL	C1	28FEB45	Welshpool	7/130	B	17SEP45
					BL	25APR48
FELTON	C1	8MAY45	Oswestry	7/142	BL	19FEB47-25AUG55
WROXETER	C1	7JUL45	Shrewsbury	7/162	B	2JAN47-20OCT54
					BL	15JAN59
DONINGTON	C1	17JUL45	Newport, Salop	7/164	B	18JUN46-13JUL51.
					GR	25JAN57
CLAVERLEY	C1	25AUG45	Wolverhampton	7/171	B	45-19APR53
					OR/R	25AUG45-10SEP48
BECKBURY	C1	26SEP45	Shifnal	7/179	R	18JUL47-28OCT53
					B	11NOV48
MONK-HOPTON	C1	20OCT45	Bridgnorth	7/181	BL	8FEB54-20MAR54
					B	18JAN55-28NOV57
NESCLIFFE	C1	18NOV45	Shrewsbury	7/190	B	22DEC46-18FEB59.
					GR	53-15JUL57
					BL	1JUN51- 9JUL59
CRESSAGE	C1	25NOV45	Shrewsbury	7/194	B	20APR48- 7AUG55
NORTON	C1	25NOV45	Shifnal	7/194	R	3JUN48-23NOV50
UPPINGTON	C1	26APR46	Wellington	7/230	B	48- JAN53.
ALVELEY	C1	27JUN46	Bridgnorth	7/246	R	9FEB48
BROOMFIELD	C1	27JUN46	Ludlow	7/246	GR	22AUG48- 8DEC55
					B	18JUL49-23SEP53
					GY/GR	9MAY53
DIDDLEBURY	C1	27JUN46	Ludlow	7/246	B	1AUG46-14AUG57
					BL	22AUG48-21SEP53
					GR	23OCT48-23SEP53.
					R	14JAN57-28MAR57
LLANDINAM	C1	27NOV46	Newtown	7/281		
CORRIS	C1	27NOV46	Machynlleth	7/281		
LLLANSILLIN	C1	24MAY47	Oswestry	9/43		Note 1.
LLANSILLIN	C1				BL	15MAR50-25DEC53
MIDDLE	C1	24MAY47	Shrewsbury	9/44	B	6AUG48-14APR59
					GR	20JUN56- 57
					BL	8SEP59
PULVERBATCH	C1	24MAY47	Shrewsbury	9/44	B	13JUN48- 2MAY55
ALBERBURY	C1	15JUN47	Shrewsbury	9/53	B	27OCT50- 3NOV50
					BL	JUN52-19FEB54
FORD	C1	15JUN47	Shrewsbury	9/54	B	10MAY50- 7APR59.
TALIESIN	C1	15JUN47	Welshpool	9/54	B	22AUG52
					GR	10OCT56
					BL	11AUG59
LLANDRINIO	C1	15JUN47	Oswestry	9/55	B	9NOV49-26NOV52
BRIDGENORTH-LOW-TOWN	C1	3SEP47	Bridgnorth	9/75	B	28SEP47-11JUL48
					BL	21FEB49- 57.
					GR	59
DAWLEY-GREEN	C1	3SEP47	Shifnal	9/76	Y	19JAN48-13MAR48
					BR	3AUG48- 57
ASHLEY	C1	11SEP47	Market Drayton	9/78	OR/BR	30MAR51
					BR/R	12JAN52-16JUL55
					GR	10SEP59
CLEE-HILL	C1	10CT47	Ludlow	9/85	B	48
					BL	14SEP48- 3FEB52
ABBEY-FOREGATE	C1	5OCT47	Shrewsbury	9/86	B	25NOV47-15NOV48
					BL	10DEC48-13MAY58.
					GR	27AUG53-21JUL57
CASTLE-FOREGATE	C1	5OCT47	Shrewsbury	9/86	B	9JUL49
					GR	9JUN58
COLEHAM	C1	5OCT47	Shrewsbury	9/86	B	1DEC47-25MAR59

Salop

FRANKWELL	C1	5OCT47	Shrewsbury	9/86	B	16JUN48- 7OCT58
					GR/BR	10MAY49
BRIMFIELD	C1	19OCT47	Ludlow	9/92	BL	58-14MAY59
CHURCH-STRETTON	C1	9NOV47	Shrewsbury	9/96	B	31JAN48-12AUG49
					B/GR	9APR49-22JAN54
					BL/B	7JUN49
WINSTANSTOW	C1	12NOV47	Shrewsbury	9/97	BL	29JUN48- 8OCT49
RODINGTON	C1	12NOV47	Shrewsbury	9/98	GR	20MAY48-29JUL51
CHESWARDINE	C1	16DEC47	Market Drayton	9/107	B	15MAY48- 2DEC53
					BL	16MAY59
HINSTOCK	C1	16DEC47	Market Drayton	9/107	B	10FEB51- 2FEB53.
					GR	22FEB58
MARBURY	C1	3MAR48	Whitchurch	9/129		
SMETHCOTT	C1	3MAR48	Shrewsbury	9/129		
KINNERLEY	C1	9MAR48	Oswestry	9/131	B	18DEC50-29JAN53
MUNSLOW	C1	3JUN48	Shrewsbury	9/155	B	49-29APR58
CALVERHALL	C1	28AUG48	Whitchurch	9/177		
CHELMARSH	C1	28AUG48	Bridgnorth	9/178	B	17JUL49- 8AUG51.
HANMER	C1	28AUG48	Whitchurch	9/178	B	8JAN49- 6DEC49
					BL	19JAN53
DAWLEY	C1	11OCT48	Shifnal	9/186	B	9NOV48
					R/BR	7FEB49
					Y	1MAY49- 5FEB51
WOORE	C1	15DEC48	Market Drayton	9/199	B	54
					BL	20JAN59
MONTFORD	C1	24JAN49	Shrewsbury	9/207A	GR	7MAR57
LOPPINGTON	C1	31MAY49	Shrewsbury	10/2	GR	13NOV55- 3APR56
					B	15MAY58
TREGYNON	C1	4JUN49	Newtown	10/6	B	1JAN54- 7APR57
WORFIELD	C1	13JUN49	Wolverhampton	10/14	B	30OCT49-15JAN51.
WISTANSTOW	C1	26SEP49	Shrewsbury	10/42	BL	17JAN50-22MAR54
					GR	1NOV50-27FEB55
WHITTINGTON	C1	15FEB50	Oswestry	10/66	BL	7JUL56
GARTHILL	C1	15FEB50	Shrewsbury	10/68		
WESTON	C1	28MAR50	Shrewsbury	10/78		
DUDLESTON	C1	1MAY50	Ruabon	10/87	B	13JUL50-26AUG56.
ST-MARTINS	C1	1MAY50	Ruabon	10/87	GR	?
ASTON-ON-CLUN	C1	11JUN50	Shrewsbury	10/92	B	22JUL50-15MAR51
BORTH	C1	6AUG50	Aberystwyth	10/103		
COCKSHUTT	C1	8NOV50	Ellesmere	10/119	BL	55
					GR	13MAR56
WORTHEN	C1	18NOV50	Shrewsbury	10/122	B	15DEC52- 8APR59.
					BL	29JAN55
					GR	14OCT57
YOCKLETON	C1	18NOV50	Shrewsbury	10/122		
HOPTON-CASTLE	C1	12FEB51	Ludlow	10/153	BL	12FEB53- NOV53
RICHARDS-CASTLE	C1	12FEB51	Ludlow	10/153		
TILSTOCK	C1	19MAR51	Whitchurch	10/176	BL	29JUN51.
					B	23OCT59
NEWTON	C1	24APR51	Shrewsbury	10/191	B	57
NEWTON-SALOP	C1	24APR51	Shrewsbury	10/191	B	3JUL57
					GR	16JUL56-16JUL58.
WESTBURY-SALOP	C1	24APR51	Shrewsbury	10/191	Y	54
					B	11MAY55
					BL	11MAY55- 56
ABERMULE	C1	28APR52	Newtown	11/45		
LLANWDDYN	C1	28APR52	Oswestry	11/45		
HADLEY	C1	18MAY52	Wellington	11/50	GR	3NOV56
					BL	9JUL58
KINNERSLEY	C1	18MAY52	Wellington	11/50	B	54-30MAR56.
					GR	20MAR58
THE-LODGE	C1	18MAY52	Ruabon	11/50	BL	30SEP53

Salop   114.

LLANGEDWIN	C1	18MAY52	Oswestry	11/51		
LLANDYSSIL	C1	18MAY52	Welshpool	11/52		
EGLWYSFACH	C1	18MAY52	Welshpool	11/52		
LLANEGRYN	C1	18MAY52	Welshpool	11/52		
PENNAL	C1	18MAY52	Welshpool	11/52		
TALLYLLYN	C1	18MAY52	Welshpool	11/52		
DINAS-MOWDDY	C1	5JUN52	Shrewsbury	11/62	B	30DEC52- 30CT54.
COALBROOKDALE	C1	JUL52	Wellington	11/82	B	52-17AUG59
					BL	28MAY58
CAERWYS	C1	JUL52	Newtown	11/82		Sent in error?
CARNO	C1	JUL52	Newtown	11/82		
LITTLE·BROMPTON	C1	DEC52	Shrewsbury	11/124	GR	56
RUSHBURY	C1	DEC52	Shrewsbury	11/124	GR	1JUL58
BAYSTON·HILL	C1	JAN53	Shrewsbury	11/132	GR	12SEP54
HANWOOD	C1	JAN53	Shrewsbury	11/132	B	55
PONTESBURY	C1	JAN53	Shrewsbury	11/132		
EDGMOND	C1	FEB53	Newport	11/137		
LITTLE·BROMPTON	C1	FEB53	Shrewsbury	11/147		
LLYNCLYS	C1	APR53	Oswestry	11/157	B	23JUN54
SELATTYN	C1	APR53	Oswestry	11/158	GR	23AUG56- 57.
GARTHMILL	C1	APR53	Shrewsbury	11/159	BL	6OCT53
BICKERTON	C1	APR53	Whitchurch	11/160	BL	20FEB60
BERRIEW	C1	MAY53	Shrewsbury	11/173	B	7APR57-20NOV58.
					BL	21AUG58-24AUG58
NEW-MILLS	C1	JUN53	Newtown	11/189		
LLANRHAIADR·YN·MOCHNANT	C1	OCT53	Oswestry	11/230		
LLANSAINTFFRAID·YN·MECHAN	C1	OCT53	Oswestry	11/230	BL	15OCT53-15OCT56
					GR	6MAY59
LLANYBLODWELL	C1	OCT53	Oswestry	11/230		
LLANYMYNECH	C1	OCT53	Oswestry	11/230	B	16JAN51-24DEC54
					BR	53
					GR	3SEP56
STANTON·LACEY	C1	OCT53	Ludlow	11/241		
ALVERLEY	C1	OCT53	Bridgnorth	11/244	GR	25FEB56
BURWARTON	C1	OCT53	Bridgnorth	11/244	GR	17NOV53
					Y	27JUL54-13NOV56.
CLAVERLEY	C1	OCT53	Bridgnorth	11/244		
BURLTON	C1	OCT53	Shrewsbury	11/248		
LLANFECHAM	C1	OCT53	Oswestry	11/248		
MARSH-BROOK	C1	OCT53	Shrewsbury	11/248	BL	48
					GR	25JAN54- 56
PENLEY	C1	OCT53	Shrewsbury	11/248		
BERRINGTON	C1	JAN54	Shrewsbury	12/20	GR	10OCT54-22MAR55
					BL	14MAY57
BURLTON	C1	JAN54	Shrewsbury	12/20	B	21FEB55
					GR	6MAR55
LEBOTWOOD	C1	JAN54	Shrewsbury	12/20	BL	16MAR57- 7SEP59
PRESTON·GOBBALDS	C1	JAN54	Shrewsbury	12/20		Note 2.
PRESTON·GUBBALLS	C1				GR	25JUL54-10AUG57
STAPLETON	C1	JAN54	Shrewsbury	12/20	B	25SEP55
UPTON·MAGNA	C1	JAN54	Shrewsbury	12/20		
CRIGGION	C1	JAN54	Shrewsbury	12/21		
YOCKLETON	C1	JAN54	Shrewsbury	12/21		
GRINSHILL	C1	FEB54	Shrewsbury	12/27		
TAL-Y-BONT	C1	FEB54	Aberystwyth	12/27		
COALPORT	C1	APR54	Wellington	12/47		
SHERIFF-HALES	C1	APR54	Newport	12/48	B	4JUN54.
ADDERLEY	C1	APR54	Market Drayton	12/50		

Notes: 2. Probably not used - see below (re-cut?)

Salop

Office	Class	Date	Via	Ref	Color	Period
MORDA	C1	MAY54	Oswestry	12/57	BL	5JUL55- 3JAN57
					B	7APR59-12SEP59
EASTHOPE	C1	JUN54	Shrewsbury	12/74	BR	10SEP54- 57
WATERS-UPTON	C1	JUN54	Wellington	12/74		
CROSS-HOUSES	C1	JUN54	Shrewsbury	12/76		
DITTON	C1	JUN54	Bewdley	12/80a	BR	57
TONG	C1	AUG54		12/98	GR	17MAR56
WESTON	C1	AUG54		12/98		
CONDOVER	C1	DEC54	Shrewsbury	12/108	GR	21MAR55-29DEC56
					BL	20JUL57- 1DEC57
					B	29NOV57-16AUG58.
SILVERDALE	C1	27OCT54	"To Mr Beaufort Oswestry"	12/129	B	19FEB5? Note 3.
GLAZELEY	C1	15NOV54	Bridgnorth	12/136		
BOW·ST	C1	27JAN55	Aberystwyth	12/153	BL/B	22JUL55-27JUN59
					GR	26NOV57-21JAN58
BICTON-HEATH	C1	10MAR55	Shrewsbury	12/169	GR	57-23SEP59.
					BL/B	22MAR59-21APR59
CHILDS-ERCAL	C1	20MAR55	Market Drayton	12/173	GR	22FEB58
HARLEY	C1	25MAR55	Wellington	12/176		
ADBASTON	C1	30MAR55	Newport	12/180		
LLANGYNOG	C1	30MAR55	Oswestry	12/188		
CLUNGUNFORD	C1	20APR55	Shrewsbury	12/189	GR	55
LLWYDIARTH	C1	2MAY55	Oswestry	12/190		
GOBOWEN	C1	2MAY55	Oswestry	12/191	BL	15DEC57-29SEP58
PRIORS-LEE	C1	2MAY55	Shifnal	12/191	GR	57
DAWLEY-BANK	C1	2MAY55	Wellington	12/192	BL	12DEC57
					GR	27APR59
HORSEHAYS	C1	2MAY55	Wellington	12/192	B	29APR57- 1APR58.
LITTLE-DAWLEY	C1	2MAY55	Wellington	12/192		
BOMERE-HEATH	C1	15JUN55	Shrewsbury	12/210	B	9MAR57- 5MAR59
					BL	12APR58- 1DEC58
BASCHURCH	C1	15JUN55	Shrewsbury	12/213	GR	11OCT55-31DEC58
					B	57-17JUL58.
HADNALL	C1	21JUN55	Shrewsbury	12/229	GR	2MAR58
ALBRIGHTON	C1	10AUG55	Shrewsbury	12/231		
GRAVEL	C1	10AUG55	Shrewsbury	12/231		
HALF-WAY·HOUSE	C1	10AUG55	Shrewsbury	12/231	BL	56-20JUL57
					B	14OCT57- 8APR59.
LEA-CROSS	C1	10AUG55	Shrewsbury	12/231		
PONTESFORD·BRIDGE	C1	10AUG55	Shrewsbury	12/231	B	4JAN57-30JUL58
					BL	6JAN57
WYKEN	C1	1SEP55	Bridgnorth	12/235		
MIDDLETON	C1	8SEP55	Ludlow	12/241		
CEMMAES	C1	8NOV55	Shrewsbury	12/266	GR	31DEC55
					B	8JUL57
SHAWBURY	C1	8NOV55	Shrewsbury	12/266		
EATON-CONSTANTINE	C1	30NOV55	Wellington	12/274	BL	8JUN57-10JUN57
					BL/GR	7JUL58
CLEE-HILL	C1	17DEC55	Ludlow	12/278	BR	3JAN57
					BL/B	14DEC57- 5MAR58.
					BL	2MAR58
					B	3APR58
JACKFIELD	C1	26DEC55	Wellington	12/287		
PONTFATHEW	C1	28DEC55	Welshpool	12/288		
CAERSWS	C1	5JAN56	Newtown	12/292	BL	22APR58
HARMER-HILL	C1	8JAN56	Shrewsbury	12/294		
ASHFORD-CARBONEL	C1	27FEB56	Ludlow	12/317		

Notes: 3. Sent to the Surveyor - a Staffs office.

Salop   116.

MORETON	C1	27FEB56	Newport	12/317	GR	11NOV56-25JAN59.
					B	25JAN59
ORLETON	C1	27FEB56	Ludlow	12/317	B	2FEB58-14SEP58
CLUN	C1	22MAR56	Shrewsbury	12/325		
LYDBURY-NORTH	C1	22MAR56	Shrewsbury	12/325		
GRINDLEY-BROOK	C1	23MAR56	Whitchurch	12/330	BL	57- 9APR59.
STOTTESDON	C1	3JUN56	Bewdley	13/15	R	2DEC56
					B	19JAN58
WENTNOR	C1	27JUN56	Shrewsbury	13/30		
PENEGOES	C1	27JUN56	Shrewsbury	13/35		
FRODESLEY	C1	12SEP56	Shrewsbury	13/63		
LLANSILIN	C1	12SEP56	Oswestry	13/63	GY/B	18APR59
					BL/B	4MAY59.
LLYNCLYS	C1	12SEP56	Oswestry	13/63	BL	6MAR57-19JUN58
STANTON	C1	12SEP56	Shrewsbury	13/64		
LLANRHAIADR-YN -MOCHNANT	C1	12SEP56	Oswestry	13/69	BL	18JAN59
WEST-FELTON	C1	14OCT56	Shrewsbury	13/85		
KINNERLEY	C1	8NOV56	Oswestry	13/91	GR	29JAN58
LLANYMYNECH	C1	8NOV56	Oswestry	13/91	GR	15MAR57
					BL	15JUL58-15AUG58
WORFIELD	C1	9DEC56	Bridgnorth	13/106	B	57-23MAR58.
LLANVAIR	C1	17DEC56	Ludlow	13/111		
ALVELEY	C1	1JAN57	Bridgnorth	13/116		
MUNSLOW	C1	1JAN57	Shrewsbury	13/122	B	31MAY58-31AUG58.
PAINS·LANE	C1	4MAR57	Wellington	13/162		
ACTON-BURNELL	C1	12MAR57	Shrewsbury	13/169	B	?
DINAS-MOWDDY	C1	17MAR57	Shrewsbury	13/180	BL	15SEP59
BICTON-HEATH	C1	23MAR57	Shrewsbury	13/191	B	22MAR59- 27SEP59
RUYTON	C1	7APR57	Shrewsbury	13/208	BL/B	20SEP57-11FEB59.
ACKLETON	C1*	12APR57	Bridgnorth	13/213		
BILLINGSLEY	C1*	12APR57	Bridgnorth	13/213		
HARPSWOOD	C1*	12APR57	Bridgnorth	13/213		
HIGLEY	C1*	12APR57	Bridgnorth	13/213		
NEWTON	C1*	12APR57	Bridgnorth	13/213		
OLDBURY	C1*	12APR57	Bridgnorth	13/213		
QUAT	C1*	12APR57	Bridgnorth	13/213		
QUATFORD	C1*	12APR57	Bridgnorth	13/213		
MORVILLE	C1*	12APR57	Bridgnorth	13/214	B	3SEP58- 4SEP58.
WILLEY	C1*	12APR57	Bridgnorth	13/214		
NORTON	C1*	12APR57	Market Drayton	13/214		
GRAVEL	C1*	23APR57	Shrewsbury	13/216		
LLANDINARN	C1*	23APR57	Shrewsbury	13/216		
PRESTON-GOBALDS	C1*	23APR57	Shrewsbury	13/216		Note 4.
PRESTON-GUBBALLS	C1*				GR	10AUG57- 58
SHAWBURY	C1*	23APR57	Shrewsbury	13/216		
ALBERBURY	C1*	4MAY57	Shrewsbury	13/227	BL	13APR59
NEENTON	C1*	16MAY57	Bridgnorth	13/231	GR	28APR58.
BAYSTON-HILL	C1*	5JUN57	Shrewsbury	13/249	B	57-20SEP59.
OLD-HALL	C1*	13JUN57	Ludlow	13/258		
BEGUILDY	C1*	13JUN57	Ludlow	13/258		
BROMFIELD	C1*	13JUN57	Ludlow	13/258		
FELINDRE	C1*	14JUL57	Ludlow	13/271		
BRONYGRATH	C1*	10JUL57	Ruabon	13/277		
LLWYNGWRIL	C4	7AUG57	Caernarvon	14/8		Note 5.
MEOLE-BRACE	C4	28SEP57	Shrewsbury	14/37		
CAPEL-ARTHOG	C4	22OCT57	Corwen	14/61		

Notes: 4. Probably not used - see below.
                5. Probably intended for Corwen.

Salop

PENLEY	C4	3NOV57	Shrewsbury	14/69		
CUMMINS-COCH	C4	24NOV57	Shrewsbury	14/86		
PRESTON BROCKHURST	C4	24NOV57	Shrewsbury	14/86		
ADMASTON	C4	28NOV57	Wellington	14/90	BL	9DEC58.
GREAT-BOLAS	C4	28NOV57	Wellington	14/90		
LONG STANTON	C4	28NOV57	Wellington	14/90		
WROKWARDINE	C4	28NOV57	Wellington	14/90		
TRENCH-LANE	C4	28NOV57	Wellington	14/90		
BURTON	D4	30NOV57	Wellington	14/91		
EYTON	D4	30NOV57	Wellington	14/91		
LEIGHTON	D4	30NOV57	Wellington	14/91	B	14MAY59-18MAY59.
MARBURY	D4	30NOV57	Whitchurch	14/91		
PRESTON	D4	30NOV57	Wellington	14/91		
LILLIES·HALL	C4	14JAN58	Newport	14/124		
BUCKNELL	C4	27JAN58	Shrewsbury	14/132		
MANAUGHTY	D1	31MAR58	Shrewsbury	14/177		
PERKINS-GREEN	D1	3MAR58	Shrewsbury	14/177		
DORRINGTON	D1	22APR58	Shrewsbury	14/204	B	26MAR59-15SEP59.
					BL	16SEP59
ASH	D4	22JUL58	Whitchurch	16/2		
BETTISFIELD	D1	22JUL58	Whitchurch	16/2		
CHORLTON	D1	22JUL58	Whitchurch	16/2		
REDBROOK	D1	22JUL58	Whitchurch	16/2		
CARDINGTON	D1	28AUG58	Shrewsbury	16/26		
CHIRBURY	D1	20SEP58	Shrewsbury	16/48		
CALVERHALL	D1	24SEP58	Whitchurch	16/49		
CRESSAGE	D1	23OCT58	Shrewsbury	16/64		
LLANBRYNMAIR	D1	25OCT58	Shrewsbury	16/68		
CASTLE·FOREGATE	D1	5NOV58	Shrewsbury	16/83	BL	11FEB59.
LLANYMAWDDY	D1	8NOV58	Shrewsbury	16/84	B	15SEP59
WESTBURY SALOP	D2	7JAN59	Shrewsbury	16/134		
THE-BRIDGES	D1	27JAN59	Shrewsbury	16/149		
CHURCH-STOKE	D1	16FEB59	Shrewsbury	16/160		
MORETON SALOP	D2	15APR59	Newport	18/28		
CROSS-HOUSES	D1	25APR59	Shrewsbury	18/33		
EDSTASTON	D1	14MAY59	Shrewsbury	18/42		
DIDDLEBURY	D1	4JUN59	Ludlow	18/54		
WIXHALL·SALOP	D1	23JUL59	Whitchurch	18/81		
MAESBURY	D1	28JUL59	Oswestry	18/83		
PENYBONT·FAWR	D1	28JUL59	Oswestry	18/83		
RHYDYCROESAN	D1	28JUL59	Oswestry	18/83		
WELCH·FRANKTON	D1	28JUL59	Oswestry	18/83		
ARLEEN	D4	28JUL59	Oswestry	18/84		
HENGOED	D4	28JUL59	Oswestry	18/84		
KNOCKIN	D4	28JUL59	Oswestry	18/84		
PANT	D4	28JUL59	Oswestry	18/84		
SARNAN	D4	28JUL59	Oswestry	18/84		
TREFONNEN	D1	3AUG59	Oswestry	18/84		
DELIFE	D4	3AUG59	Newport, Mon	18/85		

Salop

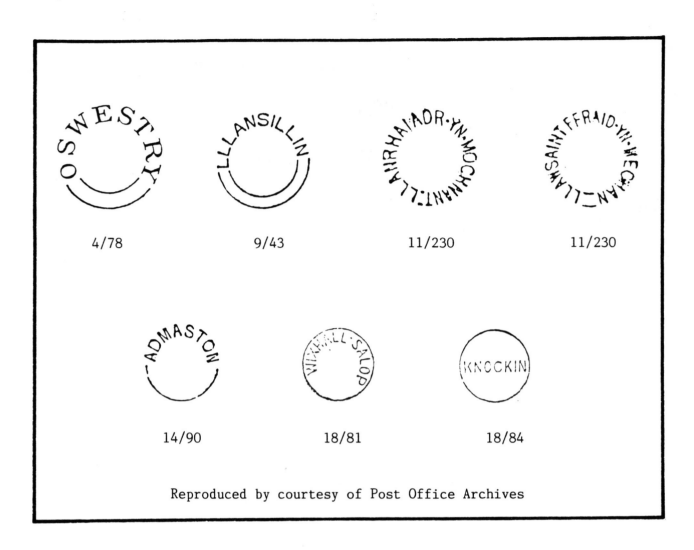

4/78   9/43   11/230   11/230

14/90   18/81   18/84

Reproduced by courtesy of Post Office Archives

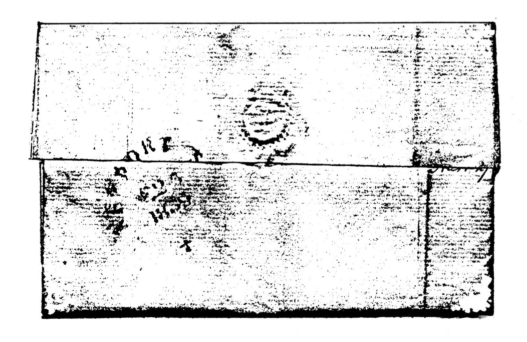

The UDC of NEWPORT-SALOP is known used to 19th November 1839. A CDS was issued on 31st December 1839 but the letter above shows use of a skeleton (or 'traveller') datestamp on 26th December, five days before the CDS was issued. Newport was a post town.

Salop

Similar Sans-serif (C1) Marks of Shropshire (1)

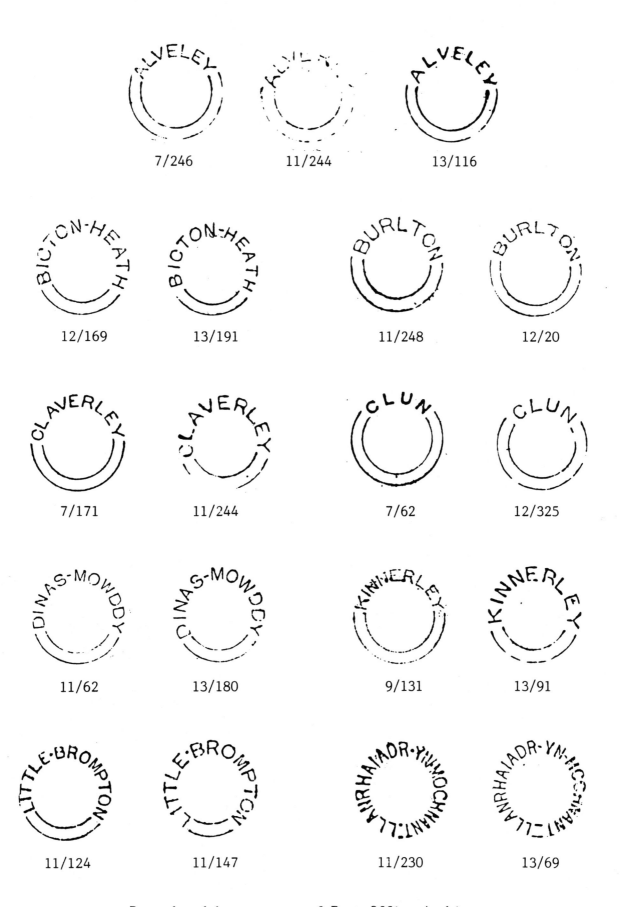

Reproduced by courtesy of Post Office Archives

Salop 120.

Similar Sans-serif (C1) Marks of Shropshire (2)

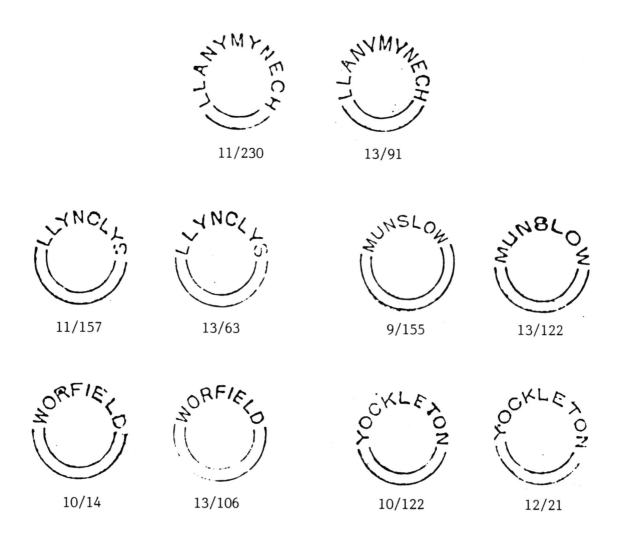

Reproduced by courtesy of Post Office Archives

BROSELEY (7/50)

Unusual use of an undated stamp as a cancellation on a ride letter.

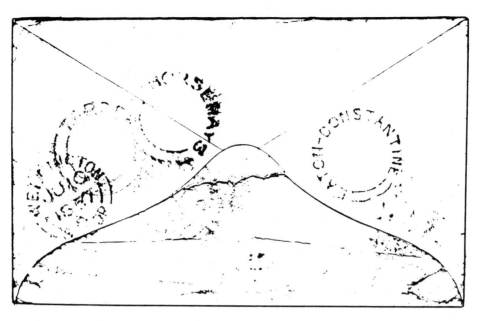

A letter with three UDCs - it was posted at TARDEBIGG (Worcs 11/229) and passed through HORSEHAYS (12/192) before reaching its address at EATON CONSTANTINE (12/274)

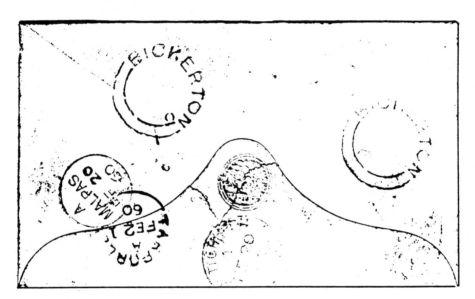

BICKERTON (11/160) in blue ink, the stamp having been struck twice for no apparent reason. By 1860, the office was again under Whitchurch after a spell under Chester.

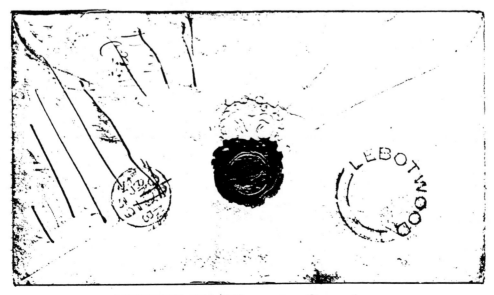

LEBOTWOOD (12/20), under Shrewsbury.

Salop

Above: BOW ST (12/153), a sub-office of Shrewsbury but 70 miles distant.

Below: CASTLE FOREGATE (16/83), an office in the centre of Shrewsbury.

STAFFORDSHIRE

BILSTON (73). Pre-proof books, 1/26
(CDS 15FEB38)

Bradley/Bradeley 11/106 14/256
Coppice 12/262
Coseley 5/174 7/270 12/299
Deepfield 12/262
Prince's End 9/1 14/185 14/243 See TL27.

BRIERLEY HILL (995). + (CDS 19FEB49) See TL10.

Brockmoor + 16/119
Hart Street + 16/119

BURTON-ON-TRENT (152).

Branston(e) 12/3
Caldwell/Cauldwell $\underline{2}$ 12/198 16/86
Dunstall 12/176
Eggin(g)ton $\underline{2}$ 10/7
Hartshorne $\underline{2}$ 11/197 16/86
Hilton $\underline{2}$ 12/275 16/87
Horninglow 9/71
Horninglow Street + 16/86
Lullington $\underline{2}$ 7/75 16/86
Midway $\underline{2}$ 11/105
Milton $\underline{2}$ 13/103
Needwood (Forest) 16/67
New(h)all $\underline{2}$ 7/75 16/87
New Street +
Newton (Solney) $\underline{2}$ 7/6 16/86
Repton $\underline{2}$ 7/6 16/87
Rolleston 10/34
Rosliston $\underline{2}$ 12/272 12/288
Stapenhill $\underline{2}$ 7/75 16/86
Swadlin(g)cote $\underline{2}$ 10/192
Tat(t)enhill 12/3
Tutbury 5/169 9/54 (CDS 24MAY51)
Victoria Crescent 12/222
Walton-on-Trent $\underline{2}$ 10/274 18/30
Willington $\underline{2}$ 10/7 16/86
Winshill $\underline{2}$ 13/103
Wooden Box/Woodville $\underline{2}$ 7/75 9/117 (CDS 11DEC54).

CHEADLE (175). See TL3&30.

Alton 7/3 13/15 See TL3&30.
Tean 7/17 12/260 (CDS 7JUL57)
See TL3&30.

ECCLESHALL (273).

Blackwater 13/23
Standon 10/193 See TL12&34.
Wetwood 13/51

FAZELEY (297). 1/53 (CDS 24DEC41)
See TL2&7.

Kingsbury $\underline{4}$ 9/178 16/113
See TL2&7.
Wilmcott/Wilnecote $\underline{4}$ 9/177
10/139 16/113 See TL2&7.

LEEK (448). 1/203* (CDS 8SEP38)

Wetley Rocks 7/172 7/192

LICHFIELD (457).

Alrewas + 9/14 (CDS 25FEB57)
Barton(-under-Needwood) +
9/14 (CDS 28MAR50) See TL18.
Burntwood 7/28* 9/128 16/113
Elford 7/179 14/111 See TL39.
Hanbury 9/156 See TL13.
Harleston/Harlaston 11/189
See TL39.
Kings Bromley 5/182 See TL20&25.
New Inn 9/155 See TL13.
Shenstone 7/140 16/106
(CDS 13MAR57)
Whittington 7/257 16/113
Yoxall 5/182 See TL19.

+ indicates an office which used a straight line (or P.P.) stamp after 1840.

An underlined number, eg $\underline{2}$, indicates an office outside Staffs - see key at end.

Staffs

NEWCASTLE-UNDER-LYME (546).

Audley 9/183 (CDS 8APR56)
Barthomley <u>1</u> 10/275
Betley 9/183
Burslem (551) 4/74 (CDS 14OCT44) See TL21.
Chesterton 9/146 12/336 12/341
Cobridge (550) 4/74 See TL21.
Endon 11/248 See TL38.
Etruria (554) 4/74 14/120 See TL21.
Golden Hill 10/122 16/64 See TL21.
Hanford 11/132
Hanley (549) 4/74 7/100 (CDS 14OCT44) See TL21.
Hartshill 11/248 See TL21.
Keele 7/247
Kidsgrove 10/275 14/120 See TL21.
Knutton Heath 11/260
Lane Delph (552) 4/74 See TL21.
Lane End=Longton (553) 4/74 (CDS 14OCT44) See TL21.
Lawton <u>1</u> 1/103 (CDS 21NOV39) See TL21.
Longport (555) 4/74 13/230 See TL21.
Madeley 9/183 18/96
Maer 12/74
Norton-in-the-Moors 9/126 9/132 See TL35.
Penkhull 11/82 See TL21.
Shelton (556) 4/74 See TL21.
Silverdale 12/129 (CDS 17NOV59)
Smallthorn 13/83 14/242 See TL35.
Trentham 10/162 13/40 (CDS 12SEP56) 18/3 See TL40.
Trent Vale 11/181 See TL40.
Tunstall (548) 4/74 9/6 (CDS 28JAN47) See TL21.
Whitmore Station 9/43
Wolstanton 7/247 See TL21.

PENKRIDGE (605). 1/144 (CDS 1JUL37) See TL4.

Wheaton Aston 10/55 See TL4&6.

RUGELEY (660). 1/164 (CDS 5SEP38)

Admaston 9/156
Armitage 12/34
Brereton 9/44
Colton 7/174 13/151
Colwich 12/199
Gentleshaw 14/79
Great Heywood (661) 1/63 (CDS 23MAR57)
      See TL17&23.
Hamstall Ridware 12/34
Hednesford 12/166 See TL29&37.
Hill Ridware 7/142 11/19
Hixon 12/83
Longdon + 13/149 (CDS 27MAR57) 16/126
Shirleywich + (662) 12/337 See TL5.
Wols(e)ley Bridge (663) Pre-proof books, 1/204
      4/111 13/154 See TL17&23.

STAFFORD (730). 1/183
      (CDS 11SEP34)

Aston 13/43
Bednal 14/220
Bishopswood 13/197
Caverswall 13/161
Church Eaton 7/76 (CDS 12MAR51)
      16/126
Dunstone 14/220
Foregate +
Ga(i)ley 14/215
Gayton 14/215
Gnosall 11/103
Hopton 13/191
Oakamoor 16/121
Rickerscote 14/220
Stretton (-Penkridge) 11/103
      11/156 See TL14.
Tixall 11/103
Walton 9/156 16/62
Weston (-on-Trent) 11/103
      12/82? 14/252

STOKE-ON-TRENT (547). 4/74
      (CDS 14OCT44) See TL21.

Blurton 12/336
Fenton 13/47
Milton 12/97
Mow Cop <u>1</u> 13/14
New Chapel 12/96
Northwood 12/81? 18/96
Rode Heath <u>1</u> 12/96
Smallwood <u>1</u> 12/96

STONE (745).

Barlaston 11/105
Blythe Marsh 13/161 See TL31.
Draycot(t) (-in-the-Moors)
      11/105 See TL31.
Forsbrook 2/44 14/258 See TL31.
Hilderstone 9/235
Ipstones 10/94 (CDS 27JAN58)
      See TL31.
Kingsley 12/324 See TL31.
Leigh 10/122 See TL31.
Mil(l)wich 9/235 9/243
Moddershall 13/161
Norton Bridge 12/337
Sandon 9/235
Swynnerton 9/107
Tittensor 14/8

+ indicates an office which used a straight line stamp after 1840.

An underlined number, eg <u>2</u>, indicates an office outside Staffs - see key at end.

Staffs

TAMWORTH (774). 2/140 (CDS 21FEB40) Note 1.

Clifton (Campville) 10/274 (CDS 22MAR56) 16/106
Middleton 4 13/237
Newton (Regis) 4 12/51
Polesworth 4 10/3

TIPTON (799). + 4/9 (CDS 22JUL39)

Great Bridge 9/236 9/242 14/231
Ocker Hill + 14/231 14/243
Tipton Green + 7/261 14/150 (CDS 22JUN58)
Tividale + 14/231

UTTOXETER (827). See TL33.

Abbots Bromley (828) 1/2 (CDS 25MAR57) See TL24.
Cubley 2 13/38
Doveridge 2 11/224 See TL16.
Etwall 2 7/16 13/278 See TL16.
Marchington 12/77
Newborough 11/181
Sudbury (829) + 2 13/201 See TL16.

WALSALL (834). 1/203 (CDS 8SEP38)

Aldridge 5/169 (CDS 7FEB57) 16/106
Bloxwich 5/197 (CDS 6JUN56)
Brownhills 12/241 (CDS 25OCT59)
Cannock 5/178 (CDS 12MAR51) See TL26,29&37.
Church Bridge 12/166 See TL37.
Pelsall 12/241
Stonall 9/178
Upper Stonall 13/129
Willenhall (039) 5/198 (CDS AUG53) See TL22
                                          & Note 2.

Wyrley Bank 12/241

WEDNESBURY (850).

Charleymount 13/197
Darlaston 5/121 (CDS 3JUN52)
Kingshill 12/74
Moxley 11/157
Wood Green 13/197

WEST BROMWICH (868).

Churchfield 14/256
High Street + 14/256
Hill Top 9/129 13/171 14/256
Spon Lane + 14/256.

WOLVERHAMPTON (905).

Albrighton 3 4/106 (CDS 28MAR50)
                          See TL9&28.
Bilston Road + 14/269
Bre(e)wood + 5/152 (CDS 14SEP49)
                          See TL15.
Chapel Ash 9/134 14/269
Claverley 3 7/171 11/244
           (CDS 1JAN57) See TL8.
Codsall 9/59 9/64
Codsall Wood 18/57
Compton 11/3 13/278*
Coven 11/156 12/192
Dudley Row/Road 9/131
Essington 18/72
Ettingshall 14/269
Ford Houses 16/106
Gornal 2/50 5/38 12/337 See TL1.
Horseley Field(s) + 9/131
Monmore Green +
Oaken 12/244
Pattingham 7/66 14/269
                          See TL9&11.
Penn 9/129
Pennfields 12/114
Portobello 12/104
Shareshill 9/176
Short Heath 12/104 16/106
Stafford Street 9/131
Tettenhall 4/106 12/20 12/34
The Wergs 12/199
Trysull + 7/93 14/269
Walsall Road 16/3
Wednesfield 7/182 13/129
Wednesfield Heath 12/114
Whitmore Reans/Reams 16/3
Wombourne 7/68 14/269
Worcester Street 12/62
Worfield 3 5/88 5/108 5/113
           10/14 13/106 See TL8.

ASHBOURNE (28), Derbys

Alstonefield 7/28 14/43
Ellastone 7/184 14/43
Ilam 7/28 14/43
Mayfield 7/184 14/77
Rocester 7/184

BEWDLEY (68), Worcs

Upper Arley 10/47 Note 3.

+ indicates an office which used a straight line (or P.P.) stamp after 1840.

An underlined number, eg 4, indicates an office outside Staffs - see key at end.

Staffs

BIRMINGHAM (75), Warks

Birchfield(s) 9/44
Cape of Good Hope 11/129 14/192
Great Barr + 12/137
Hampstead/Hamstead 13/51 13/278*
Hampstead Road /Row 10/193
Handsworth + 12/7 (CDS 28JUN55)
Harborne 7/17 13/278*
Harborne Heath 12/93
Little Aston 12/331
Oscott 12/331 14/105
Perry 12/331
Queeslet 13/48 16/113
Smethwick (034) + (CDS 21MAY55)

BUXTON (155), Derbys

Longnor 7/227

CONGLETON (216), Ches

Knypersley 11/105 (CDS 20SEP58)

DUDLEY (263), Worcs

Blackheath 12/155
Himley 10/153 16/141
Kingswinford 5/182 (CDS 4JUL51)
Lower Gornal 12/252 12/261
Old Hill 7/171 16/142
Pensnett 7/161
Rowley Regis 7/142
Sedgley 9/64 9/92 (CDS 27JUN56)
Swindon 12/50
Wall Heath 12/83
Woodsetton 12/336.

KIDDERMINSTER (415), Worcs

Broom 14/258 Note 4.

MARKET DRAYTON (509), Salop

Ashley 9/78

NEWPORT (565), Salop

Sheriff Hales 12/48 Note 5.

SHIFNAL (705), Salop

Weston (-under-Lizard) 12/98

STOURBRIDGE (750), Worcs

Brettell Lane + 12/37 See TL36.
Coalbourn Brook 16/144 16/158
Cradley 5 7/205 16/118
                    See TL32.
Cradley Heath (no UDC)
Enville 7/204 18/43
Kinver + (CDS 21MAY51)
Quarry Bank 11/229 See TL32.
Stourton 11/229 14/151
Wordsley + 10/176 14/149.

Notes:

1. Partly Warks until 1890.
2. UDC sent to Wolverhampton.
3. Transferred to Worcestershire in 1894/95.
4. In Staffs until 1844 but see Worcs section.
5. Transferred to Shropshire in 1894/5.

+ indicates an office which used a straight line (or P.P.) stamp after 1840.

KEY to offices not in Staffordshire

1 is in Cheshire
2 is in Derbyshire
3 is in Shropshire
4 is in Warwickshire
5 is in Worcestershire.

TRANSFERS - Staffordshire

TL 1. Gornal from Wolverhampton to Dudley, possibly in 1837/40.

2. Fazeley no longer a post town from 23APR49. (Night mail to Birmingham and Day Mail to Tamworth). Kingsbury and Wilnecot under Tamworth.

3. Cheadle reduced to a sub-office under Stone on 10MAY49.

4. Penkridge reduced to a sub-office under Stafford on 10MAY49. Wheaton Aston (if it had opened by that date) was probably transferred to Wolverhampton.

5. Shirleywich from Rugeley to Stafford on 13AUG49.

6. Wheaton Aston from Wolverhampton to Stafford on 7JAN50.

7. Both Day and Night Mails for Fazeley to be sent to Tamworth from 3NOV50 following introduction of Gloucester and Tamworth TPO on 1NOV50.

8. Claverley and Worfield from Wolverhampton to Bridgnorth on 9JUN51.

9. Albrighton and Pattingham from Wolverhampton to Shifnal on 9JUN51.

10. Brierley Hill became a post town on 10OCT51.

11. Pattingham from Shifnal to Wolverhampton on 26NOV51.

12. Standon from Eccleshall to Stone on 23SEP52.

13. Hanbury and New Inn from Lichfield to Burton on Trent on 6APR53.

14. Stretton from Stafford to Wolverhampton, perhaps early in 1853.

15. Brewood from Wolverhampton to Stafford on 13JUN53. In AUG53 it was announced that it had been "reduced to a sub-office".

16. Etwall, Doveridge and Sudbury from Uttoxeter to Derby on 18JUL53.

17. Great Heywood and Wolseley Bridge to Stafford on 30JUL53.

18. Barton under Needwood from Lichfield to Burton on Trent on 8AUG53.

19. Yoxall from Lichfield to Burton on Trent on 15AUG53.

20. Kings Bromley from Lichfield to Rugeley on 15AUG53.

21. Stoke on Trent became a post town on 24JAN54. Fifteen offices were transferred from Newcastle to Stoke at that time.

Staffs

TL22.		Willenhall from Walsall to Wolverhampton on 28OCT54.
23.		Great Heywood and Wolseley Bridge from Stafford to Rugeley on 18JAN55.
24.		Abbots Bromley from Uttoxeter to Rugeley by 1855.
25.		Kings Bromley from Rugeley to Lichfield on 21MAY55.
26.		Cannock from Walsall to Rugeley on 21MAY55.
27.		Princes End from Bilston to Tipton on 12JUN55.
28.		Albrighton from Shifnal to Wolverhampton on 27JUL55.
29.		Cannock and Hednesford from Rugeley to Walsall on 2AUG56.
30.		Cheadle (and delivery) from Stone to Stafford on 1JAN57.
31.		Blythe Marsh, Forsbrook, Draycot(t), Ipstones, Kingsley and Leigh from Stone to Stafford on 13JAN57.
32.		Quarry Bank, Cradley and Cradley Heath from Stourbridge to Brierley Hill on 1JUN57.
33.		Uttoxeter reduced to a sub-office under Derby on 23NOV57.
34.		Standon from Stone to Eccleshall on 5DEC57.
35.		Smallthorn and Norton in the Moors from Newcastle under Lyme to Stoke on 30JUL58.
36.		Brettell Lane from Stourbridge to Brierley Hill on 10SEP58.
37.		Cannock, Church Bridge and Hednesford from Walsall to Stafford on 11MAR59.
38.		Endon from Newcastle under Lyme to Stoke on 1AUG59.
39.		Elford and Harleston from Lichfield to Tamworth on 1JAN60.
40.		Trentham and Trent Vale from Newcastle under Lyme to Stoke on 15MAR60.

Staffs

STAFFORDSHIRE

WOLSELEY BRIDGE	C3D	by 23			B	5AUG23- 9APR40	
BILSTON	C3C	pre-25			B	17FEB25-17MAR27	
WALSALL	C2*	13FEB28	Walsall	1/203	R	7APR28-29MAR38	
					OR/BR	13APR31	
LEEK	C2*	(Locally altered - see Note 1.)			B	31- 35	
LAWTON	C2*	14JUN28	Lawton	1/103	B	32- 38	
ABBOTS BROMLEY -	C3	26MAR29	Abbots Bromley	1/2	R	19JUL34-19OCT40	
					OR/BR	15AUG38	
					B	24JAN43- 9JUL56	
					GR	4JAN56-15JAN57	
GREAT HEYWOOD	C3	26MAR29	Great Heywood	1/63	B	29DEC37-28OCT56.	
WOLSELEY BRIDGE -	C3	26MAR29	Wolseley Bridge	1/204	B	17SEP29-15APR34	
BILSTONE	C2*	31AUG29	Bilston	1/26	B	8SEP31- 4AUG37	
PENKRIDGE	C2*	20DEC29	Penkridge	1/144	B	?	
					CrimR	21DEC32- 1MAY35	
					BR	8DEC35	
FAZELEY	C2*	9AUG31	Fazeley	1/53	R	35-22JAN41.	
					B	1APR41	
RUGELEY	C2*	15AUG31	Rugeley	1/164	B	2JAN32-15AUG38	
STAFFORD	C2*	12SEP31	Stafford	1/183	B	29DEC31- 7FEB34	
TAMWORTH	C2	28APR35	Tamworth	2/140	R/OR	30JUL36-28DEC37.	
GORNAL	C2	12OCT37	Wolverhampton	2/50	B	10MAY40 Note 2.	
FORSBROOK	C2	21MAR38	Forsbrook	2/44	B	11MAY38-25MAR50	
ALBRIGHTON	C2	30MAR39	Wolverhampton	4/106	B	20SEP39- 2SEP48	
					R	22APR41	
TETTENHALL	C2	30MAR39	Wolverhampton	4/106	B	29SEP39-24APR46	
TIPTON	C2	19JUN39	Birmingham	4/9		Note 3.	
BURSLEM	C2	23JAN40	Newcastle-u-L	4/74	B	7JUL40-20MAY44.	
					R	11NOV40	
COBRIDGE-STAFFS.	C2	23JAN40	Newcastle-u-L	4/74	B	26APR44- 50	
					dkBL	30APR47	
ETRURIA	C2	23JAN40	Newcastle-u-L	4/74	B	19APR41- 44	
HANLEY-STAFFS.	C2	23JAN40	Newcastle-u-L	4/74	B	13MAY40-16JUL44	
LANE-DELPH	C2	23JAN40	Newcastle-u-L	4/74	B	21AUG41-23MAR52.	
					GR	2FEB55	
LANE-END	C2	23JAN40	Newcastle-u-L	4/74	B	8FEB40-14AUG44	
LONGPORT-STAFFS.	C2	23JAN40	Newcastle-u-L	4/74	B	3MAR45- 7FEB50	
SHELTON-STAFFS.	C2	23JAN40	Newcastle-u-L	4/74	B	25DEC44- NOV49	
					GR	24FEB51-27JUL58.	
					BL	20JUN52- 59	
					GR/Gy	22AUG57-23NOV58	
					BL/GR	29OCT58	
STOKE-UPON-TRENT	C2	23JAN40	Newcastle-u-L	4/74	B	40-13JUL43.	
TUNSTALL	C2	23JAN40	Newcastle-u-L	4/74	B	21DEC40- 1NOV45	
WOLSELEY-BRIDGE	C2	4FEB41	Wolseley Bridge	4/111	B	5MAY42- 2MAY46	
GORNAL	C2	18OCT41	Dudley	5/38	B	20AUG42-19OCT45	
WARFIELD	C2	23APR42	Wolverhampton	5/88		Note 4.	
WORFIELD	C2	26JUL42	Bracknell	5/108		Note 5.	
WORFIELD	C2	3SEP42	Wolverhampton	5/113	B	10SEP42- 30OCT49.	
DARLASTON	C2	24OCT42	Darlaston	5/121	B	9JUN43	
					R	24NOV46- 3APR47	
					BL/GR	4MAY49-26APR52	
					BL	5MAR49-14APR51	

Notes:
1. 21mm dia, arcs 2mm apart in place of mileage. Known without mileage or arcs in 1829.
2. See also 5/38.
3. A straight line stamp continued in use.
4. Spelling error - see below.
5. Missent - returned for re-issue.

Staffs   130.

Name	Class	Date	Town	Ref	Colour	Period
BREEWOOD	C2	12APR43	Wolverhampton	5/152	B	12DEC44-29NOV48
TUTBURY	C2	11JUL43	Burton on Trent	5/169	B	5APR45-17JUL46.
ALDRIDGE	C2	11JUL43	Walsall	5/169	B	3FEB44-29SEP49
COSELEY	C2	4AUG43	Bilstone	5/174	B	44
CANNOCK	C2	30AUG43	Walsall	5/178	B	16JUN47
KINGSWINFORD	C2	19SEP43	Dudley	5/182	R	2JAN45-17OCT45
					B	20FEB47-20OCT50.
KINGS-BROMLEY	C2	19SEP43	Lichfield	5/182	GR/B	17SEP45
					BL	26MAR53
YOXALL	C2	19SEP43	Lichfield	5/182	B	12APR45- 4SEP48
					BL	21JUN59
BLOXWICH	C2	16NOV43	Walsall	5/197	B	45- 5JUN48
WILLENHALL	C2	16NOV43	Wolverhampton	5/198	R	22JAN44- 9JUN53
ALTON	C2	6DEC43	Cheadle	7/3	B	26NOV45- 6FEB48
					BL	1DEC49
					GR	11MAY56
					BL/GR	57
NEWTON	C2	19DEC43	Burton on Trent	7/6	B	19DEC44- 45
REPTON	C2	19DEC43	Burton on Trent	7/6	B	22FEB44-10FEB53
ETWALL	C2	13JAN44	Uttoxeter	7/16	B	27FEB44-29MAR47
					BL/GR	2DEC44
					GR	4APR53- 7FEB56.
TEAN	C2	13JAN44	Cheadle	7/17	B	5MAY45-19JUN55
					BL	4NOV52
					GR	12NOV55
HARBORNE	C2	13JAN44	Birmingham	7/17	BL	4MAY46- 4MAY56
					B	15MAY46- 6JUN49
ALSTONEFIELD	C2	21FEB44	Ashbourne	7/28	R	22JAN46- 9FEB53.
					B	5OCT47
					GR	8NOV48
ILAM	C2	21FEB44	Ashbourne	7/28	R	11NOV45-12JUL55
BURNTWOOD	C2				B	47
PATTINGHAM	C1	31MAY44	Wolverhampton	7/66	OR	3NOV48-12JUN50
WOMBORNE	C1	6JUN44	Wolverhampton	7/68	B	50
NEWALL	C1	28JUN44	Burton on Trent	7/75	B	21JUN45-25AUG47
LULLINGTON	C1	28JUN44	Burton on Trent	7/75	B	18SEP45-23MAY49
STAPENHILL	C1	28JUN44	Burton on Trent	7/75	B	4DEC50
WOODEN-BOX	C1	28JUN44	Burton on Trent	7/75	B	30AUG47 Note 6.
CHURCH-EATON	C1	28JUN44	Stafford	7/76	B	16AUG45-29APR47
TRYSULL	C1	4SEP44	Wolverhampton	7/93	OR	31JUL49
					BL/GR	4JAN55
HANLEY-STAF	C1M	14OCT44	Newcastle-u-L	7/100	B	49
SHENSTONE	C1	18APR45	Lichfield	7/140	B	46?
					GR	13FEB46-17JUL47
					BL	5JAN49-22MAY53
					GR/BL	6SEP52
HILL-REDWARE	C1	8MAY45	Rugeley	7/142	B	17MAY47 Note 7.
ROWLEY-REGIS	C1	8MAY45	Dudley	7/142	B	7MAR46- 8JUL59.
					OR	7AUG48-16DEC49
PENSNETT	C1	7JUL45	Dudley	7/161	B	29SEP47-18SEP48
					GR	13JUN55-14DEC57
OLD-HILL	C1	25AUG45	Dudley	7/171	R	46
					BR	4NOV52
					R/BR	19MAY54
					B	18SEP58
CLAVERLEY	C1	25AUG45	Wolverhampton	7/171	B	45-19APR53
					R	10AUG46-28JUL47
					OR	25AUG45-10SEP48
WHITLEY-ROCKS	C1	29AUG45	Leek	7/172		Note 8.

Notes: 6. Re-named "Woodville" - see 9/117.
         7. Incorrect spelling - see also 11/19.
         8. Spelling error - re-issued at 7/192.

Staffs

COLTON	C1	9SEP45	Rugeley	7/174		
ELFORD	C1	26SEP45	Lichfield	7/179	BL	20SEP48-18JUN52
WEDNESFIELD	C1	10OCT45	Wolverhampton	7/182		
MATHFIELD	C1	25OCT45	Ashbourne	7/184	B	18AUG54 Note 9.
					BL	26JUN56
ELLASTONE	C1	25OCT45	Ashbourne	7/184	B	25SEP48- 5APR58.
					BL	18DEC5?
					BR	53
ROCESTER	C1	25OCT45	Ashbourne	7/184	B	15APR50-14OCT51
WE TLEY-ROCKS	C1	17NOV45	Leek	7/192	B	30JAN48- 3FEB50
					BL	27APR50- 56
ENVILLE	C1	5JAN46	Stourbridge	7/204	B	25FEB46-27JUL49.
CRADLEY	C1	10JAN46	Stourbridge	7/205	B	7AUG47-18NOV50
					BR	18SEP53
LONGNOR	C1	8APR46	Buxton	7/227	BR/R	28JUN48
					R/OR	10JUL52
WOLSTANTON	C1	27JUN46	Newcastle Staff	7/247	B	24MAY47- 6JUL52
KEELE	C1	27JUN46	Newcastle Staff	7/247	GR	16DEC57
WHITTINGTON	C1	25JUL46	Lichfield	7/257	BL/GR	15AUG46
					OR/Y	13OCT47
					B	16JUN48-14FEB50
TIPTON-GREEN	C1	25AUG46	Tipton	7/261	OR/R	17APR47-26MAY49.
					GR	4FEB56
COSELEY	C1	29SEP46	Bilston	7/270	B	21AUG48
PRINCES-END	C1	1JAN47	Bilston	9/1		
TUNSTALL	C1M	28JAN47	Newcastle Staff	9/6	BL	60
ALREWAS	C1	22FEB47	Lichfield	9/14		
BARTON	C1	22FEB47	Lichfield	9/14	B	28FEB47-26JAN50
WHITMORE-STATION	C1	24MAY47	Newcastle Staff	9/43	GR	23SEP47
					GR/Gy	23JUN52
					BL	53
					BL/B	25NOV53
BIRCHFIELDS	C1	24MAY47	Birmingham	9/44	B	10SEP52- 56.
					BL	23MAY53-21JAN60
BRERETON	C1	24MAY47	Rugeley	9/44		
TUTBURY	C1	15JUN47	Burton on Trent	9/54	B	26APR50-16NOV50.
CODSALL	C1	2JUL47	Wolverhampton	9/59		Note 10.
SEDGELEY	C1	24JUL47	Dudley	9/64		Note 11.
CODSALL	C1	24JUL47	Wolverhampton	9/64	B	6SEP49
HORNINGLOW	C1	17AUG47	Burton on Trent	9/71	B	17AUG47- 2JUN48
ASHLEY	C1	11SEP47	Market Drayton	9/78	OR/BR	30MAR51
					BR	12JAN52
					R	16JUL55
					GR	10SEP59
SEDG LEY	C1	19OCT47	Dudley	9/92	B	30SEP49-14MAR54
					GR	12JAN56 Note 12.
SWYNNERTON	C1	16DEC47	Stone	9/107	B	21DEC53
WOODVILLE	C1	27JAN48	Burton on Trent	9/117		
NORTON-IN-THE-MOORS	C1	12FEB48	Newcastle Staff	9/126		Note 13.
BURNTWOOD	C1	3MAR48	Lichfield	9/128	B	29AUG53-30AUG53
PENN	C1	3MAR48	Wolverhampton	9/129	Grey/B	6OCT59
HILL-TOP	C1	3MAR48	West Bromwich	9/129	BL/GR	14JAN57-17JAN57
HORSELEY-FIELD	C1	9MAR48	Wolverhampton	9/131	B	3APR51-12AUG52

Notes:
9. Normally spelt "Mayfield".
10. 9/59 and 9/64 are similar but different stamps: all use shown against the latter.
11. Spelling error - re-issued at 9/92.
12. Re-issued stamp with letter filed out.
13. Appears identical to 9/132.

Staffs

Name	Type	Date	Office	Ref	Colour	Date
STAFFORD-ST	C1	9MAR48	Wolverhampton	9/131	R	15APR52
					Y/BR	19MAR53
					Grey	12APR59.
DUDLEY·ROAD	C1	9MAR48	Wolverhampton	9/131	BL	51
NORTON-IN-THE-MOORS	C1	9MAR48	Newcastle Staff	9/132	OR	1JAN49-16JUL52
					R	13JUN52
CHAPEL-ASH	C1	12MAR48	Wolverhampton	9/134	OR/BR	2AUG48-30OCT49
					OR	19APR50-11MAY50
					R	12APR51
CHESTERTON	C1	4MAY48	Newcastle Staff	9/146		
NEW-INN	C1	3JUN48	Lichfield	9/155	B	4OCT55
					GR	29APR57-19AUG57
WALTON	C1	3JUN48	Stafford	9/156	GR	3APR49
HANBURY	C1	3JUN48	Lichfield	9/156	B	6AUG51
					GR ·	6DEC55
ADMASTON	C1	3JUN48	Rugeley	9/156		
SHARESHILL	C1	24AUG48	Wolverhampton	9/176		
WILMCOTT	C1	28AUG48	Fazeley	9/177	B	20MAR50 Note 14.
STOUALL	C1	28AUG48	Walsall	9/178		Note 15.
KINGSBURY	C1	28AUG48	Fazeley	9/178	R	49
MADELEY	C1	4OCT48	Newcastle Staff	9/183	B	52
					dkBL	27OCT54
					GR	13MAY57
					GR/B	4JAN58
AUDLEY	C1	4OCT48	Newcastle Staff	9/183	BR/OR	1DEC51
BETLEY	C1	4OCT48	Newcastle Staff	9/183	B/R	6APR50- 6SEP58
SANDON	C1	28MAR49	Stone	9/235	B	4SEP55
					GR	26MAY50-21APR57
MILLWICK	C1	28MAR49	Stone	9/235		Note 16.
HILDERSTONE	C1	28MAR49	Stone	9/235	BL	10JAN53
GREAT-BRIDGE	C1	28MAR49	Tipton	9/236		Note 17.
GREAT-BRIDGE	C1	5APR49	Tipton	9/242	R/BR	20APR54
					R	54
					GR	3NOV55
MILLWICH	C1	5APR49	Stone	9/243		
POLESWORTH	C1	31MAY49	Tamworth	10/3	B	NOV50-22JUN58.
					R	20MAR55
					BL	59
WILLINGTON	C1	4JUN49	Burton on Trent	10/7	B	4JUL49
EGGINTON	C1	4JUN49	Burton on Trent	10/7		
WORFIELD	C1	13JUN49	Wolverhampton	10/14	B	30OCT49-15JAN51.
ROLLESTON	C1	23AUG49	Burton on Trent	10/34	B	9SEP51- 1FEB53
UPPER-ARLEY	C1	1NOV49	Bewdley	10/47		
WHEATON-ASTON	C1	13DEC49	Penkridge	10/55	BL	22JUN53-26NOV55
IPSTONES	C1	14JUN50	Stone	10/94		
LEIGH	C1	18NOV50	Cheadle	10/122	GR	8FEB57- 7JAN58.
GOLDEN-HILL	C1	18NOV50	Newcastle Staff	10/122	BL	1MAR52
WILNECOTE	C1	9JAN51	Tamworth	10/139	OR	14OCT54
					R/BR	5JUN55
HIMLEY	C1	12FEB51	Dudley	10/153	GR	8JAN56
TRENTHAM	C1	1MAR51	Newcastle Staff	10/162	BL	52-15DEC55

Notes: 14. Obsolete spelling - see 10/139.
15. Incorrect spelling of 'Stonall'.
16. Spelling error - re-issued at 9/243.
17. 9/236 and 9/242 are similar but different stamps: all use shown against the latter.

Office	Class	Date	Parent	Ref	Colour	Date/Period
WORDSLEY	C1	1MAR51	Stourbridge	10/176	BL	54
					B	6MAY55
SWADLINGCOTE	C1	24APR51	Burton on Trent	10/192	GR	11OCT51
STANDON	C1	24APR51	Eccleshall	10/193		
HAMPSTEAD-ROAD	C1	24APR51	Birmingham	10/193	B	5JUL52-30DEC59
					GR	6MAY56-11MAY58
					BL/GR	20SEP56- 9SEP59
						Note 18.
CLIFTON	C1	6OCT51	Tamworth	10/274	Gy/BL	25NOV51
					B	29MAR56
WALTON·ON·TRENT	C1	6OCT51	Burton on Trent	10/274	B	20DEC51-25JUN53
KIDSGROVE	C1	6OCT51	Newcastle Staff	10/275		
BARTHOMLEY	C1	6OCT51	Newcastle Staff	10/275		
COMPTON	C1	9JAN52	Wolverhampton	11/3		
HILL-RIDWARE	C1	6FEB52	Rugeley	11/19	B	2SEP54
PENKHULL	C1	JUL52	Newcastle Staff	11/82	BL	24APR53
WESTON	C1	SEP52	Stafford	11/103		
GNOSALL	C1	SEP52	Stafford	11/103	OR	23MAY53
					GR	10JAN56
						Note 19.
STRETTON	C1	SEP52	Stafford	11/103		
TIXALL	C1	SEP52	Stafford	11/103		
BARLASTON	C1	SEP52	Stone	11/105	B	21DEC59
DRAYCOT	C1	SEP52	Stone	11/105		
MIDWAY	C1	SEP52	Burton on Trent	11/105		
BRADELEY	C1	SEP52	Bilston	11/106		
KNYPERSLEY	C1	30OCT52	Congleton	11/105		
CAPE·OF·GOOD·HOPE	C1	JAN53	Birmingham	11/129	B	19AUG53- 57.
					BL	23SEP57
HANFORD	C1	JAN53	Newcastle Staff	11/132		
COVEN	C1	APR53	Wolverhampton	11/156		
STRETTON	C1	APR53	Wolverhampton	11/156	R	?
MOXLEY	C1	APR53	Wednesbury	11/157	B	9JUN53
NEWBOROUGH	C1	JUN53	Uttoxeter	11/181	BL	16MAY59
TRENT-VALE	C1	JUN53	Newcastle Staff	11/181	BL	9OCT57
					B	14JUL58-28OCT58.
HARLESTON	C1	JUN53	Lichfield	11/189		
HARTSHORNE	C1	JUL53	Burton on Trent	11/197		
DOVERIDGE	C1	AUG53	Uttoxeter	11/224	GR	25OCT59
STOURTON	C1	OCT53	Stourbridge	11/229	BL/GR	59
QUARRY-BANK	C1	OCT53	Stourbridge	11/229		
CLAVERLEY	C1	OCT53	Bridgnorth	11/244		
ENDON	C1	OCT53	Newcastle Staff	11/248	B	5APR54
					GR	55
HARTSHILL	C1	OCT53	Newcastle Staff	11/248	BL&GR	17JUN55
KNUTTON·HEATH	C1	NOV53	Newcastle Staff	11/260		
BRANSTON	C1	DEC53	Burton on Trent	12/3	B	30DEC55- 8APR59
TATTENHILL	C1	DEC53	Burton on Trent	12/3	B	3DEC58-26NOV59
					BL	16OCT59
HANDSWORTH	C1	DEC53	Birmingham	12/7	B	19FEB54- 55
TATTENHALL	C1	JAN54	Wolverhampton	12/20		Note 20.
TETTENHALL	C1	FEB54	Wolverhampton	12/34	GR	7MAR55
					B	20DEC55
HAMSTALL·RIDWARE	C1	MAR54	Rugeley	12/34		
ARMITAGE	C1	MAR54	Rugeley	12/34	B	57

Notes:
18. Commonly spelt as "Hamstead".
19. 11/103 and 11/156 appear to be identical.
20. Spelling error - re-issued below.

Staffs

Office	Type	Date	County/Town	Ref	Colour	Dates
BRETTEL-LANE	C1	MAR54	Stourbridge	12/37	OR	26DEC56
					B	19NOV57- 8SEP58
					BL/B	15FEB58- 4OCT58.
SHERIFF-HALES	C1	APR54	Newport	12/48	B	4JUN54
SWINDON	C1	APR54	Dudley	12/50		
NEWTON	C1	APR54	Tamworth	12/51		
WORCESTER-ST.	C1	MAY54	Stoke on Trent	12/62	B	17MAY58-18DEC58
						Note 21.
MAER	C1	JUN54	Newcastle Staff	12/74	BL	57
					B	9MAY59
KINGS·HILL	C1	JUN54	Wednesbury	12/74		
MARCHINGTON	C1	JUN54	Uttoxeter	12/77	BL	14FEB59
NORTHWOOD	C1	cJUN54		12/81	B	14JUN58-15JUN58
						Note 22.
WESTON	C1	cJUN54		12/82		Note 23.
WALL-HEATH	C1	cJUN54		12/83	BL	23FEB56 Note 24.
HIXON	C1	cJUN54		12/83		Note 25.
HARBORNE·HEATH	C1	20JUL54		12/93	BL	13OCT54 Note 26.
					B	5DEC55-14FEB60.
RODE·HEATH	C1	cAUG54		12/96		Note 27.
NEWCHAPEL	C1	cAUG54		12/96		Note 27.
SMALLWOOD	C1	cAUG54		12/96		Note 27.
MILTON	C1	cAUG54		12/97	BL	28JUL56 Note 27.
WESTON	C1	12AUG54		12/98		Note 23.
PORTOBELLO	C1	22AUG54		12/104	B	4OCT58 Note 28.
SHORT·HEATH	C1	22AUG54		12/104	B	5AUG58 Note 28.
PENNFIELDS	C1	16SEP54		12/114	GR	11MAY57- 9APR58
					BL	JUN58 Note 28.
WEDNESFIELD·HEATH	C1	16SEP54		12/114		Note 28.
SILVERDALE	C1	27OCT54	Mr Beaufort	12/129	B	19FEB5?
GREAT-BARR	C1	7DEC54	Birmingham	12/137	OR	27JUL55
					GR	21OCT56
					B	14DEC57- 58
BLACKHEATH	C1	1FEB55	Dudley	12/155		
CHURCH·BRIDOE	C1	27FEB55	Walsall	12/166		Note 29.
HEDNESFORD	C1	27FEB55	Rugeley	12/166		
DUNSTALL	C1	25MAR55	Burton on Trent	12/176		
COVEN	C1	2MAY55	Wolverhampton	12/192		
CALDWELL	C1	17MAY55	Burton on Trent	12/198		
COLWICH	C1	17MAY55	Rugeley	12/199		
THE-WERGS	C1	17MAY55	Wolverhampton	12/199	B	11MAY59
VICTORIA·CRESCENT	C1	21JUL55	Burton on Trent	12/222		
WYRLEY-BANK	C1	8SEP55	Walsall	12/241		
PELSALL	C1	8SEP55	Walsall	12/241		
BROWNHILLS	C1	8SEP55	Walsall	12/241		
OAKEN	C1	19SEP55	Wolverhampton	12/244		
LOWER-GORNAL	C1	5OCT55	Dudley	12/252		
TEAN	C1	5NOV55	Stone	12/260		
LOWER-GORNAL	C1	5NOV55	Dudley	12/261		
DEEPFIELD	C1	5NOV55	Bilston	12/262	dkBL	23SEP59

Notes:
21. Missent - intended for Wolverhampton.
22. Probably issued to Stoke on Trent.
23. 12/82 possibly issued to Stafford.
    12/98 probably issued to Shifnal.
24. Probably sent to Dudley.
25. Probably sent to Rugeley.
26. Probably sent to Birmingham.
27. Probably sent to Stoke on Trent.
28. Probably sent to Wolverhampton.
29. Spelling error - "Brid<u>oe</u>" for "Bridge".

Staffs

COPPICE	C1	5NOV55	Bilston	12/262	B	58
ROSLINGTON	C1	30NOV55	Burton on Trent	12/272		Note 30.
HILTON	C1	4DEC55	Burton on Trent	12/275		
ROSLISTON	C1	28DEC55	Burton on Trent	12/288		
COSELEY	C1	21JAN56	Bilston	12/299	GR	31MAR56
KINGSLEY	C1	22MAR56	Stone	12/324		
LITTLE-ASTON	C1	25MAR56	Birmingham	12/331		
OSCOTT	C1	25MAR56	Birmingham	12/331		
PERRY	C1	25MAR56	Birmingham	12/331	GR	19OCT56
					BL/GR	14DEC58.
BLURTON	C1	3APR56	Stoke on Trent	12/336		
CHESTERTCN	C1	3APR56	Newcastle Staff	12/336		Note 31.
WOODSETTON	C1	3APR56	Dudley	12/336		
GORNAL	C1	3APR56	Dudley	12/337		
NORTON-BRIDGE	C1	3APR56	Stone	12/337		
SHIRLEYWICH	C1	3APR56	Stafford	12/337		
CHESTERTON	C1	16APR56	Newcastle Staff	12/341		
MOW-COP	C1	3JUN56	Stoke on Trent	13/14	BL	7MAY57-29JUN57.
ALTON	C1	3JUN56	Stone	13/15		
BLACKWATER	C1	21JUN56	Eccleshall	13/23		
CUBLEY	C1	11JUL56	Uttoxeter	13/38		
TRENTHAM	C1	14JUL56	Newcastle Staff	13/40	GR	21JUL56-16AUG56.
ASTON	C1	15JUL56	Stafford	13/43		
FENTON	C1	29JUL56	Stoke on Trent	13/47	BL/B	APR59
QUEESLET	C1	29JUL56	Birmingham	13/48		
WETWOOD	C1	5AUG56	Eccleshall	13/51		Note 32.
HAMPSTEAD	C1	5AUG56	Birmingham	13/51	BL/GR	6MAY58
SMALLTHORN	C1	14OCT56	Newcastle Staff	13/83		
WINSHILL	C1	2DEC56	Burton on Trent	13/103		
MILTON	C1	2DEC56	Burton on Trent	13/103		
WORFIELD	C1	9DEC56	Bridgnorth	13/106	B	57-23MAR58.
UPPER·STONNALL	C1	30JAN57	Walsall	13/129		
WEDNESFIELD	C1	30JAN57	Wolverhampton	13/129	B	1FEB59
LONGDON	C1	14FEB57	Rugeley	13/149		
COLTON	C1	18FEB57	Rugeley	13/151		
WOLSELEY-BRIDGE	C1	23FEB57	Rugeley	13/154		
CAVERSWALL	C1	4MAR57	Stafford	13/161		
BLYTHE-MARSH	C1	4MAR57	Stone	13/161	BL	7MAY57
MODDERSHALL	C1	4MAR57	Stone	13/161		
HILL-TOP	C1	17MAR57	West Bromwich	13/171		
HOPTON	C1	23MAR57	Stafford	13/191		
BISHOPSWOOD	C1	27MAR57	Stafford	13/197	GR	28MAY58
WOODGREEN	C1	27MAR57	Wednesbury	13/197		
CHARLEYMOUNT	C1	27MAR57	Wednesbury	13/197		
SUDBURY	C1	1APR57	Derby	13/201	GR	12DEC58
					B	9JAN59-16MAY59
LONGPORT	C1*	9MAY57	Stoke on Trent	13/230	B	18APR59
MIDDLETON	C1*	16MAY57	Tamworth	13/237	B	18APR59
ETWALL	C1*	15JUL57	Derby	13/278	GR	1JUN58
COMPTON	D3	cJUL57			B	28DEC59
HAMPSTEAD	D3	cJUL57			GR	4DEC59
HARBORNE	D3	cJUL57			B	?
TITTENSOR	C4	7AUG57	Stone	14/8		

Notes: 30. Spelling error - re-issued at 12/288.
31. Spelling error - re-issued at 12/341.
32. Previously Blackwater - see 13/23.

Staffs 136.

ILAM	C4	OCT57	Ashbourne	14/43		
ALSTONEFIELD	C4	OCT57	Ashbourne	14/43	BL	30NOV57
ELLASTONE	C4	OCT57	Ashbourne	14/43	B	3NOV57-12JAN59
MAYFIELD	C4	12NOV57	Ashbourne	14/77		
GENTLESHAW	C4	14NOV57	Rugeley	14/79	BL	19DEC59
OSCOTT	D4	10DEC57	Birmingham	14/105		
ELFORD	D4	23DEC57	Lichfield	14/111	BR/B	16SEP58
					GR	4DEC58
					BL	59
ETRURIA	C4	2JAN58	Stoke on Trent	14/120		
KIDSGROVE	C4	2JAN58	Stoke on Trent	14/120		
WORDESLEY	D1	18FEB58	Stourbridge	14/149		
TIPTON·GREEN R.O.	D2	20FEB58	Tipton	14/150		
STOURTON	D4	20FEB58	Stourbridge	14/151	BL	5MAR60
PRINCES-END	D1	1APR58	Tipton	14/185		
CAPE-OF·GOOD-HOPE	D1	6APR58	Birmingham	14/192	GR	20JAN59-19JAN60.
					B	59
GAYTON	D4	28APR58	Stafford	14/215		
GALEY	D4	28APR58	Stafford	14/215		
BEDNAL	D4	10MAY58	Stafford	14/220		
RICKERSCOTE	D1	10MAY58	Stafford	14/220		
DUNSTONE	D1	10MAY58	Stafford	14/220		
OCKER·HILL R.O.	D2	15MAY58	Tipton	14/231		
GREAT·BRIDGE R.O.	D2	15MAY58	Tipton	14/231		
TIVIDALE R.O.	D2	15MAY58	Tipton	14/231		
SMALLTHORN	D1	22MAY58	Stoke on Trent	14/242		
OCKER·HILL R.O	D2	31MAY58	Tipton	14/243		
PRINCES·END R.O	D2	31MAY58	Tipton	14/243	BL	58
WESTON	D4	4JUN58	Stafford	14/252		
HILL-TOP	D4	15JUN58	West Bromwich	14/256		
SPON-LANE R.O	D2	15JUN58	West Bromwich	14/256		
HIGH·STREET R.O	D2	15JUN58	West Bromwich	14/256		
CHURCHFIELD R.O	D2	15JUN58	West Bromwich	14/256		
BRADLEY	D4	15JUN58	Bilston	14/256		
BROOM	D4	15JUN58	Kidderminster	14/258		Note 34.
FORSBROOK	D1	16JUN58	Stafford	14/258		
ETTINGSHALL	D1	29JUN58	Wolverhampton	14/269		
PATTINGHAM	D1	29JUN58	Wolverhampton	14/269		
BILSTON ROAD R.O	D2	29JUN58	Wolverhampton	14/269		
CHAPEL-ASH R.O	D2	29JUN58	Wolverhampton	14/269	B	1JAN59-21DEC59
WOMBORNE	D1	29JUN58	Wolverhampton	14/269		Note 35.
TRYSULL	D4	29JUN58	Wolverhampton	14/269	B	4MAR60
WALSALL-RD R.O	D2	22JUL58	Wolverhampton	16/3		
WHITMORE·REAMS R.O	D2	22JUL58	Wolverhampton	16/3		
WALTON	D4	21OCT58	Stafford	16/62		
GOLDEN-HILL	D1	21OCT58	Stoke on Trent	16/64		
NEEDWOOD	D1	23OCT58	Burton on Trent	16/67	B	3DEC58-26NOV59.
WILLINGTON	D1	8NOV58	Burton on Trent	16/86		
NEWTON-SOLNEY	D1	8NOV58	Burton on Trent	16/86		
STAPENHILL	D1	8NOV58	Burton on Trent	16/86	B	23JUN59
HORNINGLOW·ST R.O	D2	8NOV58	Burton on Trent	16/86	B?	17JUN59
					BL	1FEB60
LULLINGTON	D1	8NOV58	Burton on Trent	16/86		
HARTSHORNE	D1	8NOV58	Burton on Trent	16/86		
CALDWELL	D1	8NOV58	Burton on Trent	16/86		
NEWHALL	D4	8NOV58	Burton on Trent	16/87		

Notes: 34. Returned by the postmaster (on the surveyor's instruction) on 31AUG58.
35. Annotated 'x': may not have been sent.

REPTON	D4	8NOV58	Burton on Trent	16/87	GR	20JAN59
					B	2AUG59
HILTON	D4	8NOV58	Burton on Trent	16/87		
FORD-HOUSES	D1	7DEC58	Wolverhampton	16/106		
SHORT-HEATH	D1	7DEC58	Wolverhampton	16/106		
SHENSTONE	D1	7DEC58	Lichfield	16/106	B	21MAR59
ALDRIDGE	D1	7DEC58	Walsall	16/106		
CLIFTON-CAMPVILLE	D1	7DEC58	Tamworth	16/106		
BURNTWOOD	D1	14DEC58	Lichfield	16/113		
WHITTINGTON	D1	14DEC58	Lichfield	16/113		
QUEESLET	D1	14DEC58	Birmingham	16/113		
KINGSBURY	D1	14DEC58	Tamworth	16/113		
WILNECOTE	D1	14DEC58	Tamworth	16/113		
CRADLEY	D4	18DEC58	Brierley Hill	16/118		
HART-STREET R.O	D2	20DEC58	Brierley Hill	16/119		
BROCKMOOR R.O	D2	20DEC58	Brierley Hill	16/119		
OAKAMOOR	D1	24DEC58	Stafford	16/121		
LONGDON STAFF.	D1	31DEC58	Rugeley	16/126		
CHURCH-EATON	D1	31DEC58	Stafford	16/126	B	18JAN59
HIMLEY	D4	21JAN59	Dudley	16/141		
OLD-HILL	D1	21JAN59	Dudley	16/142		
COALBURN-BROOK	D1	21JAN59	Stourbridge	16/144		Note 36.
COALBOURN·BROOK	D1	12FEB59	Stourbridge	16/158	BL	15SEP59
TRENTHAM	D1	17MAR59	Newcastle Staff	18/3	B	6JUN59-13MAR60
WALTON·ON-TRENT	D1	20APR59	Burton on Trent	18/30	B	3MAY59
ENVILLE	D4	14MAY59	Stourbridge	18/43		
CODSALL-WOOD	D1	8JUN59	Wolverhampton	18/57		
ESSINGTON	D1	12JUL59	Wolverhampton	18/72		
MADELEY STAFF.	D2	19AUG59	Newcastle Staff	18/96		
NORTHWOOD	D1	19AUG59	Stoke on Trent	18/96		

Notes: 36. Spelling error - re-issued below.

LEEK on a letter to Doncaster. Issued as an undated mileage stamp, the '154' mileage was removed in 1829 and the arcs subsequently added locally.

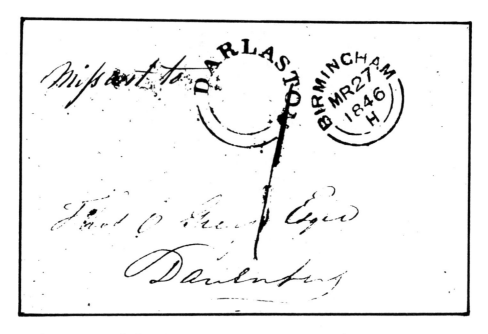

DARLASTON (5/121) in red ink used as a 'Missent' mark.

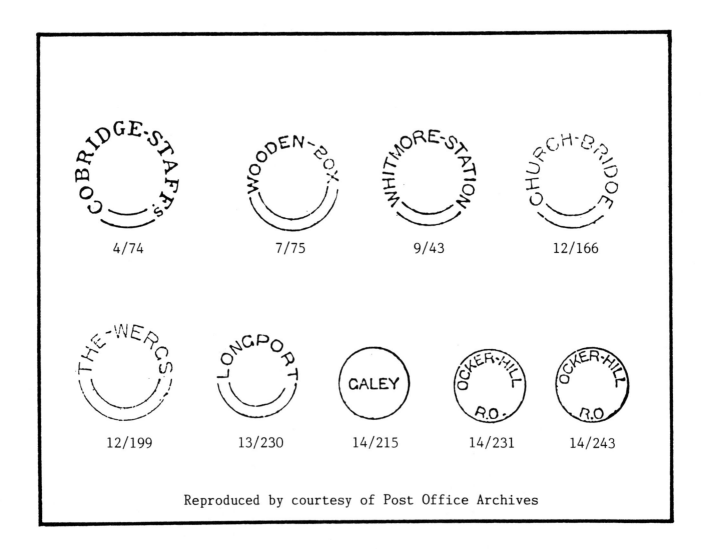

COBRIDGE-STAFFS 4/74	WOODEN-BOX 7/75	WHITMORE-STATION 9/43	CHURCH-BRIDGE 12/166
THE-WERCS 12/199	LONGPORT 13/230	GALEY 14/215	OCKER-HILL R.O. 14/231	OCKER-HILL R.O. 14/243

Reproduced by courtesy of Post Office Archives

Staffs

Similar Sans-serif (C1) Marks of Staffordshire (1)

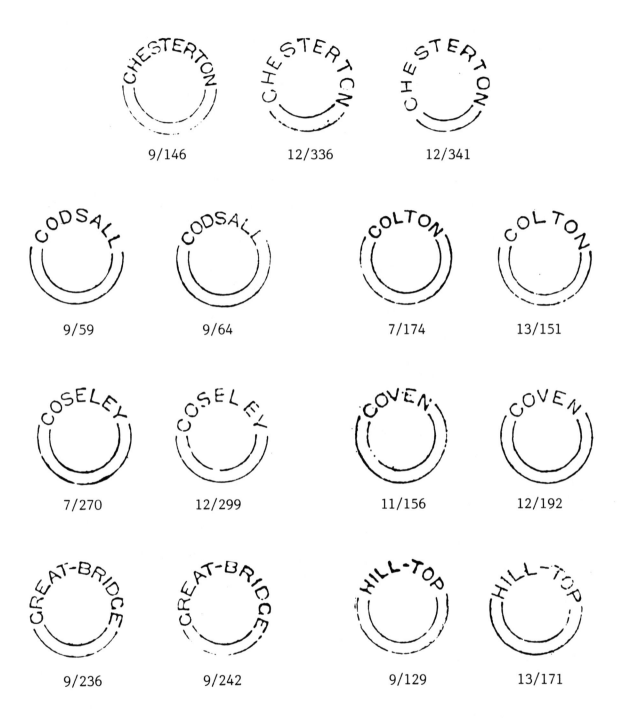

Reproduced by courtesy of Post Office Archives

Staffs 140.

Similar Sans-serif (C1) Marks of Staffordshire (2)

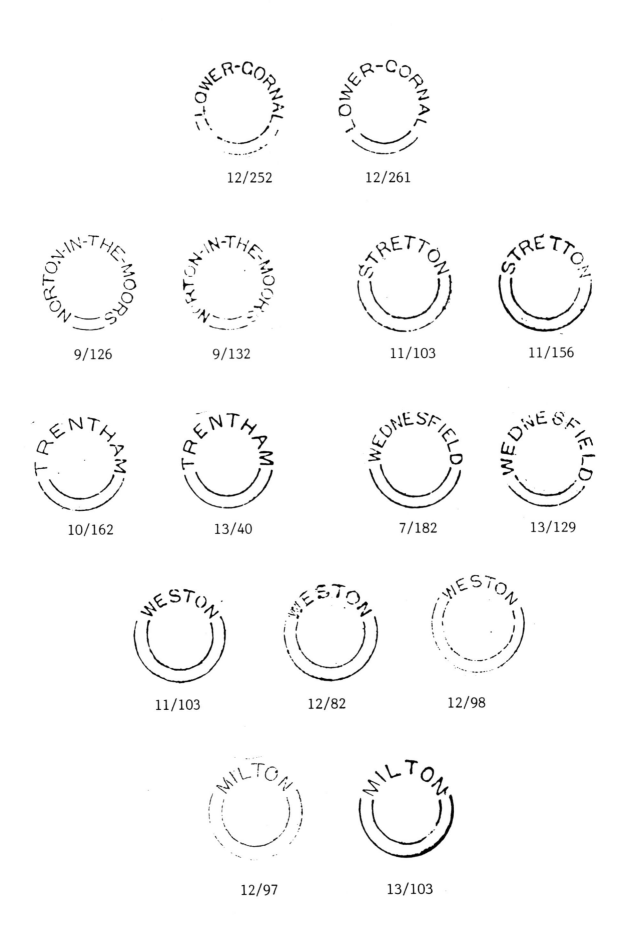

Reproduced by courtesy of Post Office Archives

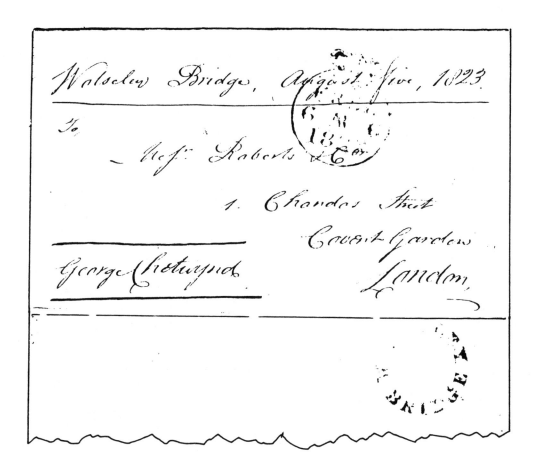

The newly-discovered early UDC of WOLSELEY BRIDGE used in 1823.
This type of seriffed stamp has not been recorded previously.

COMPTON (13/278*), the first type D3 stamp that
has been recorded from the Wolverhampton area.

Staffs 142.

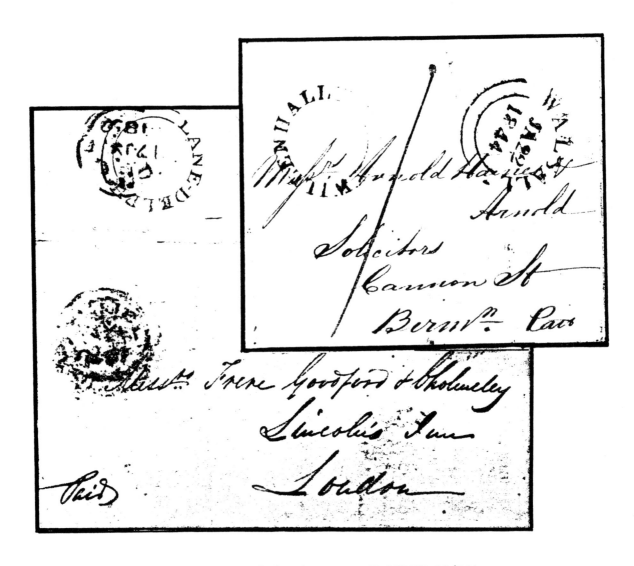

WILLENHALL (5/198) and LANE-DELPH (4/74)

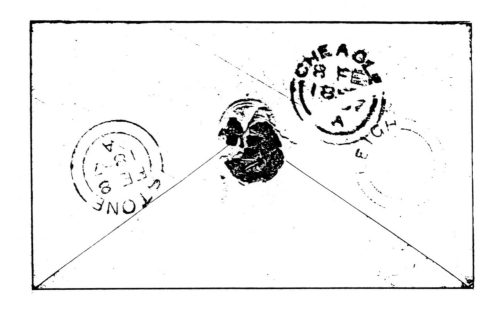

LEIGH (10/122), under Stone, in green ink.

WARWICKSHIRE

ATHERSTONE (33). Pre proof books

Appleby (Magna) + <u>1</u> 9/210 (CDS 24MAR59)
Ausley (Ansley) Boot End 11/105
Austrey 10/2 10/8
Baddesley 11/68
Chapel End 18/52
Hartshill 7/178
Hurley 9/155 16/51
Measham + <u>1</u> 9/210 16/51
Sheepy + <u>1</u> 9/210
Sibson <u>1</u> 9/51
Swepston(e) <u>1</u> 7/190 See TL11.
Twycross + <u>1</u> 9/210

COVENTRY (223).

Allesley 5/113 5/164 13/4 13/271*
Anst(e)y 9/7
Bedworth 5/164 (CDS 24MAY51) See TL3.
Berkeswell 7/171 16/82
Bishop's Street +
Brinklow 5/164
Carsley (Keresley?) 13/46
Coleshill (213) (CDS 29APR56) See TL23.
E(a)rlsdon 13/46
Fillongley 5/166 13/221
Foleshill 5/164 13/53
Hampton in Arden 11/109 18/24 See TL29.
Hill Field +
Keresley 14/207
Jordan Wells +
Lea Marston 11/12 See TL23.
Longford 13/46 18/45
Meriden 5/164
Ne(i)ther Whitacre 9/177 See TL23.
Nuneaton (957) 5/164 See TL3.
Railway Station (No mark yet found)
Ryton on Dunsmore 10/33
Sowe (Walsgrave-on-Sowe) 9/49 16/82
Spon End +
Stoke Green 18/93
Stonebridge 5/164
Stretton on Dunsmore + 5/164 See TL28.
Withybrook 12/137 13/271*
Wolston + 5/164 16/82.

KENILWORTH (950). 5/164 Note 1.
               (CDS 29MAY45)

Ashow 11/181
Baginton 9/177
Bubbenhall 13/271
Castle End Note 2.
Lower Kenilworth 14/63 14/80
Stoneleigh 12/170 16/1

KINETON (417). See TL4&9.

Chadshunt 9/84 9/93 See TL4&9?

LEAMINGTON SPA (444).
        1/101 1/105 (CDS 4JAN33)

Bishops Tachbrook 9/78 13/271
Cubbington 9/138 16/142
Harbury 9/77 14/204 See TL10.
Radford 9/138 18/78
South Parade + 14/216
Ufton 9/78 See TL10
Upper Parade + 14/111
Wappenbury 12/314
Whitnash 13/250

NUNEATON (957). 5/164
        (CDS 13JUL46) See TL3.

Astley 12/81?
Attleborough 10/274 16/161
Chilvers Coton 13/106
Shenton <u>1</u> 13/20
Stockingford + 9/96a 16/161
                Note 3.

RUGBY (659). 1/165 (CDS 9JAN40)

Ashby St Legers <u>2</u> 12/210
Bilton 12/181
Bishops Itchington 14/253
Bourton (on Dunsmore) 10/120
Catthorpe <u>1</u> 9/27 13/208
Churchover 12/330
Cotesbach <u>1</u> 12/292 See TL22.

Notes:
1. Under Coventry until c 1845.
2. Probably used the Kenilworth UDC from JUL45.
3. 9/96a sent to Hinckley in error.

+ indicates an office which used a straight line (or P.P.) stamp after 1840.

An underlined number, eg <u>1</u>, indicates an office outside Warks - see key at end.

Warks

Rugby (Cont'd)

Hill Morton 7/271
Kilsby + 2 12/232 See TL2,18&19.
Long Itchington 12/181
Long Lawford 14/234
Monks Kirby 9/178 18/80 See TL26.
Newbold on Avon 12/250
(King's) Newnham + 2 9/98 14/199
Northend 14/240
Pailton 7/142 See TL26.
Priors Marston 11/124
South Kilworth 1 12/210
Stockton 12/181
Stretton under Fosse 12/250
Thurlaston 12/321
Wormleighton 11/227 16/163
Yelvertoft 2 7/270

SHIPSTON ON STOUR (706). 1/177 (CDS 31MAR37)

Brailes 5/76 16/161
Burmington 13/236
Cherington 5/76 16/161
Ilmington 14/212
Newbold (on Stour) 14/212
Tredington 11/135 16/161

SOUTHAM (722). See TL6&10.

Gran(d)borough 9/32 See TL10,24&25.
Leamington Hastings 7/179 See TL6&10.
Marton 7/179 See TL6&10.
Napton 7/66 See TL6&10.

STRATFORD ON AVON (754).

Alcester (755) 1/2 (CDS 17MAR46) See TL8.
Alderminster 10/23
Alveston 11/159 16/163
Bearley 11/159
Bidford (on Avon) 5/167
    (CDS 4JUL51) 16/88 See TL8.
Church Street 10/198
Clifford Chambers 11/159
Eatington/Ettington 10/22 16/163
Great Alne 9/31 14/192 See TL15.
Hockley Heath + 11/26 14/134 See TL15.
Lighthorne 10/44 See TL7.
Long Marston 11/159
Luddington 14/37
Snitterfield 9/78 16/163
Studley (141) + 5/32 (CDS 27JUN54) See TL1.

Tanworth 9/151 See TL15.
Tiddington 7/87 16/163
Ullenhall 11/159 See TL15.
Welford 10/205
Wellesbo(u)rne 5/167
    (CDS 18AUG58) See TL9.
Wootton Wawen 11/159 14/192
    See TL15.

WARWICK (848).

Barford + 13/154
Butlers Marston 14/2
Claverdon 9/128
Edmonscote/Emscote 7/4
    13/227 18/36
Hampton Lucy 10/275 18/36
Haseley 7/229
Hatton 11/197 18/36
Leek Wotton 9/192
Loxley 13/253
Rowington 14/2
Tysoe 11/106
Wasperton 12/252 12/261

BANBURY (46), Oxon

Avon Dassett 9/150
Farnborough 11/191
Fenny Compton 11/191 See TL16.
Radway 10/100
Warmington 11/121

BIRMINGHAM (75).

Bickenhill 12/331 See TL30.
Curdworth + 12/331
Henley in Arden (78) 1/74
    (CDS 28MAR50)
Lapworth 12/331
Water Orton 12/331 14/192

BROMSGROVE (139), Worcs

Coughton 12/324

CHIPPING NORTON (195), Oxon

Long Compton 5/168 16/161
    See TL14.

+ indicates an office which used a straight line (or P.P.) stamp after 1840.

An underlined number, eg 2, indicates an office outside Warks - see key at end.

Warks

DAVENTRY (238), Northants

Barby 2 12/129 See TL19.
Braunston + See TL25.
Crick 2 7/246 See TL17.
West Haddon 2 + 7/211 (CDS 11JUL56) See TL20.

EVESHAM (284), Worcs

Salford Prior(s) 10/146

FAZELEY (297), Staffs

Kingsbury 9/178 16/113 See TL5.
Wilmcott/Wilnecote 9/177 10/139
           16/113 See TL5 and Note 4.

HINCKLEY (365), Leics

Bulkington 7/234 16/161 See TL13.
Wolvey 7/161 16/160 See TL13&27.

LUTTERWORTH (483), Leics

Swinford 1 7/229 See TL21.
Wibtoft 10/192 14/183
Wiley 16/143.

MORETON IN MARSH (534), Glos

Barton in/on the Heath 10/162

TAMWORTH (774), Staffs Note 4.

Middleton 13/237
Newton (Regis) 12/51
Polesworth 10/3

WELFORD (857), Northants
           (CDS 9MAR40) See TL12.

Husbands Bosworth 1 7/75 18/88
  (CDS 14OCT59) See TL12 & Note 5.
Lubenham 1 7/39 14/207 16/161
           See TL12 & Note 6.
Naseby 2 7/185 12/204 14/207
           See TL12.
North Kilworth 1 7/230 14/197
           See TL12.
Theddingworth 1 7/39 14/197
           See TL12 & Note 6.

Notes: 4. Partly in Warwickshire until 1890.
         5. See Leics Notes 1 and 2.
         6. 7/39 sent to Market Harborough.

KEY to offices not in Warwickshire

1 is in Leicestershire
2 is in Northamptonshire.

Warks   146.

TRANSFERS - Warwickshire

TL 1.   Studley from Stratford on Avon to Bromsgrove between 1841 and 1844.

2.   Kilsby from Daventry to Rugby on 27NOV46.

3.   Nuneaton (previously under Coventry) became a post town in 1847. (Bedworth did not become a sub-office of Nuneaton until 1854, three years after it became a Money Order Office.)

4.   Kineton reduced to a sub-office under Stratford on 29JUL48.

5.   Kingsbury and Wilmcott to Tamworth when Fazeley was reduced to a sub-office under Tamworth on 23APR49.

6.   Southam reduced to a sub-office under Leamington on 31JUL49.

7.   Lighthorne possibly from Stratford to Warwick at an unknown date between 1849 & 1854 but it may never have been under Stratford.

8.   Alcester and Bidford from Stratford to Bromsgrove on 5JUN51.

9.   Kineton and Wellesbourne from Stratford to Warwick on 28JUN51.

10.   Harbury, Ufton and Southam from Leamington to Rugby on 5JUL51. (Probably Grandborough, Leamington Hastings, Marton and Napton moved with Southam.)

11.   Swepstone from Atherstone to Ashby de la Zouch in 1852.

12.   Welford reduced to a sub-office under Rugby on 7MAR53. (Welford had five sub-offices at the time which would also have moved.)

13.   Wolvey and Bulkington from Hinckley to Nuneaton on 18JUL54.

14.   Long Compton may have transferred from Chipping Norton to Shipston on Stour, either in 1854 or between 1856 and 1859, or it may have been subordinate to both offices.

15.   Great Alne, Tanworth, Ullenhall, Wootton Wawen and (probably) Hockley Heath under both Stratford and Birmingham from 1854.

16.   Fenny Compton to Rugby on 31AUG54, probably from Banbury.

17.   Crick from Daventry to Rugby on 9FEB55.

18.   Kilsby from Rugby to Daventry on 9FEB55.

19.   Barby and Kilsby from Daventry to Rugby on 1JUN55.

20.   West Haddon from Daventry to Rugby on 24FEB56.

21.   Swinford from Lutterworth to Rugby on 24FEB56.

22.   Cotesbach from Rugby to Lutterworth on 17MAR56.

23.   Coleshill, (Nether) Whitacre and Lea Marston from Coventry to Birmingham on 19NOV56.

TL24.   Grandborough from Rugby to Daventry, possibly briefly in 1856.
25.   Braunston and Grandborough from Daventry to Rugby on 21FEB57.
26.   Monk's Kirby and Pailton from Rugby to Lutterworth on 16AUG58.
27.   Wolvey from Nuneaton to Hinckley on 16AUG59.
28.   Stretton on Dunsmore from Coventry to Rugby on 31AUG59.
29.   Hampton in Arden from Coventry to Birmingham on 9SEP59.
30.   Bickenhill from Birmingham to Coventry on 9SEP59.

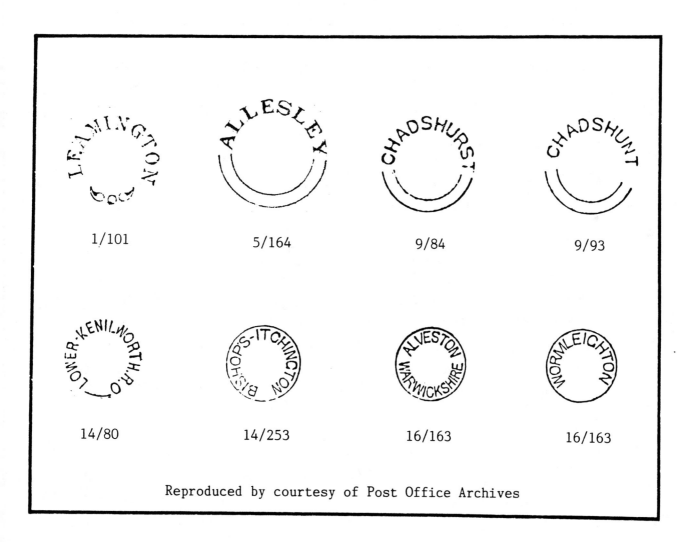

Reproduced by courtesy of Post Office Archives

Instructions No. 57, 1854.

By Command of the Postmaster General.

NOTICE TO THE PUBLIC,
AND
Instructions to all Postmasters,
ISSUING AND PAYING
MONEY ORDERS.

GENERAL POST OFFICE,
September, 1854.

ENGLAND.

Minor Money Order Offices will be opened at the undermentioned Places on the respective dates named:—

	COUNTY	Head Office (when the Office itself is not a Head Office)	
Tow Law	Durham	Darlington	2nd October.
Bramley	York	Leeds	10th do.
Cleckheaton	York	Leeds	12th do.

The Post Office at *Bedworth*, formerly under Coventry, is now a Sub-Office to *Nuneaton*.

IRELAND.

The undermentioned Major Money Order Offices will be reduced to *Minor* Offices on the respective dates named. Postmasters must, therefore, after those dates pay no Money Order issued at these Offices, unless the corresponding Advice shall have been received by them through the Chief Money Order Office, Dublin, with the Stamp of that Office affixed to the document:—

A typical notice advising the public (and postmasters) of the opening of new Money Order Offices. Although Nuneaton became a post town in 1847, it does not appear that Bedworth was transferred from Coventry to Nuneaton until September 1854, three years after it became a Money Order Office and was issued with a circular datestamp.

Warks

WARWICKSHIRE

LEAMINGTON	C3C	29DEC25	Leamington	1/101	B	5APR26-28MAY28
LEAMINGTON	C2*				B	21JUN28-27DEC29
					R	7SEP29-30OCT29
ATHERSTONE	C2*				B	29JUL28-22JAN40
HENLEY IN ARDEN	C3	29AUG28	Henley in Arden	1/74	OR/R	13SEP30- 5FEB41.
					B	31MAR41-21OCT47
					BL	18MAY49-10JAN50
AULCESTER	C2*	22MAY29	Alcester	1/2	OR/R	16OCT29-13AUG40.
					B	28MAY41- 5NOV45
					BR	22MAY44
SHIPSTONE ON STOUR	C3A	7SEP29	Shipston on S	1/177	B	6APR31-10AUG36.
LEAMINGTON	C2	27SEP30	Leamington	1/105	B	28NOV31- 9JAN33
RUGBY	C2*	14DEC31	Rugby	1/165	B	7JAN32- 3DEC38
STUDLEY	C2	30SEP41	Stratford on A	5/32	B	10NOV41- 8JUN48
					BL	20SEP49-27NOV52.
BRAILES	C2	25FEB42	Shipston on S	5/76	B	27MAY44
					BL	20SEP50-26NOV53
					BL/GR	16JUL54
CHERRINGTON	C2	25FEB42	Shipston on S	5/76	B	12MAY43
					BL	16MAY54-27JAN55
ALLESBY	C2	20AUG42	Coventry	5/113		Note 1.
ALLESLEY	C2	14JUN43	Coventry	5/164	B	23FEB44.
BEDWORTH	C2	14JUN43	Coventry	5/164	B	25JAN45-11FEB50
BRINKLOW	C2	14JUN43	Coventry	5/164	B	19MAY44-20NOV46
					BR	22OCT45
					GR	19NOV55
FOLESHILL	C2	14JUN43	Coventry	5/164	B	14SEP44-18JAN50
MERIDEN	C2	14JUN43	Coventry	5/164	B	28MAY52-15MAY59
					GR	3AUG56
					BL/B	29JUN58- 20OCT59
					GR/B	8FEB59-13FEB59.
NUNEATON	C2	14JUN43	Coventry	5/164	B	20OCT43-18DEC44.
KENILWORTH	C2	14JUN43	Coventry	5/164	B	15MAY44-12OCT53
STONEBRIDGE	C2	14JUN43	Coventry	5/164	B	23FEB44- 2MAY48
					BR	11FEB47
STRETTON-ON-DUNSMORE	C2	14JUN43	Coventry	5/164	B	20OCT43-20NOV58.
					GR	14FEB58
WOLSTON	C2	14JUN43	Coventry	5/164	B	2FEB47-13NOV56
					BR	10CT49
					GR	20OCT56-28DEC57
FILLONGLEY	C2	29JUN43	Coventry	5/166	B	19NOV48
					GR	12MAY56- JUL56
BIDFORD	C2	4JUL43	Stratford on A	5/167	B	21OCT43-30MAR47.
WELLESBORNE	C2	4JUL43	Stratford on A	5/167	R	APR41- 5DEC51
					OR	24MAY44-10JAN49
					BL	12MAR50- 4JUL55
LONG-COMPTON	C2	5JUL43	Chipping Norton	5/168	B	8NOV44-20JUL46.
					BL	22NOV56
EDMONSCOTE	C2	6DEC43	Warwick	7/4	B	31MAR46-21JUL55
LUBBENHAM	C2	18MAR44	Mkt Harborough	7/39	B	44-13MAR55
THEDDINGWORTH	C2	18MAR44	Mkt Harborough	7/39	B	14DEC44- 55
					GR	27AUG56-28FEB57.
NAPTON	C1	31MAY44	Southam	7/66	B	21AUG45-30OCT56
					GR	19MAY52
HUSBANDS-BOSWORTH	C1	28JUN44	Lutterworth	7/75	B	31OCT45-14NOV49.
					GR	8JAN56-12MAR57
					B	11FEB58
TIDDINGTON	C1	13AUG44	Stratford on A	7/87	BL	28JUL51
PAILTON	C1	8MAY45	Rugby	7/142	B	22JUL55
					GR	OCT56

Notes: 1. Incorrect spelling - corrected below.

Warks

Name			Office	Ref	Colour	Date
WOLVEY	C1	7JUL45	Hinckley	7/161	OR	3DEC50
					R	25AUG51
					BL/GR	19MAY52
					GR	54
BERKSWELL	C1	25AUG45	Coventry	7/171	B	2MAR46-21APR49
					Gy/GR	24JUL56
HARTSHILL	C1	26SEP45	Atherstone	7/178	B	30MAY47- 5MAY54
					GR	19JAN56
LEAMINGTON-HASTINGS	C1	26SEP45	Southam	7/179	B	30NOV55-14APR56.
					GR	4OCT56
					BL	JUN59
MARTON	C1	26SEP45	Southam	7/179	B	25APR52
					BL	11MAR54
NASEBY	C1	25OCT45	Welford	7/185	B	46- 5MAR55.
SWEPSTON	C1	18NOV45	Atherstone	7/190	B	12AUG46
					BR	51
					GR	3MAR56- 3MAR57.
WEST-HADDON	C1	14FEB46	Daventry	7/211	OR	29OCT49
					R	27JUL50- 51
SWINFORD	C1	20APR46	Lutterworth	7/229		
HASELEY	C1	20APR46	Warwick	7/229	B	12AUG46- 53.
NORTH-KILWORTH	C1	20APR46	Welford	7/230	B	16MAR50-24AUG53
BULKINGTON	C1	1MAY46		7/234	R	12JUL54
CRICK	C1	27JUN46	Daventry	7/246	BL	28FEB60.
YELVERTOFT	C1	29SEP46	Rugby	7/270	OR	12OCT49
HILLMORTON	C1	2OCT46	Hill-Morton	7/271		
ANSTEY	C1	28JAN47	Coventry	9/7		
CALTHORPE	C1	12MAR47	Rugby	9/27	B	17NOV48-10APR55
GREAT-ALNE	C1	19APR47	Stratford on A	9/31	BL	9JAN52
GRANBOROUGH	C1	27APR47	Southam	9/32	GR	27FEB55
SOWE	C1	7JUN47	Coventry	9/49	B	24NOV53
					BL	6APR58.
SIBSON	C1	11JUN47	Atherstone	9/51		
HARBURY	C1	11SEP47	Leamington	9/77	OR	13APR49- 2NOV55
SNITTERSFIELD	C1	11SEP47	Stratford on A	9/78	BL	50-28JAN53 Note 2.
BISHOPS-TACHBROOK	C1	11SEP47	Leamington	9/78	B	24NOV47-13NOV49.
					R	5JUL55
					OR	28JUN57
					GR	28JUL58.
UFTON	C1	11SEP47	Leamington	9/78		
CHADHURST	C1	10CT47	Kineton	9/84		Note 1.
CHADSHUNT	C1	19OCT47	Kineton	9/93		
STOCKINGFORD	C1	12NOV47	Hinckley	9/96a		
NEWNHAM	C1	12NOV47	Rugby	9/98		
CLAVERDON	C1	3MAR48	Warwick	9/128		
CUBBINGTON	C1	29MAR48	Leamington	9/138	R	8JUN48
					OR	9JUL53
RADFORD	C1	29MAR48	Leamington	9/138	BL/GR	29JUN57
AVON-DASSETT	C1	24MAY48	Bristol	9/150	B	27MAR49
					BL	? Note 3.
TANWORTH	C1	24MAY48	Stratford on A	9/151	BL	24MAR51-16JAN56
HURLEY	C1	3JUN48	Atherstone	9/155	B	5NOV49
BAGINTON	C1	28AUG48	Kenilworth	9/177	B	29JAN50-12JUL50
WILMCOTT	C1	28AUG48	Fazeley	9/177	B	20MAR50
NEITHER-WHITACRE	C1	28AUG48	Coleshill	9/177		
KINGSBURY	C1	28AUG48	Fazeley	9/178	R	49
MONKSKIRBY	C1	28AUG48	Rugby	9/178	B	5OCT50.
LEEK-WOOTTON	C1	19NOV48	Warwick	9/192		

Notes: 2. Found used as 'SNITTER FIELD'.
3. Sent to Bristol in error - should be Banbury.

Warks

Name		Date	Location	Ref		
SHEEPY	C1	1FEB49	Atherstone	9/210		
APPLEBY	C1	1FEB49	Atherstone	9/210	B	19FEB50-27MAR52
TWYCROSS	C1	1FEB49	Atherstone	9/210	GR	8JUL57-26DEC57
					B	14MAY58-27OCT59
MEASHAM	C1	1FEB49	Atherstone	9/210		
ANSTREY	C1	31MAY49	Atherstone	10/2		Note 1.
POLESWORTH	C1	31MAY49	Tamworth	10/3	B	NOV50-22JUN58
					R	20MAR55
					BL	59
AUSTREY	C1	6JUN49	Atherstone	10/8	BL	29OCT51
					B	28NOV51
EATINGTON	C1	10JUL49	Stratford on A	10/22	B	JUN49
					BL	21JUN51- 2SEP55.
					GR	8JUL53
					OR	26JUL58
ALDERMINSTER	C1	10JUL49	Stratford on A	10/23	B	50- 4FEB52.
					BL/GR	31DEC59
RYTON-ON-DUNSMORE	C1	23AUG49	Coventry	10/33	B	6AUG55
LIGHTHORNE	C1	9OCT49	Stratford on A	10/44		
RADWAY	C1	6AUG50	Banbury	10/100		
BOURTON	C1	8NOV50	Rugby	10/120		
WILNECOTE	C1	9JAN51	Tamworth	10/139	OR	14OCT54
					R/BR	5JUN55
SALFORD-PRIOR	C1	29JAN51	Evesham	10/146	BL	30APR58
					B	5DEC58
BARTON-IN-THE-HEATH	C1	1MAR51	Moreton in M	10/162	B	12AUG58
WEBTOFT	C1	24APR51	Lutterworth	10/192		
CHURCH-ST	C1	18MAY51	Stratford on A	10/198	BL	22DEC51-18JAN59
					BL/GR	11MAY52- 9APR56
					B	13FEB52
					R	JAN57-27APR57.
WELFORD-ON-AVON	C1	27MAY51	Stratford on A	10/205	OR	17APR55
ATTLEBOROUGH	C1	6OCT51	Nuneaton	10/274		
HAMPTON·LUCY	C1	6OCT51	Hampton Lucy	10/275		
LEA-MARSTON	C1	9JAN52	Coventry	11/12		
HOCKLEY·HEATH	C1	6MAR52	Stratford on A	11/26	BL	2APR52-26MAY52
					BR	17JAN56-29APR56
					B	15JUL57-24AUG57.
BADDESLEY	C1	11JUN52	Atherstone	11/68		
BOOT	C1	SEP52	Atherstone	11/105		
TYSOE	C1	OCT52	Warwick	11/106	B	29AUG56
HAMPTON-IN-ARDEN	C1	OCT52	Coventry	11/109	GR	57
					B	17MAY58
WARMINGTON	C1	DEC52	Banbury	11/121		
PRIORS-MERSTON	C1	DEC52	Rugby	11/124	BL/GR	12JAN55-17MAR57.
					GR	1MAY56
TREDINGTON	C1	JAN53	Shipston on S	11/135		
ULLENHALL	C1	APR53	Stratford on A	11/159		
WOOTTON-WALWEN	C1	APR53	Stratford on A	11/159		
CLIFFORD·CHAMBERS	C1	APR53	Stratford on A	11/159	B	56
					BL	58
LONG·MARSTON	C1	APR53	Stratford on A	11/159	R	8FEB55
					OR	12SEP56
BEARLEY	C1	APR53	Stratford on A	11/159		
ALVESTON	C1	APR53	Stratford on A	11/159		
ASHOW	C1	JUN53	Kenilworth	11/181		
FENNY-COMPTON	C1	29JUN53	Banbury	11/191	B	25OCT59
FARNBOROUGH	C1	29JUN53	Banbury	11/191	BL/GR	21OCT57
HATTON	C1	JUL53	Warwick	11/197	BL	3SEP57.
WORMLEIGHTON	C1	SEP53	Rugby	11/227		
NEWTON	C1	APR54	Tamworth	12/51		

Warks   152.

ASTLEY	C1	cJUN54		12/81		
MARTON	C1	cJUL54		12/92		
BARBY	C1	27OCT54	Daventry	12/129	BL/GR	13APR57
					BL	3SEP59
WITHYBROOK	C1	7DEC54	Coventry	12/137		
STONELEIGH	C1	20MAR55	Kenilworth	12/170		
BILTON	C1	30MAR55	Rugby	12/181	BL	12AUG55
STOCKTON	C1	30MAR55	Rugby	12/181	GR	30NOV55-18MAR57
					BL	14APR56- JUN59
					Y	17MAR57
LONG·ITCHINGTON	C1	30MAR55	Rugby	12/181		
NASEBY	C1	20MAY55	Welford	12/204	B	7MAR57
ASHBY-ST-LEGERS	C1	13JUN55	Rugby	12/210	GR	57
SOUTH·KILWORTH	C1	15JUN55	Rugby	12/210		
KILSBY	C1	10AUG55	Rugby	12/232	GR	56- 57.
					B	25APR59
					BL	26APR59- 60
NEWBOLD-ON-AVON	C1	20OCT55	Rugby	12/250	GR	16MAR56-17MAY56.
STRETTON-UNDER-						
FOSSE	C1	20OCT55	Rugby	12/250		
WASPERTON	C1	5OCT55	Warwick	12/252		
WASPERTON	C1	5NOV55	Warwick	12/261		
COTESBACH	C1	5JAN56	Rugby	12/292		
WAPPENBURY	C1	17FEB56	Leamington	12/314		
THURLASTON	C1	4MAR56	Rugby	12/321		
COUGHTON	C1	22MAR56	Bromsgrove	12/324	B	9SEP58-25FEB59.
CHURCH-OVER	C1	22MAR56	Rugby	12/330		
CURDWORTH	C1	25MAR56	Birmingham	12/331		
LAPWORTH	C1	25MAR56	Birmingham	12/331		
WATER-ORTON	C1	25MAR56	Birmingham	12/331	BL	MAY58
BICKENHILL	C1	25MAR56	Birmingham	12/331		
ALLESLEY	C1	2MAY56	Coventry	13/4		
SHENTON	C1	11JUN56	Nuneaton	13/20		
LONGFORD	C1	29JUL56	Coventry	13/46		
ERLSDON	C1	29JUL56	Coventry	13/46		Note 4.
CARSLEY	C1	29JUL56	Coventry	13/46		Note 4.
FOLESHILL	C1	7AUG56	Coventry	13/53		
CHILVERS-COTON	C1	9DEC56	Nuneaton	13/106		
BARFORD	C1	23FEB57	Warwick	13/154		
CATTHORPE	C1	7APR57	Rugby	13/208		
FILLONGLEY	C1*	29APR57	Coventry	13/221		
EMSCOTE	C1*	4MAY57	Warwick	13/227	GR	2JUL57.
BURMINGTON	C1*	16MAY57	Shipston	13/236		
MIDDLETON	C1*	16MAY57	Tamworth	13/237	B	18APR59
WHITNASH	C1*	8JUN57	Leamington	13/250		
LOXLEY	C1*	15JUN57	Warwick	13/253		
BUBBENHALL	C1*	14JUL57	Kenilworth	13/271	B	1SEP59.
BISHOPS TACHBROOK	C1*	14JUL57	Leamington	13/271		
ALLESLEY	D3	cJUL57			B	15APR59
WITHYBROOK	D3	cJUL57			BL	26SEP58.
ROWINGTON	C4	5AUG57	Warwick	14/2	B	12AUG58
BUTLERS-MARSTON	C4	5AUG57	Warwick	14/2		
LUDDINGTON	C4	28SEP57	Stratford on A	14/37		
LOWER-KENILWORTH	D2	22OCT57	Kenilworth	14/63		
LOWER·						
KENILWORTH.R.O	C4	14NOV57	Kenilworth	14/80	B	28NOV59-27DEC59.
UPPER PARADE R.O	D1	23DEC57	Leamington	14/111	B	AUG58-31DEC59
					BL	28NOV59
HOCKLEY-HEATH	D1	3FEB58	Birmingham	14/134	B	15DEC58
WIBTOFT	D4	31MAR58	Lutterworth	14/183		

Notes: 4. Mis-spellings of E̲arlsdon & Keresley?

GT ALNE	D4	6APR58	Birmingham	14/192	BL/B	29NOV59	
WOOTTON-WAWEN	D1	6APR58	Birmingham	14/192	BL/B	23AUG59	
WATER-ORTON	D1	6APR58	Birmingham	14/192			
NTH-KILWORTH	D1	13APR58	Rugby	14/197			
THEDDINGWORTH	D1	13APR58	Rugby	14/197	GR	28FEB57	
					B	18JUN59-12DEC59	
KING'S·NEWNHAM	D1	15APR58	Rugby	14/199			
HARBURY	D4	22APR58	Rugby	14/204	B	28SEP59	
LUBBENHAM	D1	22APR58	Rugby	14/207	B	30AUG58	
NASEBY	D4	22APR58	Rugby	14/207			
KERESLEY	D1	22APR58	Coventry	14/207			
NEWBOLD	D4	22APR58	Shipston on S	14/212			
ILMINGTON	D1	22APR58	Shipston on S	14/212			
SOUTH·PARADE R.O.	D2	1MAY58	Leamington	14/216	B	22MAR59-23APR59	
LONG-LAWFORD	D1	22MAY58	Rugby	14/234			
NORTHEND	D1	22MAY58	Rugby	14/240			
BISHOPS-ITCHINGTON	D1	5JUN58	Rugby	14/253			
STONELEIGH	D1	22JUL58	Kenilworth	16/1			
HURLEY	D4	30SEP58	Atherstone	16/51			
MEASHAM	D4	30SEP58	Atherstone	16/51	B	?	
SOWE	D4	5NOV58	Coventry	16/82			
WOLSTON	D4	5NOV58	Coventry	16/82	BL	58	
BERKSWELL	D1	5NOV58	Coventry	16/82			
BIDFORD	D4	23NOV58	Bromsgrove	16/88			
KINGSBURY	D1	14DEC58	Tamworth	16/113			
WILNECOTE	D1	14DEC58	Tamworth	16/113			
CUBBINGTON	D1	21JAN59	Leamington	16/142			
WILLY	D4	21JAN59	Lutterworth	16/143			
WOLVEY	D4	18FEB59	Nuneaton	16/160			
LUBENHAM	D1	18FEB59	Rugby	16/161	B	4APR59-30DEC59	
TREDINGTON	D1	18FEB59	Shipston on S	16/161			
CHERRINGTON	D1	18FEB59	Shipston on S	16/161			
LOWER·BRAILES	D1	18FEB59	Shipston on S	16/161			
LONG·COMPTON	D1	18FEB59	Shipston on S	16/161			
ATTLEBOROUGH	D1	18FEB59	Nuneaton	16/161			
BULKINGTON	D1	18FEB59	Nuneaton	16/161			
STOCKINGFORD	D1	18FEB59	Nuneaton	16/161			
WORMLEIGHTON	D1	23FEB59	Rugby	16/163			
SNITTERFIELD	D1	23FEB59	Stratford on A	16/163			
ALVESTON WARWICKSHIRE	D2	23FEB59	Stratford on A	16/163	B	13JUL59	
TIDDINGTON	D1	23FEB59	Stratford on A	16/163	BL	3JAN60	
UPPER·EATINGTON	D1	23FEB59	Stratford on A	16/163			
HAMPTON-IN-ARDEN	D1	9APR59	Coventry	18/24			
EMSCOTE	D4	29APR59	Warwick	18/36	B	1SEP59.	
HATTON	D4	29APR59	Warwick	18/36			
HAMPTON LUCY	D1	29APR59	Warwick	18/36			
LONGFORD WARW.	D2	18MAY59	Coventry	18/45			
CHAPEL END	D1	6JUN59	Atherstone	18/52			
RADFORD·SEMELE	D1	19JUL59	Leamington	18/78			
MONKS·KIRBY	D1	19JUL59	Lutterworth	18/80			
HUSBAND'S·BOSWORTH	D1	12AUG59	Rugby	18/88			
STOKE·GREEN	D1	12AUG59	Coventry	18/93			

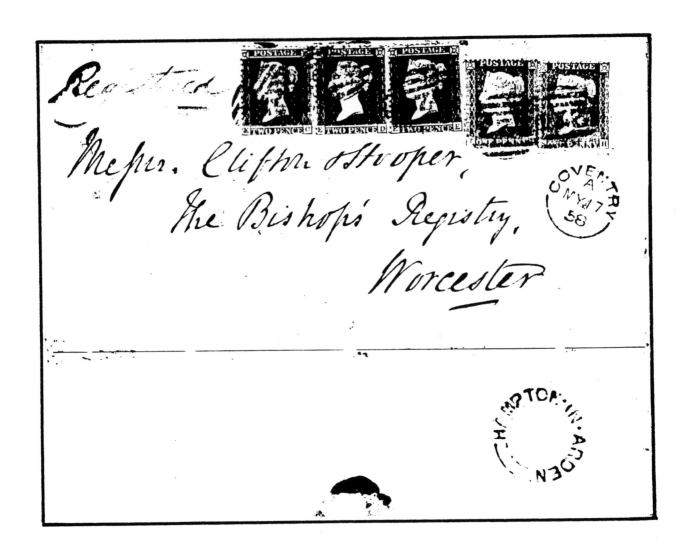

HAMPTON·IN·ARDEN (11/109) on a registered letter of 1858.

Similar Sans-serif (C1) Marks of Warwickshire

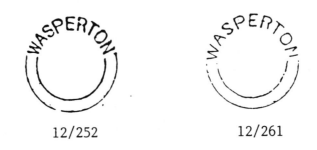

12/252   12/261

Reproduced by courtesy of Post Office Archives

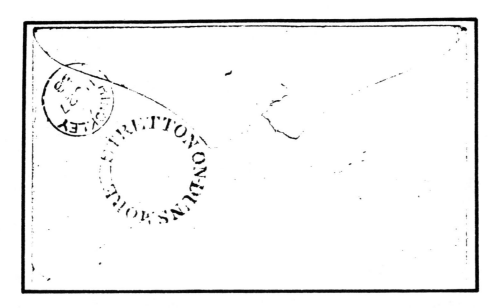

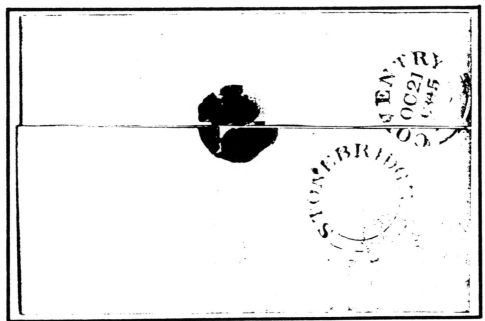

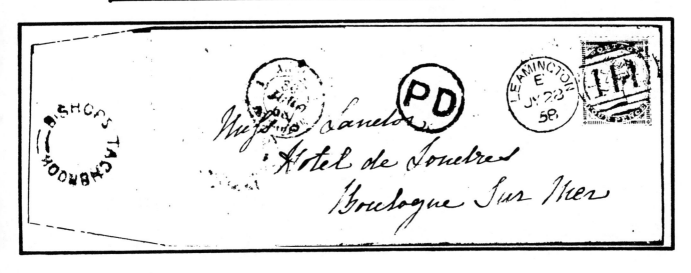

Above: STRETTON ON DUNSMORE (5/1640

Centre: STONEBRIDGE (5/164)

Below: BISHOPS TACHBROOK (13/271)

BIRMINGHAM

BIRMINGHAM (75).

Acocks Green 12/331
Alcester Lane End 12/331
Ashtead Row + (CDS MAR54) 13/250*
Aston 9/44
Aston New Town 11/106
Aston Park 12/331
Aston Road + 9/79
Balsall Heath 10/99
Bartley Green 13/197
Beech Lane 14/192
Bickenhill 12/331 See TL5.
Birchfields 9/44
Brierley Hill (995) + (CDS 19FEB49) See TL1.
Bristol Street + (CDS 22SEP58) 13/250*
Camp Hill +
Cape of Good Hope 11/129 14/192
Castle Bromwich + 12/276 13/250* 14/192
Catherine-A-Barns 12/331
Curdworth @ 12/331
Deritend + (CDS MAR54)
Duddeston Row + 5/86 14/192
Edgbaston @ 9/117 (CDS MAR54)
Elmdon @ 12/275
Erdington + 12/275
Five Ways + 14/192 (CDS 4SEP58)
Gooch Street + 11/161 14/192
Gravelly Hill 12/331
Great Barr @ 12/137
Great Hampton Street + 11/206 (CDS MAR54) 13/210
Halesowen + 9/1 (CDS 24SEP49)
Hall Green 10/2 16/142
Hampstead 13/51 13/250*
Hampstead Road 10/193
Handsworth + 12/7 (CDS 28JUN55)
Harborne 7/17 13/250*
Harborne Heath 12/93
Henley in Arden (78) (CDS 28MAR50)
Highgate 9/7 (CDS 4SEP58)
Hockley Hill + 7/129 14/140
Hollywood 14/199
Icknield Street + 12/40 14/192
Kings Heath 12/331
Kings Norton @ 12/276
Knowle + 12/275 14/105
Ladywood +
Lancaster Street + 14/192
Langley 11/248
Lapworth 12/331
Lee Crescent 11/157
Little Aston 12/331
Lozells + 9/177 14/192
Marston Green 12/331
Mere Green 13/57 13/250*.

Milpool Hill 13/250
Minworth 12/275 14/105*
Monument Lane 13/250*
Moseley 7/66 13/250*
Nechells Green 11/129
Northfield @ 12/276
Oldbury (035) + (CDS 24MAY51)
                                        12/7
Oscott 12/331 14/105
Over Witton 12/331
Parade 16/26
Penns 9/27 9/70 13/250* 14/192
Perry 12/331
Queslett 13/48 16/113
Quinton 12/129
Redhill 13/63
Saltley 11/129
Sandpits + 14/192
Selly Oak 12/331
Shirley (Street) @ 11/143 13/51
Small Heath 9/51 13/192 13/250*
                                       14/192
Smethwick (034) @ (CDS 21MAY55)
Solihull (719) + 7/17*
Sparkbrook 9/27 14/192
Stirchley 12/331 13/250*
Summer Lane + 10/116 13/250*
                                       14/192
Sutton Coldfield + (CDS 19FEB49)
Washwood Heath 12/331 13/250*
Water Orton 12/331 14/192
Wellington Road +
Wild Green 12/331
Winson Green 11/129
Yardley 7/68 13/250* 14/192

COVENTRY (223).

Coleshill (213) (CDS 29APR56)
                                       See TL3.
Hampton in Arden 11/109 18/24
                                       See TL4.
Lee Marston 11/12 See TL3.
Nether Whitacre 9/177 See TL3.

STRATFORD ON AVON (754).

Great Alne 9/31 14/192 See TL2.
Hockley Heath @ 11/26 14/134
                                       See TL2.
Tanworth 9/151 See TL2.
Ullenhall 11/159 See TL2.
Wooton Wawen 11/159 14/192
                                       See TL2.

+ indicates an office which used a straight line stamp after 1840.

@ indicates an office which used a Penny Post stamp after 1840.

TRANSFERS - Birmingham

TL 1. Brierley Hill became a post town on 1OCT51.

2. Great Alne, Tanworth, Ullenhall, Wooton Wawen and (probably) Hockley Heath under both Stratford and Birmingham from 1854.

3. Coleshill, Nether Whitacre and Lea Marston from Coventry to Birmingham on 19NOV56.

4. Hampton in Arden from Coventry to Birmingham on 9SEP59.

5. Bickenhill from Birmingham to Coventry on 9SEP59.

Note: Night Mail for Fazeley (Staffs) was sent to Birmingham between 23APR49 and 3NOV50.

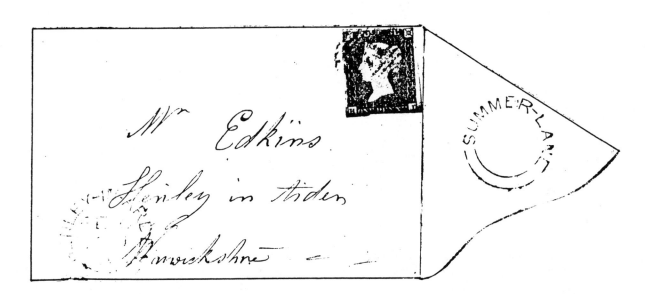

SUMMER-LANE (10/116), the mark of an office in a grocer's shop at 102 Summer Lane.

Probably the finest known strike of type D1 CAPE-OF-GOOD-HOPE (14/192).

BIRMINGHAM

Name	Class	Date	Town	Ref	Color	Dates
DUDDESTON	C2	16APR42	Birmingham	5/86		
HARBORNE	C2	13JAN44	Birmingham	7/17	BL	4MAY46- 4MAY56
					B	15MAY46- 6JUN49
SOLIHULL	C2				B	5APR38- 7FEB39
MOSELEY	C1	31MAY44	Birmingham	7/66	B	10JUN46-18JUN46
					BL	30OCT47-27JUL49
YARDLEY	C1	6JUN44	Birmingham	7/68	R	1DEC44-12APR49.
					GR	57
HOCKLEY-HILL	C1	27FEB45	Birmingham	7/129	B	13AUG45- 4AUG49
					GR	7MAY46- 4OCT57
					BL	7MAR45-19AUG57
HALESOWEN	C1	1JAN47	Birmingham	9/1	B	8FEB47-20JUN49.
HIGHGATE	C1	28JAN47	Birmingham	9/7	BL	24NOV47-26JUN58
					BL/GR	13JUN47-27SEP59
					B	29MAR51
					GR	25AUG52-18APR58.
					BR	5AUG58-27SEP59
PEUNS	C1	12MAR47	Birmingham	9/27		Note 1.
SPARKBROOK	C1	12MAR47	Birmingham	9/27	?	16JUL47
					BR	15JUN48
					R	14OCT50- 57
					OR	2DEC50
					BL	29NOV53- 6MAR55
					GR	22NOV57
GREAT ALNE	C1	19APR47	Stratford on A	9/31	BL	9JAN52
ASTON	C1	24MAY47	Birmingham	9/44	BL	5APR53-22JUN54
BIRCHFIELDS	C1	24MAY47	Birmingham	9/44	B	10SEP52- 56
					BL	23MAY53-21JAN60
SMALL-HEATH	C1	11JUN47	Birmingham	9/51	B	27MAY54-10OCT56.
PENNS	C1	13AUG47	Birmingham	9/70	R	14OCT47- 8NOV51
ASTON-ROAD	C1	18NOV47	Birmingham	9/79		
EDGBASTON	C1	15JAN48	Birmingham	9/117	B	3APR48- 8MAR59.
					GR	4FEB57-26FEB58
TANWORTH	C1	24MAY48	Stratford on A	9/151	BL	24MAR51-16JAN56
					?	13OCT57
NEITHER-WHITACRE	C1	28AUG48	Coleshill	9/177		
THE-LOYELLS	C1	28AUG48	Birmingham	9/177		Note 2.
THE-LOZELLS	C1				BL	11JUN53-12SEP53
					B	24JUL54-25JUL54
HALL-GREEN	C1	31MAY49	Birmingham	10/2	BL	14APR51
BALSALL-HEATH	C1	10JUL50	Birmingham	10/99	B	14JUL52- 56
					BL/GR	12JUL56-20DEC58
					BL	9JUL57- 7JAN59
SUMMER-LANE	C1	8NOV50	Birmingham	10/116	B	20DEC50- 5FEB51
					BL	53
					GR	12DEC56
HAMPSTEAD-ROAD	C1	24APR51	Birmingham	10/193	B	5JUL52-30DEC59
					GR	6MAY56-11MAY58
					BL/GR	20SEP56- 9SEP59
LEA-MARSTON	C1	9JAN52	Coventry	11/12		
HOCKLEY-HEATH	C1	6MAR52	Stratford on A	11/26	BL	2APR52-26MAY52
					R/BR	21MAY55
					BR	17JAN56-29APR56
					GR	29APR56
					B	15JUL57-24AUG57

Notes:
1. Probably not used - see 9/70.
2. Probably not used in this form but corrected locally - see below.

Name	Class	Date	Place	Ref	Colour	Date Range
ASTON-NEWTON	C1	OCT52	Birmingham	11/106	?	20OCT53
					GR	20NOV53-12AUG59
HAMPTON-IN-ARDEN	C1	OCT52	Coventry	11/109	GR	57
					B	17MAY58
CAPE·OF·GOOD·HOPE	C1	JAN53	Birmingham	11/129	B	19AUG53- 57.
					BL	23SEP57
NECHELLS-GN	C1	JAN53	Birmingham	11/129		
SALTLEY	C1	JAN53	Birmingham	11/129		
WINSON·GN	C1	JAN53	Birmingham	11/129	GR	4MAR58
					BL	3MAR59
SHIRLEY-BIRMINGHAM	C1	FEB53	"Mr Churchill"	11/143	B	6MAR53- 56
					BR/B	5MAR53-15MAY55.
LEE·CRESCENT	C1	APR53	Birmingham	11/157	B	7MAR53- 9MAR54
ULLENHALL	C1	APR53	Stratford on A	11/159		
WOOTTON-WALWEN	C1	APR53	Stratford on A	11/159		
GOACH-ST	C1	APR53	Birmingham	11/161		Note 3.
GT-HAMPTON-ST	C1	AUG53	Birmingham	11/206	BL	31MAR55-13APR55
					GR	22OCT56-25JUL57.
LANGLEY	C1	OCT53	Birmingham	11/248	BL	28NOV54
HANDSWORTH	C1	DEC53	Birmingham	12/7	B	19FEB54- 55.
OLDBURY	C1	DEC53	Birmingham	12/7		
ICKNIELD ST	C1	MAR54	Birmingham	12/40		
HARBORNE·HEATH	C1	20JUL54		12/93	BL	13OCT54
					B	5DEC55-14FEB60.
QUINTON	C1	27OCT54	Birmingham	12/129	B	4DEC54
GREAT BARR	C1	7DEC54	Birmingham	12/137	OR	27JUL55
					B	14DEC57- 58
CASTLE-BROMWICH	C1	4DEC55	Birmingham	12/276		
ELMDON	C1	4DEC55	Birmingham	12/275	GR	30JAN56-30JUN56
ERDINGTON	C1	4DEC55	Birmingham	12/275	GR/B	19APR58
					Grey	14FEB60.
KINGS·NORTON	C1	4DEC55	Birmingham	12/276		
KNOWLE	C1	4DEC55	Birmingham	12/275		
MINWORTH	C1	4DEC55	Birmingham	12/275	BL/GR	8DEC56
NORTHFIELD	C1	4DEC55	Birmingham	12/276	BL/GR	3APR58
ACOCKS-GREEN	C1	25MAR56	Birmingham	12/331		
ALCESTER-LANE-END	C1	25MAR56	Birmingham	12/331		
ASTON-PARK	C1	25MAR56	Birmingham	12/331		
BICKENHILL	C1	25MAR56	Birmingham	12/331		
CATHERINE-A-BARNS	C1	25MAR56	Birmingham	12/331		
CURDWORTH	C1	25MAR56	Birmingham	12/331		
GRAVELLY-HILL	C1	25MAR56	Birmingham	12/331	GR	6JUL56
					BL	59.
KINGS-HEATH	C1	25MAR56	Birmingham	12/331	BL	20NOV59
LAPWORTH	C1	25MAR56	Birmingham	12/331		
LITTLE-ASTON	C1	25MAR56	Birmingham	12/331		
MARSTON-GREEN	C1	25MAR56	Birmingham	12/331		
OSCOTT	C1	25MAR56	Birmingham	12/331		
OVER-WITTON	C1	25MAR56	Birmingham	12/331		
PERRY	C1	25MAR56	Birmingham	12/331	GR	19OCT56.
					BL/GR	14DEC58
SELLY-OAK	C1	25MAR56	Birmingham	12/331		
STIRCHLEY	C1	25MAR56	Birmingham	12/331		
WASHWOOD-HEATH	C1	25MAR56	Birmingham	12/331	B	1JAN58
WATER-ORTON	C1	25MAR56	Birmingham	12/331	BL	MAY58
WILD-GREEN	C1	25MAR56	Birmingham	12/331	GR	7MAR58.
QUEESLET	C1	29JUL56	Birmingham	13/48		
HAMPSTEAD	C1	5AUG56	Birmingham	13/51	BL/GR	6MAY58
SHIRLEY	C1	5AUG56	Birmingham	13/51	BL	4JUN57
					GR	57.

Notes: 3. Incorrect spelling of 'Gooch'.

Bham

Office	Type	Date	Town	Ref	Colour	Dates
MERE-GREEN	C1	8AUG56	Birmingham	13/57		
REDHILL	C1	12SEP56	Birmingham	13/63		
SMALL-HEATH	C1	25MAR57	Birmingham	13/192		
BARTLEY-GREEN	C1	27MAR57	Birmingham	13/197		
GT-HAMPTON-ST	C1	18APR57	Birmingham	13/210	BL/B	57- 58
					B	17MAR58- 4MAR59
					BL	23MAY58-24SEP58
					?	23MAY59
MILPOOL-HILL	C1	8JUN57	Birmingham	13/250		
ASHTED ROW	D3	cJUL57			GR/B	1NOV58
					B	6MAY59
					BL	4JUL59
BRISTOL STREET	D3	cJUL57			BL	7JUL58
CASTLE BROMWICH	D3	cJUL57	The Steel Impression		GR	11OCT58
HAMPSTEAD	D3	cJUL57	books do not record		GR	4DEC59
HARBORNE	D3	cJUL57	any type D3 marks.		B	?
MERE GREEN	D3	cJUL57			BL	15SEP59
MONUMENT LANE	D3	cJUL57			GR	17JUN58
					B	18JUN58-25AUG59
MOSELEY	D3	cJUL57			BL/B	30MAY59-19OCT59
					B	6OCT59- 6NOV59
PENNS	D3	cJUL57			B	25AUG58
SMALL HEATH	D3	cJUL57			B	3DEC59
STIRCHLEY	D3	cJUL57			B	6DEC58-18MAR59.
SUMMER LANE	D3	cJUL57			Drab	13SEP58
					BL/B	13SEP59
WASHWOOD HEATH	D3	cJUN57			B	8NOV58
YARDLEY	D3	cJUL57			BL	59
					B	?
KNOWLE	D4	10DEC57	Birmingham	14/105	B	15SEP58
OSCOTT	D4	10DEC57	Birmingham	14/105		
MINWORTH	D1?	(or D3)			GR	18OCT58
HOCKLEY-HEATH	D1	3FEB58	Birmingham	14/134	B	15DEC58
HOCKLEY-HILL.RO	D1	5FEB58	Birmingham	14/140	GR	16FEB58
					B	9MAR58-12APR58
					Drab	24JUN58-11AUG58
					BL	15DEC58- 7MAY59
BEECH-LANE	D1	6APR58	Birmingham	14/192		
CAPE-OF-GOOD-HOPE	D1	6APR58	Birmingham	14/192	GR	20JAN59-19JAN60.
					B	59
CASTLE-BROMWICH	D1	6APR58	Birmingham	14/192	B	58
DUDDESTON-ROW R.O.	D2	6APR58	Birmingham	14/192	B	2JUN58
FIVE-WAYS R.O.	D2	6APR58	Birmingham	14/192	B	26JUN58-29MAY59
					dkBL	8MAR59- 5MAR60.
					GR	59
GOOCH ST R.O.	D5	6APR58	Birmingham	14/192		
GT ALNE	D4	6APR58	Birmingham	14/192	BL/B	29NOV59
ICKNIELD-ST R.O.	D2	6APR58	Birmingham	14/192	GR	18SEP58
LANCASTER-ST R.O.	D2	6APR58	Birmingham	14/192	B	13JUL58
LOZELLS R.O.	D5	6APR58	Birmingham	14/192	B	6JAN59
PENNS	D4	6APR58	Birmingham	14/192		
SAND-PITS R.O.	D2	6APR58	Birmingham	14/192	BL	58.
SMALL-HEATH	D1	6APR58	Birmingham	14/192		
SPARK-BROOK	D1	6APR58	Birmingham	14/192	B	14JAN60
SUMMER-LANE R.O.	D2	6APR58	Birmingham	14/192	GR	12MAY58-14JAN60
WATER-ORTON	D1	6APR58	Birmingham	14/192		
WOOTTON-WAWEN	D1	6APR58	Birmingham	14/192	BL/B	23AUG59
YARDLEY	D4	6APR58	Birmingham	14/192		
HOLLYWOOD	D1	15APR58	Birmingham	14/199		
PARADE	D4	28AUG58	Birmingham	16/26	BL/B	25MAR59.
					BL	60
QUEESLET	D1	14DEC58	Birmingham	16/113		
HALL-GREEN	D1	21JAN59	Birmingham	16/142		
HAMPTON-IN-ARDEN	D1	9APR59	Coventry	18/24		

BIRMINGHAM RECEIVERS, THEIR TRADES AND LOCATIONS WHERE KNOWN

Office	Receiver	From	To
ACOCKS GREEN	Thomas Harris, Grocer Warwick Road	9APR56-	6JUN78
ALCESTER LANE END	Thomas Dedicoat	1JUL56-	91
ASHTEAD ROW	Thomas Ash, Chemist and Druggist 167, Ashtead Row Office closed 21 Mar 1866	OCT26-	21MAR66
ASTON	Frederick James Roberts, Engraver, Armourer to the Queen's Own Worcestershire Yeomanry and Clerk and Sexton to Aston Parish. Situated adjacent to Aston Park in Aston village Office closed 16 Nov 1859	NOV47-	NOV59
ASTON NEWTOWN	John Haddock, High Street, Aston	OCT52	
	John Nickolls, High Street, Aston	JUL59-	2JAN64
ASTON PARK	Same office as Aston		
ASTON ROAD	Mrs. Eliza Smith, Shopkeeper and Servants Register Office 90, Aston Road	47-	55
	John Gilison 90, Aston Road Office closed 1 Oct 1862	NOV55-	16JUN62
BALSALL HEATH	Enoch Blakemore, Boot and Shoe maker Tindal Street Office closed 26 Feb 1866	6JUN53-	22JUN64
BARTLEY GREEN	Joseph Taylor Office closed 18 May 1861	12AUG57	
BEECH LANE	William Veal, Steel Toymaker Beech Lane, Harborne (later named Beech Lanes)	1JUL56-	9MAY80
BICKENHILL	Joseph Ward, Parish Clerk	1JUL56-	24DEC97
BIRCHFIELD	Edward Moore, Sadler and Harness Maker	By 54	
BRIERLEY HILL	James Williams, Grocer and Tea Dealer High Street	By 54	
BRISTOL STREET	Thomas Picken, Stationer and Bookbinder 221, Bristol Street	By 45	
	Miss Ann Hipkins, Stationer 221, Bristol Street Office closed 30 Sep 1858	MAY49	
CAMP HILL	Robert Gillman, Provision Dealer 136 Camp Hill	DEC55-	APL63

CAPE OF GOOD HOPE	Joseph Jay Office closed 20 Apr 1870	DEC52- 63
CASTLE BROMWICH	Mrs Ann Lewis	29- 6JAN72
CATHERINE A BARNES	Oliver Hadley Office closed 9 Sep 59	9JUN56

COLESHILL	James Dale, Chemist, Grocer and Dealer in British Wines
	    Market Place, (Post Office was in High Street)
	James Dale, Druggist and Seedsman
	    Church Hill, Coleshill
		By 50
		
		14JUN54-23SEP75

CURDWORTH	Edward Cater, Wheelwright
	    Hare and Hounds, Minworth
	Joseph Spencer
	    Curdworth
		By 50- 56
		
		20NOV56- 63

DERITEND	Mrs Mary Jelfe
	    52 High Street, Deritend
	Amy Jelfe
	    51, High Street, Deritend
	John Bunce, Watch and Clockmaker
	    174, High Street, Deritend
		By 45- 49
		
		49
		
		MAY51-11DEC62

DUDDESTON ROW	Mrs Elizabeth Harris, Shopkeeper
	    18, Duddeston Row
	Jonas Bowen, Shopkeeper and Brassfounder
	    41, Duddeston Row
	    Office closed 18 Jul 1861
		By 45
		
		FEB55- 61

EDGBASTON	Miss Louisa Mewis, 'Mistress of Edgbaston Post Office' (1845 Kelly Directory)
	    Hagley Road
	John Taylor, Grocer
	    84, Hagley Road, corner of Monument Lane (now Monument Road)
	    adjacent to Ivy Bush Inn
	        Office renamed 'Hagley Road' in 1863
		By 45
		
		AUG45

ELMDON	Josiah Limbery, Victualler and Farmer Cock Inn, Elmdon	By 45
ERDINGTON	Isaac James, Shopkeeper and Fire Insurance Agent	NOV32- 61

FIVE WAYS	Thomas Price, Stationer and Printer
	    95, Broad Street
	Miss Mary Anne Pickton, Stationer and Circulating Library
	    98, Broad Street, (corner of Broad Street and Hagley Road)
		By 45
		
		APR49-30NOV75

GOOCH STREET	Mrs Charlotte Hughes, Hosier
	    Corner of Gooch Street and Benacre Street
	William Law
	    64, Gooch Street
	Henry Williams
	    64, Gooch Street
	Peter Humphreys
	    Office closed 1858
		By 54- 55
		
		JUN55-28FEB56
		
		27MAR56-15APR57
		25MAY57

HOCKLEY HEATH	Matthew Wood, Shoe maker	By50- 56
	Joseph Richmond, Tailor and Grocer	11MAY56-20DEC92
HOCKLEY HILL	Henry Machon, Tobacconist	
	120, Hockley Hill	45- 46
	John Kendrick, Chemist and Grocer	
	215, New John Street West	JUL46- 76
HOLLYWOOD	Charles Cranmore, Shopkeeper	7JUN58- 94
ICKNIELD STREET	Ann Marsh,	
	110 Icknield Street	SEP54- 61
	Office closed 17 Oct 1861 but reopened in 1865	
KINGS HEATH	William Jeffcoat, Baker	28APR56-26MAR57
	John Knowles, Grocer	27APR57-20OCT73
KINGS NORTON	Thomas Hems	By53
	Thomas Simpson, Grammar School Master	16APR55- 10CT66
KNOWLE	John Cattell, Baker	By25- 51
	Charles Cope, Wine Agent	JUL51-10MAY63
LADYWOOD	Miss Maria Rowe, Draper	
	219 Icknield Street West, Ladywood	FEB55- 6DEC79
LANCASTER STREET	W. Drury,	
	30 Lancaster Street	By35
	Richard Chapple, Dispensing Chemist and Grocer	By45
	Alfred Hood Foster, Druggist and Grocer	
	35 Lancaster Street	By49
	Robert Austin, Printer	
	34 Lancaster Street	By54- 72
LANGLEY	E.G. Jones	14NOV53
	John Green	26JAN57-31JAN57
	Enoch Hadley	10APR57- 8AUG59
LAPWORTH	Joseph Richmond, Tailor	3APR56- 7JUN66
LEE CRESCENT	Miss Mary Sears, Milliner and Dressmaker	
	176 Lee Bank Road	By54
LEE MARSTON	Robert Lingard, Farmer and Butcher	By54-24MAR74
LITTLE ASTON	Thomas Marigold, Wheelwright	11MAY56- 62
LOZELLS	Henry John Barker, Druggist and Grocer	48
	Thomas Barker, Druggist and Grocer	
	at corner of Lozells Lane and Wilton Street	DEC55- 76
MARSTON GREEN	Samuel Wheeler	1JUL56-10MAR57
	Joseph Abbey	30APR57- 30CT61
MERE GREEN	Elizabeth Johnson	15SEP56-25SEP77
MILPOOL HILL	Same Office as Alcester Lane End	

GRAVELLY HILL	Charles Willetts	9APR56- NOV58
	Priscilla Riley	9DEC58- 61
GREAT ALNE	Thomas Edwards, Shoe maker and Constable	JUL47-after71

GREAT BARR	Robert Craggs, Inn keeper
	    Scott Arms Inn, corner of Walsall Road and
	    Newton Road, Great Barr
		40- 56

	Aaron Insley	14DEC56
	William Davis	18JAN62-11MAR72
GREAT HAMPTON STREET	Edward Gunn, Druggist and Grocer Corner of Kenyon Street and Great Hampton Street	35
	William Canning, Grocer, Chemist and Drysalter 1, Kenyon Street at corner of Great Hampton Street	By 45
HALESOWEN	Miss Elizabeth Cox Hagley Street, Halesowen	By 41- 47
	William Parkes High Street, Halesowen	DEC47- 9JUN68
HALL GREEN	Henry Matthews	APR49- 62
	John Wheel	25FEB62-28APR66
HAMPSTEAD	John Mattinson	56
	Esther Mattinson	10SEP56
HAMPSTEAD ROAD	William Crane, Grocer Hampstead Row, Handsworth	MAY51- 6APR59
	Joseph Crane Office close 14 Aug 1863	25APR59- 5JUL63
HAMPTON IN ARDEN	John Tabberer Stone Bridge Inn	By 45
	Benjamin Butler, Shopkeeper Stone Bridge Inn	By 54- 64
HANDSWORTH	Samuel Sanders, Grocer, Collector of Queen's Taxes, Agent to Birmingham and District Fire Office Soho Street, Handsworth	By 45

	William White, Shopkeeper
	    Soho Street, Handsworth
	    Office Closed 11 Apr 1876 and moved to Villa Road
		NOV53- 1APR76

HARBORNE	Samuel Dugmore, Parish Clerk Office Closed 22 Apr 1862 but re-opened 1 Oct 1862	FEB44-29MAR62
HARBORNE HEATH	William Miles, Boot and Shoe maker Office closed 1861-62	OCT44
HENLEY IN ARDEN	Samuel Hoitt	By 25- 49
	John Hannett, Stationer and Bookseller	15JAN50- 73
HIGHGATE	Mrs Mary Savage, Shopkeeper 82, Highgate, Birmingham	JAN47
	Henry Lee, Grocer 196, Moseley Road, Birmingham	29DEC58- 80

MINWORTH	Edward Cater, Publican and Wheelwright 'Hare and Hounds', Minworth	By58-23DEC60
MONUMENT LANE	Same Office as 'Edgbaston'	

MOSELEY	Thomas Bird
	    Moseley Village
	Mrs. Sarah Hayes, Postmistress
	    Rear of 'Fighting Cocks' Inn
		By45
		
		9AUG52- 62

NECHELLS GREEN	Charles Hainge, Tailor 4 Nechells Park Road, Birmingham	19FEB55-30JUN83
NETHER WHITACRE	Elizabeth Silk John Silk, Plumber and Glazier Office closed 27 May 1871	30SEP48 By54
NORTHFIELD	Joseph Joice, Postmaster George Dutton, Tailor and Parish Clerk	By41- JAN54 20JAN54-30SEP77
OLDBURY	Josiah Lowe, Stationer, Printer, Bookbinder and Newsagent Birmingham Street	JAN44-30APR83
OSCOTT	William Wardell Office closed 27 Dec 1860	25DEC57-13NOV60
PARADE	Mrs. Mary Shemeld, Tobacconist 19 Parade, Birmingham	1OCT58- 74
PENNS	Joseph Martin John Allsop Office closed 14 June 1860	By49- JAN56 17JAN56
PERRY	John Oakes	9APR56- 60
QUEESLET	Thomas Parkes Office closed 23 Dec 1861	1NOV56
QUINTON	David Deeley, Shopkeeper	10MAR54-23AUG72
REDHILL	Joseph Harris Office closed 30 Aug 1883	16NOV56
SALTLEY	Richard Tibbatts, Grocer and Baker William Coles, Stationer	29DEC52-31DEC59 JAN60-11AUG80

SANDPITS	Miss Fanny Davies
	    Lower Terrace, Sandpits, Birmingham
	William White
	    29 Sandpits, Birmingham
	    17 Sandpits, Birmingham
	    123 Sandpits, Birmingham
	    Office closed 30 Sep 1858
		
		35
		
		By45
		By49
		By54

SELLY OAK	Benjamin Humphries	3APR56- 62

SHIRLEY STREET	Joseph Cary Richards
	    'Plume of Feathers' Inn, Shirley Street. Later shortened
	      to 'Shirley'.
	William Baxter
		25JUL49-27OCT61
		28OCT61-27OCT80

SMALL HEATH	Robert Lees, Shopkeeper 259 Coventry Road Thomas Tysall	By53- 56 22DEC56- 61

SMETHWICK	Joseph Vernon, Tailor, Draper and Fire Insurance Agent
	    13 Oldbury Road at corner of Brewery Street, Smethwick
	    (This portion of Oldbury Road is now named High Street)
		OCT37- 64

SOLIHULL	Ann Capener Thomas Harborne, Tailor and Registrar of Births and Deaths for Solihull High Street, Solihull Miss Pheobe Harborne, Postmistress William C. Pearman Susannah Pearman	By30 By45- 51 DEC51-25JUL57 18NOV57-24FEB58 MAR58- 71
SPARKBROOK	John Morris, Wheelwright	JUN47-16DEC75
STIRCHLEY	Chales Lamb	29APR56-20AUG64
SUMMER LANE	Gerard Blakeman, Grocer 102 Summer Lane at corner of New John Street West, Birmingham	MAY53- 66
SUTTON COLDFIELD	James Beech Mill Street, Sutton Coldfield Mrs Ann Wilkins	OCT40- 2MAY59 2DEC59-27SEP72
TANWORTH	Edward Copage, Shoe maker Tanworth Street, Tanworth	OCT46- JUL62
ULLENHALL	William Cooke, Shopkeeper Office closed 2 Jan 1862 but reopened 1 Sep 1866	JAN54- DEC61
WASHWOOD HEATH	Richard Lowe, Shopkeeper Miss Ann Windridge, Shopkeeper	6MAY56-31MAR58 1APR58- 5DEC82
WATER ORTON	Elijah Gagliss Charles Gilbert	9APR56- 4JUN58 24MAR59-10AUG66

WELLINGTON ROAD	William Bate, Baker and Flour Dealer
	    Wellington Road, off Bristol Road, Birmingham
	Richard Odams, Baker
	    Wellington Road at corner of Wellington Terrace
	Elizabeth Gordan
		
		By48
		
		By54- 58
		10OCT58- 3APR61

WILD GREEN	Thomas Wilkins, Maltster	2APR56
WINSON GREEN	Henry Adams, Tailor Lodge Road,	19APR53- DEC64
WOOTON WAWEN	Elizabeth Clarke	JAN54- 73

YARDLEY	James Chell, Master of the Free School John Green, Tailor Church Road, Yardley	44- JUL54-13MAY95	54

Some offices existed prior to or later than dates shown in these listings which only cover the period of this book.

Some offices which closed in this period were later reopened.

PENNS (9/70) - Joseph Martin was the receiver when this letter was sent. Mail was received at 8am and despatched at 7pm. It was conveyed between Birmingham and Sutton Coldfield by a mail gig and then taken to and from Penns by foot post. The Penns office also handled mail for the adjacent hamlets of Langley Heath and Warmley.

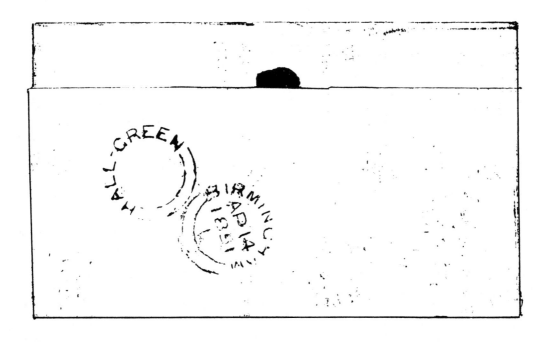

HALL-GREEN (10/2) - The only recorded example of this stamp at an office where Henry Matthews was appointed receiver in April 1849, holding the position until 1862.

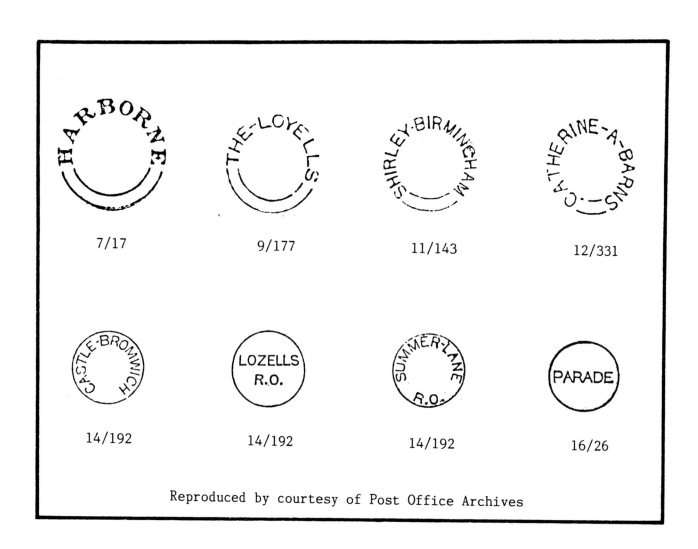

Similar Sans-serif (C1) Marks of Birmingham

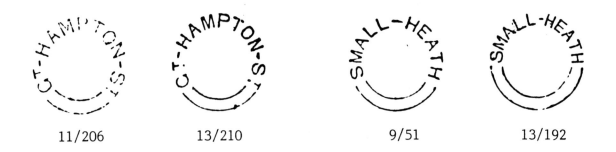

Reproduced by courtesy of Post Office Archives

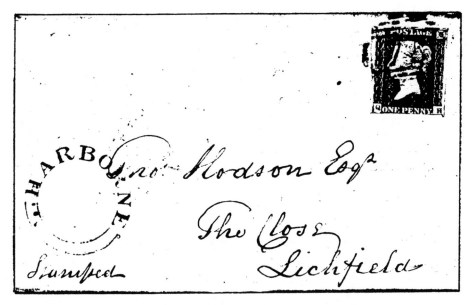

HARBORNE (7/17) - the only Birmingham C2 mark known to have been used in the 1840s.

THE LOZELLS (9/177*) - the stamp in the Steel Impression Books was wrongly cut with a letter 'Y' for 'Z' and it was probably corrected locally in Birmingham. The name of 'The Lozells' is derived from the Saxon 'Lowe' (hill) and 'Cele' (cold).

MOSELEY (7/66) in blue ink on a cover dated December 1847.

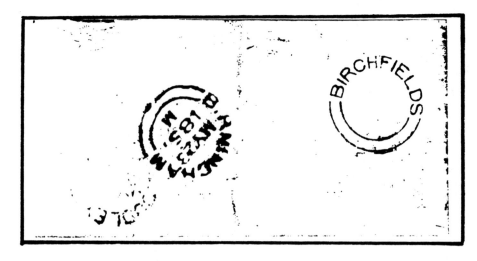

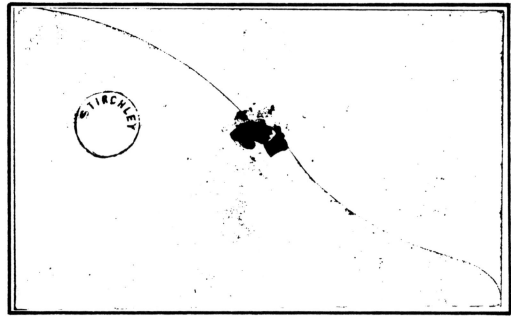

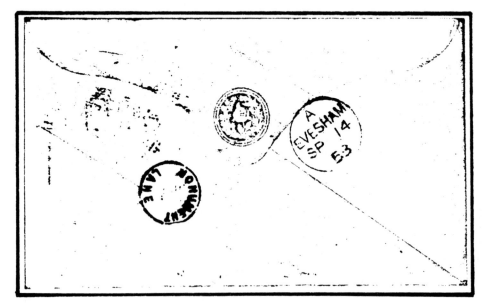

Above: BIRCHFIELDS (9/44) - then a hamlet 2½ miles north of Birmingham.

Centre: STIRCHLEY (13/250*)   Below: MONUMENT LANE (13/250*)

The issue of the unique small undated 'Creswell' stamps to some Birmingham offices - of which two are illustrated - was not recorded in the Steel Impression Books.

WORCESTERSHIRE

BEWDLEY (68).

Bayton 12/14
Ditton 2 12/80a
Lembrook 12/14
Rock 13/230
Stottesdon 2 13/15
Upper Arley 10/47
Wribbenhall 12/14

BROADWAY (137). 2/11 (CDS 19FEB38)

Stanton 3 10/163
Weston sub Edge 3 10/198

BROMSGROVE (139). 1/18 (CDS 20FEB38)

Abbots Morton 11/114 16/88
Alvechurch 7/77 (CDS 22JUN58)
Astwood Bank 11/2
Bromsgrove Station 11/229
Callow Hill 12/232
Catshill 11/229
Coughton 4 12/324
Crabbs Cross 11/230
Fairfield 14/275
Feckenham + 10/54 (CDS 25MAR57)
Finstall 16/143
Hanbury 7/146 16/88
Headless Cross 11/229
Inkberrow 11/138
Lickey End 11/229
Redditch 1/163 (CDS 10AUG44) 12/50* 18/96
Rednal 13/69
Stoke Prior 7/146 16/88
Tardebigg 11/229
Wichbold 11/229 13/36 See TL22.

DROITWICH (262). 2/139* (CDS 20JAN38)

Elmley Lovett 11/229 14/104
Hadsor 11/229
Himbleton 18/57
Tibberton 18/53.

DUDLEY (263). 1/33 (CDS 16MAR33)

Blackheath 5 12/155
Himley 5 10/153 16/141
Holly Hall 12/231
Kates Hill 10/95 16/142
Kingswinford 5 5/182 (CDS 5JUL51)
Lower Gornal 5 12/252 12/261
Netherton 9/7 16/137
                              (CDS 16DEC59)
Old Hill 5 7/171 16/142
Pensnett 5 7/161
Rowley Regis 5 7/142
Sedgley 5 9/64 9/92 (CDS 27JUN56)
Swindon 5 12/50
Wall Heath 5 12/83
Woodsetton 5 12/336

EVESHAM (284).

Bengeworth 11/241 16/148
Cleeve Prior 14/44
Dumbleton 7/21 13/281
Greenhill 11/229
Hampton 11/229 16/141
Harvington 9/2 16/148
Salford Prior(s) 4 10/146
South Littleton 9/2
Worcester Road 11/225

KIDDERMINSTER (415).

Blakebrook 11/159
Broadwater 11/241
Broom 14/258
Chaddesley Corbett + 7/40 7/133
Churchill 11/241
Cookley 7/53 14/111
Farfield 11/159
Franche 11/241 12/313
Stone 11/241
Winterfield 14/258
Wolverley 7/236 14/111

+ indicates an office which used a straight line (or P.P.) stamp after 1840.

An underlined number, eg 2, indicates an office outside Worcs - see key at end.

Worcs

MALVERN (497).

Barnards Green 12/92 See TL16&18.
Bosbury 1 7/44
Colwall 1 7/44
Colwall Green 1 14/70
Cradley 1 7/49 14/70
Leigh Sinton 9/103 14/270 16/13 See TL15&20.
Malvern Link 7/49 14/105
Malvern Wells 7/87
Newland Green 12/92 18/24 See TL16&20.
North Malvern 12/92
Stiffords Bridge 1 12/92
West Malvern 14/87 (CDS 10NOV57)

PERSHORE (611). Pre-proof books, (CDS 21OCT39)

Birlingham 9/49 16/163
Cropthorne 7/222
Defford 9/49 16/167
Eckington 7/70 See TL5&13.
Elmley 9/92
Elmley Castle 16/163
Fladbury 7/222 13/4 16/163
Peopleton 12/267 16/163
Wick 18/67 18/95
Wire Piddle 11/130 16/163

SHIPSTON ON STOUR (706). 1/177 (CDS 31MAR37)

Brailes 4 5/76 16/161
Burmington 4 13/236
Cherington 4 5/76 16/161
Ilmington 4 14/212
Newbold on Stour 4 14/212
Tredington 4 11/135 16/161

STOURBRIDGE (750).

Belbroughton 5/179 14/149
Brettell Lane 5 + 12/37 See TL21.
Careless Green 16/16
Coalbourn Brook 5 16/144 16/158
Cradley 5 7/205 16/118 See TL19.
Enville 5 7/204 18/43
Hagley 5/179 14/151 (CDS 31MAR58)
Lower Clent 11/229 14/149
Lye 7/205 14/70
Oldswinford 11/161
Quarry Bank 5 11/229 See TL19.
Stourton 5 11/229 14/151
Wollaston 11/161 14/149
Wordsley 5 + 10/176 14/149.

STOURPORT (751). 1/177
(CDS 13JAN40)

Abberley 11/152
Dunley 10/188
Hartlebury + 11/156
Holt 10/211
Shrawley 9/77

TENBURY (783). 2/139
(CDS 31OCT39) 7/40*

Bockleton 7/247
Eardeston 13/271 14/12
Kyre 12/15
Lindridge 13/271
Little Hereford 1 12/15
Rochford 14/204

WORCESTER (918).

Acton Beauchamp 13/287
Alfrick 12/3
Bevere Green 18/46
Bridge Street 9/57
Broadwas 7/15 12/77 16/113
Class Gate 9/57
Clifton on Teme 7/222 13/20
Cornmarket + 12/77
Cotheridge 12/3
Crowle 9/43
Earls Croome 12/6
Fernhill Heath 7/158 13/149
Great Witley 7/152 See TL7.
Grimley 12/77
Hallow 7/220
Hawford 7/223
Henwick 12/3
Kempsey 4/111
Knightsford Bridge 16/29
Leigh 7/273 13/149
London Road 4/111
Lower Wick 12/3
Martley 10/74
Much Cowarne 1 12/106
Ombersley 4/111 (CDS 24JUL51)
See TL2&9.
Pencombe 1 18/82
Pirton 12/6
Powick 4/111 14/7
Ripple 10/35 See TL14.
Robertsend Street 5/194 16/113
St Johns 4/111 10/121
Salwarpe 12/3

+ indicates an office which used a straight line (or P.P.) stamp after 1840.

An underlined number, eg 2, indicates an office outside Worcs - see key at end.

Worcester (Cont'd)

Sapey Bridge 9/47 12/99
Severn Stoke 5/188 16/113
Sidbury 9/57 13/258
Spetchley 12/3
Stanbrook 14/57
Stanford Bridge 12/203 14/212
Stockton 7/182 See TL7.
Stoke Lacey $\underline{1}$ 14/154
Stoulton 10/103
Tedstone Wafer $\underline{1}$ 12/6
Tithing 9/57 14/139
Upper Sapey $\underline{1}$ 12/3
Upton on Severn 1/163* (CDS 30SEP45)
Welland 12/6

BIRMINGHAM (75)

Halesowen 9/1

BROMYARD (138), Herefs See TL6.

Bishops Frome $\underline{1}$ 10/267 See TL6.

CHIPPING NORTON (195), Oxon

Long Compton $\underline{4}$ 5/168 16/161 See TL3.

GLOUCESTER (312), Glos

Redmarley 5/159 7/92 See TL4&17.
Staunton 7/163 (CDS 28MAR51)
14/90

MORETON IN MARSH (534), Glos

Blockley $\underline{3}$ 5/101 10/65
See TL11&12.
Mickleton $\underline{3}$ 9/160 See TL10.

STRATFORD ON AVON (754), Warks

Alcester $\underline{4}$ 1/2 See TL8.
Bidford $\underline{4}$ 5/167 16/88 See TL8.
Studley + 5/32 (CDS 1JUN54)

TEWKESBURY (788), Glos

Beckford 9/4
Bredon 9/170 12/315 16/58
Eldersfield 14/277
Kemerton 9/4 16/57
Longdon 7/33 16/58
Overbury 9/70 16/58
Strensham 7/79 12/315 16/58

WOLVERHAMPTON (905), Staffs

Gornal $\underline{5}$ 2/50 5/38 12/337
See TL1.

+ indicates an office which also used a straight line stamp after 1840.

KEY to offices not in Worcestershire

$\underline{1}$ is in Herefordshire
$\underline{2}$ is in Shropshire
$\underline{3}$ is in Gloucestershire
$\underline{4}$ is in Warwickshire
$\underline{5}$ is in Staffordshire.

Worcs 174.

Notes:
6. "These two stamps were returned to this office on 31Aug by the Postmaster of Kidderminster who stated he had been instructed to do so . . ."
7. See 16/13 - probably a correction.
8. Spelling error - see 16/158.
9. Probably not used - see 18/95.

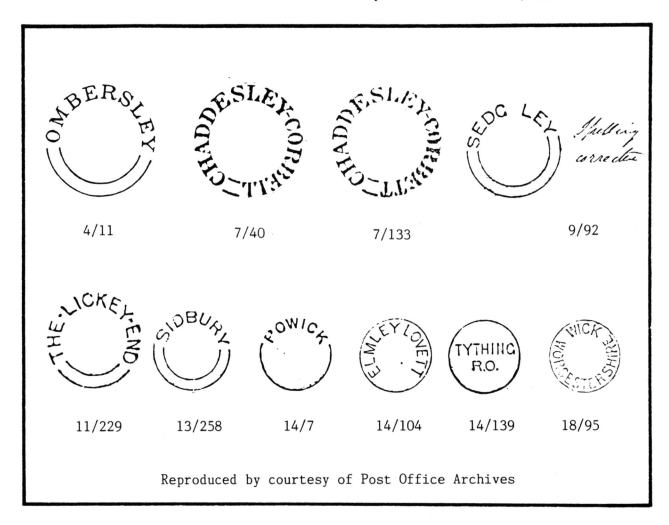

SEVERN-STOKE (5/188)

TRANSFERS - Worcestershire

TL 1. Gornal from Wolverhampton to Dudley, possibly in 1837/41.

2. Ombersley from Worcester to Stourport, probably before 1843.

3. Long Compton may have transferred from Chipping Norton to Shipston on Stour, either in 1854 or between 1856 and 1859, or it may have been subordinate to both offices.

4. Redmarley from Gloucester to Ledbury on 19OCT44.

5. Eckington from Pershore to Tewkesbury on 22MAY48.

6. Bromyard reduced to a sub-office (under Worcester) on 6AUG50. Bishops Frome would have transferred to Worcester at the same time.

7. Stockton and Great Witley from Worcester to Stourport on 5MAR51.

8. Alcester and Bidford from Stratford on Avon to Bromsgrove on 5JUN51.

9. Ombersley from Stourport to Droitwich on 27MAY52.

10. Mickleton from Moreton in Marsh to Broadway on 1NOV53.

11. Blockley from Moreton in Marsh to Broadway, perhaps briefly in the early 1850s.

12. Blockley from Broadway to Moreton in Marsh on 22JAN54.

13. Eckington from Tewkesbury to Pershore on 18JUL54.

14. Ripple from Worcester to Tewkesbury on 31AUG54.

15. Leigh Sinton from Malvern to Worcester on 1JAN55.

16. Barnards Green and Newland Green from Malvern to Worcester cJAN55.

17. Redmarley from Ledbury to Gloucester on 3NOV55.

18. Barnards Green from Worcester to Malvern on 19APR56.

19. Quarry Bank and Cradley from Stourbridge to Brierley Hill on 1JUN57. (Brierley Hill had become a post town on 10OCT51.)

20. Newland Green and Leigh Sinton from Worcester to Malvern on 14DEC57.

21. Brettell Lane from Stourbridge to Brierley Hill on 10SEP58.

22. Wichbold from Bromsgrove to Droitwich on 27AUG59.

WORCESTERSHIRE

PERSHORE	C2*				B	28- 38
					BL	23MAR38-26MAR38
DUDLEY	C2*	4MAY29	Dudley	1/33	B	15FEB32-30JUL36
AULCESTER	C2*	22MAY29	Alcester	1/2	OR/R	16OCT29-13AUG40
					B	28MAY41- 5NOV45
					BR	22MAY44
BROOMSGROVE	C3A	11AUG29	Bromsgrove	1/18	B	19MAY31-22DEC34.
SHIPSTONE ON STOUR	C3A	7SEP29	Shipston on S	1/177	B	6APR31-10AUG36
REDDITCH	C2*	24SEP29	Redditch	1/163	R	31OCT29-14AUG38
					B	29OCT40-14MAR44.
UPTON	C2*				B	13JAN30-20MAY45
STOURPORT	C2*	11MAR30	Stourport	1/177	drab	9OCT33
					B	34- 40
BROADWAY	C2	16MAR33	Broadway	2/11	B	28MAY33- 36
TENBURY	C2*	9DEC33	Tenbury	2/139	B	18OCT34-20AUG38
DROITWICH	C2*				B	8JAN37-17JUN37
GORNAL	C2	12OCT37	Wolverhampton	2/50	B	10MAY40
ST JOHN'S·WORCESTER	C2	3MAR41	Worcester	4/111	B	24JUL41- 4JUL49
LONDON-RD						
-WORCESTER	C2	3MAR41	Worcester	4/111	B	27MAY41- 48
					BL	49-23FEB59
					GR	5JUN55
KEMPSEY	C2	3MAR41	Worcester	4/111	B	41-20SEP48.
					BL	19MAR49- 5JUL59
					BL/GR	27APR49-19OCT51
					dkGR	19APR58
OMBERSLEY	C2	3MAR41	Worcester	4/111	B	2JUN41-10NOV50.
POWICK	C2	3MAR41	Worcester	4/111	B	14NOV41-14AUG46
					GR	22FEB52
STUDLEY	C2	30SEP41	Stratford on A	5/32	B	10NOV41- 8JUN48
					BL	20SEP49-27NOV52
GORNAL	C2	18OCT41	Dudley	5/38	B	20AUG42-19OCT45.
BRAILES	C2	25FEB42	Shipston on S	5/76	B	27MAY44
					BL	20SEP50-26NOV53
					BL/GR	16JUL54
CHERRINGTON	C2	25FEB42	Shipston on S	5/76	B	12MAY43
					BL	16MAY54-27JAN55
BLOCKLEY	C2	4JUN42	Moreton Marsh	5/101	OR/R	24AUG43-10AUG50
					BR	3MAR48
					GR/BL	21OCT52-26JAN53
					GR	26MAR55- 56.
REDMARLEY	C2	13MAY43	Gloucester	5/159		
BIDFORD	C2	4JUL43	Stratford on A	5/167	B	21OCT43-30MAR47
LONG COMPTON	C2	5JUL43	Chipping Norton	5/168	B	8NOV44-20JUL46
					BL	22NOV56
BELLBROUGHTON	C2	30AUG43	Stourbridge	5/179	B	45-20SEP55
HAGLEY	C2	30AUG43	Stourbridge	5/179	R	16JUL44- 10OCT51.
					OR	13AUG50-26DEC50
					R/OR	25AUG51-11NOV56
					dkBL	5AUG52
					BL/GR	2FEB54
					B	8JUN54
					BL	4OCT55
					GR	3SEP56
KINGSWINFORD	C2	19SEP43	Dudley	5/182	R	2JAN45-17OCT45
					B	21FEB47-20OCT50.

Office	Type	Date	Town	Ref	Color	Dates
SEVERN-STOKE	C2	23OCT43	Worcester	5/188	R	3OCT45-25FEB51
					R/B	9OCT45
					B	10APR51- 7MAR55
					OR	24APR56
					BL/B	11NOV57
					GR	8MAR58
ROBERTSEND-ST	C2	8NOV43	Worcester	5/194	B	8NOV43-28MAY47
					BL	49-16JUN55
					GR	15JUN55
					OR/R	19MAR57
BROADWAS	C2	13JAN44	Worcester	7/15	BR	8AUG46- 3SEP46
					B	5OCT46
					R	27OCT49-13AUG53
DUMBLETON	C2	20JAN44	Evesham	7/21	B	2MAR45-15JAN48
					BL	20DEC54
LONGDON	C2	26FEB44	Tewkesbury	7/33	BR	20DEC53
					BL	5DEC51
CHADDESLEY-CORBELL	C2	18MAR44	Kidderminster	7/40		Note 1.
TENBURY	C2M				B	13JUN46 Note 2.
BOSBURY	C1	15APR44	Great Malvern	7/44	B	26DEC47
					BL	19APR55-24OCT55
					R	25APR56-25NOV56
					BL/B	8SEP59
COLWALL	C1	15APR44	Great Malvern	7/44	B	23DEC46- 6OCT57
					BL	9MAY49- 9MAR50.
					B/GR	6OCT57
MALVERN-LINK	C1	19APR44	Great Malvern	7/49	B	24MAY46
					BL	5NOV46- 1JAN55
					OR/R	13FEB50- 1FEB57
CRADLEY	C1	19APR44	Great Malvern	7/49	B	11MAR45-21MAR50
					GR	16JUN49
					BL	13JAN52-16SEP52
					R	30JAN56-28JUL56.
					OR	26MAR57
COOKLEY	C1	11MAY44	Kidderminster	7/53		
ECKINGTON	C1	8JUN44	Pershore	7/70	B	29NOV59
ALVECHURCH	C1	1JUL44	Bromsgrove	7/77	R	45
					GR	27APR48-23MAR55.
					BR	23APR49
					BL/B	23JUL53
STRENSHAM	C1	10JUL44	Tewkesbury	7/79		
MALVERN-WELLS	C1	13AUG44	Malvern	7/87	OR	14DEC44-21JUL57
					R	48-24JAN57
					B	15AUG48
					BL	51-21DEC53
REDMARLEY	C1	22AUG44	Ledbury	7/92	B	15AUG45-14OCT52
					BR	26SEP46
CHADDESLEY-CORBETT	C2	20MAR45	Kidderminster	7/133	BL	7APR51- 3APR55
					R	22NOV55-17OCT57.
					B	10OCT59
ROWLEY-REGIS	C1	8MAY45	Dudley	7/142	B	7MAR46- 8JUL59
					OR	7AUG48-16DEC49
HANBURY	C1	14MAY45	Bromsgrove	7/146	BL	2APR52
STOKE-PRIOR	C1	14MAY45	Bromsgrove	7/146	B	15FEB48
					GR	25AUG55
					OR	8DEC55
GREAT-WITLEY	C1	14JUN45	Worcester	7/152	B	5AUG46- 4DEC47
					BL/GR	12JAN52-13JAN57
					R	21APR58
FERNHILL-HEATH	C1	28JUN45	Worcester	7/158		

Notes: 1. Spelling error - see 7/133.
2. Probably a poor strike of the CDS.

Worcs   178.

Name		Date	Place	Ref		
PENSNETT	C1	7JUL45	Dudley	7/161	B	29SEP47-18SEP48
					GR	13JUN55-14DEC57.
STAUNTON	C1	16JUL45	Gloucester	7/163		
OLD-HILL	C1	25AUG45	Dudley	7/171	R	46
					BR	4NOV52
					R/BR	19MAY54
					B	18SEP58
STOCKTON	C1	10OCT45	Worcester	7/182	GR	16SEP54
					R	14MAR55
ENVILLE	C1	5JAN46	Stourbridge	7/204	B	25FEB46-27JUL49.
CRADLEY	C1	10JAN46	Stourbridge	7/205	B	7AUG47-18NOV50
					BR	18SEP53
LYE	C1	10JAN46	Stourbridge	7/205	B	24AUG47- 51
HALLOW	C1	13MAR46	Worcester	7/220	B	5JAN47- 53.
					BL	17OCT59
CROPTHORNE	C1	17MAR46	Pershore	7/222	B	5MAR47-17FEB59
					R	56- 57
					BL	59
FLADBURY	C1	17MAR46	Pershore	7/222	BR	16OCT46
					BL	27JUL50
					GR	11DEC51- 2MAR59
CLIFTON-ON-TEME	C1	17MAR46	Worcester	7/222	B	3SEP46-25JAN50
					BL	8JUN50-10MAR55
HAWFORD	C1	20MAR46	Worcester	7/223	BL/GR	21JUL53
WOLVERLEY	C1	10MAY46	Kidderminster	7/236	B	14FEB47- 7SEP50
					BL	14DEC47-29JAN53.
BOCKLETON	C1	27JUN46	Tenbury	7/247	B	24JUN49
					Y	30AUG59
LEIGH	C1	10OCT46	Worcester	7/273		
HALESOWEN	C1	1JAN47	Birmingham	9/1	B	8FEB47-20JUN49
HARVINGTON	C1	1JAN47	Evesham	9/2	B	21JUN48
					BL	24DEC49-14NOV53.
					R	51
					BL/GR	10SEP55
					OR	14MAY57- 2JUN57
SOUTH-LITTLETON	C1	1JAN47	Evesham	9/2		
BECKFORD	C1	12JAN47	Tewkesbury	9/4	GR	23MAR55
KEMERTON	C1	12JAN47	Tewkesbury	9/4	B	19AUG47-20AUG47
					GR	18OCT52-30APR55.
NETHERTON	C1	28JAN47	Dudley	9/7	B	9AUG47
CROWLE	C1	24MAY47	Worcester	9/43	GR	49-21MAR51
					R	14MAY57
SAPEYBRIDGE	C1	1JUN47	Worcester	9/47	B	9MAY49
					GR	20JUL50
					BL	30JUN52-11APR53
DEFFORD	C1	7JUN47	Pershore	9/49	B	1AUG48
					BL/GR	15OCT55
BIRLINGHAM	C1	7JUN47	Pershore	9/49	B	20SEP58
TITHING	C1	30JUN47	Worcester	9/57	BL	19NOV50-17JAN56
					BL/B	3JUL57
					B	6JUL57-25JUL57.
BRIDGE-ST	C1	30JUN47	Worcester	9/57	R	6AUG48-23JUL49
					OR	16AUG48
					BL	15FEB53- MAY58
CLASS-GATE	C1	30JUN47	Worcester	9/57	B	2JAN48- 8MAR49
SIDBURY	C1	30JUN47	Worcester	9/57	B	1MAY48- 4NOV51
					BL	3AUG49-21MAR59.
					R	4JUL56
SEDGELEY	C1	24JUL47	Dudley	9/64		
OVERBURY	C1	13AUG47	Tewkesbury	9/70		

Worcs

Name	Type	Date	Office	Ref	Mark	Period
SHRAWLEY	C1	11SEP47	Stourport	9/77	BL	17NOV50- 7NOV59
ELMLEY	C1	19OCT47	Pershore	9/92		
SEDG LEY	C1	19OCT47	Dudley	9/92	B	30SEP49-14MAR54
					GR	12JAN56 Note 3.
LEIGHSINTON	C1	26NOV47	Great Malvern	9/103	B	20JUN48
					BL	19JUN51-28JUN55
MICKLETON	C1	20JUN48	Campden	9/160	B	7JAN49-21JUL55
					BL/B	22JAN50
					BL	27APR50
					R	3JUL57
BREDON	C1	29JUL48	Tewkesbury	9/170	B	25MAY50-14JUN52
					BR	20DEC53
RIPPLE	C1	3SEP49	Worcester	10/35		
UPPER-ARLEY	C1	1NOV49	Bewdley	10/47		
FECKENHAM	C1	13DEC49	Bromsgrove	10/54	GR	4JUL50
BLOCKLEY	C1	31JAN50	Moreton Marsh	10/65		Note 4.
MARTLEY	C1	9MAR50	Worcester	10/74	R	5SEP56
KATES-HILL	C1	14JUN50	Dudley	10/95	B	25MAY58
STOULTON	C1	6AUG50	Worcester	10/103	BL	16SEP54-31DEC58
					BL/GR	59
ST-JOHNS	C1	18NOV50	Worcester	10/121	B	15APR51-23OCT58.
					R	12JUN57-15NOV57
					BL	26MAY59
SALFORD-PRIOR	C1	29JAN51	Evesham	10/146	BL	30APR58
					B	5DEC58.
HIMLEY	C1	12FEB51	Dudley	10/153	GR	8JAN56
STANTON	C1	1MAR51	Broadway	10/163	BL	12JUN51-20MAY55
WORDSLEY	C1	19MAR51	Stourbridge	10/176	BL	54
					B	6MAY55
DUNLEY	C1	12APR51	Stourport	10/188	BR	13MAR55
					R	1APR56
WESTON-SUB-EDGE	C1	18MAY51	Broadway	10/198	BL	23JUN51
HOLT	C1	24JUN51	Stourport	10/211	GR	27OCT59- 7NOV59.
BISHOPS·FROME	C1	5OCT51	Bromyard	10/267	BL	8MAR52-30MAY55
					BL/GR	6JUN55
ASTWOOD-BANK	C1	21NOV51	Bromsgrove	11/2	B	11MAY55- 9NOV59
					GR	11MAY55
					BL	58
ABBOTS-MORTON	C1	OCT57	Bromsgrove	11/114		
WIRE-PIDDLE	C1	JAN53	Pershore	11/130	BL	19JAN54-24JAN59
					R	4DEC55-15DEC57.
					B	58
TREDINGTON	C1	JAN53	Shipston on S	11/135		
INKBERROW	C1	FEB53	Bromsgrove	11/138	R	28DEC54
ABBERLEY	C1	MAR53	Stourport	11/152		
HARTLEBURY	C1	APR53	Stourport	11/156	BL	28AUG54-17FEB59
					B	14FEB60
FARFIELD	C1	APR53	Kidderminster	11/159	BL	12MAR54
BLAKEBROOK	C1	APR53	Kidderminster	11/159	BL	25MAR59
WOLLASTON	C1	APR53	Stourbridge	11/161		
OLD-SWINFORD	C1	APR53	Stourbridge	11/161	B	19AUG58
WORCESTER-RD	C1	SEP53	Evesham	11/225		
HEADLESS·CROSS	C1	OCT53	Bromsgrove	11/229	B	18JUN58-21JUN58
TARDEBIGG	C1	OCT53	Bromsgrove	11/229	R	9JUN57
					BL	58-28JUN59
					B	11MAY59-29JUN59.
BROMSGROVE·STATION	C1	OCT53	Bromsgrove	11/229		
THE·LICKEY·END	C1	OCT53	Bromsgrove	11/229		

Notes: 3. 9/64 with the second 'E' filed out.
4. See usage of the C2 mark - 5/101.

Worcs

Name	Class	Date	Office	Ref	Color	Date2
CATSHILL	C1	OCT53	Bromsgrove	11/229	B	13DEC58
WICHBOLD	C1	OCT53	Bromsgrove	11/229		
HADZOR	C1	OCT53	Droitwich	11/229		
EMLEY-LOVETT	C1	OCT53	Droitwich	11/229		
GREENHILL	C1	OCT53	Evesham	11/229		
HAMPTON	C1	OCT53	Evesham	11/229	R	3MAY55
QUARRY-BANK	C1	OCT53	Stourbridge	11/229		
STOURTON	C1	OCT53	Stourbridge	11/229	BL/GR	59
LOWER-CLENT	C1	OCT53	Stourbridge	11/229	GR	25MAR54
					R	20NOV56
CRABBS-CROSS	C1	OCT53	Bromsgrove	11/230	BL	55-26APR58
					B	23AUG58- 9APR59
STONE	C1	OCT53	Kidderminster	11/241	BL	19MAY55
					B	10NOV58
FRANCHE	C1	OCT53	Kidderminster	11/241	BL	11OCT57
BROADWATER	C1	OCT53	Kidderminster	11/241		
CHURCHILL	C1	OCT53	Kidderminster	11/241		
BENGEWORTH	C1	OCT53	Evesham	11/241	R	3NOV53-16NOV55.
					BR	14JUL57
					BL	17DEC57
					B	6FEB58- 6JAN59.
SALWARPE	C1	DEC53	Worcester	12/3	B	29AUG59
SPETCHLEY	C1	DEC53	Worcester	12/3	R	8JUL57-14JUL57
					BL	28MAY59
					B	27OCT59
HENWICK	C1	DEC53	Worcester	12/3	R	23APR55
LOWER-WICK	C1	DEC53	Worcester	12/3	R	31MAR56- 58.
					BL	30MAR59
					B	15MAY59-15JUN59
ALFRICK	C1	DEC53	Worcester	12/3	R/OR	21SEP54-27FEB57
COTHERIDGE	C1	DEC53	Worcester	12/3	B	25NOV57
UPPER-SAPEY	C1	DEC53	Worcester	12/3	R	16MAY57-29SEP57
					B	18NOV58
TEDSTONE-WAFER	C1	DEC53	Worcester	12/6	R/BR	15OCT56-11AUG57
					BL	58
EARLS-CROOME	C1	DEC53	Worcester	12/6	B	MAR55-27APR59.
					OR	22APR56
PIRTON	C1	DEC53	Worcester	12/6	R	55
WELLAND	C1	DEC53	Worcester	12/6	B	5DEC59
BAYTON	C1	JAN54	Bewdley	12/14	B	3JAN60
LEMBROOK	C1	JAN54	Bewdley	12/14		
WRIBBENHALL	C1	JAN54	Bewdley	12/14	BL	8OCT57
KYRE	C1	JAN54	Tenbury	12/15		
LITTLE-HEREFORD	C1	JAN54	Tenbury	12/15	GR	3MAY57
BRETTEL-LANE	C1	MAR54	Stourbridge	12/37	OR	26DEC56
					B	19NOV57- 8SEP58
					BL/B	15FEB58- 4OCT58.
SWINDON	C1	APR54	Dudley	12/50		
REDDITCH	C1M				R	1JUL54 Note 2.
CORNMARKET	C1	JUN54	Worcester	12/77	B	21JAN58
					BL	21APR58
GRIMLEY	C1	JUN54	Worcester	12/77		
BROADWAS	C1	JUN54	Worcester	12/77		
DITTON	C1	JUN54		12/80a	BR	57 Note 5.
WALL-HEATH	C1	JUN54		12/83	BL	23FEB56
NORTH-MALVERN	C1	DEC54	Malvern	12/92	OR/R	14MAY56-22OCT56
NEWLAND-GREEN	C1	DEC54	Malvern	12/92	R	4AUG56
STIFFORD-BRIDGE	C1	DEC54	Malvern	12/92	R	3JAN55
					OR/R	5MAY57
BARNARDS-GREEN	C1	DEC54	Malvern	12/92	R	30OCT56

Notes: 5. Probably sent to Bewdley.

Office	Class	Date	Town	Ref	Type	Period
SAPEY-BRIDGE	C1	12AUG54	Worcester	12/99	B	55-26JAN59
					R	2JUN56- 20OCT56
					BL	10MAR55-28DEC57.
MUCH-COWARNE	C1	22AUG54		12/106		
BLACKHEATH	C1	1FEB55	Dudley	12/155		
STANFORD-BRIDGE	C1	24MAY55	Worcester	12/203	BL	2AUG55
HOLLY-HALL	C1	10AUG55	Dudley	12/231		
CALLOW-HILL	C1	11AUG55	Bromsgrove	12/232		
LOWER-GORNAL	C1	5OCT55	Dudley	12/252		
LOWER-GORNAL	C1	5NOV55	Dudley	12/261		
PEOPLETON	C1	13NOV55	Pershore	12/267		
FRANCH	C1	17FEB56	Kidderminster	12/313	BL	59
BREDON	C1	17FEB56	Tewkesbury	12/315	BL	16NOV57
					B	16JUN58
STRENSHAM	C1	17FEB56	Tewkesbury	12/315		
COUGHTON	C1	22MAR56	Bromsgrove	12/324	B	9FEB58-25FEB59
WOODSETTON	C1	3APR56	Dudley	12/336		
GORNAL	C1	3APR56	Dudley	12/337		
FLADBURY	C1	2MAY56	Pershore	13/4	GR	27JUL56-13SEP58.
					R	30JAN57
					BL	2MAR59
STOTTESDON	C1	3JUN56	Bewdley	13/15	R	2DEC56
					B	19JAN58
CLIFTON-ON-TEME	C1	11JUN56	Worcester	13/20	R	20JUN56- 20OCT56
					B	26JAN59
WICHBOLD	C1	27JUN56	Bromsgrove	13/36		
REDNAL	C1	12SEP56	Bromsgrove	13/69	BL	9FEB59
LEIGH	C1	14FEB57	Worcester	13/149	B	23AUG59
FERNHILL-HEATH	C1	14FEB57	Worcester	13/149		
ROCK	C1*	9MAY57	Bewdley	13/230	B	1JUL58
					BL	18DEC59
BURMINGTON	C1*	16MAY57	Shipston on S	13/236		
SIDBURY	C1*	13JUN57	Worcester	13/258	BL	12OCT58-21MAR59
LINDRIDGE	C1*	14JUL57	Tenbury	13/271		
EARDESTON	C1*	14JUL57	Tenbury	13/271		
DUMBLETON	C4	15JUL57	Evesham	13/281	B	11SEP58-19APR59.
ACTON-BEAUCHAMP	C4	25JUL57	Worcester	13/287		
POWICK	C4	7AUG57	Worcester	14/7	GR	52
					BL	58
					B	18JAN60
EARDESTON	C4	27AUG57	Tenbury	14/12	BL	12NOV57
CLEEVE-PRIOR	C4	6OCT57	Evesham	14/44		
STANBROOK	D4	15OCT57	Stanbrook	14/57		
CRADLEY	D4	10NOV57	Great Malvern	14/70	BL	11FEB59-24FEB59
COLWALL-GREEN	D1	10NOV57	Great Malvern	14/70		
LYE	D4	10NOV57	Stourbridge	14/70		
WEST-MALVERN	D1	27NOV57	Great Malvern	14/87	B	23JUL58
					BL	29DEC58-12APR59.
STAUNTON	C4	27NOV57	Gloucester	14/90	B	28JAN59- 8APR59
ELMLEY-LOVETT	D1	10DEC57	Droitwich	14/104		
MALVERN LINK	D1	10DEC57	Malvern	14/105	BL	58-15JAN59
					B	14JAN58-10JAN60
COOKLEY	D4	23DEC57	Kidderminster	14/111		
WOLVERLEY	D4	23DEC57	Kidderminster	14/111	B	MAY5?
TYTHING R.O.	D5	5FEB58	Worcester	14/139	B	31MAY58- 1NOV58
					BL	59
BELBROUGHTON	D1	18FEB58	Stourbridge	14/149	B	25AUG58-18OCT59.
LOWER CLENT	D1	18FEB58	Stourbridge	14/149	B	7DEC58-12MAY59
WOLLASTON	D1	18FEB58	Stourbridge	14/149		
WORDESLEY	D1	18FEB58	Stourbridge	14/149		
HAGLEY	D4	20FEB58	Stourbridge	14/151		

Worcs

Name	Class	Date	Town	Ref	Status	Date2
STOURTON	D4	20FEB58	Stourbridge	14/151	BL	5MAR60
STOKE LACEY	D1	25FEB58	Worcester	14/154		
ROCHFORD	D1	22APR58	Tenbury	14/204	BL	1MAR59
NEWBOLD	D4	22APR58	Shipston on S	14/212		
STANFORD-BRIDGE	D1	22APR58	Worcester	14/212	BL	11NOV58
ILMINGTON	D1	22APR58	Shipston on S	14/212		
BROOM	D4	15JUN58	Kidderminster	14/258		Note 6.
WINTERFIELD	D1	15JUN58	Kidderminster	14/258		Note 6.
LEIGHSINTON	D1	29JUN58	Malvern	14/270		Note 7.
FAIRFIELD	D1	9JUL58	Bromsgrove	14/275	B	3NOV59-29NOV59
ELDERSFIELD	D1	14JUL58	Tewkesbury	14/277		
LEIGH·SINTON	D1	7AUG58	Malvern	16/13	B	26AUG58
CARELESS·GREEN	D1	7AUG58	Stourbridge	16/16		
KNIGHTSFORD-BRIDGE	D1	4SEP58	Worcester	16/29	BL	9JAN59
KEMERTON	D1	7OCT58	Tewkesbury	16/57	B	14NOV58-30NOV59.
BREDON	D4	12OCT58	Tewkesbury	16/58		
LONGDON	D4	12OCT58	Tewkesbury	16/58		
OVERBURY	D1	12OCT58	Tewkesbury	16/58		
STRENSHAM	D1	12OCT58	Tewkesbury	16/58		
HANBURY	D4	23NOV58	Bromsgrove	16/88		
BIDFORD	D4	23NOV58	Bromsgrove	16/88		
STOKE-PRIOR	D1	23NOV58	Bromsgrove	16/88		
ABBOTS-MORTON	D1	23NOV58	Bromsgrove	16/88		
ROBERTSEND STREET	D1	14DEC58	Worcester	16/113	BL	30JUN59- 2FEB60.
SEVERNSTOKE	D1	14DEC58	Worcester	16/113	B	27APR59
BROADWAS	D1	14DEC58	Worcester	16/113		
CRADLEY	D4	18DEC58	Brierley Hill	16/118		
NETHERTON	D1	12JAN59	Dudley	16/137	B	8FEB59
HIMLEY	D4	21JAN59	Dudley	16/141		
HAMPTON	D4	21JAN59	Evesham	16/141		
KATES-HILL	D1	21JAN59	Dudley	16/142		
OLD-HILL	D1	21JAN59	Dudley	16/142		
FINSTAL	D4	21JAN59	Bromsgrove	16/143	B	59
COALBURN-BROOK	D1	21JAN59	Stourbridge	16/144		Note 8.
BENGEWORTH	D1	27JAN59	Evesham	16/148	B	16MAR59-21OCT59
					BL	60
HARVINGTON	D1	27JAN59	Evesham	16/148	B	30NOV59
COALBOURN-BROOK	D1	12FEB59	Stourbridge	16/158	BL	15SEP59
TREDINGTON	D1	18FEB59	Shipston on S	16/161		
CHERRINGTON	D1	18FEB59	Shipston on S	16/161		
LOWER·BRAILES	D1	18FEB59	Shipston on S	16/161		
LONG·COMPTON	D1	18FEB59	Shipston on S	16/161		
BIRLINGHAM	D1	23FEB59	Pershore	16/163		
FLADBURY	D1	23FEB59	Pershore	16/163		
PEOPLETON	D1	23FEB59	Pershore	16/163		
WYRE-PIDDLE	D1	23FEB59	Pershore	16/163		
ELMLEY-CASTLE	D1	23FEB59	Pershore	16/163		
DEFFORD	D4	1MAR59	Pershore	16/167	BL/B	59
					BL	22NOV59
NEWLAND-GREEN	D1	9APR59	Malvern	18/24		
ENVILLE	D4	14MAY59	Stourbridge	18/43		
BEVERE-GREEN	D1	21MAY59	Worcester	18/46		
TIBBERTON	D1	6JUN59	Droitwich	18/53		
HIMBLETON	D1	8JUN59	Droitwich	18/57		
WICK-WORC	D1	5JUL59	Pershore	18/67		Note 9.
PENCOMBE	D1	28JUL59	Worcester	18/82		
WICK WORCESTERSHIRE	D2	17AUG59	Pershore	18/95		
REDDITCH	D1	19AUG59	Bromsgrove	18/96		

Similar Sans-serif (C1) Marks of Worcestershire

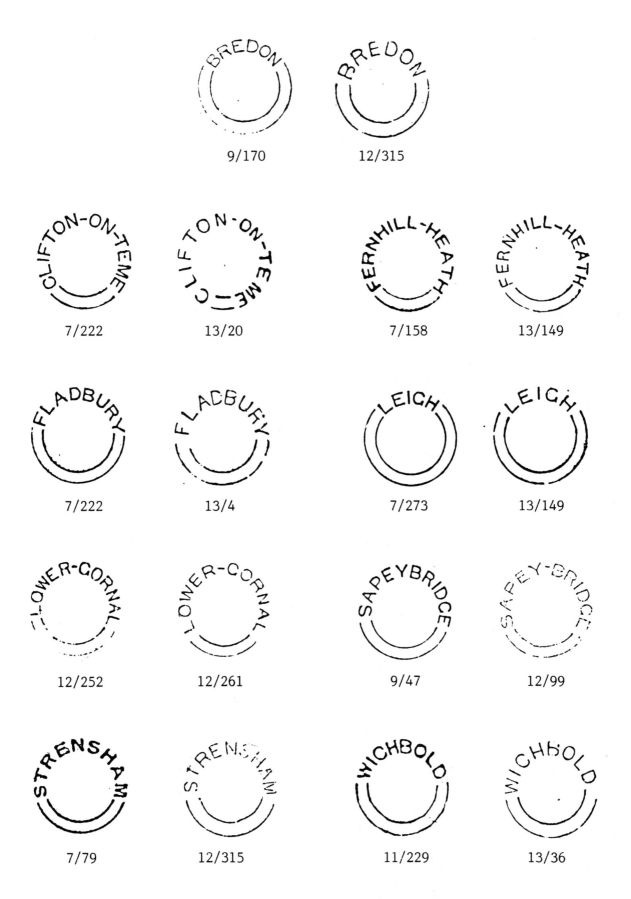

Reproduced by courtesy of Post Office Archives

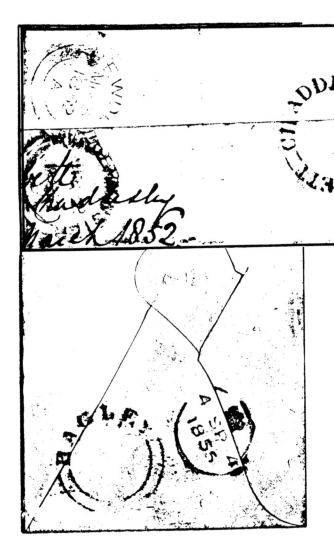

Above: CHADDESLEY-CORBETT (7/133)

Centre: HAGLEY (5/179) in green ink.
(This mark is known in at least seven different colours between 1844 & 56.)

Below: BELLBROUGHTON (5/179) - this stamp was issued at the same time as Hagley and used under the same post town but is only known in black ink.

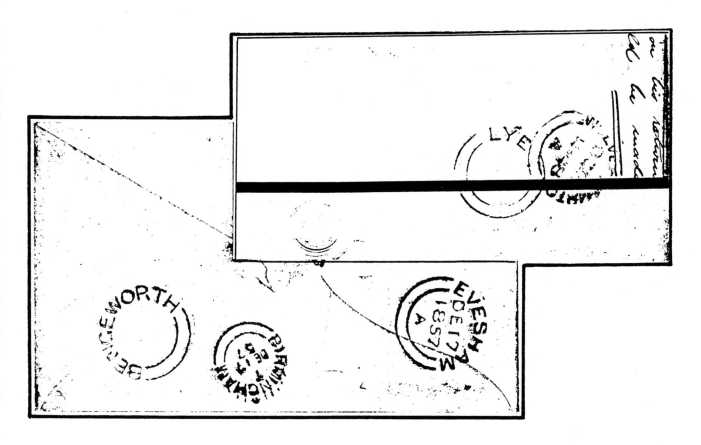

Above: LYE (7/205)

Below: BENGEWORTH (11/241)

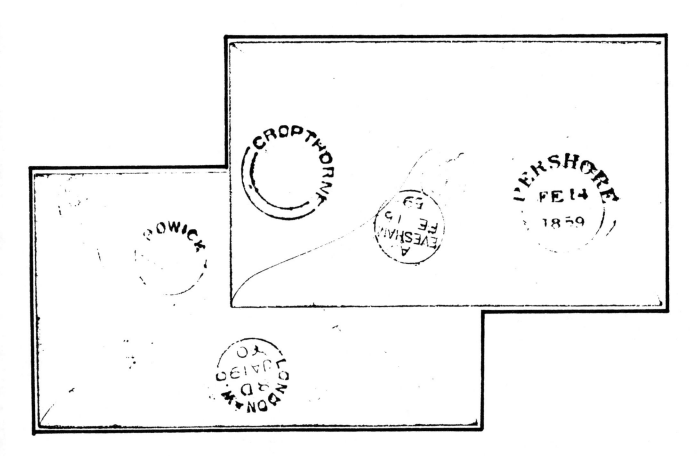

Above: CROPTHORNE (7/222)

Below: POWICK (14/7)

RAILWAY SUB-OFFICES (RSOs)

The following minor offices, from the date stated, received some or all of their mail from a Travelling Post Office (TPO) and their UDC therefore may not be found used in conjunction with the circular datestamp of the expected post town.

On and from 28DEC57 to receive mail through the Tamworth & Shrewsbury TPO :

Aston on Clun	Little Brompton
Beguildy	Lydbury
Brampton Bryan	Marshbrook
Bromfield	Munslow
Church Stretton	Newton
Clun	Old Hall
Clungunford	Onibury
Diddlebury	Rushbury
Felindre	Stanton Lacey
Hopton Castle	Wistanstow
Knighton	

On and from 17OCT59 to receive mail through the Tamworth & Shrewsbury TPO :

Eardisland	Shobden
Kingsland	Titley
Pembridge	Wigmore
Staunton Arrow	

* * * * *

MONEY ORDER OFFICES

Before postal orders were introduced in 1881, small sums of money could be safely transmitted through the post by means of a Money Order. The essential difference between a Money Order and the more familiar Postal Order was that a Money Order had to specify the office at which payment would be made. The Post Office then advised that office of the impending Order and recorded the details in London. It was a cumbersome and generally unprofitable procedure but popular with the public, especially "the poorer classes", it was said, "who employ it for the purpose of making remittances of small sums to their friends". Money Orders survived the introduction of Postal Orders for the transfer of larger sums of money only because of their greater security. Further information on Money Orders may be found in James Mackay's 'Registered Mail of the British Isles' and M.J. Daunton's account of the 'Royal Mail, the Post Office since 1840'.

Before November 1844, all Money Order Offices (M.O.O.s) were at post towns. To widen the scope of the service, some of the larger sub-offices became M.O.O.s between 1844 and 1849 and, on 1st October 1849, all existing M.O.O.s were designated 'Major' Money Order Offices. Thereafter, many more sub-offices became M.O.O.s and, until 1st October 1859, were classed as either 'Major' or 'Minor', most falling into the latter category. Since the amount that could be transmitted by means of a Money Order before 1860 was limited to £5, it is probable that the category of 'major' or 'minor' was determined by the amount of cash the office could hold. After 1st October 1859, the distinction ceased.

The relevance of the Money Order procedure to sub-offices using UDCs was that they were thereafter required to hold a datestamp to strike on Money Orders. Although in London and the larger provincial offices special datestamps were provided, including the designation "M.O.O." or something similar, the sub-offices were issued with normal double arc circular datestamps. Whether it had been the Post Office's intention that they should also use these datestamps to backstamp letters is not known but it seems unlikely that sub-postmasters would have been expected either to hold two stamps or repeatedly to take out and re-insert date slugs as the duty required. Whatever the intention, virtually all sub-offices issued with a CDS ceased to use a UDC.

The issue date of circular datestamps to sub-offices that became M.O.O.s - as well as to the smaller post towns that originally used UDCs - is included in each county's Office List for they indicate the probable last date of UDC usage at each office concerned. In isolated cases, where a further UDC was issued after the CDS issue, one can expect to find that the office was subsequently downgraded and ceased to be a M.O.O., sometimes when it was placed under a different post town. A few sub-postmasters were either conscientious or misguided and, for a while, continued to strike undated stamps on letters while, at the same time one presumes, using their datestamps solely on Money Orders.

The list below, by county, is of sub-offices that were originally issued with a UDC but, before 1860, upgraded to M.O.O.s and provided with a CDS. Only at Birmingham were any designated as 'Major' Money Order Offices between 1st October 1849 and 1st October 1859 and these are indicated; all others were 'Minor' M.O.O.s. For convenience, the list indicates the CDS issue dates (also shown in the Office Lists) and it should be noted that, although most datestamps were issued a few weeks before a M.O.O. was officially established, some were sent out many months earlier while a few were not issued until shortly afterwards. Collectors may find it rewarding to seek out early strikes of datestamps at these small offices.

DERBYSHIRE

Money Order Office	Post Town	M.O.O. Establ'd	Date of CDS Issue	Notes
Baslow	Chesterfield	1NOV56	14OCT56	
Bolsover	Chesterfield	1OCT59	23JUL59	
Brailsford	Derby	1JUL68	26JUN50	See Note 1.
Castle Donnington	Derby	1OCT49	26SEP49	
Castleton	Bakewell	1AUG57	20JUL57	
Chapel-en-le-Frith	Stockport	1MAR51	20FEB51	
Clay Cross	Chesterfield	1FEB51	26DEC50	
Dronfield	Sheffield	1AUG56	29JUL56	
Duffield	Derby	1FEB51	26DEC50	
Eckington	Chesterfield	1OCT57	21SEP57	
Glossop	Manchester	1MAR49	23MAY47	See Note 2.
Hartington	Ashbourne	1DEC57	1DEC57	
Hathersage	Bakewell	1MAY56	16APR56	
Heanor	Belper	2MAR57	5MAR57	
Ironville	Alfreton	1NOV52	SEP52	
Kegworth	Derby	1AUG56	16APR56	
Long Eaton	Derby	1DEC57	21SEP57	
Melbourne	Derby	1OCT49	26SEP49	
Ockbrook	Derby	1FEB51	26DEC50	
New Mills	Stockport	13JAN54	FEB54	
Ripley	Alfreton	1APR51	20FEB51	
Smalley	Derby	1MAR56	31JAN56	
Stapleford	Derby	1JUL58	5JUN58	
Staveley	Chesterfield	2JUN51	26DEC50	
Stony Middleton	Bakewell	1JUL58	9APR58	
Tideswell	Bakewell	1MAR51	20FEB51	

Notes:

1. Possibly intended as a M.O.O. in 1850 but not established.
2. Classed as a 'Major' M.O.O. after 1st October 1849.

GLOUCESTERSHIRE

Money Order Office	Post Town	M.O.O. Establ'd	Date of CDS Issue	Notes
Badminton	Chippenham	8JUL51	28MAR51	
Blakeney	Newnham	2JUN56	11JUN56	
Blockley	Moreton in M.	1AUG57	1SEP57	
Chipping Sodbury	Chippenham	1APR50	28MAR50	
Cinderford	Newnham	1MAR51	7MAR51	
Frampton on Severn	Dursley	18JUN51	28MAR51	See Note 3.
Lea	Gloucester		28MAR51	See Note 4.
Mitcheldean	Gloucester	16JUN51	28MAR51	
Nailsworth	Stroud	1MAR49	16JAN49	See Note 2.
Newent	Gloucester	1APR50	28MAR50	
Painswick	Gloucester	1MAR49	16JAN49	See Note 2.
Parkend	Lydney	1JAN59	30DEC58	

GLOUCESTERSHIRE (Continued)

Money Order Office	Post Town	M.O.O. Establ'd	Date of CDS Issue	Notes
Staunton	Gloucester	1JUL51	28MAR51	See Note 5.
Stow on the Wold	Moreton in M?	1FEB51	31MAY49	
Thornbury	Gloucester?	1MAR49	29JAN49	See Note 2.
Winchcombe	Cheltenham?	1OCT49	12SEP49	
Wickwar	Wotton u Edge	3JUL51	28MAR51	

Notes:

3. Served from Stonehouse after 13th January 1854.
4. Struck from the list of M.O.O.s in June 1851.
5. M.O.O. "abolished" on 21st October 1857.

HEREFORDSHIRE

Money Order Office	Post Town	M.O.O. Establ'd	Date of CDS Issue	Notes
Bodenham	Leominster	13JUN51	21MAY51	See Note 6.
Eardisley	Hereford	10FEB51	26DEC50	
Kentchurch	Hereford	7FEB51	26DEC50	
Kingsland	Leominster	1APR59	5APR59	
Lea	Gloucester		28MAR51	See Note 4.
Letton	Hereford	Not known	26DEC50	
New Radnor	Kington	1JUL55	28JUN55	
Pembridge	Leominster	11JUN51	21MAY51	
Pen y Bont	Kington	Not known	28JUN55	
Shobden	Leominster	Not known	23JUL59	
Staunton Arrow	Leominster	Not known	16JAN60	
Titley	Leominster	Not known	23JUL59	
Weobley	Hereford	10FEB51	26DEC50	
Whitchurch	Monmouth	1JUL51	28MAR51	

Notes:

6. Ceased as an M.O.O. in January 1852.

LEICESTERSHIRE

Money Order Office	Post Town	M.O.O. Establ'd	Date of CDS Issue	Notes
Appleby Magna	Atherstone	1APR59	24MAR59	
Bottesford	Nottingham	1JUL56	6JUN56	
Desford	Leicester	10OCT58	29SEP58	
Kibworth Harcourt	Mkt Harborough	1MAY56	2MAY56	
Market Bosworth	Hinckley	1APR50	28MAR50	
Mountsorrel	Loughborough	1APR57	20MAR57	
Shepshed	Loughborough	1MAR58	17MAR58	
Whitwick	Ashby de la Zouch	1AUG56	15JUL56	
Wigston	Leicester	1JUL58	15JUN58	

NORTHAMPTONSHIRE

Money Order Office	Post Town	M.O.O. Establ'd	Date of CDS Issue	Notes
Braunston	Rugby	24JUN51	24MAY51	
Brixworth	Northampton	3MAR51	24FEB51	
Crowland	Peterborough	2AUG52	JUL52	
Desborough	Kettering	10OCT57	30SEP57	See Note 7.
Guilsborough	Northampton	15MAR51	24FEB51	
Kingscliffe	Wansford	1AUG51	19AUG51	
Long Buckley	Daventry	24JUN51	24MAY51	
Rothwell	Kettering	1MAR58	20FEB58	
Syresham	Brackley	1JAN59	7DEC58	
West Haddon	Rugby	1JUL56	11JUL56	

Notes:

7. M.O.O. discontinued on 1st March 1858.

NOTTINGHAMSHIRE

Money Order Office	Post Town	M.O.O. Establ'd	Date of CDS Issue	Notes
Basford	Nottingham	10OCT55	10OCT55	
Beeston	Nottingham	1JUN52	26MAY52	
Bingham	Nottingham	6JUL46	27APR43	See Note 2.
Bottesford	Nottingham	1JUL56	6JUN56	
Collingham	Newark	10OCT58	24SEP58	
Eastwood	Nottingham	1FEB51	26DEC50	
Hucknall Torkard	Nottingham	1DEC57	1DEC57	
Hyson Green	Nottingham	1JAN59	8NOV58	
Ilkeston	Nottingham	2JUN51	23MAY51	
Radcliffe on Trent	Nottingham	1MAR58	20FEB58	
Sutton in Ashfield	Alfreton	1MAR51	20FEB51	See Note 8.
Warsop	Mansfield	2JUN56	11JUN56	

Notes:

8. Under Mansfield from July 1854.

OXFORDSHIRE

Money Order Office	Post Town	M.O.O. Establ'd	Date of CDS Issue	Notes
Bampton	Witney	5FEB51	26DEC50	
Brill	Tetsworth	1MAY56	16APR56	
Charlbury	Enstone	3FEB51	26DEC50	
Deddington	Woodstock	6MAR47	19JAN47	See Note 2.
Dorchester	Wallingford	8MAR51	24FEB51	
Ensham	Oxford	1AUG51	26DEC50	
Kidlington	Oxford	1SEP52	24APR51	

OXFORDSHIRE (Continued)

Money Order Office	Post Town	M.O.O. Establ'd	Date of CDS Issue	Notes
Lower Heyford	Woodstock	1OCT57	6OCT57	
St Clements	Oxford	1DEC56	8NOV56	
Shiplake	Reading	Not known	18JAN58	
Watlington	Tetsworth	1APR51	4MAR51	

SHROPSHIRE

Money Order Office	Post Town	M.O.O. Establ'd	Date of CDS Issue	Notes
Acton Burnell	Shrewsbury	1APR59	8DEC58	
Albrighton	Wolverhampton	1APR50	28MAR50	
Aston on Clun	Shrewsbury	6JUN51	4JUL51	See Note 9.
Baschurch	Shrewsbury	1JAN59	16OCT58	
Berriew	Shrewsbury	1JAN59	7DEC58	
Brampton Bryan	Shrewsbury	Not known	23DEC57	
Bromfield	Shrewsbury	Not known	23DEC57	
Broseley	Shifnal	15MAR51	12MAR51	
Cemmaes	Shrewsbury	1APR58	22APR58	
Church Stretton	Shrewsbury	10OCT49	19SEP49	
Churchstoke	Shrewsbury	1SEP56	27AUG56	See Note 10.
Claverley	Bridgnorth	2FEB57	1JAN57	
Clun	Shrewsbury	2MAR57	7FEB57	
Dawley	Shifnal	20MAR51	12MAR51	
Hanmer	Whitchurch	1FEB58	27JAN58	
Hodnet	Mkt Drayton	18JUN51	24MAY51	
Knighton	Presteign	9JUN51	21MAY51	See Note 11.
Leintwardine	Ludlow	1APR58	23DEC57	
Little Brampton	Shrewsbury	Not known	23DEC57	
Llanbrynmair	Shrewsbury	2JAN60	17SEP59	
Llanfyllin	Oswestry	15FEB51	29JAN51	
Llanidloes	Shrewsbury	6MAR47	28JAN47	See Note 2.
Llanrwst	Oswestry	1APR49	20FEB49	See Note 2.
Llanymynech	Oswestry	1OCT58	20SEP58	
Lydbury	Shrewsbury	Not known	23DEC57	
Madeley	Shifnal	24JUN51	24MAY51	See Note 12.
Minsterley	Shrewsbury	1MAY56	8APR56	
Much Wenlock	Ironbridge	6DEC44	14OCT44	See Notes 2&13.
Newton	Shrewsbury	Not known	23DEC57	
Oakengates	Wellington	1SEP56	8AUG56	
Onibury	Shrewsbury	Not known	18JAN58	
Prees	Shrewsbury	2MAR57	9DEC56	
Wem	Shrewsbury	1MAR49	20FEB49	See Note 2.
Wistanstow	Shrewsbury	Not known	23DEC57	

Notes:

9. An earlier CDS, 'ASTON', issued on 21st May 1851.
10. M.O.O. discontinued on 1st January 1859.
11. Served from Shrewsbury from December 1852.
12. Served from Wellington from September 1852.
13. Served from Wellington from October 1852.

MOOs

STAFFORDSHIRE

Money Order Office	Post Town	M.O.O. Establ'd	Date of CDS Issue	Notes
Abbots Bromley	Rugeley	1APR57	25MAR57	
Albrighton	Wolverhampton	1APR50	28MAR50	
Aldridge	Walsall	2MAR57	7FEB57	See Note 14.
Alrewas	Lichfield	2MAR57	25FEB57	
Audley	Newcastle u Lyme	1MAY56	8APR56	
Barton u Needwood	Burton on Trent	1APR50	28MAR50	
Bloxwich	Walsall	2JUN56	6JUN56	
Brewood	Wolverhampton	10OCT49	14SEP49	
Brownhills	Walsall	2APR60	25OCT59	
Burslem	Newcastle u Lyme	6NOV44	14OCT44	See Note 2.
Cannock	Walsall	20MAR51	12MAR51	See Note 15.
Church Eaton	Stafford	20MAR51	12MAR51	See Note 14.
Claverley	Bridgnorth	2FEB57	1JAN57	
Clifton Campville	Tamworth	1APR56	22MAR56	See Note 14.
Darlaston	Wednesbury	6JUN52	3JUN52	
Great Heywood	Rugeley	1APR57	23MAR57	
Hanley	Newcastle u Lyme	6NOV44	14OCT44	See Note 2.
Ipstones	Stafford	1FEB58	27JAN58	
Kingswinford	Dudley	7JUL51	4JUL51	
Knypersley	Congleton	10OCT58	20SEP58	
Lane End/Longton	Newcastle u Lyme	6NOV44	14OCT44	See Notes 2&16.
Longdon	Rugeley	1JUL57	27MAR57	See Note 14.
Sedgley	Dudley	1JUL56	27JUN56	
Shenstone	Lichfield	1APR57	13MAR57	See Note 14.
Silverdale	Newcastle u Lyme	2JAN60	17NOV59	
Tipton Green R.O.	Tipton	1JUL58	22JUN58	
Trentham	Newcastle u Lyme	1SEP56	12SEP56	See Note 17.
Tunstall	Newcastle u Lyme	6MAR47	28JAN47	See Note 2.
Tutbury	Burton on Trent	24JUN51	24MAY51	
Upper Tean	Stafford	1JUL57	7JUL57	
Willenhall	Walsall	1JUL53	AUG53	
Woodville	Burton on Trent	2NOV54	11DEC54	

Notes:

14. M.O.O. discontinued on 1st January 1859.
15. Establishment in doubt; also established as a M.O.O. on 1st September 1856.
16. Re-named in September 1848.
17. M.O.O. discontinued on 1st April 1859.

WARWICKSHIRE

Money Order Office	Post Town	M.O.O. Establ'd	Date of CDS Issue	Notes
Alcester	Stratford on Avon	6JUL46	17MAR46	See Note 2.
Appleby Magna	Atherstone	1APR59	24MAR59	
Bedworth	Coventry	24JUN51	24MAY51	
Bidford	Stratford on Avon	15JUL51	4JUL51	See Note 18.
Braunston	Rugby	24JUN51	24MAY51	
Husbands Bosworth	Rugby	10OCT59	14OCT59	
Wellesbourne	Warwick	10OCT58	18AUG58	
West Haddon	Rugby	1JUL56	11JUL56	

Notes:

18. M.O.O. discontinued March 1852.

BIRMINGHAM

Money Order Office	Post Town	M.O.O. Establ'd	Date of CDS Issue	Notes
Ashtead Row	Birmingham	21FEB54	MAR54	See Note 19.
Bristol Street	Birmingham	1OCT58	22SEP58	
Coleshill	Birmingham	6APR57	29APR56	
Deritend	Birmingham	22FEB54	MAR54	See Note 19.
Edgbaston	Birmingham	22FEB54	MAR54	See Note 19.
Five Ways	Birmingham	1OCT58	4SEP58	
Great Hampton St	Birmingham	22FEB54	MAR54	See Note 19.
Halesowen	Birmingham	1OCT49	24SEP49	
Handsworth	Birmingham	1JUL55	28JUN55	
Henley in Arden	Birmingham	1APR50	28MAR50	
Highgate	Birmingham	1APR59	4SEP58	
Oldbury	Birmingham	24JUN51	24MAY51	See Note 20.
Smethwick	Birmingham	1JUN55	21MAY55	
Sutton Coldfield	Birmingham	1MAR49	19FEB49	See Note 19.

Notes:

19. Established as a 'Major' M.O.O.
20. Became a 'Major' M.O.O. on 1st April 1852.

WORCESTERSHIRE

Money Order Office	Post Town	M.O.O. Establ'd	Date of CDS Issue	Notes
Alcester	Stratford on Avon	6JUL46	17MAR46	See Note 2.
Alvechurch	Bromsgrove	1JUL58	22JUN58	
Cradley Heath	Stourbridge	1AUG54	JUL54	
Feckenham	Bromsgrove	1APR57	25MAR57	
Hagley	Stourbridge	1APR58	31MAR58	
Halesowen	Birmingham	1OCT49	24SEP49	
Kingswinford	Dudley	7JUL51	4JUL51	
Kinver	Stourbridge	2JUN51	21MAY51	
Malvern Wells	Malvern	1DEC57	10NOV57	
Netherton	Dudley	2JAN60	16DEC59	
Ombersley	Stourport	4AUG51	24JUL51	
Redditch	Bromsgrove	6NOV44	10AUG44	See Note 2.
Sedgley	Dudley	1JUL56	27JUN56	
Staunton	Gloucester	1JUL51	28MAR51	See Note 5.
Studley	Bromsgrove	2JAN55	1JUN54	See Note 21.
Upton on Severn	Worcester	1OCT45	30SEP45	See Note 2.

Notes:

21. CDS (originally issued as 'STUDELEY') replaced on 27th June 1854.

ALPHABETICAL INDEX TO MIDLAND OFFICES

WITH UNDATED CIRCULAR MARKS

Abberley	172	Ash	108	Bartestree	45
Abbey Dore	45	Ashbourne	14	Barthomley	124
Abbey Foregate	107	Ashby de la Zouch	57	Bartley Green	156
Abbots Morton	171	Ashby Parva	57	Barton (in Fabis)	83
Abbotts Bromley	125	Ashby St Legers	72 143	Barton in the Heath	30 145
Abermule	108	Ashford	14	Barton Seagrave	70
Ab Kettleby	58	Ashford Carbonel	106	Barton St Michael(s)	29
Abthorpe	71	Ashleworth	29	Barton u Needwood	123
Ackleton	106	Ashley	106 126	Barwell	57
Acocks Green	156	Ashover	14	Baschurch	107
Acton Beauchamp	172	Ashow	143	Basford	83
Acton Burnell	107	Ashtead Row	156	Basingfield	83
Adbaston	106	Ashton Keynes	29	Baslow	14
Adderbury	95	Astley	143	Bassingham	83
Adderley	106	Aston (B'ham)	156	Bath Road	29
Admaston (Salop)	108	Aston (Ludlow)	106	Bayston Hill	107
Admaston (Staffs)	124	Aston (Stafford)	124	Bayton	171
Ailburton	30	Aston Blank	30	Bearley	144
Alberbury	107	Aston Cross	31	Beckbury	107
Albrighton (Salop)	107	Aston New Town	156	Beckford	31 173.
Albrighton (Wolves)	108 125	Aston on Clun	106	Beckingham	83
Alcester	144 173	Aston Park	156	Beckley	94
Alcester Lane End	156	Aston Road	156	Bednal	124
Alderley	31	Astwood Bank	171	Bedworth	143
Alderminster	144	Atherstone	143	Beech Lane	156
Alderton	29	Attleborough	143	Beeston	83
Aldridge	125	Audley	124	Beguildy	106
Aldsworth	30	Aus/Ansley Boot End	143	Beighton	16
Alfrick	172	Austrey	143	Belbroughton	172
Allensmore	45	Avening	30	Belgrave	57
Allesley	143	Avon Dassett	94 144	Belgrave Gate	57
Allexton	57	Awre	30	Belper	14
Alrewas	123	Aynho	70	Belton	58
Alstonefield	14 125	Babworth	84	Benefield	70
Alton	123	Badby	70	Bengeworth	171
Alvaston	15	Baddesley	143	Benson	96
Alvechurch	171	Badminton	30	Berkeley	29
Alveley	106	Baginton	143	Berkeswell	143
Alvescot	96	Bagthorpe	83	Berriew	107
Alveston	144	Bakewell	14	Berrington	107.
Alwalton	71	Balderton	83	Berrow	45
Ambergate	14	Balsall Heath	156	Besthorpe	83
Ampney Crucis	29	Bamford	14	Betley	124
Andoversford	29	Bampton	95	Bettisfield	108
Ansley/Ausley	143	Barby	70 145	Beulah	46
Anstey (Leics)	57	Barford	144	Bevere Green	172
Anst(e)y (Warks)	143	Barkestone	58 83	Beverstone	30
Apethorpe	71	Barlaston	124	Bibury	31
Apperley	31	Barlborough	14	Bickenhill	144 156
Appleby Magna	16 58 143	Barlow	14	Bickerton	108
Arleen	106	Barnack	72	Bicton Heath	107
Arlingham	30	Barnards Green	172	Bidford (on Avon)	144 173
Armitage	124	Barnby Moor	84	Billesdon	57
Arnold	83	Barnsley	29	Billingsley	106
Arthingworth	58 72	Barnwell	70	Bilston	123
Ascot Wychwood	94	Barrington	31 94	Bilston Road	125
Asfordby	58	Barrow on Soar	57	Bilton	143

Index

Bingfield Heath	96
Bingham	83
Birch	46
Birchfields	126 156
Birlingham	172
Bishopstone	45
Bishopswood	124
Bishops Cleeve	29
Bishops Frome	45 173
Bishops Itchington	143
Bishops Tachbrook	143
Bisley	30
Bitteswell	57
Blaby	57
Blackheath	126 171
Blackmarston	45
Blackthorn	94
Blackwater	123
Bladon	95
Blakebrook	171
Blakeney	30
Blakesley	71
Blatherwick	72
Bletchington	94
Blidworth	83
Blisworth	70
Blockley	30 173
Bloxham	94
Bloxwich	125
Blurton	124
Blyth	84
Blythe Marsh	124
Bobbers Mill	83
Bockleton	172
Boddington (Glos)	29
Boddington (N'thants)	70
Bodenham	46
Bodicott	94
Bolsover	14
Bomere Heath	107
Bonsall	15
Borlestree	45
Borrowash	15
Borth	108
Bosbury	46 172
Botley/Botley Green	94
Bottesford	58 83
Boughton	70
Bourton (Warks)	143
Bourton on the Hill	30
Bourton on the Water	30
Bowbridge	30
Bow Street	108
Bozeat	71
Brackley	70
Bradwell	14
Brad(e)ley	123
Brailes	144 172
Brailsford	15
Bramcote	15 84
Brampton Bryan	46 106
Brampton Moor	14
Branston (Leics)	58
Branston(e) (Staffs)	123
Brassington	15
Braunston (Leics)	58
Braunston (N'thants)	70 145
Braunstone	57
Breadsall	15
Bredon	31 173
Bredwardine	45
Breedon	15 57
Brereton	124
Brettell Lane	126 172
Bre(e)wood	125
Bridge Casterton	59
Bridge St (Hereford)	45
Bridge St (N'thants)	70
Bridge St (Worcester)	172
Bridgnorth	106
Bridgnorth Low Town	106
Brigstock	71
Brill	95
Brimfield	46 106
Brimington	14
Brimpsfield	29
Brimscombe (Port)	30
Brinklow	143
Brinsley	14 84
Bristol Street	156
Britwell Salome	95
Brixworth	70
Brize Norton	95
Broadbottom	16
Broadwas	172
Broadwater	171
Broadway	171
Broadwell	30
Brockmoor	123
Brockthorpe	29
Brockworth	29
Brokenborough	30
Bromfield	106
Bromsgrove	171
Bromsgrove Station	171
Bromyard	45
Bronllys	46
Bronygarth	108
Brookend	30
Brook Street	15
Broom	126 171
Broseley	107
Broughton (N'thants)	70
Broughton (Notts)	83
Brownhills	125
Bruntingthorpe	57
Brynllis	46
Bubbenhall	143
Buckminster	58
Bucknell	107
Bugbrook	71
Bulkington	145
Bulwell	83
Bulwick	72
Bunny	83
Burbage	57
Burghill	45
Burlton	107
Burmington	144 172
Burnaston	15
Burntwood	123
Burrough on the Hill	58
Burslem	124
Burton (Salop)	108
Burton Hill	30
Burton Joyce	83
Burton Latimer	70
Burton Overy	57
Burwarton	106
Butlers Marston	144
Butterley	14.
Buxton	14
Byfield	70
Caersws	108
Cainscross	30
Caldwell	16 123
Callow Hill	171
Calver	14
Calverhall	108
Calverton	83
Cambridge	29
Cannock	125
Can(n) Office	107
Canon Pyon	45
Capel Arthog	108
Cape of Good Hope	126 156
Cardington	107
Careless Green	172
Carey	46
Carlbridge	95
Carlton (Nottingham)	83
Carlton (Worksop)	84
Carlton upon Trent	83
Carno	108
Carrington	83
Carsley	143.
Castleton	14
Castle Bromwich	156
Castle Donnington	15 58
Castle Foregate	107
Castor	71
Catherine-A-Barns	156
Catshill	171
Catthorpe/Calthorpe	59 143
Caunton	83
Cavendish Bridge	15 58
Caversham	96
Caversham Hill	96
Caverswall	124
Cemmaes	107
Chaddesden	15
Chaddesley Corbett	171

Index

Chadlington	94	Clifford Chambers	144	Crabbs Cross	171
Chadshunt	143	Clifton	83	Cradley (Herefs)	46 172
Chalford	30	Clifton (Campville)	125	Cradley (Worcs)	126 172
Chalgrove	95	Clifton Hampden	95	Cranford	70
Chapel Ash	125	Clifton on Teme	172	Cransley	71
Chapel Brampton	70	Clipston	58 72	Creaton	70
Chapel End	143	Clown	14	Credenhill	45
Chapel en le Frith	14	Clun	106	Cresbrook	14
Charfield	31	Clungunford	107	Cressage	107
Charlbury	94	Clyro	46	Crich	14
Charlesworth	16	Coalbourn Brook	126 172	Crick	70 145
Charleymount	125	Coalbrookdale	108	Criggion	107
Charlton (Glos)	30	Coaley	29	Croft	57
Charlton (N'thants)	72 95	Coalport	108	Cromford	15
Charlton Kings	29	Coalville	57	Cromhall	31
Charterville	95	Coates (Glos)	30	Cropthorne	172
Checkendon	94	Coates (N'thants)	71	Cropredy	94
Chedworth	29	Cobridge	124	Cropwell Butler	83
Chellaston	15	Cock Gate	46	Crosshands	31
Chelmarsh	106	Cockshutt	106	Cross Houses	107.
Cher(r)ington	144 172	Codnor	14	Croughton	70
Chesterton (N'thants)	70	Codsall	125	Crow Hill	46
Chesterton (Staffs)	124	Codsall Wood	125	Crowland	71
Cheswardine	106	Cold Overton	58	Crowle	172
Childs Ercal	106	Coleford	29	Crowmarsh	96
Chilton	95	Coleham	107	Croxton Kerrial	58
Chilvers Coton	143	Coleorton	57	Crudwell	30
Chilwell	83	Colesbourne	29	Cubbington	143
Chinnor	95	Collingham	83	Cubley	16 125
Chipping Norton	94	Colston Bassett	83	Cuckney	83
Chipping Sodbury	31	Colton	124	Cuddesden	95
Chipping Warden	72 94	Colwall	46 172	Culworth	72 94
Chirbury	108	Colwall Green	46 172	Cummins/Commins Coch	107
Chorlton	108	Colwich	124	Cumnor	95
Church Bridge	125	Combe Hill	29	Curbridge	95
Church Broughton	15	Compstall	16	Curdworth	144 156
Church Eaton	124	Compton	125	Cuxham	95
Churchfield	125	Condover	107	Daglingworth	29
Churchill (Oxon)	94	Congleton	126	Darlaston	125
Churchill (Worcs)	171	Connington	71	Darley	15
Churchover	143	Cookley	171	Daventry	70
Church Stoke	108	Coppice	123	Dawley	107
Church St	144	Corby	71	Dawley Bank	108
Church Stretton	107	Cornmarket	172	Dawley Green	107
Cinderford	30	Corris	107	Deanshanger	72.
Cinder Hill	83	Corse Lawn	31	Deddington	95
Clanfield	95	Cosby	57	Deene	71
Clarborough	84	Coseley	123	Deepfield	123
Class Gate	172	Cosgrove	72	Defford	172
Claverdon	144	Cossington	57	Denby	14
Claverley	108 125	Coston	58	Derby Road	83
Claybrooke	57	Cotesbach	59 143	Derwent	14
Claydon	94	Cotgrave	83	Desborough	70
Claypole	83	Cotheridge	172	Desford	57
Clayworth	84	Cottesbrooke	70	Diddlebury	106
Clay Cross	14	Cottesmore	58	Didmarton	30
Clearwell	31	Coughton	144 171	Dilwyn	46
Clee Hill	106	Countesthorpe	57	Dinas Mowddy	107
Cleeve Prior	171	Coven	125	Dingeston	31
Clifford	45	Cowley	29	Diseworth	16 57

Ditton	108 171	Ecton	70	Farthingstone	71
Docklow	46	Edensor	14	Fazeley	123
Donington	106	Edgbaston	156	Feckenham	171
Dorchester	96	Edgmond	106	Felindre	106
Dore	16	Edgworth	29	Felton	106
Dormington	45	Edmonscote	144	Fenny Compton	94 144
Dorrington	107	Edstaston	107	Fenton	124
Doveridge	16 125	Edwinstowe	84	Fernhill Heath	172
Down Ampney	31	Eggin(g)ton	16 123	Fifield	94
Draycott (Derbys)	15	Eglwysfach	108	Filkins	96
Draycot(t) (Staffs)	124	Egmanton	83	Fillongley	143
Drayton (N'thants)	70	Eign	45	Finedon	70
Drayton (Oxon)	96	Eign Street	45	Finstall	171
Droitwich	171	Eldersfield	31 173	Fiskerton	83
Dronfield	16	Elford	123	Five Ways	156
Duckmanton	14	Elkesley	84	Fladbury	172
Dudbridge	30	Ellastone	14 125	Flintham	83
Duddeston Row	156	Ellesmere	106	Flore	71
Duddington	72	Elmdon	156	Foleshill	143
Dudleston	108	Elmley	172	Ford (Glos)	29.
Dudley	171	Elmley Castle	172	Ford (Salop)	107
Dudley Road	125	Elmley Lovett	171	Ford Houses	125
Duffield	15	Elton (N'thants)	70	Forsbrook	124
Dumbleton	31 171	Elton (Notts)	83	Forthampton	31
Dunham on Trent	83	Empingham	59	Fossbridge	29
Dunkirk	30	Emscote	144	Fosters Booth	71
Dunley	172	Enderby	57	Fotheringhay	70
Dunstall	123	Endon	124	Fownhope	45
Dunstone	124	English Bicknor	29	Frampton on Severn	29
Dylife	107	Ensham	94	Franch	171
Dymock	31 45	Enstone	94	Frankwell	107
Dyrham	31	Enville	126 172	Fretherne	30
Eagle	83	Epperstone	83	Fritchley	14
Eakring	83	Erdington	156	Fritwell	94
Eardeston	172	Erlsdon	143	Frocester	30
Eardisland	46	Erwood	46	Frodesley	107
Eardisley	45	Essington	125	Frowlesworth	57
E(a)rlsdon	143	Etruria	124	Gaddesby	58
Earls Barton	71	Ettingshall	125	Ga(i)ley	124
Earls Croome	172	Ettington	144	Gamston	84
Earl Shilton	57	Etwall	16 125	Garsington	95
Eastcombe	30	Evenjobb	45	Garthmill	107
Easthope	107	Evenley	70	Garway Common	46
Eas(t)ington	30	Everton	84	Gayton	124
Eastleach Turville	31	Ewelme	96	Geddington	70.
Eastnor	45	Exton	58	Gentleshaw	124
Easton	72	Eyam	14	Gilmorton	57
Easton Maudit	70	Eydon	70	Glasbury	46
Eastwell	58	Eye (Herefs)	46	Glatton	71
Eastwood	83	Eye (N'thants)	71	Glazeley	106
East Bridgeford	83	Eyton	108	Glenfield	57
East Haddon	70	Fackley	83	Glossop	16
East Leake	57 84	Fairfield (Derbys)	14	Gnosall	124
East Markham	84	Fairfield (Worcs)	171	Gobowen	106
East Stoke	83	Fairford	31	Golden Hill	124
Eatington	144	Farfield	171	Gooch Street	156
Eaton Bishop	45	Farnborough	94 144	Goodrich	46
Eaton Constantine	108	Farndon	83	Goring	96
Eckington (Derbys)	14	Farnsfield	83	Goring Heath	96
Eckington (Worcs)	31 172	Farthinghoe	70	Gornal	125 173
				Gosford	94

Index

Gotham	15 84	Hamstall Ridware	124	Helpston	72
Granby	84	Hanbury (Staffs)	123	Hempstead	29
Grandborough	144	Hanbury (Worcs)	171	Hengoed	106
Gravel	107	Handley	14	Henley in Arden	144 156
Gravelly Hill	156	Handsworth	126 156	Henley on Thames	94
Great Alne	144 156	Hanford	124	Henwick	172
Great Barr	126 156	Hanley	124	Heyford	71
Great Billing	70	Hanmer	108	Heyford Warren	95
Great Bolas	108	Hannington	70	Hickling	58 85
Great Bowden	58	Hanwood	107	Higham	14
Great Bridge	125	Harborne	126 156	Higham Ferrers	70
Great Brington	70	Harborne Heath	126 156	Higham on the Hill	57
Great Easton	58 71	Harbury	143	Highgate	156
Great Glen	57	Harby	58	High Cross Street	57
Great Hampton Street	156	Hardingstone	70	High Ercall	108
Great Harrowden	71	Haresfield	29	High Street (W Brom)	125
Great Hazeley	95	Harewood End	46	High Town (Herefs)	45
Great Heywood	124	Hargrave	72	Highley	106
Great Longstone	14	Harleston	123	Highnam	29
Great Milton	95	Harlestone	70	Hilderstone	124.
Great Tew	94	Harley	108	Hill Morton	144
Great Witley	172	Harmer Hill	107	Hill Ridware	124
Greenhill (Derbys)	16	Harnhill	29	Hill Top	125
Greenhill (Worcs)	171	Harpole	71	Hilton	16 123
Greenhill Lane	14	Harpswood	106	Himbleton	171
Green Lane	15	Harrington	70	Himley	126 171
Greens Norton	71	Harthill	85	Hinstock	106
Greenway	45	Hartington	14	Hixon	124
Greetham	58	Hartlebury	172	Hoarwithy	46
Grendon	70	Hartpury	29	Hoby	58
Gretton	58 71	Hartshill (Staffs)	124	Hockley Heath	144 156
Grimley	172	Hartshill (Warks)	143	Hockley Hill	156
Grindleford Bridge	14	Hartshorne	16 123	Hodnet	106
Grindley Brook	108	Hartwell	70	Holbrook	15
Gringley	84	Hart Street	123	Holloway	15
Grinshill	107	Harvington	171	Holly Hall	171
Groby	57	Haseley	144	Hollywood	156
Grosmont	45	Hasfield	29	Holme	71
Guilsborough	70	Hasland	14	Holme Lacey	45
Hackenthorpe	16	Hassop	14	Holmer	45
Hackleton	70	Hathern	57	Holt (Oxon)	95
Haddenham	95	Hatherop	31	Holt (Worcs)	172
Hadfield	16	Hathersage	14	Holymoorside	15
Hadley	108	Hatton	144	Holywell St	94
Hadnall	107	Hawford	172	Hook Norton	94.
Hadsor	171	Hawkesbury Upton	31	Hope	16
Hagley	172	Hawling	29	Hope Mansell	29 46
Halesowen	156 173	Hayfield	16	Hopton	124
Halfway House	107	Hazelbeach	70	Hopton Castle	106
Hallaton	58	Hazlewood	14	Horninglow	123
Hall Green	156	Headington	94	Horninglow Street	123
Hallow	172	Headless Cross	171	Horseferry Bridge	29
Hambledon	94	Heage	14	Horsehays	108
Hambleton	58	Heanor	14	Horseley Fields	125
Hampstead	126 156	Heath (Derbys)	14	Horsepath	95
Hampstead Road	126 156	Heath/Hethe (Oxon)	94	Horsley	30
Hampton	171	Hednesford	124	Hoton	57
Hampton Bishop	45	Heeley	16	Houghton on the Hill	57
Hampton in Arden	143 156	Hellidon	70	Hoveringham	83
Hampton Lucy	144	Helmdon	70	How Caple	46

Hucclecote	29	Kingsland	46	Leintwardine	46 106
Hucknall (Huthwaite)	14 84	Kingsley	124	Leire	57
Hucknall (Torkard)	83	Kingsthorpe	70	Lembrook	171
Hugglescote	57	Kingstone	15 84	Lenton	83
Hulland	14	Kingstone Blount	95	Leominster	46
Humberstone	57	Kingswinford	126 171	Leonard Stanley	30
Humberstone Gate	57	Kingswood	31	Letton	45
Hundred House	45	Kings Acre	45	Letwell	84
Hungarton	57	Kings Bromley	123	Lew	95
Huntley	29	Kings Caple	46	Lewknor	95
Hurley	143	Kings Heath	156	Lickey End	171
Husbands Bosworth	59 71 145	Kings Norton	156	Lighthorne	144
Hyson Green	83	Kings Stanley	30	Lilleshall	106
Ibstock	57	Kings Sutton	72 95	Linby	83
Ibston	96	Kington	45	Lindridge	172
Ickford	95	Kinnerley	106	Linton	46
Icknield Street	156	Kinnersley	108	Lionshall	45
Iffley	94	Kirkby	83	Littledean	30
Ilam	14 125	Kirklington	83	Littlemore	94
Ilkeston	16 83	Kirk Ireton	15	Littleover	15.
Ilmington	144 172	Kirk Langley	15	Littleworth	30
Inkberrow	171	Kirtlington	94	Little Addington	71
Intake	16	Kneesal	83	Little Aston	126 156
Ipsden	96	Knighton	106	Little Brington	70
Ipstones	124	Knightsford Bridge	172	Little Brom/Brampton	107
Irchester	71	Knockin	106	Little Dawley	108
Ironbridge	107	Knowle	156	Little Eaton	15
Ironville	14	Knutton Heath	124	Little Harrowden	71
Irthlingborough	70	Knypersley	126	Little Hereford	47 172
Isham	71	Kyre	172	Little Houghton	70
Islip (N'thants)	71	Lamport	70	Little Marcle	45
Islip (Oxon)	94	Lancaster Street	156	Little Rissington	31 94
Jackfield	108	Lane Delph	124	Little Sodbury	30
Kates Hill	171	Lane End (Bucks)	96	Little Somerford	30
Keele	124	Lane End/Longton	124	Litton	14
Kegworth	15 58	Langham	58	Llanbadarn Fynydd	45
Kelham	83	Langley	156	Llanbrynmair	108
Kelmarsh	70	Langwith	16 83	Llandinam	108
Kemerton	31 173	Lapworth	144 156	Llandogo	29
Kempsey	172	Lawton	124	Llandrinio	106
Kempsford	31	Laxton	58 72	Llandyssil	108
Kenilworth	143	Lea (Derbys)	15	Llanegryn	108
Kentchurch	45	Lea (Herefs)	29 46	Llanfecham	106
Keresley	143	Lea Cross	107	Llanfyllin	106
Ketley	108	Leafield	95	Llangammarch	46.
Ketton	59	Lea Marston	143 156	Llangarran	46
Kibworth Harcourt	57	Leamington Spa	143	Llangedwin	106
Kiddington	95	Leamington Hastings	144	Llangorse	45
Kidlington	94	Lechlade	31	Llangrove Common	46
Kidmore End	96	Leckhampton	29	Llangynog	106
Kidsgrove	124	Ledbury	45	Llanrhaiadr-yn-M'nt	106
Kilburn	14	Leebotwood	107	Llanrwst	106
Killamarsh	15	Lee Crescent	156	Llansaintffraid-yn-M	106
Kilsby	70 144	Leek	123	Llansillin	106
Kimberley	83	Leek Wotton	144	Llanvair (Waterdine)	106
Kingham	94	Leigh (Worcs)	172	Llanwddyn	106
Kingsbury	123 145	Leigh (Staffs)	124	Llanwrtyd	46
Kingscliffe	71	Leigh Sinton	172	Llanyblodwell	106
Kingscote	31	Leighterton	31	Llanymawddy	107
Kingshill	125	Leighton	108	Llanymynech	106

Index

Llwydiarth	106	Maidwell	70	Minety	30
Llwyngwril	108	Maisemore	29	Minsterley	107
Llynclys	106	Malvern Link	172	Minster Lovell	95
Llyswen	46	Malvern Wells	172	Minsterworth	29
Lockington	15 58	Manaughty	107	Minworth	156
Lois Weedon	71	Mansfield Road	83	Miserden	29
London Road (Glos)	29	Mansfield Woodhouse	83	Misson	84
London Road (Worcs)	172	Manton	58	Misterton	84
Longdon (Staffs)	124	Maple Durham	96	Mitcheldean	29
Longdon (Worcs)	31 173	Mapperley	83	Mixbury	95
Longford (Derbys)	15	Mappleton	14	Moddershall	124
Longford (Warks)	143	Marbury	108	Molesworth	71
Longhope	29	Marchington	125	Money Ash	14
Longney	29	Marden	45	Monk Hopton	106
Longnor	14 126	Market Bosworth	57	Monks Kirby	59 144
Longport	124	Market Overton	58	Montford	107
Longtown	46	Markfield	57	Montpellier	29
Long Buckby	70	Marple	16	Monument Lane	156
Long Compton	94 144 173	Marshbrook	107	Moor Green	83
Long Crendon	95	Marshfield	31	Morcott	58.
Long Eaton	15	Marsh Gibbon	94	Morda	106
Long Itchington	144	Marston Green	156	Moreton	106
Long Lawford	144	Marston Montgomery	14	Moreton in Marsh	30
Long Marston	144	Marston St Lawrence	70	Moreton on Lug	45
Long Newnton	30	Marton	144	Morville	106
Long Stanton	108	Martley	172	Mosborough	15
Loppington	107	Mathfield/Mayfield	14 125	Moseley	156
Lound	84	Matlock Bath	15	Moulton	70
Lowdham	83	Matlock Bridge	15	Mountsorrel	57
Lower Benefield	70	Matlock Village	15	Mowsley	58
Lower Clent	172	Mattersey	84	Mow Cop	124
Lower Eagleton	45	May(s) Hill	31	Moxley	125
Lower Gornal	126 171	Mears Ashby	70	Much Cowarne	47 172
Lower Guiting	30	Measham	16 58 143	Much Dewchurch	46
Lower Heeley	16	Medbourne	58	Much Marcle	31 45
Lower Heyford	95	Melbourne	15	Much Wenlock	107
Lower Kenilworth	143	Mellor	16	Muggington	15
Lower Milton	94	Melton Mowbray	58	Munslow	107
Lower Wick	172	Meole Brace	107	Muston	58 83
Lowick	71	Mere Green	156	Nailstone	57
Loxley	144	Meriden	143	Nailsworth	30
Lozells	156	Meysey Hampton	31	Nantmel	45
Lubenham	58 72 145	Mickleover	15	Napton	144
Luckington	30	Mickleton	30 173	Narborough	57
Luddington (N'thants)	71	Middle	107	Naseby	71 145.
Luddington (Warks)	144	Middleton (Derbys)	15	Nassington	71
Ludgershall	95	Middleton (N'thants)	71	Nechells Green	156
Lullington	16 123	Middleton (Salop)	106	Needwood	123
Lutterworth	57	Middleton (Warks)	125 145	Neenton	106
Lydbrook	31 46	Middleton Cheney	72 94	Ne(i)ther Whitacre	143 156
Lydbury	106	Middleton Stoney	94	Neithrop	94
Lyddington	58	Midway	16 123	Nescliffe	107
Lydney	30	Milford	15	Netherseal	15 57
Lye	172	Millfield	71	Netherton	171
Lyndon	58	Milpool Hill	156	Nether Broughton	58
Mackworth	15	Milton (Derbys)	16 123	Nettlebed	94
Madeley (Salop)	107	Milton (N'thants)	70	Nettleton	30
Madeley (Staffs)	124	Milton (Staffs)	124	Newbold	15
Madley (Herefs)	45	Milton u Wychwood	94	Newbold on Avon	144
Maer	124	Mil(l)wich	124	Newbold on Stour	144 172
Maesbury	106	Minchinhampton	30		

Index

Newbold Verdon	57	Oaksey	29	Pensnett	126 171
Newborough (N'thants)	72	Ockbrook	15	Pen y Bont	45
Newborough (Staffs)	125	Ocker Hill	125	Penybont Fawr	106
Newbridge on Wye	46	Oddington	31 94	Peopleton	172
Newent	29	Old	70	Perkins Green	107
Newerne	30	Oldbury (B'ham)	156	Perry	126 156
Newhall	16 123	Oldbury (Salop)	106	Pershore	172
Newland (Glos)	31	Old Brampton	15	Peterborough	71
Newland (Oxon)	95	Old Brinsley	14	Peterchurch	45
Newland Green	172	Old Glossop	16	Pinxton	14
Newnham (Glos)	30	Old Hall	107	Pirton	172
Newnham (Warks)	144	Old Hill	126 171	Pitchcombe	30
Newport (Salop)	106	Old Lenton	83	Pitsford	70
Newthorpe	83	Old Radford	83	Pitt Court	31
Newton (Bridgnorth)	106	Old Sodbury	31	Pittville	29
Newton (Notts)	83	Oldswinford	172	Pleasley	16 83
Newton (Regis)	125 145	Ollerton	84	Plumtree	83
Newton (Shrewsbury)	107	Ombersley	172	Polebrook	71
Newton Solney	16 123	Onibury	106	Polesworth	125 145
New Basford	83	Ordsall	84	Pontesbury	107.
New Chapel	124	Orleton	46 106	Pontesford Bridge	107
New Fletton	71	Orlingbury	71	Pontfathew	108
New Hincksey	94	Orston	83	Pontrilas	45
New Inn	123	Oscott	126 156	Pooll Hill	46
New Lenton	83	Osmaston (Ashbourne)	14	Portobello	125
New Mills (Derbys)	16	Osmaston (Derby)	15	Portway	45
New Mills (Salop)	108	Oundle	70	Potterspury	72
Normanton	14	Overbury	31 173	Powick	172
Normanton on Soar	57 84	Overseal	15 57	Prees	107
Northend	144	Over Witton	156	Prestbury	29
Northfield	156	Oxendon	58 72	Preston	108
Northgate Street	29	Oxford St, Leicester	57	Preston Brockhurst	107
Northleach	30	Oxton	83	Preston Capes	70
Northwood	124	Packington	15 57	Preston Gubballs	107
North Aston	95	Pagenhill/Packenhill	30	Princes End	123
North Cerney	29	Pailton	59 144	Priors Lee	107
North Kilworth	59 71 145	Pains Lane	108	Priors Marston	144
North Leigh	95	Painswick	30	Pulverbatch	107
North Luffenham	58	Pant	106	Purton	29
North Malvern	172	Parade	156	Quarndon	15
North Newington	94	Park Corner	94	Quarry Bank	126 172
North Nibley	31	Parkend	30	Quat	106
North Stoke	96	Park End St	94	Quatford	106
Norton (Derbys)	16 83	Parwich	14	Quedgeley	29
Norton (Glos)	29	Pattingham	108 125	Queslett	126 156.
Norton (Mkt Drayton)	106	Pattishall	71	Quennington	31
Norton (Sheffield)	16	Paulerspury	71	Quinton	156
Norton (Shifnal)	107	Peak Forrest	16	Quorn(don)	57
Norton Bridge	124	Pelsall	125	Radbourne	15
Norton Cannon	45	Pembridge	46	Radcliffe	83
Norton in the Moors	124	Pencombe	47 172	Radford (Notts)	83
Norwell	83	Pencraig	46	Radford (Warks)	143
Nuneaton	143	Penegoes	107	Radway	94 144
Nuneham	94	Penkhull	124	Rampton	83
Nuttall	83	Penkridge	124	Ramsden	95
Nympsfield	30	Penley	107	Ranby	84
Oakamoor	124	Penn	125	Randwick	30
Oaken	125	Pennal	108	Ranskill	84
Oakengates	108	Pennfields	125	Ratcliffe	57
Oakham	58	Penns	156	Raunds	71
Oakley	95				

Index

Ravenstone	15 57	Sandhurst	29	Slimbridge	29
Rearsby	57	Sandiacre	15 84	Smalley	15
Redbrook (Glos)	31	Sandon	124	Smallthorn	124
Redbrook (Salop)	108	Sandpits	156	Smallwood	124
Redditch	171	Sapey Bridge	173	Small Heath	156
Redhill	156	Sapperton	29	Smethcott	107
Redmarley	29 46 173	Sarnan	106	Snarestone	57
Redmile	58 83	Saundby	84	Sneinton	83
Rednal	171	Saul	30	Sneinton Elements	84
Remenham Hill	94	Sawley	15	Snelston	14
Rempstone	57 84	Sawtry	71	Snitterfield	144
Repton	16 123	Saxondale	83	Solihull	156
Respidge	30	Scaldwell	70	Somerby	58
Retford	84	Scalford	58	Sommerstown	94
Rhydycroesan	106	Scarcliffe	16 83	Souldern	70 95
Richards Castle	46 106	Seagrave	57	Southgate Street	29
Rickerscote	124	Sedgley	126 171	Southwell	84
Riddings	14	Selattyn	106	South Cerney	29
Ridgway	15	Selly Oak	156	South Croxton	57
Ringstead	71	Selston	14 84	South Kilworth	59 144.
Ripley	14	Severn Stoke	173	South Leverton	84
Ripple	31 172	Shardlow	15	South Littleton	171
Riseley	70	Shareshill	125	South Luffenham	59
Risley	15	Shawbury	107	South Muskham	83
Roade	70	Shearsby	58	South Newington	94
Robbers/Bobbers Mill	83	Sheepscombe	30	South Parade	143
Robertsend St	172	Sheepy	58 143	South Stoke	96
Rocester	14 125	Shelton (Notts)	83	South Wingfield	14
Rochford	172	Shelton (Staffs)	124	Sowe	143
Rock	171	Shenington	94	Sparkbrook	156
Rodborough	30	Shenstone	123	Spetchley	173
Rode Heath	124	Shenton	58 143	Spondon	15
Rodington	107	Shepshed	57	Spon Lane	125
Rolleston	123	Sherborne	30	Spratton	70
Rosliston	16 123	Sheriff Hales	106 126	Stadhampton	96
Rotherfield Greys	94	Sherstone	30	Stafford	124
Rotherfield Peppard	94	Shilton	95	Stafford Street	125
Rothley	57	Shiplake	96	Stanbrook	173
Rothwell	70	Shiplake Row	96	Standlake	95
Rowington	144	Shipston on Stour	144 172	Standon	123
Rowley Regis	126 171	Shipton Moyne	30	Stanford	57 84
Rowsley	15	Shipton u Wychwood	94	Stanford Bridge	173
Ruardean	30	Shirebrook	16 83	Stanground	71
Ruddington	83	Shirley (St)	156	Stanton (Broadway)	31 171
Rudge (now Edge)	30	Shirleywich	124	Stanton (Coleford)	29.
Rufford	84	Shobden	46	Stanton (Salop)	107
Rugby	143	Short Heath	125	Stanton by Dale	15
Rugeley	124	Shortwood	30	Stanton Harcourt	95
Rushbury	107	Shrawley	172	Stanton Lacey	106
Rushden	70	Shucknell	45	Stanton St John	95
Rushton	70	Shurdington	29	Stanwick	70
Ruyton	107	Sibford	94	Stapenhill	16 123
Ryhall	59	Sibson	58 143	Stapleford	15 84
Ryton on Dunsmore	143	Sidbury	173	Stapleton	107
Saddington	58	Siddington	29	Station Rd (Worksop)	84
Salford Prior(s)	145 171	Sileby	57	Staunton	29 173
Salperton	30	Silverdale	124	Staunton Arrow	46
Saltley	156	Silverstone	71	Staunton on Wye	45
Salwarpe	172	Skegby	83	Staveley	15
Sandford	95	Skenfrith	45	Staverton	29
		Slawston	58		

Index

Steeple Aston	95
Stifford(s) Bridge	46 172
Stinchcombe	31
Stirchley	156
Stockingford	143
Stockton (Warks)	144
Stockton (Worcs)	173
Stockwith	84
Stokenchurch	95
Stoke (Notts)	83
Stoke Bruerne	71
Stoke Green	143
Stoke Lacey	47 173
Stoke on Trent	124
Stoke Prior (Herefs)	46
Stoke Prior (Worcs)	171
Stoke Row	94
Stonall	125
Stone (Glos)	29
Stone (Worcs)	171
Stonebridge	143
Stonehouse	30
Stoneleigh	143
Stone Gravels	15
Stonesfield	95
Stoney Stanton	57
Stoney Middleton	14
Stottesdon	108 171
Stoulton	173
Stourport	172
Stourton	126 172
Stow on/in the Wold	30
Stratton	29
Stratton Audley	94
Strelly	84
Strensham	31 173
Stretton (Oakham)	59
Stretton (Penkridge)	124
Stretton en le Fields	15 57
Stretton on Dunsmore	143
Stretton under Fosse	144
Stroud Green	30
Studley	144 173
Sturton	84
St Briavels	31
St Clements	94
St Giles	94
St Johns	172
St Martins	108
St Marys Bridge	15
St Pauls	29
St Weonards	46
Sudborough	71
Sudbury	16 125
Sugwas Pool	45
Summertown	94
Summer Lane	156
Sutton (Notts)	83
Sutton Bonnington	57 84
Sutton in Ashfield	83
Sutton (on the Hill)	15
Sutton St Nicholas	45
Swadlin(g)cote	16 123
Swannington	57
Swanwick	14
Swarkeston(e)	15
Swepstone	58 143
Swinbrook	31 94
Swinderby	83
Swindon	126 171
Swinford	57 145
Swithland	57
Swyncombe	94
Swynnerton	124
Syresham	70
Syston	57
Tackley	95
Taddington	14
Taliesin	108
Tallyllyn	108
Tal y Bont	108
Tamworth	125
Tansley	15
Tanworth	144 156
Tardebigg	171
Tarrington	45
Tat(t)enhill	123
Taynton	29
Tean	123
Tedstone Wafer	147 173
Tenbury	172
Tetsworth	95
Tettenhall	125
Theddingworth	58 72 145
The Bridges	107
The Broad	46
The Flat	30
The Lodge	108
The Trumpet	45
The Wergs	125
Thornbury	30
Thorney	71
Thornton	57
Thoroton	84
Thorpe	14
Thorpe Langton	58
Thorpe Malsor	70
Thorpe Mandeville	72 94
Thrapston(e)	71
Thringstone	57
Thrussington	57
Thulston	15
Thurgarton	83
Thurlaston (Leics)	57
Thurlaston (Warks)	144
Thurmaston	57
Thurnby	57
Tibberton	171
Tibshelf	14
Ticknall	15
Tiddenham	31
Tiddington	144
Tideswell	14
Tiffield	71
Tilstock	108
Tilton on the Hill	57
Tintwistle	16
Tipton	125
Tipton Green	125
Tirley	31
Tissington	14
Titchmarsh	71
Titley	45
Tittensor	124
Tividale	125
Tixall	124
Toddenham	30
Tollerton	84
Tong	107
Tortworth	31
Towcester	71
Tredington	144 172
Trefonnen	106.
Tregynon	108
Trench Lane	108
Trentham	124
Trent Vale	124
Trowell	84
Trysull	125
Tuffley	30
Tugby	57
Tunstall	124
Tupton	15
Turnditch	15
Tur Langton	58
Turville	94
Tutbury	123
Twining Green	31
Twycross	58 143
Tysoe	144
Tything	173
Uckington	29
Ufton	143
Uley	30
Ullenhall	144 156
Ullesthorpe	57
Unston	16
Upper Arley	125 171.
Upper Assendon	94
Upper Parade	143
Upper Sapey	47 173
Upper Stonall	125
Upper Wolvercote	94
Upper Worton	95
Uppingham	58
Uppington	108
Upton (Notts)	83
Upton Magna	107
Upton on Severn	173
Upton St Leonards	30
Victoria Crescent	123
Vowchurch	45
Wadenhoe	71
Walcote	57

Index

Walesby	84	West Felton	107	Withington (Glos)	29
Walford	46	West Haddon	70 145	Withington (Herefs)	45
Walgrave	70	West Hallam	15	Withybrook	143
Walkeringham	84	West Kington	30	Witney	95
Wall Heath	126 171	West Malvern	172	Wixhall	108
Walsall	125	Wetley Rocks	123	Wollaston (N'thants)	71
Walsall Road	125	Wetwood	123	Wollaston (Worcs)	172
Waltham on the Wolds	58	Whaley Bridge	16	Wollaton	84
Walton (Herefs)	45	Whaplode Drove	71	Wols(e)ley Bridge	124
Walton (Leics)	57	Whatton	84	Wolstanton	124
Walton (Staffs)	124	Wheatley	95	Wolston	143
Walton on Trent	16 123	Wheaton Aston	124	Wolverley	171
Wanlip	57	Whilton	70	Wolvey	57 145
Wansford	71	Whissendine	58	Wombourne	125
Wappenbury	143	Whitchurch (Herefs)	46	Woodborough	84
Warborough	96	Whitchurch (Oxon)	96	Woodchester	30
Wardington	94	Whitchurch (Salop)	108	Woodcote	94
Wargrave	94	Whitebrook	29	Wooden Box/Woodville	16 58 123
Warmington (N'thants)	71	Whitecroft	30	Woodford	71
Warmington (Warks)	94 144	Whitfield (Derbys)	16	Wood Green	125.
Warsop	83	Whitfield (Glos)	29	Woodhouse Eaves	57
Washwood Heath	156	Whitfield (N'thants)	70	Woodsetton	126 171
Wasperton	144	Whitminster	30	Woodside	30
Waterloo Street	57	Whitmore Reans/Reams	125	Woodstock	95
Waterstock	95	Whitmore Station	124	Woolhope	45
Water Newton	71	Whitnash	143	Woolstone	29
Water Orton	144 156	Whitney	45	Woolvercot	95
Waters Upton	108	Whittington (Derbys)	15	Woonton	45
Watford	70	Whittington (Salop)	106	Woore	106
Watlington	95	Whittington (Staffs)	123	Wooton	95
Watton	84	Whittlebury	71	Wootton	70
Wednesfield	125	Whittlesey	71	Wootton Wawen	144 156
Wednesfield Heath	125	Whitwell	15 84	Worcester Road	171
Welch Frankton	106	Whitwick	57	Worcester Street	125
Weldon	71	Wibtoft	57 145	Wordsley	126 172
Welford (N'thants)	71	Wichbold	171	Worfield	108 125
Welford (Warks)	144	Wick	172	Worksop	84
Welland	173	Wicken	72	Wormbridge	45
Wellesbourne	144	Wickwar	31	Wormleighton	144
Wellingborough Rd	70	Wigmore	46	Worthen	107
Wellington (Herefs)	45	Wigston	57	Wotton under Edge	31
Wellington Place	70	Wilbarston	58 72	Wribbenhall	171
Wellow	83	Wilby	70	Wrockwardine	108
Welton	70	Wild Green	156	Wroxeter	107
Wem	107	Wiley	57 145	Wroxton	94.
Wenlock	107	Willenhall	125	Wyken	106
Wentnor	107	Willey	106	Wymeswold	57
Weobley	45	Willington	16 123	Wymondham	58
Werrington	71	Wilmcott/Wilnecote	123 145	Wyrley Bank	125
Westbury	107	Wilton	46	Wysall	84
Westbury on Severn	30	Winchcombe	29	Wytham	95
Westhide	45	Wingerworth	15	Yardley	156
Westhorpe	84	Winshill	16 123	Yardley Gobion	72
Weston (Shrewsbury)	107	Winson	30	Yardley Hastings	70
Weston (Stafford)	124	Winson Green	156	Yarndon/Yarnton	95
Westonbirt	30	Winster	15	Yate	31
Weston Favell	70	Winstone	29	Yaxley	71
Weston on the Green	95	Winterfield	171	Yelvertoft	72 144
Weston sub Edge	31 171	Winthorpe	83	Yockleton	107
Weston (under Lizard)	107 126	Wire Piddle	172	Yorkley	30
Weston under Penyard	30 46	Wistanstow	107	Youlgrave	14
West Bridgford	84	Witcombe	30	Yoxall	123

THE MIDLAND (GB) POSTAL HISTORY SOCIETY

Founded 1975

President: The Reverend Christopher M. Beaver

Chairman: Roger Broomfield

Secretary: Eric Lewis

Treasurer: Mrs Elizabeth Lewis

Editor, 'Midland Mail': John Soer, 51D Barkham Road, Wokingham, Berks RG41 2RG

County Editors:

Derbyshire	Harold Wilson
Gloucestershire	John Hine
Herefordshire	Roger Broomfield
Leicestershire (& Rutland)	John Soer
Northamptonshire	Derek Smeathers
Nottinghamshire	Dennis Humphreys
Oxfordshire	Martin Scroggs
Shropshire	Guy Bridges
Staffordshire	Chris Beaver & Richard Farman
Warwickshire	Alan Godfrey
Birmingham	Eric & Elizabeth Lewis
Worcestershire	Chris Jackson

Co-ordinating Editor: John Calladine, Dunley House, Cranham, Gloucester GL4 8HQ
(phone 01452-862218)

The Society meets monthly on Saturday afternoons between September and April. Many meetings are in the centre of Birmingham, close to New Street Station, but other venues include Worcester and Shrewsbury (a joint meeting with The Shropshire Postal History Society). The December meeting is traditionally at The Bass Museum, Burton on Trent. The Society also holds a biennial meeting with The Somerset and Dorset Postal History Group in Gloucestershire. Visitors may attend any meeting.

The Society's bulletin, 'Midland Mail', appears five times a year and is sent free to members. It includes details of forthcoming meetings, comprehensive reports of displays given to the Society, news of research projects and illustrated articles on all aspects of postal history. 'Midland Mail' and the Society's publications have all gained awards at Stampex.

Membership details are available from the Treasurer, Mrs Elizabeth Lewis, at:

27, Rathbone Road,
Smethwick
Warley
West Midlands B67 5JG

* * * * *

NEW INFORMATION

If you are able to update the information in this book by reporting usage beyond the span of dates listed or, perhaps, have seen a UDC that is apparently not listed, please send complete details, including the type, proof book reference (if known) and ink colour, to the appropriate member at the addresses given below:

Derbyshire: Mr H.S.Wilson, 17 Heath Avenue, Littleover, Derby DE23 6DJ

Gloucestershire: Mr J.F.Hine, c/o Dunley House, Cranham, Gloucester GL4 8HQ

Herefordshire: Mr R.W.Broomfield, 78 Court Road, Malvern, Worcs WR14 3EG

Leicestershire (& Rutland): Mr J.Soer, 51D Barkham Road, Wokingham, Berks RG41 2RG

Northamptonshire: Mr D.Smeathers, 20 Pound Lane, Great Billing, Northampton NN3 4DX

Nottinghamshire: Mr D.Humphreys, 35 Lambourne Drive, Wollaton, Nottingham NG8 1GR

Oxfordshire: Mr M.Scroggs, Thatchways, High St, Lower Brailes, Banbury, OX15 5HW

Shropshire: Mr G.Bridges, 59 Abbey Foregate, Shrewsbury SY2 6BQ

Staffordshire: The Rev C.M.Beaver, 70 Filance Lane, Penkridge, Stafford ST19 5JT

Warwickshire: Mr A.D.Godfrey, 43 Seymour Road, Alcester, Warwickshire B49 6JY

Birmingham: Mr E.Lewis, 27 Rathbone Road, Smethwick, Warley, West Midlands B67 5JG

Worcestershire: Mr C.R.Jackson, 49 Mason Road, Headless Cross, Redditch, B97 5DT

DID YOU KNOW?

Did you know that The Midland (GB) Postal History Society has produced two further publications?

THE UNDATED STRAIGHT LINE AND NUMBERED RECEIVING HOUSE MARKS
OF THE MIDLAND COUNTIES, 1840-1860. (December 1988)

THE LOCAL POSTS OF THE MIDLAND COUNTIES TO 1840
(October 1993)

Enquiries about these books may be addressed to the Co-ordinating Editor (please see the previous page) or to Messrs Vera Trinder Ltd, 38 Bedford Street, London WC2E 9EU

* * * * *